TANGLED WEB

Tales

of

Digital

Crime

from the

Shadows

of

Cyberspace

RICHARD POWER

A Division of Macmillan USA

201 West 103rd Street, Indianapolis, Indiana 46290

Tangled Web: Tales of Digital Crime from the Shadows of Cyberspace

International Standard Book Number: 0-7897-2443-x

Library of Congress Catalog Card Number: 00-106209

Printed in the United States of America

First Printing: September 2000

02 01 00   4 3 2 1

Trademarks

Warning and Disclaimer

Associate Publisher
Tracy Dunkelberger

Acquisitions Editor
Kathryn Purdum

Development Editor
Hugh Vandivier

Managing Editor
Thomas Hayes

Project Editor
Tonya Simpson

Copy Editor
Michael Dietsch

Indexer
Erika Millen

Proofreader
Benjamin Berg

Team Coordinator
Vicki Harding

Design Manager
Sandra Schroeder

Cover Designer
Anne Jones

Interior Designer
Trina Wurst

Product Marketing Manager
Amy Neidlinger

Publicity
Gardi Ipema Wilks

Layout Technicians
Ayanna Lacey
Heather Hiatt Miller
Stacey Richwine-DeRome

Contents at a Glance

Table of Contents

Foreword

Our world has been changing dramatically, and we haven't being paying much attention. Sure, we know how computer technology and networking have increased productivity and that the Internet has become an enabling technology similar to the invention and development of electricity as a power source. We are all aware of how much money has been made by Internet startups, through online stock trading and through business-to-business networking.

What few are aware of are the dangerous waters we are treading.

We live in a society quite capable of providing sufficient physical security. Banks have vaults and alarm systems; office buildings have controlled access and guards; government installations have fences and much better armed guards when appropriate. Jewelry shop owners remove their wares from window displays and lock them in a vault each night. Stores in poor neighborhoods use video cameras full-time and have bars or grates over windows when closed.

But the online world is not so secure. A company that spent millions installing a state-of-the-art alarm system might not even have a single employee tasked with computer security. Companies that do spend money install the equivalent of network burglar alarms, intrusion detection systems, but then do not hire anyone to monitor the IDS console. The firewalls that are the equivalent to the guard at the entryway to the networks get configured for performance, not security. At best, the majority of organizations pay only lip service to computer security.

Tangled Web makes these points abundantly clear. Through surveys, case studies, and stories about the few successful prosecutions, *Tangled Web* exposes the depth of our vulnerability to online theft, penetration, abuse, and manipulation. Even as the business world migrates to a fully online presence, we remain stuck with our heads in the sand, hoping that what we can't see won't hurt us.

But what we *can* see—the adolescent hacker "owning" computers for use in chat rooms, stealing credit cards to pay for new computer equipment, using your network to deliver spam email advertisements for pornographic sites—is only the tip of the iceberg. Defacement of Web servers by a hacktivist may garner 30 seconds in the evening news, but such public attacks are not the real problem.

In *Tangled Web*, you will learn about the details that you didn't see on the evening news. For example, how two hackers' systems were found to have the commands that brought down the AT&T phone network in 1990 (and you thought it was just a software bug). Or how, exactly, a Russian went about getting his hands on more than $10 million wired from Citibank. Or how an electronic entrepreneur was prepared to sell 84,000 credit card numbers, burned on a CD and encrypted with a key taken from a novel about the Mafia.

The CSI/FBI surveys in the beginning of the book present statistics on the growing awareness of the threat to our security. The participants in the series of surveys, over a five-year period, show increasing awareness of not just the level of threat, but also the ability to place a dollar amount on the damages caused by various forms of electronic malfeasance. As you read through these chapters, you might be surprised to see that the greatest threat to your company's resources has remained exactly the same over the years, while the threat of Internet attacks has continued to rise.

And yet, the incidents and statistics reported in *Tangled Web* detail just the parts that we do know about. The chapter on corporate espionage, for example, provides abundant details about the cases of information theft that we know about. But this is like bragging about capturing a single truck loaded with cocaine at the border, when tens of thousands of tons actually wind up in the noses of addicts each year.

The true extent of computer crime is still unknown. Most organizations still refuse to share information about computer crime with law enforcement. And, for every system penetration or instance of unauthorized use discovered, there are probably ten or more left unnoticed.

Individual hackers have their own resources and what they can garner from friends, associates, and the Internet to work with. Just imagine what it would be like if you could take what is essentially an amateur computer security specialist and provide unlimited resources to him or her, including training, access to classified intelligence, the fastest computers and network links, and cooperation with a cadre of other dedicated and enthusiastic individuals. What you would have then would look like the information warfare teams already in existence in more than 20 countries worldwide.

When these teams perform an intrusion, it is unlikely that it will be noticed. They are after not attention but information or future control. They have a better understanding of the systems they are attacking, and they have the time and patience necessary to do a thorough job without leaving behind any traces of the attack. It is the unseen and unheard-of attacks that any organization with any critical online resources should be afraid of. And, if you think this is beyond the capacities of most large nation-states, just read about how a small group called the Phonemasters completely compromised a regional phone company to the point that they could do anything they wanted, even warning criminals of wiretaps placed on their phone lines. Even as the phone company was implementing better security, the Phonemasters were creating back doors into the compromised systems that would let them get around the enhanced security.

Instead of improving our defenses, the marketplace has generally chosen to go with fluff. The security chosen by most companies today is like that on a fishing shack on a backcountry lake: a sign saying "Protected by Smith and Wesson." I have visited companies where a firewall, intended to protect an e-commerce business, was still in its packing crate, and ones where the ID systems were merely there to show to visiting investors. And the most popular products in use are not the most secure by far.

Today, the number-one and number-two (in sales) firewalls use a technique known as stateful packet filtering, or SPF. SPF has the dual advantages of being fast and flexible, and this is why it has become so popular. Notice that I didn't even mention security, as this is not the number-one reason people chose these firewalls. Instead, SPF is popular because it is easy to install and doesn't get in the way of business as usual. It is as if you hired a guard for the entry to your building who stood there waving people through as fast as possible.

Marketing plays an even greater role in the failure of security. Microsoft, unfortunately for the world, owns the desktop market and is busily going after the server market as well. On the desktop, Microsoft features, such as Outlook and Windows Script Host, turn every desktop into a potential relay for viruses like Melissa and ILOVEYOU, or a source for denial of service attacks. NT Web servers, which can with great effort be made relatively secure, get hacked three times more often than any type of Unix Web server, and yet make up only one-fifth of the Web servers installed today. Instead of building and shipping truly secure systems, Microsoft talks about what it can do. And what it actually does is introduce amazingly flexible and complex products that even its own engineers admit are based on undocumented source code.

If I haven't already moved you to pay attention to security, I certainly expect that *Tangled Web* will do it. This book can be used as a tool to convince management of the extent of the risk—not simply that there is a real risk, but how damaging it can be to ignore that risk. Not just in financial terms, which is real enough and well-documented here, but also in terms of winding up with a security breach detailed above the fold of the *New York Times*.

If you are a security professional, you will, in most cases, know that your company is not spending enough money and attention on security. Buy this book and give it to your managers. Read it yourself, so you can be armed with stories and statistics about those who ignored the risk instead of managing it. Learn about successful prosecutions and what evidence proved significant, so instead of being a just a victim, you will have at least a chance to strike back.

As Richard Power writes in the epilogue, the stories about computer crime continue to unfold. Even so, what you have in your hands is the single, most complete description in existence today. And perhaps, someday in the not-too-distant future, we can be proud instead of embarrassed of our security, because we chose not to ignore the problem but to get serious about it instead.

Rik Farrow
July 2000

"Since it is universally believed that man is merely what his consciousness knows of itself, he regards himself as harmless and so adds stupidity to iniquity. He does not deny that terrible things have happened and still go on happening, but it is always 'the others' who do them…Even if, juristically speaking, we were not accessories to the crime, we are always, thanks to our human nature, potential criminals…None of us stands outside of humanity's collective shadow. Whether the crime occurred many generations back or happens today, it remains the symptom of a disposition that is always and everywhere present—and one would therefore do well to possess some 'imagination for evil,' for only the fool can permanently disregard the conditions of his own nature. In fact, negligence is the best means of making him an instrument of evil. Harmlessness and naivete are as little helpful as it would be for a cholera patient and those in his vicinity to remain unconscious of the contagiousness of the disease."

—Carl Jung, *The Undiscovered Self*

Acknowledgments

Tangled Web itself is an acknowledgement of some of the many bright and dedicated individuals who have helped reveal what lurks in the shadows of cyberspace. Their names and affiliations are strewn throughout the text. There are others, too, who are not mentioned, or could not be mentioned, who have made significant contributions.

Without the foresight and daring of Patrice Rapalus, the director of the Computer Security Institute (CSI), I would not have been able to accomplish as much as I have in this field. Indeed, all those who take information security seriously owe her a debt of gratitude whether they are aware of it or not.

Tangled Web is the result of several years of intense focus but was produced on a harrowing schedule in an insanely short span of weeks. Without the creative vision, professionalism, and humor of Kathryn Purdum and Hugh Vandivier, my editors at Macmillan, it would not have been possible to do the impossible. Michael Dietsch, Tonya Simpson, Benjamin Berg, and others at Macmillan also worked hard and well on this project.

I also want to thank Christina Stroz, Doron Sims, and Scott Hamilton, three students at York Prep High School in New York, who navigated their way through the maze of the U.S. Federal court system, located some court documents vital to this book (although they had been given the wrong docket number), and photocopied them for me.

Crime, War, and Terror in the Information Age

PART I

Welcome to the Shadow Side of Cyberspace

In 1991, Alvin Toffler's *The Third Wave* proclaimed the dawn of the Information Age. One decade later, cyberspace is an extraordinary extension of the human experience.

You can play the stock market on-line. You can apply for a job on-line. You can shop for lingerie on-line. You can work on-line. You can learn on-line. You can borrow money on-line. You can engage in sexual activity on-line. You can barter on-line. You can buy and sell real estate on-line. You can purchase plane tickets on-line. You can gamble on-line. You can find long-lost friends on-line. You can be informed, enlightened, and entertained on-line. You can order a pizza on-line. You can do your banking on-line. In some places, you can even vote on-line.

Indeed, the human race has not only brought its business to cyberspace, it has brought its exploration of the psyche there, too. And in the digital world, just as everywhere else, humanity has encountered its shadow side. Information Age business, government, and culture have led to Information Age crime, Information Age war, and even Information Age terror.

You can perform financial fraud on-line. You can steal trade secrets on-line. You can blackmail and extort on-line. You can trespass on-line. You can stalk on-line. You can vandalize someone's property on-line. You can commit libel on-line. You can rob a bank on-line. You can frame someone on-line. You can engage in character assassination on-line. You can commit hate crimes on-line. You can sexually harass someone on-line. You can molest children on-line. You can ruin someone else's credit on-line. You can disrupt commerce on-line. You can pillage and plunder on-line. You could incite to riot on-line. You could even start a war on-line.

Types of Cybercrime

There is a broad spectrum of cybercrimes, including

- Unauthorized access by insiders (such as employees)
- System penetration by outsiders (such as hackers)
- Theft of proprietary information (whether a simple user ID and password or a trade secret worth tens of millions of dollars)
- Financial fraud using computers
- Sabotage of data or networks
- Disruption of network traffic (for example, denial of service attacks)
- Creation and distribution of computer viruses, Trojan horses, and other types of malicious code
- Software piracy
- Identity theft
- Hardware theft (for example, laptop theft)

In Chapter 3 and Chapter 4, you will see that these and other cybercrimes are both widespread and costly.

In the United States, much of this criminal activity falls under the scope of the Computer Fraud and Misuse Act (Title 18, Section 1030) and the Economic Espionage Act (Title 18, Section Chapter 90) of the Federal Criminal Code. (See Appendix A.)

The Computer Fraud and Abuse Act makes it a federal crime to intentionally access a computer without authorization or by exceeding authorization and thereby obtain information to which the person is not entitled. The statute covers unlawfully accessing not only government or government-related computers to obtain information generated or owned by the federal government (especially secret information), but also any computers used in interstate or foreign commerce.

The Act was passed and signed into law in 1986. It was amended in 1988, 1989, 1990, 1994, and 1996 to fine-tune some of the language as well as address new developments.

Many of the cases you will read about in *Tangled Web* are covered under the Computer Fraud and Abuse Act. In some cases, government or university computers were hit; in other cases, financial institutions or phone companies were hit. In numerous cases, computers in multiple environments (including government, university, financial, telecommunications, and others) were hit.

Most states also have their own computer crime laws. For example, Iowa's code annotated section 716A.9 reads:

A person commits computer theft when the person knowingly and without authorization accesses or causes to be accessed a computer, computer system, or computer network, or any part thereof, for the purpose of obtaining services, information or property or knowingly and without authorization and with the intent to permanently deprive the owner of possession, takes, transfers, conceals or retains possession of a computer, computer system, or computer network or any computer software or program, or data contained in a computer, computer system, or computer network.

The Economic Espionage Act (EEA), passed and signed into law in 1996, makes it a federal crime to profit from the misappropriation of someone else's trade secret. Although the EEA is not exclusively a "computer crime law," it specifically includes language about unauthorized "downloads," "uploads," and "e-mails" in addition to language about more traditional methods such as "photocopies" and "deliveries." (Economic espionage is increasingly computer-based crime. For more on the EEA and cases prosecuted under it, see Chapter 10.)

Some cybercrimes reach everywhere and hurt everyone:

- Electronic commerce crime (like the theft of hundreds of thousands of credit card records) threatens the Internet boom that has fueled the unprecedented economic recovery the United States has experienced over the past decade.

- Economic espionage (like the theft of biotech secrets stored in digital files) threatens U.S. competitiveness in the global marketplace.

- Infrastructure attacks (like an assault against a nation's power grid) threaten the safety and well-being of whole populations.

Other cybercrimes, such as identity theft or cyberstalking, strike at individual citizens, exposing them to financial, psychological, and even physical harm.

Of course, a wide range of unsavory activity also occurs on-line, which, although not illegal, could lead to serious financial losses. For example, an employee's inappropriate use of a corporate e-mail system could lead to a costly sexual harassment suit.

Types of Cybercriminals

In 1994, I stood in the doorway of a crowded auditorium at a computer security conference organized by the National Institute of Standards and Technology (NIST) and the National Security Agency (NSA). Donn B. Parker, formerly of SRI International and currently with SRI spin-off venture Atomic Tangerine (www.atomictangerine.com), one of the great pioneers in the information security field, was delivering a seminal discourse on "The Wild West of NetSec."

Much of what Parker foretold that bright autumn morning has come to pass. For example, automated hacking tools have contributed to a drop in the skill level required to launch serious attacks. But something struck me as incongruous. During one portion of his presentation, Parker outlined a psychological profile of "hacker youths" based on his own first-hand research and interviews. I didn't doubt the conclusions he drew. Certainly, juvenile hackers could wreak havoc and mayhem. Certainly, psychological factors were at play in criminality of any kind. And yet, I asked myself, "What's wrong with this picture?"

It wasn't Parker's presentation at all; it was the palpable denial that pervaded the huge hall. There was something more to the story than adolescent hackers. There was a different and far more insidious problem that was rarely spoken of in public.

The stereotypical youthful hacker simply provided a convenient foil, a scapegoat, a placeholder for the professional criminals and foreign intelligence agents that would be conducting similar on-line break-ins. These digital hired guns would not be seeking the technological adventure; they would be seeking technological advantage.

Thereafter, I kept my eye on the big picture. Yes, it is the youthful hacker who usually ends up on the front page of the newspaper, but the professional doesn't make as many mistakes as that impetuous, adolescent transgressor. Professionals use stealth and superior skill to accomplish clandestine missions. Evidence of their activity is rarely detected. When professionals are detected, the targeted organizations rarely admit to their activities. They are afraid the bad press would scare off their investors, clients, and the like.

Just as diverse types of cybercrime occur, diverse types of cybercriminals perpetrate them.

Dishonest or disgruntled insiders (such as employees, ex-employees, contractors, temporary workers) want to sell your trade secrets, commit financial fraud, or just destroy your data or networks for revenge.

The term *hackers*, of course, has become somewhat hackneyed. Some in cyberculture distinguish between *hackers* and *crackers*. The politically correct use refers to those who break in simply to explore as *hackers* and to those who break into systems to steal or destroy information as *crackers*. But even those hackers who break in just to explore are guilty of at least breaking and entering.

For example, if you heard a noise in the middle of the night and turned on the light to discover someone crawling around your bedroom, it wouldn't really matter to you that the intruder was a student of interior design in search of inspiration, would it?

Professional spies and saboteurs are perhaps the most elusive of foes. They work for rival governments and competing corporations. They are paid. They are very adept. They can bring down your company, topple your government, or crash your stock market. They are rarely caught.

Career criminals are increasingly involved in cyberspace. Just as they became involved in trucking, casinos, and banking, organized criminal enterprises are eyeing e-commerce. And just as organized crime will go after e-commerce, petty criminals will target the financial resources of private individuals through on-line manipulation.

Terrorists might well target critical infrastructures such as the telephone system, the power grid, or the air traffic control system. These systems are run on computers and are vulnerable to cyberattacks.

Tangled Web is a journey into the shadows of cyberspace.

Inside the Mind of the Cybercriminal

E veryone is fascinated by cybercrime. They want to know "why." But as I outlined the contents of *Tangled Web* and typed "Inside the Mind of the Cybercriminal," I thought, "That will be a short chapter." Why? Well, for three reasons.

First, why indulge in too much probing about the psychological roots of cybercrime or even the conscious motivations of the cybercriminals themselves in a world where so little time is spent looking for the psychological roots or conscious motivations behind genocide, for example, or child abuse?

Second, crime is crime, whether committed in the physical world or in cyberspace. If you trespass, you trespass, whether you hop a chain-link fence or a firewall. If you steal a pharmaceutical formula, you steal pharmaceutical formula, whether it's printed on paper or stored on a file server. Many people don't get this simple truth. *Crime is crime*.

Why should the psychological roots or the conscious motivation involved in cybercrimes be any different than those involved in physical-world crimes?

If you told someone you had done some serious research on the psychological roots of "hacking" or "cracking," he would probably be intrigued. He would want to hear all about it. But if instead you told the same person that you had done some serious research on the psychological roots of trespassing and burglary, he would probably start looking at his watch and concocting a cover story for making a quick exit.

Third, there simply isn't very much reliable information.

I will share two expert views with you, though: Sarah Gordon, of IBM's Thomas Watson Research Center, and Atomic Tangerine's Donn Parker have both looked long and hard at these questions. Let's take a look at what they've found out.

"Stereotyping Can Be Dangerous"

Sarah Gordon is the real deal. She is one of the most fascinating people at work in information security. Those who know—on both sides of the law—take Sarah Gordon very seriously. No one has spent more time researching the motivation of hacker and virus writers.

Consider *Forbes ASAP*'s profile of the profiler.

> Sarah Gordon's credentials as an antivirus expert, one adept at dealing with the lethal creations of young hackers, are impeccable. She spent years debugging her own personal computers while she worked as a juvenile crisis counselor. Since 1997 she has worked at the preeminent antivirus lab in the country, IBM's Thomas J. Watson Research Center, in Hawthorne, New York.
>
> "The lab," she says, "is located deep within the IBM research facility. Its door is unmistakable. It's covered with warnings. I even put up a poster that warns: 'Alien Autopsy Room.' It's a reminder of the serious nature of what goes on in there.
>
> "Security is tight, but then it has to be. This lab contains one of the most complete virus collections in the world. Whereas hacker tools can cause havoc in the wrong hands, viruses don't need any hands; once they are launched, they spread very much like a biological virus. Only by applying the appropriate antiviral agent can they be stopped."[1]

Gordon agreed to answer some of my questions for *Tangled Web*.

"What is it that leads a kid into his computer," I ask Gordon, "instead of into the mall?"

"In the early '80s to '90s, computers were not commonplace in U.S. households," she replies. "The number of kids who could actually use computers was pretty small. Most kids still hung out at malls for socialization and leisure. Now, however, leisure and socialization are taking place via the Internet, and there are computers in many more households. So it's natural that more kids would be getting into computers. You don't have to drive to get there. There is a lot more to be found on the Internet than at the local mall, too.

"Now, think about the case in other countries," Gordon says. "In many countries, there aren't malls, school social events, etc., so young people and Internet socialization is a natural mix. Another thing that the Internet provides is communication without having to

---

1. "@Work with the IBM Antivirus Expert," by Evantheia Schibsted, *Forbes ASAP*, April 6, 1998.

really 'connect,' and for young people who may be somewhat insecure in social relationships, this provides excellent 'cover.' Or did you mean what leads kids to do 'bad things' on computers? This is a whole other, very complex topic."

"Have you, in all your experience," I ask, "seen any common denominators of any significance among those the media would describe as 'hackers'?"

"Well, I'm a hacker," she replies, "(remember, not all hacking is criminal), so I'd have to examine what I have in common with the rest. I'd say we all share a curiosity about computer systems."

"Have you in all your experience seen any common denominators of any significance in those who write viruses?"

"That 'curiosity' factor, again. The difference is that the virus writer who makes his virus available is making available 'the gift that keeps on giving.' Remember, there is a differentiation between a virus writer and a virus distributor. And, there is a differentiation between a distributor and the person who actually places the virus into action. These are subtle but important differences, especially as we begin to consider legislation related to viruses."

"What do you think would lead someone to write a virus rather than hack," I ask, "or is one the outgrowth of the other?

"One is definitively *not* the natural outgrowth of the other," Gordon asserts. "For years people have said viruses are boring. I don't think this is totally accurate. Viruses are interesting, especially if you don't understand them, and it is very cool to see a virus in action for the first time.

"That said, once you understand them, they *are* boring. And, once you have passed through doing this boring stuff and realize that it has the potential to really cause disruption and damage to real people, you tend to age out of it. Historically, most virus writers have cycled through this progression; this aging out marks the end of the foray into the underground.

"Hacking," she continues, "(actual hacking, not what is done by scripters) requires a much more thorough understanding of systems and is interesting. The information you get and the people you meet in the subculture tend to be much more interesting. People who get involved in hacking, serious hacking that is, don't generally 'age out' of it. They may use the skills to move into legitimate work, which some people may question the 'rightness' of."

Another important factor, according to Gordon, is that virus writing is relatively easy and can be done by people with little (if any) system knowledge. Some virus writers are now starting to take advantage of network connectivity, and some are making a transition more quickly to hacking via the commonly distributed hacking tools and techniques, but not to a great degree. Still, Gordon says, it is increasing.

So the two worlds, she believes, are beginning to overlap somewhat. And due to the nature of the digitally connected world, even a little overlap makes for a big impact. Basically, making a program replicate is so easy (and so irresponsible) that most hackers don't want any part of it.

"What are the differences between the common denominators for hackers and viruses writers?" I continue.

"Hackers," Gordon observes, "usually have a much higher skill level and understanding of systems in general. Virus writers I've met at DEFCON generally have a very elementary technical knowledge of viruses and tend to ask and go over the same material year after year."

Gordon's work makes a point that it is wrong to stereotype either hackers or virus writers. But nevertheless, I ask her if she had seen some motivation or aggregate of similar motivations that are prevalent or at least significant among hackers and virus writers.

"I think stereotyping can be dangerous. I have found that it's inaccurate to say all virus writers are unethical; it is wrong and inaccurate to say all hackers are criminals.

"But if there is a motivation prevalent among hackers," Gordon observes, "it's that curiosity thing again…just wanting to understand how things work!

"Virus writers tend to age out of virus writing; hackers tend to develop more integrated knowledge and transition into working with computers in some capacity related to systems."

I also ask Gordon if she had any comment on the motivations behind David Smith's creation and launching of Melissa or the motivations of de Guzman or whomever is found to be responsible for the Love Letter Worm.

"Generally, people who write viruses do not conceptualize the potential impact of that action on other people," she states. "It is much like a video game, where things happen but they are not 'real.' People get caught up in 'the game' of it, and only when they come face to face with the consequence do they realize it was not a game at all. It takes that face-to-face confrontation, or, simply aging out, to make them stop.

"Most of them do age out," she continues. "However, sometimes older people continue in this 'game,' seemingly not recognizing the consequence of their actions, or not caring. This doesn't mean they intentionally wanted to cause problems, although it certainly may. As for Smith, I have no idea whether he wanted to cause any specific types of problems. However, I am reasonably sure that Mr. David Smith had no idea of what the impact of that virus would be.

"This is not to say he is not responsible," Gordon says. "He has admitted he released it, and he has to take responsibility for that. And sure, he understood the code well enough, but to really understand the implications of its interaction with this huge monster we call 'the Net,' no. That's a whole different thing. It's something we as a society have not yet begun to address."

For more of Sarah Gordon's insights on the motivation of hackers and virus writers and related subjects, go to www.badguys.org and review some of her papers on the subject.

"Intense Personal Problems" Are the Key

In his excellent book, *Fighting Computer Crime: A New Framework for Protecting Information*, Donn Parker reveals some of the motivations that different types of cybercriminals had expressed to him in his interactions with them.

Here are a couple examples:

- "The bank desperately needed my information security consulting services but did not realize it. I was going to demonstrate how easy it was to engage in the first step in a funds transfer and show them the results so that they'd hire me to help. The first step was so easy that I decided to try the next step to see if it could be done as well, then the bank would be even more impressed. Nobody noticed what I had done. The next step was so easy as well, that I decided to see how far I could go. I never thought that I could succeed in doing the entire crime. I planned to return the money that I stole and appear as a hero."

- "I knew that if I did not destroy our competitor's computer center, I would be laid off from my computer operator job, and the affair that I was having with the president's wife would end. After all, he supplied the gasoline."[2]

Parker remarks that cybercriminals (just like physical-world criminals) need to rationalize their crimes.

> For example, the bank embezzler in Minneapolis didn't modify his bank balance. He merely modified the computer program so that it ignored his bank account overdraft for a while. According to him, no money was actually stolen and no one was losing anything—as long as he replenished his account before anyone noticed.

> International intellectual property pirates often rationalize their espionage and theft by claiming that it is okay to break the laws of foreign countries as long as they do not break the laws of their own country. Besides, they feel justified because other countries are so rich and theirs is so poor.[3]

---

2. *Fighting Computer Crime: A New Framework for Protecting Information*, Donn Parker, page 147, John Wiley & Sons, Inc., 1998.

3. *Fighting Computer Crime*, pages 146, 148.

According to Parker, although there is no way to describe "a typical cybercriminal," there are some common traits.

In psychological terms, Parker asserts, they can exhibit *differential association syndrome*. For example, an embezzler may start by taking only small things like paper clips, paper, and pencils to use at home. "Everyone does it." But the embezzler's thefts will escalate until he is stealing thousands of dollars from the company's bank account.

The same is true with the theft of computer services. Two programmers ended up in jail for running their own side business on company computers. "But," they said, "everyone does it." Well, yes, other employees used the company's computers for sending personal e-mail messages or playing games, but these two guys ended up utilizing three-fourths of the organization's mainframe computer to run their sheet-music business.

Parker observes that cybercriminals also frequently tend to anthropomorphize the computers they attack and yet feel that attacking a computer does no harm to other people.

> Most of the cybercriminals I have encountered could not engage in a person-to-person crime if their lives depended on it. They could not look victims in the eye and rob them or attack them, but [they] have no problem attacking or robbing a computer because a computer does not look back or exhibit anguish. Cybercriminals often distinguish between the unacceptable practice of doing harm to people and the impersonal acts of doing harm to or through computers. Yet, many receive a measure of satisfaction in their crimes by personifying the computers they attack, viewing them as adversaries and deriving some enjoyment from ripping them off.[4]

Many cybercriminals exhibit the Robin Hood syndrome, rationalizing that they are taking from victims who, in their view, can afford it. But, as Parker remarks, there is a twist to it. In cybercrime terminology, the Robin Hood syndrome doesn't refer to "stealing from the rich to give to the poor," but rather "stealing from the rich and keeping the booty."

> The victims of cybercrime are often organizations that—at least in the criminal's mind—can afford to suffer a relatively small loss to help solve the criminal's intense personal problems.[5]

These "intense personal problems" are the key, according to Parker, for unlocking the mind of the cybercriminal.

> Despite the common view that greed usually motivates individuals to commit business crime, I have found that most cybercriminals are attempting to solve intense personal problems. At the time that a criminal perpetrates the crime, he is indeed attempting to achieve some type of gain. Law enforcement and the news media usually interpret this as greed or the desire for high living, but my interviews with criminals indicate that intense need, rather than greed, causes them to commit crimes. The problems that they are attempting to resolve run

---

4. Fighting Computer Crime, page 141.

5. Fighting Computer Crime, page 142-3.

the usual gamut of human difficulties: problems with a marriage or love relationship, failure to progress as fast as others in a career path, a need for money
to settle outstanding debts, feeding addictions, and so on. Overall, the cybercriminal perceives himself as a problem solver rather than as a criminal.[6]

The problem of sport or joy-riding hackers, unlike disgruntled employees or fraud-
sters, demands special attention.

Many of them are juveniles and, therefore, should be handled differently.
Furthermore, many joy riders, whether juvenile or adult, really are misguided and do
not mean to do harm or even see anything wrong or dangerous in their "explorations."

There is a lot of evidence that these intruders have some serious problems.

In 1996, while working at SRI International, Parker concluded a study based on interviews with more than 80 hackers in the United States and Europe.

Common traits that emerged from Parker's study of youthful hackers included:

- Precociousness, curiosity, and persistence
- Habitual lying, cheating, stealing, and exaggerating
- Juvenile idealism, e.g., "power to the people," "if it feels good, do it."
- Hyperactivity
- Drug and alcohol abuse

And as the 1990s wore on, Parker observes, hacker culture took a turn for the worse.

During the interviews, it became clear that, the once honorable pursuit of
hacking (as described by Stephen Levy in his 1984 book, *Hackers*) had largely
disappeared. In today's hacker culture, malicious hackers regularly engage in
fabrications, exaggerations, thievery, and fantasy. They delight in presenting
themselves to the media and general public as idealistic do-gooders, champi-
ons of the underdog, the "little guys" working against the big computer vendors and doing good deeds along the way. Juvenile hackers often fantasize
their roles as Clark Kents who become Supermen of cyberspace.
Unfortunately, their public persona is far from the truth.

Although malicious hackers range in age from preteen to senior citizens, they
are characterized by an immature excessively idealistic attitude. Regardless of
age, they act like irresponsible kids playing cops and robbers in a fantasy
world that can suddenly turn real when they are caught. [7]

For your further consideration, I have also included a computer crime adversarial
matrix originally developed for the FBI as an investigative, profiling tool.

---

6. Fighting Computer Crime, page 142.

7. Fighting Computer Crime, page 162-3.

Table 2.1 Computer Crime Adversarial Matrix—Organizational Characteristics

Categories of Offenders	Organization	Recruitment/Attraction	International Connections
Crackers			
Groups	Unstructured organization with counterculture orientation	Peer group attraction	Interact and correspond with other groups around the world
Individuals	None; these people are true loners	Attracted by the intellectual challenge	Subscribe to cracker journals and may interact on cracker bulletin boards
Criminals			
Espionage	Supported by hostile intelligence services	In most cases, money; some cases of ideological attraction; attention	Use computer networks to break into target computers around the world
Fraud/abuse	May operate as small organized crime group or as a loner	Money; power	Use wire services to transfer money internationally
Vandals			
Strangers	Loner or small group; may be quite young	Revenge; intellectual challenge; money	Use of computer networks and phone systems to break into target computers
Users	Often employee or former employee	Revenge; power; intellectual challenge; disgruntlement	None

Source: "Computer Crime: A Crimefighter's Handbook" by David Icove, Karl Seger, and William VonStorcb (ISBN: 1-56592-086-4).

Table 2.2   Computer Crime Adversarial Matrix—Operational Characteristics

Categories of Offenders	Planning	Level of Expertise	Tactics/Methods Used
		Crackers	
Groups	May involve detailed planning	High	Enter target computers via computer networks; exchange information with other crackers and groups
Individuals	Study networks before attempts are made	Medium to high; expertise gained through social networks	Use networks but more likely to use trial and error online than to do careful research and planning; use BBSs to share accounts on other systems
		Criminals	
Espionage	Same characteristics as crackers	High	May contract with crackers to conduct information and data collection
Fraud/abuse	Careful planning prior to crime	Medium to high, although is typically more experienced at fraud than at computer programming	May use more traditional intrusion methods such as wire tapping and trapdoors; will break into systems using basic methods
		Vandals	
Strangers	Not much planning; more a crime of opportunity	Varies	Looks around until able to gain access to system
Users	May involve detailed planning and execution	Varies; may have high level of expertise	Trap doors and Trojan horse programs; data modification

Source: "Computer Crime: A Crimefighter's Handbook" by David Icove, Karl Seger, and William VonStorch (ISBN: 1-56592-086-4).

Table 2.3 Computer Crime Adversarial Matrix—Behavioral Characteristics

Categories of Offenders	Motivation	Personal Characteristics	Potential Weaknesses
		Crackers	
Groups	Intellectual challenge; peer group fun; in support of a cause	Highly intelligent individuals; counterculture orientation	Do not consider offenses crimes; talk freely about actions
Individuals	Intellectual challenge; problem solving; power; money; in support of a cause	Moderately to highly intelligent	May keep notes and other documentation on actions
		Criminals	
Espionage	Money and a chance to attack the system	May be crackers operating in groups or as individuals	Becomes greedy for more information and then becomes careless
Fraud/abuse	Money or other personal gain; power offenders	Same personal characteristics as other fraud	Becomes greedy and makes mistakes
		Vandals	
Strangers	Intellectual challenge; money; power	Same characteristics as crackers	May become too brazen and make mistakes
Users	Revenge against organization; problem solving; money	Usually has some computer expertise	May leave audit trail in computer logs

Source: "Computer Crime: A Crimefighter's Handbook" by David Icove, Karl Seger, and William VonStorch (ISBN: 1-56592-086-4).

Table 2.4   Computer Crime Adversarial Matrix—Resource Characteristics

Categories of Offenders	Training Skills	Minimum Equipment Needed	Support Structure
		Crackers	
Groups	High level of informal training	Basic computer equipment with modem	Peer support group
Individuals	Expertise gained through experience	Basic computer equipment with modem	BBS; information exchanges
		Criminals	
Espionage	Various levels of expertise	Basic computer equipment with modem; in some cases, uses more sophisticated devices	Support may come from sponsoring intelligence agency
Fraud/Abuse	Some programming experience	Computer with modem or access to target computer	Peer group; possible organized crime enterprise
		Vandals	
Strangers	Range from basic to highly skilled	Basic computer with modem	Peer group support
Users	Some computer expertise; knowledge of programming ranges from basic to advanced	Access to targeted computer	None

Source: "Computer Crime: A Grimefighter's Handbook" by David Icove, Karl Seger, and William VonStorcb (ISBN: 1-56592-086-4).

Been Down So Long It Looks Like Up To Me: The Extent and Scope of the Cybercrime Problem

In May 2000, the FBI reported that crime in the United States dropped for a record eighth straight year in 1999, with homicides, assaults, robberies, and other serious offenses falling by 7%. The FBI, which has been compiling criminal data since the 1930s, has never before reported a drop in the crime rate for eight successive years.

Unfortunately, although the crime rate in the physical space of the United States might be decreasing, the crime rate in cyberspace is increasing.

The following four diverse sources provide some fascinating data:

- *CSI/FBI Computer Crime and Security Survey*
- Computer Emergency Response Team's (CERT) statistics on incidents, vulnerabilities, alerts, and so on
- Dan Farmer's Internet Security Survey
- WarRoom Research's Information Security Survey

The *CSI/FBI Computer Crime and Security Survey*

In the summer of 1995, I received a call from FBI Special Agent Pat Murphy, a member of the San Francisco FBI's newly formed Computer Intrusion Squad. The S.F. unit was only the second one established in the entire country. (Washington, D.C. was the first; New York was the third.)

The FBI's regional Computer Intrusion Squads investigate violations of the Computer Fraud and Abuse Act (Title 18, Section 1030), including intrusions to public switched networks, major computer network intrusions, privacy violations, industrial espionage, pirated software, and other crimes.

A few days later, I met with Murphy and Supervisory Special Agent George Vinson on the 13th floor of the Federal Office Building on 450 Golden Gate Avenue in the Tenderloin. They had a lot of questions. How bad is the computer crime problem? How often are corporations attacked? Which computer crimes are the most common? What kinds of financial losses are being incurred?

I told Murphy and Vinson that they were asking the important questions, but that no one had the answers. Furthermore, the answers would be hard to come by. Corporations are loath to admit bad news.

I suggested that we could conduct an anonymous survey of CSI members (information security practitioners in Fortune 500 companies and large government agencies). I invited Murphy and Vinson to submit the questions that they wanted answered. That's how simply it began.

The *CSI/FBI Computer Crime and Security Survey* was undertaken as a public service by the Computer Security Institute (CSI), with the participation of the San Francisco Federal Bureau of Investigation's (FBI) Computer Intrusion Squad. This ongoing effort aims to raise the level of security awareness as well as to assist in determining the scope of computer crime in the United States.

The success of the survey is unprecedented in the field of information security.

Now in its fifth year, the annual release of the results of the *CSI/FBI Computer Crime and Security Survey* is a major international news story, covered widely in the mainstream print and broadcast media. The CSI/FBI is, for better or worse, the most widely cited research on the extent and scope of cybercrime and related security problems. Furthermore, throughout the year, the survey results are referenced in numerous presentations, articles, and papers on the nature and scope of computer crime.

The CSI/FBI survey results led to my 1996 U.S. Senate testimony. The CSI/FBI survey results led to my journeys to South Africa, Japan, Brazil, Portugal, Norway, and elsewhere to deliver executive briefings on cybercrime and information warfare.

Based on responses from 643 computer security practitioners in U.S. corporations and government agencies, the findings of the *CSI/FBI 2000 Computer Crime and Security Survey* confirm the trends that have emerged over the previous years:

- Organizations are under cyberattack from both inside and outside their electronic perimeters.
- A wide range of cyberattacks have been detected.
- Cyberattacks can result in serious financial losses.
- Defending successfully against such attacks requires more than just the use of information security technologies.

Patrice Rapalus, CSI Director (and my boss), elaborates: "The trends the CSI/FBI survey has highlighted over the years are disturbing. Cybercrimes and other information security breaches are widespread and diverse. Furthermore, such incidents can result in serious damages.

"Clearly," she continues, "more must be done in terms of adherence to sound practices, deployment of sophisticated technologies, and most importantly adequate staffing and training of information security practitioners in both the private sector and government."

Bruce J. Gebhardt is in charge of the FBI's Northern California office. Based in San Francisco, his division covers 15 counties, including the continuously expanding Silicon Valley area. Computer crime is one of his biggest challenges.

"If the FBI and other law enforcement agencies are to be successful in combating this continually increasing problem," he says, "we cannot always be placed in a reactive mode, responding to computer crises as they happen. The results of the CSI/FBI survey provide us with valuable data. This information not only has been shared with Congress to underscore the need for additional investigative resources on a national level but identifies emerging crime trends and helps me decide how best to proactively and aggressively assign resources, before those 'trends' become 'crises.'"

In the midst of the media interest in the release of the fifth annual CSI/FBI survey results, several reporters asked, "What surprises you most about this year's data?"

"Well," I answered, "the only surprise is that there aren't any surprises."

For example, the number of respondents reporting their Internet connections as a frequent point of attack has increased every year for five years.

Being able to look at responses to the same questions over a period of several years provides an invaluable, unprecedented glimpse into what's really going on out there.

Here is a summation of what we have gleaned over the life cycle of the project so far.

Whom We Asked

Most respondents work for large corporations. The heaviest concentrations of respondents are in the financial services and high-tech sectors (each represents 17% of respondents). Manufacturing is the next largest industry segment (10% of respondents).

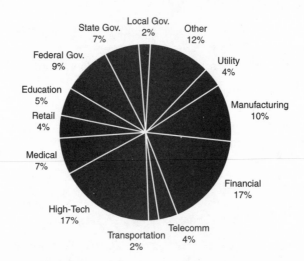

Figure 3.1 Respondents by industry sector.

Source: 2000 CSI/FBI Computer Crime and Security Survey

2000: 643 Respondents/100%

The public sector is well represented. When taken together, federal (9%), state (7%), and local (2%) government agencies comprise another 18% of respondents.

Organizations in other vital areas of the national infrastructure also responded: for example, medical institutions (7%), telecommunications (4%), and utilities (4%).

The responses come from organizations with large payrolls—for example, 30% reported 10,000 or more employees, 12% reported from 5,001 to 9,999 employees.

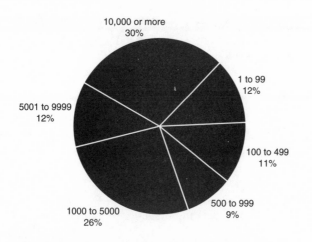

Figure 3.2 Respondents by number of employees.

Source: 2000 CSI/FBI Computer Crime and Security Survey
2000: 640 Respondents/99%

Forty-three percent of respondents in the commercial sector reported a gross income over $1 billion; 11% reported gross income of from $501 million to $1 billion. (Interestingly, these two figures are reversed from the 1999 results: Last year, 40% indicated from $501 million to $1 billion and 16% indicated over $1 billion. Further evidence of the economic prosperity of the mid-1990s?)

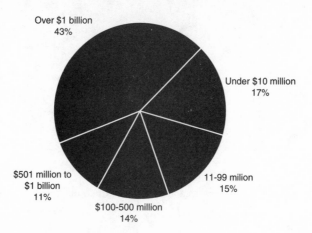

Figure 3.3 Respondents by gross income.

Source: 2000 CSI/FBI Computer Crime and Security Survey
2000: 422 Respondents/65%

Consider the 643 survey responses in regard to industry sector, number of employees, and gross income. Clearly, the results demand your attention. The types of incidents reported (whether illegal, litigious, or simply inappropriate), as well as the trends that the five-year life of the survey confirm, have the potential to do serious damage to U.S. economic competitiveness.

Unless information security is the focus of concerted efforts throughout both the public and private sector, the rule of law in cyberspace as well as U.S. leadership in the global marketplace will be undermined.

Outlaw Blues

How widespread are cyberattacks and other information security breaches?

For five years, we have asked the following question: "Have you experienced unauthorized use of computer systems within the last 12 months?" In 1996, 42% answered "yes." In 2000, 70% answered "yes." (Note: These figures are adjusted to exclude those who answered "yes," but only reported incidents of computer viruses, laptop theft, and/or some form of employee abuse of network privileges.)

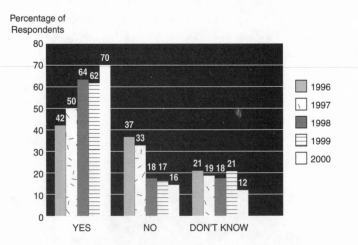

Figure 3.4 Unauthorized use of computer systems within the last 12 months.

Source: 2000 CSI/FBI Computer Crime and Security Survey
2000: 585 Respondents/91%
1999: 512 Respondents/98%
1998: 515 Respondents/99%
1997: 391 Respondents/69%
1996: 410 Respondents/96%

It is encouraging to see the precipitous decline of those who responded "no" to this question from 37% in 1996 to 16% in 2000. In 1997, 33% of respondents answered "no." In the "Briefing Notes" for the 1997 study I wrote, "After all, 'yes' and 'don't know' are probably the only honest answers to this question." In 1998, the number of respondents who answered "no" fell to 18%.

Now, in the fifth year of the survey results, the number of respondents who answered "don't know" has finally fallen: from 21% in 1999 to 12% in 2000.

What does this all mean? People are no longer living in denial. They are looking more closely at activity on their networks. Furthermore, they are using better tools to look, and they are less reluctant to answer "yes."

What about the origin of attacks? Well, although many Pollyannas still cling to the conventional wisdom that "80% of the problem is insiders, only 20% of the problem is outsiders," the number of respondents reporting their Internet connections as a frequent point of attack has increased every year: rising from 37% in 1996 to 59% in 2000. Meanwhile, the number of respondents citing their internal systems as frequent points of attack actually fell from 51% in 1999 to 38% in 2000.

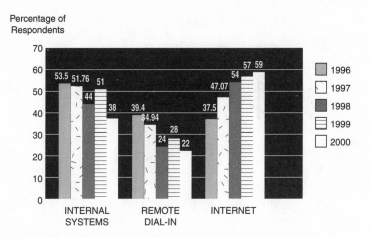

Figure 3.5   Internet connection is increasingly cited as a frequent point of attack.

Source: CSI/FBI 2000 Computer Crime and Security Survey

2000: 443 Respondents/68%
1999: 324 Respondents/62%
1998: 279 Respondents/54%
1997: 391 Respondents/69%
1996: 174 Respondents/40%

The conventional wisdom about 80% of perpetrators being insiders and 20% being outsiders is simply no longer supported by the data. It isn't that the threat from insiders has decreased; it is simply that the threat from the outside has risen dramatically because of the rise of the Internet as a means of business communication.

In the 1965 ballad "Outlaw Blues," Bob Dylan boasted, "Don't ask me nothin' about nothin', I just might tell you the truth."

Types of Cyberattack

For the last four years, we have asked the question, "Which of the following types of electronic attack or misuse has your organization detected within the last 12 months?"

In 2000, respondents reported a wide range of attacks and abuses. Here are some examples:

- 11% detected financial fraud
- 17% detected sabotage of data and/or networks
- 20% detected theft of proprietary information
- 25% detected system penetration from the outside
- 27% detected denial of service
- 71% detected unauthorized access by insiders
- 79% detected employee abuse of Internet access privileges
- 85% detected viruses

To Report or Not to Report

The aim of the annual *CSI/FBI Computer Crime and Security Survey* is not only to gather data on the dark side of cyberspace but to foster greater cooperation between law enforcement and the private sector so that both can provide a viable deterrent to cybercrime.

For the first three years, only 17% of those who suffered serious attacks reported them to law enforcement. In the 1999 survey, 32% answered that they had reported such incidents to law enforcement. In 2000, the percent of respondents who reported intrusions to law enforcement dropped to 25%.

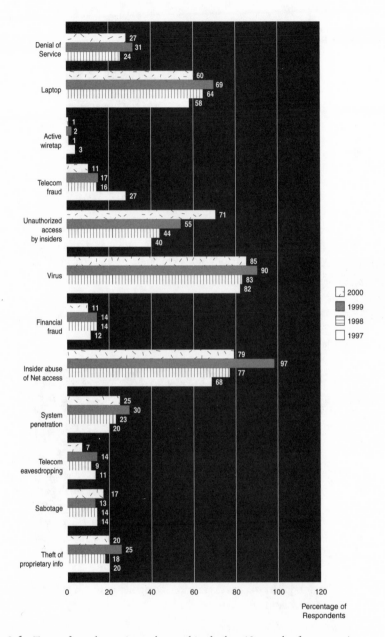

Figure 3.6 Types of attack or misuse detected in the last 12 months (by percent).

Source: 2000 CSI/FBI Computer Crime and Security Survey

2000: 581 Respondents/90%
1999: 405 Respondents/78%
1998: 458 Respondents/89%
1997: 492 Respondents/87%

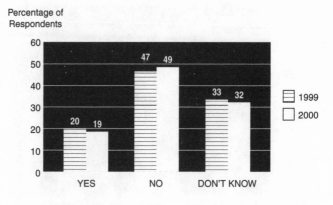

Figure 3.7   Has your WWW site suffered unauthorized access or misuse within the last 12 months? Ninety-five percent of respondents have WWW sites; 43% provide electronic commerce services via their WWW sites; only 30% were doing e-commerce in 1999.

Source: 2000 CSI/FBI Computer Crime and Security Survey

2000: 603 Respondents/93%
1999: 479 Respondents/92%

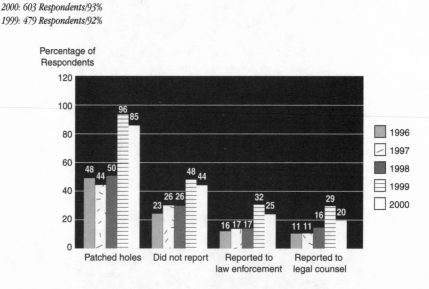

Figure 3.8   If your organization has experienced computer intrusion(s) within the last 12 months, which of the following actions did you take?

Source: 2000 CSI/FBI Computer Crime and Security Survey

2000: 407 Respondents/63%
1999: 295 Respondents/57%
1998: 321 Respondents/72%
1997: 317 Respondents/56%
1996: 325 Respondents/76%

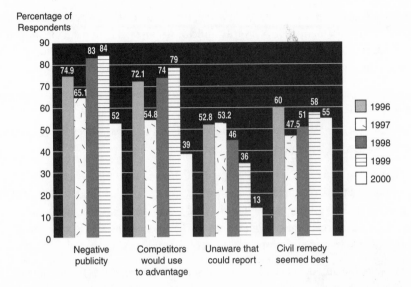

Percentage of
Respondents

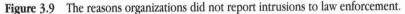

Figure 3.9   The reasons organizations did not report intrusions to law enforcement.

Source: 2000 CSI/FBI Computer Crime and Security Survey

2000: 209 Respondents/32%
1999: 107 Respondents/20%
1998: 96 Respondents/19%
1997: 142 Respondents/25%
1996: 64 Respondents/15%

Dr. Dorothy Denning of Georgetown University (Washington, D.C.) comments that a smaller percentage of companies reported incidents to law enforcement in 2000 than in 1999, but the number was still greater than for preceding years, and the percentage citing negative publicity or concern about competitors using it to advantage decreased. "Thus," she says, "the decline in reporting from last year could be due to other factors, such as the cost of dealing with an investigation or expectation that an investigation will not be successful."

Indeed, as Dr. Denning observed, it does seem that, at least among CSI/FBI survey respondents, the taboos against reporting are dropping precipitously. The percent of respondents that cited "negative publicity" fell from 84% to 52%; the percent that cited fear that "competitors would use news of the intrusion to gain competitive advantage" fell from 79% to 39%.

Rik Farrow (www.spirit.com), a CSI faculty member, adds some insight.

"The FBI has completed several prosecutions where the identity of the cybervictims was never divulged. This is an encouraging sign for those who fear adverse publicity. At the same time, a person who caused a tremendous amount of damage and gets convicted can expect to receive a much lighter sentence than a person found with a small amount of marijuana. A security director who works for a bank mentioned that the bank prefers to go after civil penalties when possible, as these penalties (plus the cost of paying defense lawyers) are likely to be much more severe."

The Truth Is Out There

The *CSI/FBI Computer Crime and Security Survey* is a non-scientific, informal but narrowly focused poll of information security practitioners.

The survey is, at best, a series of snapshots that give some sense of the "facts on the ground" at a particular time. The findings are in large part corroborated by data from other reputable studies, as well as by real-world incidents documented in open source publications. I also suggest that the findings of the CSI/FBI survey are also strengthened by having five straight years of data to draw on.

CSI offers the survey results as a public service. The report is free to anyone who requests a copy. The participation of the FBI's San Francisco office has been invaluable. It has provided input into the development of the survey itself and acted as our partner in the effort to encourage response. But CSI has no contractual or financial relationship with the FBI. It is simply an outreach and education effort on the part of both organizations. CSI foots the bill for the project and is solely responsible for the results.

Hopefully, somewhere in the mix of real-world horror stories and data points contained in this report, there is something relevant to the information protection needs of your organization that will help you make your quadrant of cyberspace safer for creation, communications, and commerce.

A Note on Methodology

Questionnaires with business reply envelopes were sent by U.S. post to 4,284 information security professionals; 643 responses were received for a 15% response rate.

In 1999, 521 responses were received (14% of 3,670 questionnaires sent). In 1998, 520 responses were received (13% of 3,890 questionnaires sent). In 1997, 563 responses were received (11% of 4,899 questionnaires sent). In 1996, 428 responses were received (8% of 4,971 questionnaires sent).

The responses were anonymous. Job titles of those queried range from information security manager to data security officer to senior systems analyst. Organizations surveyed include corporations, financial institutions, government agencies, and universities in the United States.

Relevant Data from Other Sources

I've culled the following data from serious research undertaken by some diverse entities.

CERT/CC Statistics

The Computer Emergency Response Team (CERT) at Carnegie Mellon University, founded in the wake of the Morris Worm incident (see Chapter 5), is one of the principal players in the dissemination of Internet security information. Such information includes warnings about imminent or ongoing attacks and alerts about patches that close security breaches in operating systems and applications. The CERT data included here is compiled from the many calls the team receives from sysadmins throughout cyberspace on a 24-7 basis.

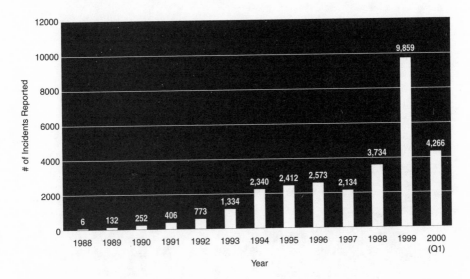

Figure 3.10 Number of incidents reported.

Source: CERT/CC Statistics 1988-2000

Total incidents reported (1988-2000): 30,261

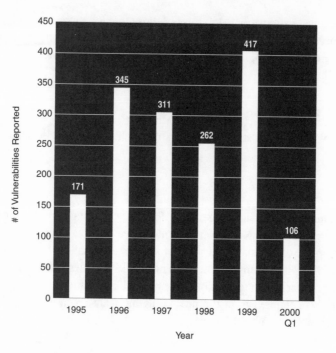

Figure 3.11 Vulnerabilities reported.

Source: CERT/CC Statistics 1988-2000

Total vulnerabilities reported (1988-2000): 1,612

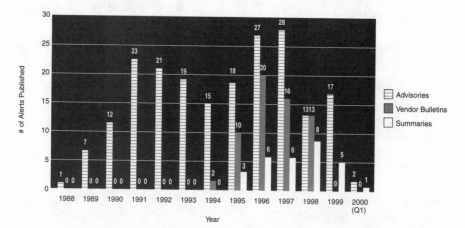

Figure 3.12 Security alerts published.

Source: CERT/CC Statistics 1988-2000

Total security alerts published (1988-2000): 293

Dan Farmer's Internet Security Survey

Dan Farmer is a leading, although controversial, Internet security expert. Farmer authored the SATAN tool for scanning and exposing network and Internet vulnerabilities. Farmer's "Internet Security Survey" is compiled from an audacious and unsolicited scan of Internet Web sites he conducted in 1996.

According to Farmer, the "red" designation refers to sites that are "wide open to any potential attacker," and the "yellow" designation refers to sites that have "problems that are less serious although still of great concern."

Table 3.1   Internet Security Survey Summary

Type of Site	Total # of Hosts Scanned	Total % Vulnerable	% Yellow	% Red
Banks	660	68.33	32.73	35.61
Credit unions	274	51.09	30.66	20.44
U.S. Federal sites	47	61.70	23.40	38.30
Newspapers	312	69.55	30.77	38.78
Sex	451	66.08	40.58	25.50
Totals	**1,734**	**64.94**	**33.85**	**31.08**
Random group	**469**	**33.05**	**15.78**	**17.27**

Source: Dan Farmer, www.fish.com
The total number of hosts in the individual categories does not add up to the "Total" number of hosts because of multi-homed hosts.

WarRoom Research's Information Security Survey

WarRoom Research is a group of competitive intelligence and information security consultants based in the Washington, D.C. area. Its data is compiled, as is much of the CSI/FBI data, from Fortune 500 corporations. The tables in this section answer the following questions.

Have you detected attempts to gain computer access to any of your computer systems from "outsiders" in the past 12 months?

Yes	119	58.0%
No	25	12.2%
Don't know	<u>61</u>	<u>29.8%</u>
	205	100.0%

Table 3.2 Vulnerability Breakdown by Site Type (in Percents)

Site Type	Denial of Service	FTP	Yellow Web	INND	REXD access	Sendmail	Red Web	YPupdated	statd
Banks	57.12	0.15	9.85	3.18	0.15	9.70	1.52	0.91	29.39
Credit unions	43.43	0.00	8.03	1.46	0.00	4.01	0.73	1.09	16.42
U.S. Federal sites	44.68	0.00	36.17	0.00	0.00	12.76	2.12	6.38	31.91
Newspapers	52.88	0.32	14.42	2.24	0.00	16.67	1.28	0.64	30.77
Sex	56.54	0.00	6.65	1.33	0.00	11.97	0.67	0.00	18.85
Totals	**53.63**	**0.12**	**10.32**	**2.19**	**0.06**	**10.67**	**1.1**	**0.81**	**24.91**
Random group	**28.14**	**0.00**	**1.92**	**0.64**	**0.64**	**7.25**	**0.00**	**0.64**	**13.65**

Source: Dan Farmer, www.fish.com
(The Denial of Service and Yellow Web vulnerabilities were "yellow" vulnerabilities, and the others were counted as red vulnerabilities.)

If yes, how many successful unauthorized accesses from "outsiders" have you detected? (developed table)

1–10	41	41.8%
11–0	24	24.5%
21–30	16	16.3%
31–40	10	10.2%
41–50	5	5.1%
>50	2	2.0%
	98	100.0%

If you experienced computer system intrusions by someone from outside your organization, indicate the type of activity performed by the intruder performed.

Manipulated data integrity	41	6.8%
Installed a sniffer	40	6.6%
Stole password files	34	5.6%
Probing/scanning of system	88	14.6%
Trojan logons	35	5.8%
IP spoofing	29	4.8%
Introduced virus	64	10.6%
Denied use of services	38	6.3%
Downloaded data	49	8.1%
Compromised trade secrets	59	9.8%
Stole/diverted money	2	0.3%
Compromised e-mail/documents	76	12.6%
Publicized intrusion	3	0.5%
Harassed personnel	27	4.5%
Other (specified)	18	3.0%
	603	100.0%

How many "insiders" have been caught misusing your organization's computer systems? Running their own ventures on company systems, abuse of online accounts, personal record keeping, etc. (developed table)

Unknown	20	9.8%
0	56	27.3%
1–5	24	11.7%
6–10	46	22.4%

11–15	32	15.6%
16–20	13	6.3%
21–25	9	4.4%
>25	5	2.4%
	205	100.0%

If yes, what disciplinary action was taken?

Oral admonishment	70	54.3%
Written admonishment	27	20.9%
Suspended	7	5.4%
Resigned	8	6.2%
Fired	11	8.5%
Referred to law enforcement	2	1.6%
Out of court settlement	0	0.0%
No action	4	3.1%
Other (specified)	0	0.0%
	129	100.0%

Conclusions

These three diverse sources offer different perspectives on the same problems. The CERT data reflects what is being reported at the sysadmin level within the Internet community. The Farmer data reflects the level of vulnerability out there as determined by a rogue hacking expert working on his own. The WarRoom Research data is a second opinion to the CSI/FBI survey data on the state of information security in corporate America. Taken together, these three very distinct avenues of research all lead to the same conclusion: Cybercrime is real, and the problem is not being adequately addressed.

Let It Bleed: The Cost of Computer Crime and Related Security Breaches

What is the cost of computer crime? How do you tabulate it? These are burning questions that don't have easy answers.

For the last four years of the *CSI/FBI Computer Crime and Security Survey*, we have asked the question, "Which of the following types of electronic attack or misuse has caused your organization financial losses within the last 12 months?"

In 1997, 75% of respondents said their organizations had suffered financial losses. In 1998, 73% acknowledged losses. In 1999, the number of respondents citing financial losses dropped to 51%. In 2000, the number of respondents acknowledging financial losses climbed back up to 74%.

Every year there is a drop-off between those willing to acknowledge suffering financial losses and those willing to put a price tag on them.

In 1997, only 59% of respondents were willing or able to quantify some of their financial losses. In 1998, only 42% were willing or able. In 1999, only 31% were willing or able. In 2000, only 42% were willing or able.

In 2000, the losses from these 273 respondents totaled $265,589,940 (the average annual total over the last three years was $120,240,180).

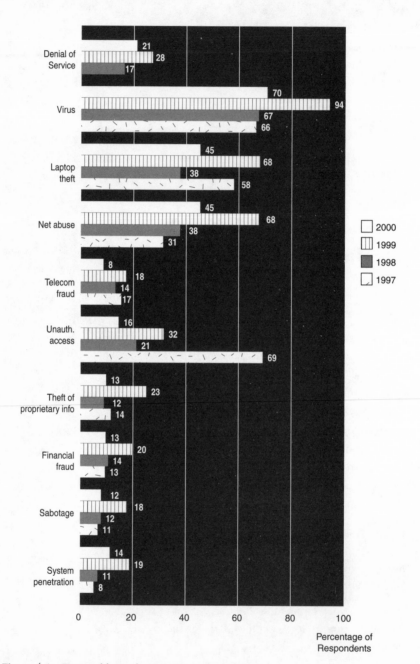

Figure 4.1   Financial losses by type or attack or misuse.

Source: 2000 CSI/FBI Computer Crime and Security Survey
2000: 477 Respondents/74%
1999: 265 Respondents/51%
1998: 376 Respondents/73%
1997: 422 Respondents/75%

In 2000, financial losses in 8 of 12 categories were larger than in any previous year. Furthermore, financial losses in four categories were higher than the combined total of the three previous years. For example, 61 respondents quantified losses due to sabotage of data or networks for a total of $27,148,000; the total financial losses due to sabotage for the previous years combined totaled only $10,848,850.

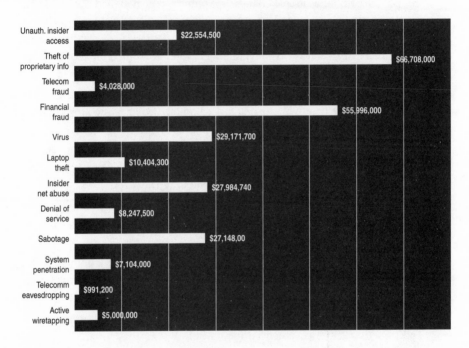

Unauth. insider access	$22,554,500
Theft of proprietary info	$66,708,000
Telecom fraud	$4,028,000
Financial fraud	$55,996,000
Virus	$29,171,700
Laptop theft	$10,404,300
Insider net abuse	$27,984,740
Denial of service	$8,247,500
Sabotage	$27,148,00
System penetration	$7,104,000
Telecomm eavesdropping	$991,200
Active wiretapping	$5,000,000

Figure 4.2   Dollar amount of losses by type.

Source: 2000 CSI/FBI Computer Crime and Security Survey

2000: 273 Respondents/42%

As in previous years, the most serious financial losses occurred through theft of proprietary information (66 respondents reported $66,708,000) and financial fraud (53 respondents reported $55,996,000).

In December 1999, I spoke on "Estimating the Cost of Cybercrime" at a National Security Forum on "International Cooperation to Combat Cyber Crime and Terrorism." Sponsored by the Consortium for Research on Information Security and Policy (CRISP), the gathering was held at the Hoover Institute Center for International Security and Cooperation (CISAC) on the campus of Stanford University.

I shared the financial losses cited in the CSI/FBI survey up until that point, but I also offered them a bit of collateral evidence to put our data in some perspective.

I reviewed the "In Case You Missed It" news items that I ran in the *Computer Security Alert* for a two-year period from November 1997 to November 1999. I was looking for news items that cited specific dollar amounts for financial losses due to cyberattacks and other information security breaches.

I found only eleven out of several hundred.

- The so-called Phonemasters gained access to telephone networks of AT&T, British Telecommunications, GTE, MCI, Southwestern Bell, and Sprint. (For a case study on the Phonemasters, refer to Chapter 7.) Their customers included private investigators, so-called information brokers, and—by way of middle-men—the Sicilian Mafia. According to the FBI, they accounted for about at least $1.85 million in financial losses to the businesses mentioned.

- Nikita Rose, a 26-year-old woman, was sentenced in federal court in connection with accessing a computer to defraud Salomon Brothers Investor Fund of $538,325 in shareholder funds.

- Jay Satiro, an 18-year-old high school dropout, was arrested after AOL officials contacted authorities. A complaint filed against Satiro said he altered AOL data and programs that would cost about $50,000 to repair.

- Fifty-one people were arrested on charges of hacking into a Chinese railway's computer system. The scheme affected more than 8,000 tickets, worth $54,000, before it was uncovered.

- A Chinese court sentenced twin brothers to death for hacking into a bank's computer system and stealing 720,000 yuan, in China's first cyber bank robbery.

- Shakuntla Devi Singla, 43, the first woman convicted of computer hacking in the United States, was sentenced for trashing a U.S. Coast Guard personnel database. It took 115 Coast Guard employees, including network administrators, more than 1,800 hours to restore the lost data. The recovery effort cost $40,000.

- The Royal Canadian Mounted Police, which conducted a 14-month investigation, said a hacker broke into the computer systems at the National Aeronautics and Space Administration (NASA) Center, the National Oceanographic and Atmospheric Association (NOAA), and Hughes STC. One victim reported US$50,000 in damage caused to files.

- In China, an alleged hacker is under arrest for stealing information from his employer and selling it to rival companies for 100,000 yuan.

- A disgruntled computer programmer has been arraigned for allegedly zapping his old firm's computer system in retaliation, causing losses of $10 million. Timothy Lloyd worked as the computer network programmer for Omega Engineering Corp., which produces high-tech measurement and control instruments used by the U.S. Navy and NASA.

- A temporary computer technician was charged with breaking into the computers of Forbes, Inc., publisher of *Forbes* magazine, and causing a computer crash that cost the company more than $100,000.

- Four high school students, ages 14 to 16, hacked into a Bay Area Internet server and then used stolen credit card numbers to go on a giant shopping spree at an on-line auction house. They ordered $200,000 worth of computers and had United Parcel Service deliver the equipment to vacant homes in San Carlos, where they would pick up the packages after school.

- Thousands of people who ran up huge phone bills trying to download erotic pictures to their computers will get $2.4 million in refunds from companies that rerouted their calls through the eastern European country of Moldavia. The Federal Trade Commission said the refunds were part of two settlements it reached with firms and individuals who used a supposedly free software program to connect more than 38,000 consumers to costly international telephone numbers, in effect hijacking their modems.

The total price tag for the financial losses cited in these eleven news items is $15,452,025.

Of course, two other more prominent news items carried high price tags for cyber-crimes during the same period.

- Kevin Mitnick's hacking spree cost high-tech companies at least $291.8 million over a two-year span before his capture, according to estimates provided to the FBI by NEC America, Nokia Mobile Phones, Sun Microsystems, and Novell. NEC said he stole software code worth $1.8 million, but Nokia figures he cost them at least $135 million, including $120 million in lost revenue "due to new developments being delayed in reaching market."

- David L. Smith, a 31-year-old New Jersey programmer, pleaded guilty to creating the Melissa computer virus and using an X-rated Web site to spread it through cyberspace, where it did an estimated $80 million in damages.

The total price tag for the $15,452,025 million in damages in the 11 incidents that ran as "In Case You Missed Its," plus the $291.8 million cited in the Mitnick case, plus the $80 million attributed to the Melissa virus is a whopping $387,252,025. (i.e., 13 cybercrime cases resulting in almost $400 million in losses).

In 2000, 273 CSI/FBI survey respondents reported a total of $265,589,940.

The aggregate total of financial losses reported over four years in the CSI/FBI survey is $626,309,795.

What's the point of the exercise?

When you contrast the CSI/FBI survey results with the 13 cases documented in the media, you gain some perspective: The CSI/FBI data on financial losses is conservative.

See Figure 4.3 for a table that shows the aggregate cost of computer crimes and security breaches over a 48-month period. Note that in 2000, 74% of the survey respondents acknowledged financial losses, but only 42% of respondents could quantify the losses.

How Do You Quantify Financial Losses Due to Info Security Breaches?

There is no tried-and-true methodology for quantifying financial losses due to information security breaches. In many cases, reported losses do not take into account the full impact of the incident. There simply isn't a clear-cut way to tabulate the bill for these nasty events...yet.

To help the process of developing such a methodology along, I recently elicited some remarks from several more knowledgeable individuals.

You Can't Fully Quantify the Loss if You Haven't Valued the Resource

Chris Grillo of Minnesota Power and Light (Duluth, Minnesota) lays the foundation.

"Before we can quantify costs," he says, "we first must identify the value of any given computer resource and the value of the information/data itself. Much of this value may have been identified during company disaster recovery projects or Y2K efforts."

Grillo says that many companies unfortunately have not allocated resources to identify and quantify total cost of ownership at this level. "Some may think that certain IT resources cannot be measured, but I believe that if it is observable, then it is countable, and if it is countable, then it is measurable."

He adds that the question of quantifying financial losses due to security breaches involves any loss to a computer resource that either affects the revenues or expenses of a company, including even loss from lost operating efficiencies causing increased costs or from lost opportunities to place resources elsewhere (i.e., opportunity cost).

"You can even extend this to cover the intangibles such as customer service and corporate image (for example, if customers can't perform some form of communication or electronic commerce, etc. or a Web page is defaced). Such events affect revenues and/or expenses in some way.

How money was lost

How money was lost	Respondents w/ Quantified Losses				Lowest Reported				Highest Reported				Average Losses				Total Annual Losses			
	'97	'98	'99	'00	'97	'98	'99	'00	'97	'98	'99	'00	'97	'98	'99	'00	'97	'98	'99	'00
Theft of proprietary info	21	20	23	22	$1K	$300	$1K	$1K	$10M	$25M	$25M	$25M	$954,666	$1,677,000	$1,847,652	$1,136,409	$20,048,000	$33,545,000	$42,496,000	$66,708,000
Sabotage of data or networks	14	25	27	28	$150	$400	$1K	$1K	$1M	$500K	$1M	$15M	$164K	$86K	$163,740	$535,750	$4,285,850	$2,142,000	$4,421,000	$27,148,000
Telecom eavesdropping	8	10	10	15	$1K	$1K	$1K	$200	$100K	$200K	$300K	$500K	$45,423	$56K	$76,500	$33,346	$1,181,000	$562,000	$765,000	$991,200
System penetration by outsider	22	19	28	29	$200	$500	$1K	$1K	$1.5M	$500K	$500K	$5M	$132,250	$86K	$103,142	$172,448	$2,911,700	$1,637,000	$2,885,000	$7,104,000
Insider abuse of Net access	55	67	81	91	$100	$500	$1K	$240	$100K	$1M	$3M	$15M	$18,304	$56K	$93,530	$164,837	$1,006,750	$3,720,000	$7,576,000	$27,984,740
Financial fraud	26	29	27	34	$5K	$1K	$10K	$500	$2M	$2M	$20M	$21M	$957,384	$388K	$1,470,592	$617,661	$24,892,000	$11,239,000	$39,706,000	$55,996,000
Denial of service	n/a	36	28	46	n/a	$200	$1K	$1K	n/a	$1M	$1M	$5M	n/a	$77K	$116,250	$108,717	n/a	$2,787,000	$3,255,000	$8,247,500
Spoofing	4	n/a	n/a	n/a	$1K	n/a	n/a	n/a	$500K	n/a	n/a	n/a	$128K	n/a	n/a	n/a	$512,000	n/a	n/a	n/a
Virus	165	143	116	162	$100	$50	$1K	$100	$500K	$2M	$1M	$10M	$75,746	$55K	$45,465	$61,729	$12,498,150	$7,874,000	$5,274,000	$29,171,700
Unauthorized insider access	22	18	25	20	$100	$1K	$1K	$1K	$1.2M	$50M	$1M	$20M	$181,437	$2,809,000	$142,680	$1,000,050	$3,991,605	$50,565,000	$3,567,000	$22,554,500
Telecom fraud	35	32	29	19	$300	$500	$1K	$1K	$12M	$1.5M	$100K	$3M	$647,437	$539K	$26,655	$157,947	$22,660,300	$17,256,000	$773,000	$4,028,000
Active wiretapping	n/a	5	1	1	n/a	$30K	$20K	$5M	n/a	$100K	$20K	$5M	n/a	$49K	$20K	$5M	n/a	$245,000	$20,000	$5,000,000
Laptop theft	165	162	150	174	$1K	$1K	$1K	$500	$1M	$500K	$1M	$1.2M	$38,326	$332K	$86,920	$6,899	$6,132,200	$5,250,000	$13,038,000	$10,404,300

Total Annual Losses: $100,119,555 $136,822,000 $123,779,000 $265,586,240

Grand Total of Losses Reported (1997-2000): $626,306,795

Figure 4.3 The cost of computer crime.

Source: Computer Security Institute
CSI/FBI 2000 Computer Crime and Security Survey

"To estimate the costs," Grillo continues, "I would look at the total cost of ownership of my resources. We do this for accounting purposes, so why not build a total cost of ownership (TCO) chart of accounts? The costs could be categorized many ways."

Grillo suggests putting various costs into the following categories:

- Capital costs, such as hardware, software, networks, servers, switches.
- Administration costs, such as management of the assets, security monitoring and follow-up, legal assistance, audit department.
- Technical support costs, when all the people call the help desk, documentation of the calls, end-user training, etc.
- End user operational costs, such as the management of user data of resources breached, awareness training of users.

Although you have many ways to look at the costs for quantification, you can also use some more obvious methods to determine costs, such as just asking your customer or including the concept of risk in the equation. For example, you may ask the owner of the asset what you would need to pay him for the asset. This would at least give you a starting point for the "negotiation" of what you should be insuring the item for. (For example, if you own a piece of art, you might not insure it for the total replacement value. Instead, you might pick a lower number to at least cover most of the costs if it were stolen; at least you wouldn't feel so bad about losing everything.) Also, you can evaluate the likelihood of that happening and then determine what you should pay to protect the asset.

For example, Grillo suggests, consider a trade secret.

"How much would you accept to sell this trade secret to someone right now? $1 billion. What is the likelihood that the trade secret would be used to develop a marketable product? 75%. You would end up having a market value (adjusted) to about $750 million."

He also offers an example using a more tangible asset.

"How much would it cost to replace the server and data stored on the server? $150,000. What are the odds that there will be a security breach that will completely compromise this secret? 10%. What should I pay to secure or insure it? 10% times $150,000 equals $15,000. Okay, let's estimate and insure it for $15,000 and use this cost as part of the loss."

Grillo continues, "If opportunities are lost or delays due to a computer resource loss occur causing financial loss, I would consider using an impact of delay analysis. In this analysis I would 'bracket' estimates of delay into ranges with their associated costs based on the above methods. For example, what would the cost be if our electronic commerce site were down for one day? One week? One month?"

System Penetration from the Outside

A hacker crawls all over your networks for days or weeks, deploying sniffers; using network resources for storage, computational power, or access to other organizations; etc. How do you begin to quantify the financial losses involved?

Marcus Ranum of Network Flight Recorder (www.nfr.com) takes a stab at it.

"First, I would itemize into categories of sub-loss:

- Downtime/lost opportunity/business
- Staff time (their salaries)
- Consultants (if used)
- Legal time (hourly)

"It might be a reasonable approach to break it up in terms of phases of the clean-up:

- Detection
- Response
- Repair
- Prosecution"

Ranum continues, "You would say, 'We spent $1,120 on consultants detecting what the hacker did. Following that, we spent $2,200 on consultants helping our staff respond and backtrack the hacker. We spent $3,000 on reinstalling the operating system on our firewall. We spent $2,929 on consultants assisting our legal counsel in preparing to prosecute the hacker.'

"For each type of expense you could break it into those phases, 'We had no legal expenses during detection, no legal expenses during response, we notified and briefed legal counsel of the situation during repair at a cost of $39,393 for their hourly services, and we had costs of $81,238 preparing to prosecute the hacker.'"

Ranum concludes, "The expenses here are going to break down pretty evenly between figuring out what they did and fixing what they did. One might want to argue that some of the expenses during the repair phase would belong to the victim, since they might be valuable for the infrastructure in the absence of the attack (i.e., 'I should have done it anyway'). So you would also end up saying, 'We bought a new tape silo for backups at a cost of $331,311.'"

Unauthorized Access from the Inside

What kind of financial losses would be involved if an insider—maybe an employee, maybe a contractor on-site—accesses sensitive information (for example, trade secrets, sales data, marketing plans, R&D) over the network, downloads it, and then sells it to your competitor?

Ranum comments that it's the "same paradigm." He says to discover that the situation occurred (detection), figure out what happened (response), figure out the business impact of the access and put things in place to prevent it again (repair), and perhaps prosecute, which is lots of work.

"The bulk of the expense in an unauthorized access by an insider is going to be determined by what they did. Fixing insider attacks is not as big a deal, because they don't need to do as much damage to get the information they need. They're also less likely to put Trojan horses and all that kind of stuff all over the network."

Sabotage of Data or Network Operations

What kinds of financial losses would be involved if a critical server or network is trashed, whether from the inside or the outside?

Ranum comments that downtime is the main factor in sabotage. Determining who did it, how/when, are the secondary factors. "If there are no backups, then I guess you'd need to somehow try to establish the value of the system and re-create the data on it. (Though if the victim tried to claim the system was critical but they had not been keeping backups, I'd be amazed if they didn't get laughed at in court)."

Malicious Code

How do you begin to quantify a serious hit from Melissa? How would you calculate damage?

Ranum answers, "Again, it's how do you detect what systems it's been on, how do you repair it, and how do you prevent it afterwards? Obviously, the cost of prevention shouldn't be part of the damages. For a viral outbreak, the costs to consider are the cost of restoring the data and downtime. Of course, if there is lost data that can be much more costly."

But Ranum finds little sympathy for anyone who suffers significant loss of data.

"It's always the victim's fault if they lose data! If the data is important, you should have enough copies of it that you would only lose a very small increment of work."

Don't Underestimate "Soft Costs"

Keith Allan Rhodes of the U.S. General Accounting Office stresses the importance of not underestimating "soft costs."

"You have asked the profound question," Rhodes observes, "because this analysis of cost is what forms the basis for deciding whether the security effort is worth the effort.

One can generate a baseline personnel cost estimate for any of the cases you've mentioned. On the surface, this seems fairly easy, but it is also a very incomplete estimate of the costs.

"For example," he says, "you have a Web site, and it gets hacked, and you have to rebuild it. Simple enough. Ten staffers work one day to bring the site back up ($1 \times 10 = 10$ staff days). Of the 10 staff, you had one manager, one systems administrator, one Web administrator, one network engineer, two content specialists, and four other staff members. Figure their billing rates or cost rates and do the math. When you get your final number, you have the direct personnel costs of bringing that single site back up from that particular breach. The complexity here is figuring out who exactly was involved for how long—for example, was the staff all local or were there headquarters staff as well?"

Rhodes adds that a lot is not covered by this calculation.

"In all of your scenarios (outsider, insider, sabotage, malicious code) there will be some level of investigation. The cost of investigation is based on how much energy you expend to investigate and whether the people and resources that are applied to the investigation are yours or someone else's. Again, this becomes a somewhat straightforward equation. How many people? For how long? At what cost?"

He cautions that this cost is clear only if you are talking about resources that are used only for this single event. "If the resources you use to investigate this breach are part of a permanent security team, then you have to factor in the personnel costs of having an information security team. Now you're factoring in the administrative overhead associated with a permanent security cadre."

Rhodes adds that you can't ignore the hidden cost of outside law enforcement. For example, the Melissa case included local, state, and federal law enforcement resources.

The U.S. Justice Department's "Cost of Crime" Web page (http://www.ojp.usdoj. gov/ovc/ncvrw/1999/cost.htm) shows statistics, he reports. "For example, in 1997, $0.5 billion was lost in robberies, $7 billion was lost in arsons, etc. These quantifiable costs are clearly understood. They correspond to our discussion of the costs to bring a site back up.

"But it is the 'softer' costs that really break the bank," Rhodes says. "For example, personal crime loss estimates of $105 billion annually in medical costs, lost earnings, and public program costs related to victim assistance. When pain, suffering, and the reduced quality of life are assessed, the cost increases to an estimated $450 billion annually.

"This may seem trivial," he says, "but it's not. Violent crime results in lost wages equivalent to one percent of American earnings, three percent of U.S. medical spending, and 14 percent of injury-related medical spending."

Rhodes adds that you should also add in insurers' losses of $45 billion annually due to crime (roughly $265 per American adult). The U.S. government pays $8 billion annually for restorative and emergency services to victims, plus perhaps one-fourth of the $11 billion in health insurance payments.

"The statistics on computer-related crime have to include these kinds of 'soft' costs, which means that corporations or organizations that are hit need to understand their value as well."

He cites an example. "Let's say you and I are corporate officers in P&R, Inc. One of our 'trusted' business planners is on the road and is standing at a payphone, speaking with her/his spouse about a change in schedule. All is fine, until s/he turns around to see the void that was once her/his briefcase and her/his laptop.

"So we begin a reconstruction period. Let's say s/he has written up a five-year corporate business plan. The plan and its backup data are all on her/his laptop, which s/he has with him/her. How do you quantify the cost of re-creating that lost business plan? How do you quantify the loss if it falls into the hands of your competitors?

"Furthermore, if, in all the scenarios you've mentioned, the organization is actually trying to successfully prosecute the perpetrator, the litigation will probably be time-consuming and very costly—especially if the litigation is part of a corporate abuse scenario."

Rhodes uses another example. "Let's say a person uses the corporate intranet for sexual harassment or child pornography. Now you're talking about litigation against your corporation or you personally as the head of the corporation. Remember, if you are a corporate officer, and your corporation does something illegal, you can be held both criminally and civilly liable for the corporation's actions."

If We Can Quantify Losses, We Can Calculate ROI

Keith Allan Rhodes points out another benefit of being able to put a price tag on financial losses due to such security breaches.

"Finally, what we are trying to figure out is the return on investment (ROI) on a security team or any security apparatus that one chooses. Is any of this worth it? If no one goes to jail? Is any of this worth it if my site still gets hacked? Is this just the price of doing business—a risk to be factored into any and all business decisions? This is one aspect of business decisions that most organizations do not face.

"Security is the price of doing business," he adds. "How secure you are is a function of the business risk you are willing to take.

"For example," Rhodes continues, "we all know that wireless service is rife with fraud. (If you can't hijack a cell phone, you better get out of the hijacking business.)

"You can break a cell phone if your teeth have enough fillings. However, the wireless services are booming, obviously at a rate that far outstrips the risk. Part because the wireless service providers can pass their losses directly on to the land of the great unwashed who do not make the connection between higher access fees and phone fraud.

"Just because the phone company was 'nice' enough to remove the unauthorized use from your bill does not mean you're not going to have to pay."

Hackers, Crackers, and Virus Writers

PART II

Did the 1990s Begin with a Big Lie?

CHAPTER 5

*T*angled *Web* focuses on seminal events that occurred from the mid-1990s on. The historic events and individuals touched on in this chapter relate to what I call "prehistory." By *prehistory*, I mean the years prior to the commercialization of the Internet, the spawning of the World Wide Web, and the dawn of e-commerce.

Three "prehistoric" subjects are covered in this chapter: some deep background on the mysterious 1990 Martin Luther King Day telecommunications system failure; a brief timeline of the long, wild ride of "superhacker" Kevin Mitnick; and the momentous attack by the Morris Worm in 1988. Indeed, there are other cybercrime events from the 1980s and early 1990s. They are well documented elsewhere.

Each of the three vignettes included here offers numerous lessons learned and unlearned.

The First Serious Infrastructure Attack?

On January 15, 1990, Martin Luther King Day, AT&T's long-distance telephone-switching system crashed, affecting service nationwide. The event lasted for nine long hours, and approximately 70 million phones calls went uncompleted. Many telephone company security professionals and law enforcement agents believed the system was brought down by denizens of the electronic underground, although no charges have ever been brought. The official statements that were made regarding the MLK Day crash insisted that it was due to a software glitch.

Spurred on by the MLK Day crash, law-enforcement agencies across the country coordinated efforts in a "hacker crackdown." The U.S. Secret Service, the Chicago Task Force, and the Arizona Organized

Crime and Racketeering Unit (a.k.a. Operation Sundevil) conducted numerous raids on hackers from Texas to New York. Legendary "cyberpunks" from the Legion of Doom (LOD) and the Masters of Deception (MOD), two notorious gangs of hackers, were arrested.

The events surrounding the busting up of LOD and MOD are recorded in *Hacker Crackdown* by Bruce Sterling (see Appendix C).

The following first-person account by an unimpeachable, but anonymous, source sheds light on hitherto unpublished aspects of the MLK Day phone system crash investigation.

I have omitted the names of the two hackers mentioned. I have also omitted references to the particular branch of military service involved.

> There had been a kid from Legion of Doom who got caught up in New York. He went by the hacker handles of ████████ and ██████████████.
>
> He got caught by NYNEX, the local phone company. The police and the judge scared the hell out of him and told him he was either going to jail or into the military service. So he decided to join the U.S. ████████.
>
> Subsequently, a military investigator got a phone call from someone known to the investigator and working in NYNEX security. The caller said, "Hey, it's me, but this is an 'anonymous' tip; you've got a problem. His name is ████ ████████ and he is going through basic training right now."
>
> The military investigator started running sources, roommates, etc. You can test to find out what kind of career path you're going to get onto in the ████████. He wanted to get into computers and tested so well he didn't have to go to school.
>
> He could go directly to his assignment. Well, he told this source that he was going to ████████████████████████ headquarters. He said, "I can't wait to mess with those computers."
>
> The investigators changed his assignment and sent him to an ████████ base in Florida for "combat communications," which meant he had to live in tents, etc.
>
> One of the sources the investigators ran at the ████████ base told them that ████ was selling phone calls in the day room of the lounge at the barracks.
>
> If you wanted to make a phone call, you would go to ████ and he would make the phone call for you and you could talk long-distance for hours without paying for it.
>
> The investigators started working with the U.S. Secret Service and the U.S. Attorney in ████████, Florida.
>
> A call came into the investigators saying, "We wanted to give you guys a heads-up. We know you're working this case and that you're about to execute a search warrant. The rumor on the street is that something big is going to happen next week, but we don't know what it is. You may want to plan on executing your search warrant early next week."

So the military investigators planned on executing the search warrant on Wednesday. Well, on Monday, AT&T died. Suddenly, they got a lot of interest.

BellSouth, AT&T, Bell Labs, and others showed up. The military investigators had all these technical advisers to execute this search warrant on this little teeny barracks room. They got his Apple IIC and his 300 baud modem. They went through his notebooks. The BellSouth and Bellcore guys were perusing the pages, and they said "Oh my God, this is the command, this is the command that took the system down. This kid had access."

One of the phone company guys went out of the room and around the corner to where the phones were and called his superiors.

Well, one of the ██████ investigators went out and around too and listened to his side of the phone conversation. He said, "Don't know if the kid did it, but he had the access and he had the command."

When the investigators interviewed the kid, he said he had been studying for a calculus test, and ██████ (a.k.a. ██████) gave him a call about 15 minutes after AT&T went down, and all ████ said was "got 'em!" and hung up.

No one ever faced criminal charges in regard to precipitating the MLK Day crash. AT&T insists it was a "software problem." It is, indeed, the official version of the story. It is the line that Sterling toes in his otherwise excellent book.

Did the 1990s begin with a big lie? Was AT&T's "admission of error" just a cover-up for some vulnerability that it was simply not safe to acknowledge? Was the MLK Day AT&T phone system crash really the first real hacker attack on an infrastructure target?

Perhaps we'll never know for sure. I am inclined to believe the tale related to me by my anonymous source.

Public Cyberenemy No. 1?

Kevin Mitnick (a.k.a. Condor) is the most legendary cybercriminal in the brief history of cyberspace. His story spans three decades and continues today.

In 1981, Kevin Mitnick, 17, was convicted and placed on parole for stealing computer manuals from a Pacific Bell switching station.

In 1982, Mitnick gained national notoriety for breaking into the North American Air Defense Command computer. He also seized temporary control of three central phone company offices in Manhattan and gained access to all the phone switching centers in California. He reprogrammed someone's home phone so that each time that person picked up the phone, a recording asked for a coin deposit.

In 1988, for months, Kevin Mitnick, 25, secretly monitored the e-mail of MCI and Digital Equipment security officials. Digital Equipment accused him of causing $4 million worth of damage to computer operations and stealing $1 million worth of software. Mitnick was convicted and received a one-year jail sentence at the low-security federal prison in Lompoc, California.

In 1993, California state police issued a warrant for the arrest of Kevin Mitnick. They accused him of wiretapping calls from the FBI to the California Department of Motor Vehicles and using law-enforcement access codes gleaned from the wiretaps to illegally gain entry to the drivers license database.

On Christmas Day, 1994, Kevin Mitnick, 31, broke into Tsutomu Shimomura's system at the San Diego Supercomputer Center. Shimomura's subsequent pursuit through cyberspace led to Mitnick's arrest in January 1995.

In 1996, in Los Angeles, Kevin Mitnick pleaded guilty to one federal charge of cellular phone fraud and admitted to violating probation on an earlier computer fraud conviction.

In 1997, Mitnick was sentenced to nearly two years in prison for parole violations and using stolen cellular phone numbers to dial into computer databases. He was awaiting trial on 25 counts of computer and wire fraud, possessing unlawful access devices, damaging computers, and intercepting electronic messages in an unrelated case.

Hackers broke into Yahoo!, the busiest site on the Internet, and posted an ominous holiday greeting. A group calling itself the PANTS/HAGIS alliance claimed it had planted a computer virus that would cause widespread damage on Christmas Day if Mitnick was not freed.

In December 1998, *Wired* reported that Mitnick said a three-month delay in the start of his trial would still not give his defense adequate to time to review the government's case against him. "I don't think it is possible to be ready by April 20th," Mitnick said in a rare telephone interview. He added, "I don't like being stuck here in jail, especially without a bail hearing."

In March 1999, Mitnick, who admitted causing millions of dollars in damage to companies whose computer systems he penetrated, pleaded guilty to five felony charges in U.S. district court. Mitnick had been in prison since his arrest in North Carolina in 1995. Although he was sentenced to three years and ten months, he was credited for time served.

On January 21, 2000, he was released from prison after having served 1,792 days in federal prison (almost five years).

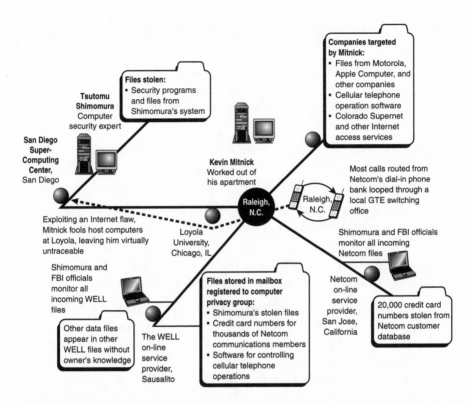

Figure 5.1 Mitnick's last crime spree.

Source: The San Francisco Chronicle.

In April 2000, a federal judge canceled Mitnick's participation on a computer security panel at the Utah Information Technologies Association "Net Trends 2000: The Digital Revolution" conference. Mitnick's prison release agreement prohibits him from "consulting or advising" on computer-related activity. He is under "supervision" until January 20, 2003.

According to the prosecutors, Mitnick's hacking spree cost high-tech companies at least $291.8 million over a two-year span before his capture. (See Chapter 3.)

Many in the media and in law enforcement portrayed Mitnick as public cyberenemy No. 1. Conversely, many in the electronic underground and its sympathizers portrayed Mitnick as a victim and a human rights *cause célèbre*. Of course, the truth lies somewhere in between and is much more poignant than either caricature.

For further details of the Mitnick case, I refer you to three books (see Appendix C):

- *Cyberpunk: Outlaws and Hackers on the Computer Frontier* by Katie Hafner and John Markoff

- *Takedown: The Pursuit and Capture of Kevin Mitnick, America's Most Wanted Computer Outlaw—By the Man Who Did It* by Tsutomu Shimomura with John Markoff

- *The Fugitive Game: Online with Kevin Mitnick* by Jonathan Littman

The Worms Crawl In, the Worms Crawl Out...

In 1988, Robert Tappan Morris, Jr., a 23-year-old graduate student in computer science at Cornell and the son of a National Security Agency (NSA) computer security expert, wrote an experimental, self-replicating, self-propagating program called a *worm* (99 lines of code, not including object files) and injected it into the Internet. He chose to release it from MIT, to disguise the fact that the worm came from Cornell.

Morris soon discovered that the program was replicating and reinfecting machines at a much faster rate than he had anticipated: There was a bug. Ultimately, many machines at locations around the country either crashed or became "catatonic." Invisible tasks were overloading VAX and Sun machines across the country and preventing users from using the machines effectively, if at all. Eventually, system administrators were forced to cut off many of their machines from the Internet entirely in an attempt to curtail the source of infection.

When Morris realized what was happening, he contacted a friend at Harvard to discuss a solution. Eventually, they sent an anonymous message from Harvard over the network, instructing programmers how to kill the worm and prevent reinfection. However, because the network route was clogged, this message did not get through until it was too late. Computers were affected at many sites, including universities, military sites, and medical research facilities. The estimated cost of dealing with the worm at each installation ranged from $200 to more than $53,000.

The primary difference between worms and other illicit computer programs (often referred to as *viruses*) is the method of operation the programs use to reproduce and spread. When a standard computer virus enters a system, it alters a system file or some other convenient file that will likely be used sometime in the near future. The alteration to this file usually is the addition of commands that will activate the virus wherever it is on the computer. The virus will then perform its nefarious deeds. The major distinction here, at least in comparison with worms, is that, until the user activates the virus, the virus is dormant on the computer. Moreover, until the altered file is called, the virus cannot perform any activity.

A worm, on the other hand, is far more powerful. When a worm gains access to a computer (usually by breaking into it over the Internet), it launches a program that searches for other Internet locations, infecting them if it can. At no time does the worm need user assistance (accidental or not) to operate its programming. Moreover, the worm travels over the Internet, so all machines attached to an infected machine risk attack. Considering the connectivity of the Internet on the whole, this includes a huge number of computers whose only defense is the sealing of the security gaps that the worm uses to enter. Secondly, worms can spread with no assistance. After the worm discovers an Internet connection, all that it must do is download a copy of itself to that location and continue running as normal.

The Morris worm took advantage of holes in two Unix programs: sendmail and finger. People at the University of California at Berkeley and MIT had copies of the program and were actively disassembling it (returning the program back into its source form) to try to figure out how it worked.

Teams of programmers worked nonstop to come up with at least a temporary fix, to prevent the continued spread of the worm. After about 12 hours, the team at Berkeley devised steps that would help retard the spread of the virus. A team at Purdue University discovered another method and widely published it. The information didn't get out as quickly as it could have, however, because so many sites had completely disconnected themselves from the network.

After a few days, things slowly began to return to normal, and everyone wanted to know who had done it all. Morris was later named in *The New York Times* as the author (though this hadn't yet been officially proven, there was a substantial body of evidence pointing to Morris).

What the Morris Worm Did to Systems

The worm didn't alter or destroy files, save or transmit the passwords that it cracked, or make special attempts to gain root or superuser access in a system (and didn't use the privileges if it managed to get them). The worm didn't place copies of itself or other programs into memory to be executed at a later time. (Such programs are commonly referred to as *timebombs*.) The worm didn't attack machines other than Sun 3 systems and VAX computers running 4 BSD Unix (or equivalent) or machines without connections to the Internet. (In other words, computers without an Internet address were not attacked. Modems do not count as Internet connectors in this respect.) The worm didn't travel from machine to machine via disk or cause physical damage to computer systems.

Actually, the intention of the worm (judging from decompiled versions of its code and the statements of its designer) was to do nothing at all. At least, nothing visible. The worm was designed simply to spread itself to as many computers as possible without giving the slightest indication of its existence. If the code worked correctly, it would have been only a tiny process continually running on computers across the Internet.

However, the code didn't work perfectly. Apparently, at the time the virus was released, the code still contained a number of bugs. In addition, experts believe that the programmer underestimated the degree to which the worm would propagate.

The result is that these seemingly innocuous processes, which didn't take up much processor time individually, began to strain systems as more and more processes infected the same machines. At a surprisingly swift rate, an infected machine began to slow down as more and more copies of the worm each tried to perform its function.

In the following example, you can see the effects of the worm infection. Table 5.1 is representative of infections all across the country.

Table 5.1   Diary of a Worm Attack on a Single System[1]

All the following events occurred on the evening of Nov. 2, 1988

Time	Event
6:00 p.m.	At about this time the worm is launched.
8:49 p.m.	The worm infects a VAX 8600 at the University of Utah (cs.utah.edu).
9:09 p.m.	The worm initiates the first of its attacks to infect other computers from the infected VAX.
9:21 p.m.	The load average on the system reaches 5. (Load average is a measure of how hard the computer system is working. At 9:30 at night, the load average of the VAX was usually 1. Any load average higher than 5 causes delays in data processing.)
9:41 p.m.	The load average reaches 7.
10:01 p.m.	The load average reaches 16.
10:06 p.m.	At this point there are so many worms infecting the system that no new processes can be started. No users can use the system anymore.

1. Adapted from "A Tour of the Worm," a paper by Donn Seely, (http://sunsite.org.uk/packages/athena/virus/seely.n)

Time	Event
10:20 p.m.	The system administrator kills off the worms.
10:41 p.m.	The system is reinfected and the load average reaches 27.
10:49 p.m.	The system administrator shuts down the system. The system is subsequently restarted.
11:21 p.m.	Reinfection causes the load average to reach 37.

In short, in under 90 minutes from the time of infection, the worm had made the infected system unusable. This same scenario occurred to more than 6,000 machines across the country. Although the worm caused no physical damage, between $100,000 and $10 million was lost due to lost access to the Internet at an infected host, according to the U.S. General Accounting Office.

What the Morris Worm Demonstrated

It's hard to have a computer program shut down 60,000 computers across the country, including those at research and military installations, without having a few people figuring out that something must be very wrong with the status quo. The 1988 worm proved to be no exception. The worm pointed out several glaring security holes in Unix networks that would probably have gone unknown, or at least been ignored as not very significant, had not the worm been so graphic in its exploitation of such "little" bugs.

There are even those who suggest thanking Morris for his actions because they provided a serious wake-up call to system administrators around the country. Of course, other people have pointed out that he might have found other ways of delivering the same message. Before late 1988, computer security was not a major concern of the Internet community—at least, not to the degree it was after November 2. The worm did not exploit several other bugs, but they were discovered during a close reinspection of operating systems and (hopefully) patched up. In addition to trying to find all the security holes in a system, several other discoveries were made, thanks to the worm.

First, access to certain files should be granted only to those who need said access. One of the worm's attacks took advantage of the fact that the file containing the encrypted passwords of all the users was publicly readable in most systems. This meant that the worm could compare various encryptions of possible passwords against the encrypted passwords in this file without triggering security warnings that would normally occur if a large number of incorrect login attempts were detected.

In addition, systems almost always kept the file in the same place, making the worm's job much easier. Fortunately, most computer networks have corrected this oversight.

Many network administrators found that having a variety of different computers running on their network was an advantage because an infection on one machine will most likely not be able to run on a large number of different machines. Therefore, such an attack is less likely to incapacitate those networks with the greatest diversity. (Of course, this limits software compatibility within a network, but we are concentrating on security right now and will ignore this for now.)

Another less technical lesson learned from the worm is that sharing research on something such as battling the worm (as MIT and Berkeley did in their attempts to decompile the program) is immensely helpful. Such a network of computer geeks and gurus ended up being the vanguard of the assault on the worm.

Beware of reflex reactions to computer problems. When system administrators discovered that the worm was using sendmail to penetrate their systems, many responded by shutting down their mail servers. This proved to be a cure that was worse than the disease. The worm had several other attack methods, and so was not really hampered by the loss of the mail utility.

The loss of the mail systems served only to delay mail that described how to defeat the worm and fix the bugs from reaching some sites. Logging information is vital in discovering the source of infections such as the worm. Many sites were hampered because they couldn't tell where the worm was coming from and how it was entering the system. (Of course, 99% of the time, most log information is unused, and because several applications require logs of their own, this can cause quite a pile of usually useless information. Once again, it is a trade-off.)

Robert T. Morris was convicted of violating the Computer Fraud and Abuse Act (Title 18) and sentenced to three years of probation; 400 hours of community service; a fine of $10,050; and the costs of his supervision. His appeal, filed in December 1991, was rejected the following March.

For the further details of the Morris worm case, refer to *Cyberpunk* by Katie Hafner and John Markoff.

Conclusion

Well, the problems highlighted here are still with us.

As you will read in Chapter 12, infrastructure attacks against targets such as the telecommunications system, the power grid, and the air traffic control system are a very real possibility. Chapters 6 and 8 point out that lone hackers are still capable of making enough mischief to draw the ire of law enforcement and give them a wild chase through cyberspace. Finally, Chapter 9 demonstrates that the Morris Worm was only the first malicious program to take down whole networks of networks.

Joy Riders: Mischief That Leads to Mayhem

O ne of the greatest misconceptions among the many who hamper the defense of cyberspace is the idea that all hacking is done only by juvenile joy riders: i.e., youthful geniuses bent on embarrassing law enforcement and the military. Of course, one of the ways in which this misconception is spread is through the mainstream media. Most cases that reach the light of day usually do end up involving juvenile hackers.

Why? Well, cases involving true cyberterrorists, information warriors, intelligence agencies, and corporate spies slip below the surface of the headlines. They are lost in the murky waters of "classified operations" or are swept under thick corporate carpets. (You'll read more about such cases in Chapter 10 and Chapter 12.)

Juvenile hackers or other "sport hackers" (a term used to describe hackers who break into systems for the same reasons but aren't minors) end up in the newspapers because they get caught. They also end up in the headlines because they seek the limelight. Furthermore, acknowledging their activities doesn't open a Pandora's box for the government agency or the corporation that was hit. If a government agency acknowledged an intelligence operation conducted by another country, there could be serious diplomatic or even military consequences. If a major corporation acknowledged a hack attack in which trade secrets were compromised seemingly by another corporation, there would be a public relations debacle: for example, their stock could dive, law suits could get filed, etc.

Nevertheless, juvenile or sport hackers, or *joy riders*, have wreaked a lot of havoc and mayhem over the years.

Here are some of the details of three high-profile stories, stretching from 1994 to 1999, that illustrate some of the lessons learned and unlearned along the way.

The Rome Labs Case: Datastream Cowboy and Kuji Mix It Up with the U.S. Air Force

The Rome Air Development Center (Rome Labs), located at Griffiss Air Force Base (New York), is the U.S. Air Force's premier command-and-control research facility.

Rome Lab researchers collaborate with universities, defense contractors, and commercial research institutions on projects involving artificial intelligence systems, radar guidance systems, and target detection and tracking systems.

On March 28, 1994, Rome Labs's system administrators (sysadmins) noticed that a *password sniffer*, a hacking tool that gathers user's login information, had been surreptitiously installed on a system linked to the Rome Labs network. The sniffer had collected so much information that it filled the disk and crashed the system, according to James Christy, who was director of Computer Crime Investigations for the Air Force Office of Special Investigations.

The sysadmins informed the Defense Information Systems Agency (DISA) that the Rome Labs network had been hacked into by an as yet unknown perpetrator. The DISA Computer Emergency Response Team (CERT), in turn, informed the Air Force Office of Special Investigations (AFOSI) of the report of an intrusion. The AFOSI, in turn, informed the Air Force Information Warfare Center (AFIWC), headquartered in San Antonio, Texas.

An AFOSI team of cybercrime investigators and security experts was dispatched to Rome Labs. They reviewed audit trails and interviewed the sysadmins. The conclusions that they reached in their preliminary investigation were very disturbing.

Two hackers had broken into seven different computers on the Rome Labs network. They had gained unlimited access, downloaded data files, and secreted sniffers on every one of them. The seven sniffers had compromised a total of 30 of Rome Labs's systems.

These systems contain sensitive research and development data.

System security logs disclosed that Rome Labs's systems had been actually been hacked into for the first time on March 23, five days before the discovery made on March 28.

The investigation went on to disclose that the seven sniffers had compromised the security of more than 100 more user accounts by capturing user logons and passwords. Users' e-mail messages had been snooped, duplicated, and deleted. Sensitive battlefield simulation program data had been pursued and purloined. Furthermore, the perpetrators had used Rome Labs's systems as a jumping-off point for a series of hack attacks on other military, government, and research targets around the world. They broke into user accounts, planted sniffer programs, and downloaded massive quantities of data from these systems as well.

The investigators offered the Rome Labs commanding officer the option of either securing all the systems that had been hacked or leaving one or more of them open to attack. If they left a few systems open, they could monitor the comings and goings of the attackers in the hope of following them back to the their point of origination and identifying them.

The commander opted to leave some of the systems open to lay a trap for the intruders.

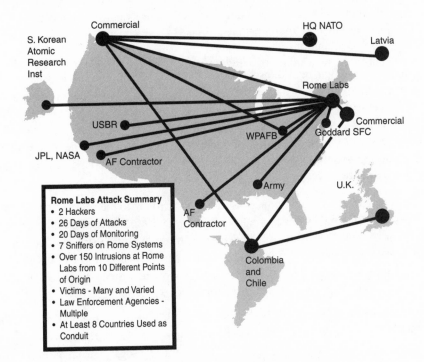

Figure 6.1   More than 100 downstream victims from the Rome Labs attacks.

Source: U.S. Air Force Office of Special Investigations

Investigators Wrestle with Legal Issues and Technical Limitations

Using standard software and computer systems commands, the attacks were initially traced back one leg of their path. The majority of the attacks were traced back to two commercial Internet service providers, cyberspace.com, in Seattle, Washington and mindvox.phantom.com, in New York City.

Newspaper articles indicated that the individuals who provided mindvox.phantom.com's computer security described themselves as "two former East Coast Legion of Doom members."

The Legion of Doom (LoD) was a loose-knit computer hacker group that had several members convicted for intrusions into corporate telephone switches in 1990 and 1991. Because the agents did not know whether the owners of the New York Internet service provider were willing participants or merely a transit point for the break-ins at Rome Labs, they decided not to approach them. Instead, they simply surveiled the victim computer systems at Rome Labs's network to find out the extent of the intruders' access and identify all the victims.

Following legal coordination and approval with Headquarters, AFOSI's legal counsel, the Air Force General Counsel's Office, and the Computer Crime Unit of the Department of Justice, real-time content monitoring was established on one of Rome Labs's networks. Real-time content monitoring is analogous to performing a wiretap because it allows you to eavesdrop on communications, or in this case, text. The investigative team also began full keystroke monitoring at Rome. The team installed a sophisticated sniffer program to capture every keystroke performed remotely by any intruder who entered the Rome Labs.

This limited context monitoring consisted of subscribing to the commercial ISPs' services and using only software commands and utilities the ISP authorized every subscriber to use. The team could trace the intruder's path back only one leg. To determine the next leg of the intruder's path required access to the next system on the hacker's route. If the attacker was using telephone systems to access the ISP, a court-ordered "trap and trace" of telephone lines was required.

Due to time constraints involved in obtaining such an order, this was not a viable option. Furthermore, if the attackers changed their path, the trap and trace would not be fruitful. During the course of the intrusions, the investigative team monitored the hackers as they intruded on the system and attempted to trace the intruders back to their origin. They found the intruders were using the Internet and making fraudulent use of the telephone systems, or "phone phreaking."

Because the intruders used multiple paths to launch their attacks, the investigative team was unable to trace back to the origin in real-time due to the difficulty in tracing back multiple systems in multiple countries.

In my interview with James Christy for this book, he provided fascinating insight into the deliberations over what capabilities could be used to pursue the investigation.

"The AFIWC worked the Rome Labs case with us," Christy says. "They developed the Hackback tool right at Rome." According to Christy, Hackback is a tool that does a finger back to the system the attack came from, then launches a scripted hack attack on that system, surveils the system, finds the next leg back, and then launches a scripted attack on that system. Hackback was designed to follow them all the way back over the Internet to their point of origination.

"Well, AFIWC developed this tool," Christy continues, "but we told them, 'Hey, you can't use that 'cause it's illegal. You're doing the same thing as the hacker is doing: You're breaking into systems.' They said, General Minihan [who was at that time the head of the NSA] says, 'We're at war, we're going to use it.' My guys had to threaten to arrest them if they did. So we all said, 'Let's try something.'"

Christy tells me there was a big conference call involving the DoJ, the Secret Service, the FBI, AFOSI, and the guys that were up at Rome Labs. "We all claimed exigent circumstances, a hot pursuit. Scott Charney [who was at that time the head of DoJ's computer crime unit] gave us the approval to go run Hackback one time. We did it, but it didn't buy us anything. The hackers weren't getting into those nodes via the Internet. They were getting in through telephone dial-ups. So it dead-ended where we already knew it was coming from."

Datastream Cowboy's Biggest Mistake

As the result of the monitoring, the investigators could determine that the hackers used the nicknames Datastream and Kuji. With this clue, AFOSI Computer Crime Investigators turned to their human intelligence network of informants that surf the Internet. The investigators levied their informants to identify the two hackers using the handles Datastream and Kuji.

"Our investigators went to their sources," Christy recalls, "saying, 'Help us out here, anybody know who these guys are?' And a day and a half later, one of these sources came back and said, 'Hey, I got this guy. Here's his e-mail!'"

According to Christy, these informants have diverse motivations. Some of them want to be cops; some of them want to do the right thing; some of them simply find hacking exciting; some of them have pressure brought to bear on them because of their own illegal activities.

Indeed, whatever the motivation, on April 5, 1994, an informant told the investigators he had a conversation with a hacker who identified himself as Datastream Cowboy.

The conversation was via e-mail and the individual stated that he was from the United Kingdom. The on-line conversation had occurred three months earlier. In the e-mail provided by the informant, Datastream indicated he was a 16-year-old who liked to attack .mil sites because they were so insecure.

Datastream had even provided the informant with his home telephone number for his own hacker bulletin board systems he had established.

Bragging of his hacking feats, as Christy explains, was Datastream Cowboy's big mistake.

"It was the only way we solved the case," he said. "If we had to rely on surveillance alone, we never would have traced it back to them because of all the looping and weaving through South America. We would have been working with multiple countries.

"Did these South American countries have laws against hacking?" Christy continues. "No. Would the South Americans have been able to do a trap and trace? Maybe not. Remember, they were using telephone lines."

The Air Force agents had previously established a liaison with New Scotland Yard who could identify the individuals living at the residence associated with Datastream's telephone numbers.

New Scotland Yard had British Telecom initiate monitoring of the individual's telephone lines with pen registers. A pen register records all the numbers dialed by the individuals at the residence. Almost immediately, monitoring disclosed that someone from the residence was phone phreaking through British Telecom, which is also illegal in the United Kingdom.

Within two days, Christy and the investigative team knew who Datastream Cowboy was. For the next 24 days, they monitored Datastream's online activity and collected data.

During the 26-day period of attacks, the two hackers, Datastream Cowboy and Kuji, made more than 150 known intrusions.

Scotland Yard Closes in on Datastream Cowboy

New Scotland Yard found that every time an intrusion occurred at Rome Labs, the individual in the United Kingdom was phone-phreaking the telephone lines to make free telephone calls out of Britain. Originating from the United Kingdom, his path of attack was through systems in multiple countries in South America and Europe, and through Mexico and Hawaii; occasionally he would end up at Rome Labs. From Rome Labs, he was able to attack systems via the Internet at NASA's Jet Propulsion Laboratory in California and its Goddard Space Flight Center in Greenbelt, Maryland.

Continued monitoring by the British and American authorities disclosed that on April 10, 1994, Datastream successfully penetrated an aerospace contractor's home system. The attackers captured the contractor's logon at Rome Labs with sniffer programs when the contractor logged on to home systems in California and Texas. The sniffers captured the addresses of the contractor's home system, plus the logon and password for that home system. After the logon and password were compromised, the attackers could masquerade as that authorized user on the contractor's home system. Four of the contractor's systems were compromised in California and a fifth was compromised in Texas.

Datastream also used an Internet Scanning Software (ISS)[1] attack on multiple systems belonging to this aerospace contractor. ISS is a hacker tool developed to gain intelligence about a system. It attempts to collect information on the type of operating system the computer is running and any other available information that could be used to assist the attacker in determining what attack tool might successfully break into that particular system. The software also tries to locate the password file for the system being scanned, and then tries to make a copy of that password file.

The significance of the theft of a password file is that, even though password files are usually stored encrypted, they are easily cracked. Several hacker "password cracker" programs are available on the Internet. If a password file is stolen or copied and cracked, the attacker can then log on to that system as what the systems perceive is a legitimate user.

Monitoring activity disclosed that, on April 12, Datastream initiated an ISS attack from Rome Labs against Brookhaven National Labs, Department of Energy, New York. Datastream also had a two-hour connection with the aerospace contractor's system that was previously compromised.

1. ISS is now a multimillion dollar company that sells ID Software. The company denies its hacker roots and that it hires hackers.

Kuji Hacks into Goddard Space Flight Center

On April 14, 1994, remote monitoring activity of the Seattle ISP conducted by the Air Force indicated that Kuji had connected to the Goddard Space Flight Center through an ISP from Latvia. The monitoring disclosed that data was being transferred from Goddard Space Flight Center to the ISP. To prevent the loss of sensitive data, the monitoring team broke the connection. It is still not known whether the data being transferred from the NASA system was destined for Latvia. (Latvia as a destination for sensitive data was, of course, something that concerned investigators. After all, the small Baltic nation had only recently become independent of Russian domination. It had been a part of the former U.S.S.R.)

Further remote monitoring activity of cyberspace.com disclosed that Datastream was accessing the National Aero-Space Plane Joint Program Office, a joint project headed by NASA and the Air Force at Wright-Patterson Air Force Base, Ohio. Monitoring disclosed a transfer of data from Wright-Patterson traversing through cyberspace.com to Latvia.

Apparently, Kuji attacked and compromised a system in Latvia that was just being used as conduit to prevent identification. Kuji also initiated an ISS attack against Wright-Patterson from cyberspace.com the same day. He also tried to steal a password file from a computer system at Wright-Patterson Air Force Base.

Kuji Attempts to Hack NATO HQ

On April 15, real-time monitoring disclosed Kuji executing the ISS attack against NATO Headquarters in Brussels, Belgium, and Wright-Patterson from Rome Labs. Kuji did not appear to gain access to any NATO systems from this particular attack. However, when interviewed on April 19 by AFOSI, a systems administrator from NATO's SHAPE Technical Center in the Hague, Netherlands, disclosed that Datastream had successfully attacked one of SHAPE's computer systems from the ISP mindvox.phantom.com in New York.

After authorities confirmed the hacker's identity and developed probable cause, New Scotland Yard requested and obtained a search warrant for the Datastream Cowboy's residence. The plan was to wait until the individual was online at Rome Labs, and then execute the search warrant. The investigators wanted to catch Datastream online so that they could identify all the victims in the path between his residence and Rome Labs. After Datastream got online at Rome Labs, he accessed a system in Korea, downloaded all data stored on the Korean Atomic Research Institute system, and deposited it on Rome Labs's system.

Initially, it was unclear whether the Korean system belonged to North or South Korea. Investigators were concerned that, if it did belong to North Korea, the North Koreans would think the logical transfer of the storage space was an intrusion by the U.S. Air Force, which could be perceived as an aggressive act of war. During this time frame, the United States was in sensitive negotiations with the North Koreans regarding their nuclear weapons program. Within hours, it was determined that Datastream had hacked into the South Korean Atomic Research Institute.

At this point, New Scotland Yard decided to expand its investigation, asked the Air Force to continue to monitor and collect evidence in support of its investigation, and postponed execution of the search warrant.

Scotland Yard Knocks on Datastream Cowboy's Door

On May 12, investigators from New Scotland Yard executed their search warrant on Datastream's residence.

When they came through the door, 16-year-old Richard Pryce (a.k.a. Datastream Cowboy) curled up in the fetal position and wept.

The search disclosed that Datastream had launched his attacks with only a 25 MHz, 486 SX desktop computer with only a 170 megabyte hard drive. This is a modest system, with limited storage capacity. Datastream had numerous documents that contained references to Internet addresses, including six NASA systems and U.S. Army and U.S. Navy systems with instructions on how to loop through multiple systems to avoid detection.

At the time of the search, New Scotland Yard detectives arrested and interviewed Datastream. Detectives stated that Datastream had just logged out of a computer system when they entered his room. Datastream admitted to breaking into Rome Labs numerous times as well as multiple other Air Force systems (Hanscom Air Force Base, Massachusetts, and Wright-Patterson). (He was charged with crimes spelled out in Britain's Computer Misuse Act of 1990.)

Datastream admitted to stealing a sensitive document containing research regarding an Air Force artificial intelligence program that dealt with Air Order of Battle. He added that he searched for the word *missile*, not to find missile data but to find information specifically about artificial intelligence. He further explained that one of the files he stole was a 3–4 megabyte file (approximately three to four million characters in size). He stored it at mindvox.phantom.com's system in New York because it was too large to fit on his home system.

Datastream explained he paid for the ISP's service with a fraudulent credit card number that was generated by a hacker program he had found on the Internet. Datastream was released on bail following the interview.

This investigation never revealed the identity of Kuji. From conduct observed through the investigators' monitoring, Kuji was a far more sophisticated hacker than the teenage Datastream. Air Force investigators observed that Kuji would only stay on a telephone line for a short time, not long enough to be traced successfully. No informant information was available except that Computer Crime Investigators from the Victoria Police Department in Australia had seen the name Kuji on some of the hacker bulletin-board systems in Australia.

Unfortunately, Datastream provided a great deal of the information he stole to Kuji electronically. Furthermore, Kuji appears to have tutored Datastream on how to break into networks and on what information to obtain. During the monitoring, the investigative team could observe Datastream attack a system and fail to break in. Datastream would then get into an online chat session with Kuji, which the investigative team could not see due to the limited context monitoring at the Internet service providers. These chat sessions would last 20–40 minutes. Following the on-line conversation, the investigative team would then watch Datastream attack the same system he had previously failed to penetrate, but this time he would be successful. Apparently Kuji assisted and mentored Datastream and, in return, received stolen information from Datastream. Datastream, when interviewed by New Scotland Yard's Computer Crime Investigators, told them he had never physically met Kuji and only communicated with him through the Internet or on the telephone.

Kuji's Identity Is Finally Revealed

In 1996, New Scotland Yard was starting to feel some pressure from the glare of publicity surrounding the upcoming hearings in the U.S. Senate, chaired by Sam Nunn (D-Georgia). Two years had passed since the arrest of the Datastream Cowboy, and yet Kuji was still at large.

New Scotland Yard investigators went back to take a closer look at the evidence they had seized and found a phone number that they hadn't traced back to its origin. When they did trace it, they discovered Kuji's true identity. Ten days after Jim Christy's initial testimony concerning the Rome Lab intrusions, 21-year-old Matthew Bevan (a.k.a. Kuji) was finally apprehended.

In court, Pryce pleaded guilty to 12 hacking offenses and paid a nominal fine of 1,200 British pounds.

But Bevan, whose father was a police officer, "lawyered-up."

After 20 hearings in which the defense challenged the Crown's evidence, the prosecution made a "business decision" and dropped the charges.

Bevan is now a computer security consultant. His Web site, www.bogus.net/kuji, features an archive of news media coverage of the Rome Labs case, a timeline of his exasperating and successful legal maneuvers, photographs of his arresting officers, and scanned headlines from the London tabloids.

In my interview with Bevan, I asked him about the motivation in the attack on Rome.

"My quest," he tells me, "was for any information I could find relating to a conspiracy or cover-up of the UFO phenomenon. I was young and interested in the UFO stuff that I had read and of course as I had the access to such machines that were broken (i.e., with poor security) it was a natural progression to seek out information.

"Also," Bevan continues, "I was bullied almost every day of my school life; the hacking world was pure escapism. I could go to school, endure the day, come home, and log on to another world. Somewhere I could get respect, somewhere that I had friends.

"At school I may have been bullied but in the back of my mind was 'Well, I hacked NASA last night, and what did you do?'"

I also asked Bevan if he wanted to set the record straight in regard to how authorities handled the case or how the media reported it.

"One of the biggest concerns that I have about the reporting of the case relates to the InfoWar aspect," he says. "It is suggested that we were taken to the brink of WWIII because of an attack on the Korean nuclear research facility. A Secret Service agent here alleged that bombers were already on their way to Korea to do a preemptive strike as it was thought that when they discovered the attack, said to have come from a U.S. military computer, they would retaliate.

"In the evidence presented in the case," Bevan says, "there was a snippet of a log that shows Datastream Cowboy logging into said facility with the user ID of 'sync,' and as the user has no Unix shell associated with it, the login is terminated. Nowhere else in the logs is any record of the intrusion being successful, and in my opinion the logs do not reflect that. Being called 'the single biggest threat to world peace since Adolf Hitler' is a tad annoying, but then even the layman can see that is just hype and propaganda."

Who Can Find the Bottom Line?

A damage assessment of the intrusions into the Rome Labs's systems was conducted on October 31, 1994. The assessment indicated a total loss to the United States Air

Force of $211,722. This cost did not include the costs of the investigative effort or the recovery and monitoring team.

No other federal agencies that were victims of the hackers (for example, NASA) conducted damage assessments.

The General Accounting Office conducted an additional damage assessment at the request of Senator Nunn. (See GAO Report, *Information Security: Computer Attacks at Department of Defense Pose Increasing Risks* [AIMD-96-84], May 22, 1996.)

Some aspects of this investigation remain unsolved:

- **The extent of the attack.** The investigators believe they uncovered only a portion of the attack. They still don't know whether the hackers attacked Rome Labs at previous times before the sniffer was discovered or whether the hackers attacked other systems where they were not detected.

- **The extent of the damage.** Some costs can be attributed to the incident, such as the cost of repair and the cost of the investigative effort. The investigation, however, was unable to reveal what they downloaded from the networks or whether they tampered with any data. Given the sensitive information contained on the various computer networks (at Rome Labs, Goddard Space Flight Center, the Jet Propulsion Laboratory, Wright-Patterson AFB, or the National Aero-Space Plane Program), it is very difficult to quantify the loss from a national security perspective.

HotterthanMojaveinmyheart:[2] The Case of Julio Cesar Ardita

On March 29, 1996, the U.S. Justice Department announced it had charged Julio Cesar Ardita (a.k.a. "El Griton"), a 21-year-old Argentine, with breaking into Harvard University's computer network and using it as a staging platform for many other hacks into sites throughout cyberspace. Like Kuji and the Datastream Cowboy, Ardita targeted sites belonging to NASA, DoD, several American universities, and those in other countries (for example, Korea, Mexico, Taiwan, Chile, and Brazil). Like Kuji and the Datastream Cowboy, Ardita gained unauthorized access to important and sensitive information in his explorations. In Ardita's case, the research information that was compromised involved satellites, radiation, and energy-related engineering.

Peter Garza of Evidentdata (Ranchero Cucamonga, California) was a special agent for the Naval Criminal Investigative Services. He led the digital manhunt that ended in Buenos Aires.

---

2. During Ardita's hacks, he created two script files that he named Hotterthanthemojaveinmyheart and InfamousAngel. These filenames were taken from the songs of Iris Dement. For more information on her work, go to www.irisdement.com.

Garza described Ardita as a dedicated hacker. "Ardita was no ordinary script kiddie," Garza tells me. "He didn't run automated hacking scripts downloaded from someone else's site. He did his hacking the old-fashioned way. He used a terminal emulator program, and he conducted manual hacks. He was prodigious. He had persistence and stamina. Indeed, I discovered records of ten thousand sessions on Ardita's home computer after it was seized. During the technical interviews we did of Ardita in Argentina (after his arrest), he would describe all-night sessions hacking into systems all over the Internet.

"Early on in the investigation," Garza adds, "I had guessed this would be a solvable case because of this persistence. I had guessed that because this was such a prolific hacker, he had to use the same file names, techniques, and hiding places just so that he would be able to remember where he left collected userids and passwords behind on the many hacked systems. Also, I hoped the hacker was keeping records to recall the hacked sites. Records that would help further the investigation if we were successful in tracking the hacker down. It was gratifying that I was right on both counts. Records on his seized computer, along with his detailed paper notes, helped us reconstruct much of what he had done."

Like the investigation that led to the identification and arrest of the Rome Labs hackers, the pursuit that led to the identification and arrest of Ardita accelerated the learning curve of those responsible for tracking down cybercriminals and bringing them to justice.

The following account, drawn from my interview with Garza and the court affidavit written by Garza himself in support of the criminal complaint against Ardita, sheds light on the details of the investigations and the groundbreaking work that the case required.

How the Search for "El Griton" Began

Sysadmins at a U.S. Navy research center in San Diego detected that certain system files had been altered. Taking a closer look, they uncovered certain files, including a sniffer he left behind, the file that contained the passwords he was logging, and a couple programs he used to gain root access and cover up his tracks.

This evidence enabled Garza to construct a profile of the hacker.

Coincidentally, and fortuitously, Garza and other naval security experts happened to be at the San Diego facility for a conference on the day that the intrusion was detected. They worked late into the night.

They succeeded in tracking the as-yet-unidentified hacker to a host system administered by the Faculty of Arts and Sciences (FAS) at Harvard University, Cambridge, Massachusetts. The hacker was making unauthorized use of accounts on the FAS host and trying to access other systems connected to Harvard's network via the Internet.

(As early as July 1995, host computers across the United States as well as in Mexico and the United Kingdom reported both successful and unsuccessful hacking attempts seeming to originate from the FAS Harvard host. But this U.S. Navy investigation that commenced in late August would lead to Ardita's arrest.)

Although it was impossible at first to determine the hacker's true identity because he was using the legitimate account holders' identities as his aliases or covers, investigators could distinguish the hacker from other users of the FAS Harvard host and the Internet through certain distinctive patterns of illicit activity. But to track the hacker all the way back to his point of origination, Garza was going to need a court order for a wiretap.

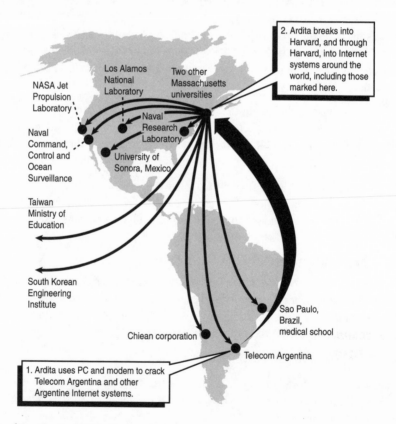

Figure 6.2 The hacker's path.

Source: U.S. Justice Department

"I called the U.S. Attorney's office in Boston on a Thursday and asked if we could have the court order in place by Monday," Garza recounts. "They laughed. Six months was considered the 'speed of light' for wiretap approval. But we started to put the affidavit together anyway, and got it okayed in only six weeks, which at that time was unheard of."

Indeed, the work of Garza and the others to obtain a wiretap in the 1995 Ardita case laid a lot of the groundwork that made it possible for investigators in the 1999 "Solar Sunrise" case (which I describe later in this chapter) to obtain wiretap approval in one day.

Ardita's Biggest Mistake

By the end of September, as Garza explains, the investigators detected a change in the hacker's behavior. "He had been dialing into the Harvard network via telephone lines. But by September, he had stopped dialing in, yet he was still active on the network. Our investigation revealed that in the beginning, he had been breaking into a PBX of an off-shore company, located in Argentina, and from there dialing into Harvard, and then from Harvard hacking elsewhere around the Internet. The change came when he broke into Telecom Argentina to get free Internet access. He would telnet from there to Harvard and then from Harvard keep hacking other sites.

"We were able to look at where he was coming from on the Internet," he explains, "and we saw a cluster of connections from different universities and other organizations in Argentina. We hadn't tracked it back to his residence yet, but at least we knew he was either coming in through Argentina or he actually was someone living in Argentina."

Breaking into Telecom Argentina turned out to be Ardita's biggest mistake.

"We had been trying to get the phone company down there to do a phone trace because we follow the trail to a bunch of dial-ups," Garza tells me. "But each one we tracked back to Argentina ended up in a modem pool, so we needed somebody down there to trace it the next step back. We couldn't get them to act fast enough until he broke into the phone system, then they acted because they were afraid of what he could do. So, in just a couple of days, they got a court order and traced the calls back to Ardita's residence."

The investigation had begun in August; Ardita was identified as the suspect in December.

On December 28, 1995, acting on information supplied by Telecom Argentina, Argentine law enforcement seized Ardita's computer files and equipment at his home in Buenos Aires.

No Ordinary Wiretap

"This is a case of cyber-sleuthing, a glimpse of what computer crime fighting will look like in the coming years," said U.S. Attorney Donald K. Stern in the official U.S. DoJ statement announcing the criminal charges filed against Ardita. "We have made enormous strides in developing the investigative tools to track down individuals who misuse these vital computer networks."

He was not indulging in hyperbole. The wiretap used in the Ardita was no ordinary wiretap. Intruder Watch was a specialized module of a Network Intrusion Detector, developed at Lawrence Livermore Lab in California. And, as Garza explains, it was the first of its kind.

"There had been four other wiretaps on a computer crime case," Garza says, "but they weren't tapping the network, they were tapping a modem line. In that instance, what was captured had to be manually reviewed and filtered, then only what was relevant to the case agents."

But with a thousand users online simultaneously, Garza insisted, they just couldn't do it that way. Practicality demanded that they quickly filter what was happening on the network. Legal considerations demanded that they minimize the intrusion on the privacy of authorized users.

Intruder Watch provided the answer to the dilemma. It intercepted only those communications that fit the patterns identified as the hacker's. "Even when communications contained the identifying patterns of the intruder," Stern observed, "we limited our initial examination to 80 characters around the tell-tale sign to further protect the privacy of innocent communications."

Although Ardita's hack of Telecom Argentina had identified him without evidence supplied through Intruder Watch, the breakthrough wiretap provided plenty of evidence on his activities. For example, as Garza recollects, Ardita got online with some of his hacker buddies on what turned out to be a bulletin board near Carnegie Mellon and gave them the phone number to his bulletin board down in Argentina.

Debriefing "El Griton"

Tracking down Ardita, and putting an end to his hacking adventures, took four months. But, as Garza relates, almost an entire year passed before U.S. investigators could actually interview the now-infamous young man.

"It took us a while to go through the mutual legal assistance treaty process," Garza explains. "Hacking wasn't illegal in Argentina. Interruption of telecommunications was, however, illegal under their penal code. So we went with that, and they agreed to hold all of his computers and everything until we got down there. But it took a while to go through our State Department and their equivalent. We finally got down there in October 1996."

Garza and other U.S. officials conducted six sessions with Ardita going into detail about his activities. These in-depth discussions allowed Garza to size up "El Griton."

"He claimed, as many hackers do, that he was doing it simply because he could," Garza tells me. "He said he was inquisitive. He claimed he was researching security. He kept insisting that he was just hacking for the good of mankind. But we walked him through what he had done. He had been phone-phreaking from the PBX of that multinational corporation. He was making calls to his girlfriend. He was making calls into Harvard. To the tune of approximately $15,000.

"We asked him, 'Isn't that just plain theft?' It had shattered his self-image of the 'White Hat Hacker.' He broke down in tears. I didn't get the sense from talking to him that he was very sophisticated people-wise. He wasn't a genius either, he was just talented and very persistent."

Of course, there is a lingering question in the minds of some regarding the Ardita case because his father just happened to be a retired Argentine military colonel "assigned" to the Argentine legislature. Could "El Griton" have been the pawn of some larger online intelligence-gathering operation? No such evidence has been produced. But it's one of those "coincidences" that just kind of gnaws at you.

In December 1997 (yes, another year later), the Ardita case was finally brought to conclusion. Because hacking wasn't a crime in Argentina, it wasn't covered under the existing extradition treaty with Argentina. But Ardita agreed to waive extradition. His father, after all, was in the Argentine military, and the case was probably something of an embarrassment.

He voluntarily traveled to the United States and pleaded guilty. The agreement worked out between the U.S. Attorney's office in Boston and Mario Crespo, Ardita's lawyer, recommended that Ardita receive a three-year probation and a fine of $5,000.

Considering the resources that went into the case, Garza acknowledges, "Ardita got off with pretty light sentence. There was criticism. But the U.S. prosecutors felt that in this case, since they could not extradite him, the stalemate would have just dragged on."

The Solar Sunrise Case: Mak, Stimpy, and Analyzer Give the DoD a Run for Its Money

In January 1998, tensions between the United States, the United Nations, and Iraq were on the rise. Saddam Hussein had expelled the UN weapons inspectors, dominating the headlines, precipitating an international crisis, and pushing the United States to the brink of renewed military action in the Persian Gulf.

On February 3, the Automated Security Incident Monitors (ASIM), the USAF's intrusion detection system, detected a root-level compromise on an Air National Guard computer system located at Andrews Air Force Base in Maryland.

On February 4, the Air Force's Computer Emergency Response Team (AFCERT) at Kelly Air Force Base in Texas detected additional compromises of systems at other Air Force Bases including Kirtland in New Mexico, Lackland in Texas, and Columbus in Mississippi.

The intruders would gain entrance to a site with tools from some .edu site (often a DNS server), and then obtain root access using the statd vulnerability. After they gained root access, the intruders would install a sniffer program to collect user passwords and create a backdoor to get back into the system. Intriguingly, the intruders would then eradicate the statd vulnerability (see CERT Advisory CA-97.26) by downloading a patch and exit the system without exploring any further.

Although the targeted systems were not classified, they were all involved in the military build-up being undertaken in regard to the Iraqi weapons inspection crisis. If the targeted systems were damaged, it could impede the flow of transportation, personnel, and medical supplies. If the Iraqis were gathering, aggregating, and analyzing the data from the targeted systems, they could use it to surmise the U.S. military's plans.

Could these intrusions be the first indications of impending information warfare with the Iraqis? Clearly, the intrusions had to be taken seriously.

Martha Stansell-Gamm, head of the U.S. Department of Justice's Computer Crime and Intellectual Property (CCIP) section, provides some insight into the ensuing probe.

"One of the singular aspects of Solar Sunrise was that it was such a multi-agency investigation," she says. "The Ardita case, for example, involved both the Navy and the FBI, but the Navy quite clearly took the lead. In the Rome Labs case, it was the Air Force that drove the investigation. But Solar Sunrise involved Army, Navy, Air Force, FBI, NASA, CIA, NSA, and others.

"Everybody was working on different pieces of it," Stansell-Gamm adds. "Everybody agreed to meet around our kitchen table at CCIP to figure out what we had, then come up with a plan and coordinate the effort. We didn't do it because somebody said so; we did it because it just made sense to everybody to do it that way. Everybody learned something whenever we got together. It was one way for us at CCIP to make sure that the needs of the investigators were being met. It was simply the most efficient way to go as far and as fast as possible and it just sort of happened."

The unprecedented interagency cooperation bore fruit.

They obtained 19 court orders in fewer than 10 days. And amazingly, a Title III wiretap was written, approved by DoJ, and sworn to in one day.

The intruders in the Solar Sunrise case didn't turn out to be Iraqi information warriors on a some kind of cyber-Jihad after all. Like Datastream Cowboy, Kuji, and El Griton, they turned out to be youthful joy riders.

The big mistake that led to the identification and capture of the intruders was a doozy. They had ftp'd sniffer output (i.e., user names and passwords) from the hacked system at Andrews AFB directly to Sonic.net, an ISP in Northern California. Then they ftp'd the purloined data to their own user accounts at Sonic using their own home PCs.

"They" turned out to be two 16-year-olds (a.k.a. Stimpy and Mak). Indeed, they had already come to the attention of the ISP's sysadmin. Harvard and MIT had complained about attempted intrusions by the two hackers.

Authorities put a wiretap in place to capture Stimpy's keystrokes after the two logged on to their accounts at Sonic. A pen register verified that calls were being made to Sonic from Stimpy's home phone line at the same time that the accounts were being accessed. Furthermore, physical surveillance at Mak's residence identified the occupants of the house at the time of the connection.

The evidence had to show guilt beyond a reasonable doubt. Without the confirmation provided by correlating the evidence from the wiretaps, the pen registers, and the physical surveillance, the accused might have argued that someone else had hacked into their accounts and used them to undertake the attacks.

The investigation had been going well, but a serious problem developed. John Hamre, an undersecretary of defense, blundered in a briefing with reporters. He let it slip out that the suspects were kids living in Northern California. That meant investigators had to race to execute their search warrants before Mak and Stimpy were tipped off by hearing about themselves on the evening news. The time difference between the coasts proved helpful as search warrants were executed early that evening.

Special Agent Chris Beeson of the San Francisco FBI Computer intrusion squad, armed and wearing a bulletproof vest (standard operating procedure), was the first law enforcement officer through the door of Stimpy's bedroom. Stimpy was on-line at the time. The kid simply looked up at Beeson and kept typing on the keyboard until he was pulled away from the computer.

"Their rooms were a mess," Beeson recounts. "They were actually cleaner after we left then when we got there. The scene was typical of teenagers. Pepsi cans. Half-eaten cheeseburgers. It is not like what you see on TV. We don't turn everything upside down. When we do a search, we take pictures when we get there and pictures when we leave. After we go through everything, we put it all in nice neat piles."

In Mak's room, the investigators found a fictional essay he had written.

> About two days ago, one of my friends was raided by the FBI and they were working up to an arrest. Apparently, he hacked NASA. The Feds. Why they bother to messing with us, I don't know. But if I could get a chance I would go to the informer's house and politely knock on his door. When he answered I would kindly say "hello," then I would put a .45 to his head and tell him to get on the ground.

> I would have the political prisoners and other friends rig a ten block radius with explosives and then call the FBI and order the release of our friend and a helicopter to fly us to the nearest jet strip. Their problem would be the ten house radius around, if any agent entered, they would blow and above the house I would have mercenaries that would report by radio every five minutes. If the government didn't comply one person each hour would be shot.

> I guess I am going to have to be satisfied with flooding all known government agencies and rendering their capabilities useful.

Mak's teacher had written some comments on the sheet of paper.

> Work on fade in and out of daydream. Write as if you are actually doing this.
> By the way, this is disturbing.

Both youths were arrested and interviewed. Their true identities, of course, were not disclosed because of their age.

Investigators shared a gut feeling all along that the intruders were indeed adventurous kids, but they had to assume the worst. The stakes were simply too high to take anything for granted. It was a time of international crisis and impending military action. Until proven otherwise, it had to be viewed as a threat to national security.

Meanwhile, a third Solar Sunrise hacker was still unidentified and at large. This third suspect was coming in over the Internet from Israel and launching his attacks against DoD targets from Maroon.com, a Web page hosting service in College Station, Texas. The AFOSI had set up consensual monitoring at Maroon.

The wiretap on Stimpy revealed IRC chats with the third hacker, known to Stimpy as Analyzer. Analyzer was Stimpy's mentor who coached him in hacking.

Analyzer had chutzpah. Two days after the arrest of Mak and Stimpy, he participated in an on-line interview with AntiOnline, a fascinating hacker news Web site, in which he claimed to have hacked 400 DoD sites and provided lists of dozens of logins and passwords for .mil sites.

On March 18, CNN's Jerusalem office posted the following story, with a headline that proclaimed, "Master hacker 'Analyzer' held in Israel":

> Israeli police spokeswoman Linda Menuchin said the 18-year-old suspect and two alleged accomplices were arrested Wednesday, in part based on information supplied by American authorities. U.S. Justice Department officials in Washington identified the ringleader as Ehud Tenebaum, an Israeli citizen, and said he has been charged with illegally accessing hundreds of computer systems.
>
> The suspects were questioned for several hours at a police station in Bat Yam, a suburb of Tel Aviv, then put under house arrest, Menuchin said. Police confiscated their passports and forbade contact between them.
>
> In an interview with AntiOnline, an online magazine that deals with Internet security issues, one of the teens, nicknamed "Makaveli," gave this explanation for what he and his cohorts had done: "It's power, dude. You know, power," he said.
>
> He said he began hacking as a challenge and concentrated on U.S. government sites because "I hate organizations."
>
> Though he mused in his interview that "chaos" was a "nice idea," the Analyzer claimed that his intrusions were actually innocent and that he even helped targets by "patching" weaknesses in their systems to prevent future intrusions.
>
> He admitted teaching other hackers how to target U.S. military systems.
>
> "Since I was going to retire, I was going to teach someone of my knowledge and guide him," the Analyzer said.[3]

The swift and committed assistance of Israeli law enforcement was essential to the success of the effort to bring Analyzer to justice.

Ehud Tennebaum, 19, and several other Israeli hackers (members of an Israeli hacker group that called itself "The Enforcers") were charged with hacking the computer systems of the Pentagon and NASA. They pleaded innocent.

Tennebaum's lawyer said his client broke no law when he penetrated the Internet sites of American and Israeli institutions, including the Knesset, because there was no notice on the sites declaring them off-limits.

Conclusion

The true cost of these three capers will never be adequately tabulated. Some questions will remain unanswered. Certainly, they amounted to an extraordinary series of

---

3. "Master hacker 'Analyzer' held in Israel," CNN, March 18, 1998.

shakedown cruises for investigators in law enforcement and the military. Along the way, they broke new ground and cultivated it. For example, they honed their investigative skills, developed new forensic tools, and established protocols for handling multi-agency and multi-country investigations. But perhaps the most striking common denominator in all three cases is that the juvenile hackers involved used known vulnerabilities for which CERT advisories had been issued and patches were available.

What's the point? Law enforcement and the military are clearly getting better at investigating, making arrests, and prosecuting such crimes, but the organizations targeted are not getting any better at preventing them. In Chapters 15, 17, and 18, I will discuss some of the reasons for this strange state of affairs.

Grand Theft Data: Crackers and Cyber Bank Robbers

I n late 1999 and early 2000, a spate of electronic commerce crimes made front-page headlines.

- In late 1999, Visa USA wrote a letter to financial institutions informing them that a hacker stole more than 485,000 credit card records from an "e-commerce site" and then secretly stashed the database on a U.S. government agency's Web site.

- In January 2000, someone believed to be a Russian hacker, identified only as Maxim, released as many as 25,000 credit card numbers stolen from CD Universe, an on-line music retailer.

  Maxim claims to have stolen 300,000 card numbers from CD Universe and allegedly attempted to extort $100,000 from the company.

- Approximately 2,000 records were stolen from SalesGate, including credit card numbers and other personal information.

- According to Loxley Information Service, a leading Thai ISP, someone hacked www.shoppingthailand.com and stole credit card information on 2,000 customers.

- RealNames, a company that substitutes complicated Web addresses with simple keywords, had to warn its users that its customer database, with as many as 20,000 records on it, had been hacked and that user credit card numbers and passwords may have been accessed.

Electronic commerce has arrived, and so has electronic commerce crime.

Here are three cases that highlight the phenomenon.

The Case of Carlos "SMAK" Salgado

In 1997, Carlos Salgado, Jr. (a.k.a. SMAK) walked into a smoking room at San Francisco International Airport carrying an encrypted CD-ROM disc with approximately 100,000 credit card numbers on it. The secret code to decrypt the CD-ROM was based on the first letters of the sentences in a specific paragraph on a specific page in Mario Puzo's *The Last Don*. He thought he was going to walk out with $260,000 in cash for the CD-ROM. Instead, FBI Special Agent Cal Dalrymple placed him under arrest and took him into custody.

On August 25, Salgado, a 37-year-old Daly City, California man, pleaded guilty to four of five counts in a federal indictment accusing him of hacking systems to gather credit card information for sale on the black market.

Salgado hacked several companies doing business on the World Wide Web, including an Internet service provider (ISP) and two other companies. Exploiting known operating system flaws and using commonly available hacking tools, Salgado gained unauthorized access to the companies' systems and harvested tens of thousands of credit card records from them.

The details of Salgado's digital adventures and the FBI investigation that brought him to justice provide a fascinating and invaluable glimpse into the shadows of cyberspace and shed light on the dark side of the electronic commerce gold rush.

One caveat before we descend into the netherworld: CSI knows the identity of the companies victimized in this case, but we will not make this information public. The FBI has gone to painstaking lengths to shield the companies involved, and making their names known would serve no good end. As the annual *CSI/FBI Computer Crime and Security Survey* has shown, negative publicity is the primary reason why so little computer crime is reported to law enforcement. Those companies that do report serious incidents should be commended, not ridiculed.

I should also note that two of the companies involved had no knowledge that they had been hacked until the FBI notified them. They were grateful for the heads-up and cooperated in the investigation.

Diary of a Computer Crime Investigation

On March 28, 1997, a technician performing routine maintenance at a San Diego–based ISP came across telltale signs of unauthorized access and discovered a packet sniffer used to collect logons. The technicians then discovered that the intruder was still logged on to the system. The relevant files were backed up. As the technicians were backing up the files, the intruder was deleting files to cover his tracks. The compromised computer was taken off-line. The unauthorized access was traced to the University of California at San Francisco (UCSF). UCSF called in the FBI.

On March 29, a customer who was to become a cooperating witness in the case notified the ISP that he had talked to a hacker using the handle SMAK via Internet Relay Channel (IRC). SMAK boasted of the hack and of gaining the credit card information. He offered to sell the credit card information along with another database of 60,000 credit card numbers.

On March 31, the San Diego office of the FBI forwarded the case to the FBI's San Francisco Computer Crime Squad. San Francisco FBI agents conducted interviews at UCSF and determined that the unauthorized access into the ISP's system originated from the compromised account of an innocent student.

In April, the FBI commenced a formal investigation. The San Diego ISP technician worked with the cooperating witness to identify SMAK. To do so, the cooperating witness continued communications with SMAK. They discussed the possibility of purchasing small samples of the credit card information. Investigators hoped the ongoing communication would provide the time to track and identify SMAK and encourage a face-to-face meeting.

During May, SMAK and the cooperating witness conversed on the IRC. SMAK sent a file with more than 50 credit card numbers as an encrypted attachment to an e-mail message. The message and attachment were received at an FBI-controlled address. SMAK bragged about his successful hacks and the purloined credit card information.

Each communication was recorded and maintained as evidence.

In May, SMAK sent an e-mail message to the cooperating witness:

```
There may be a delay in our business together of a day or
so. It's not necessarily a bad thing. Let me explain.
This morning I was reading a business magazine article
about on-line transactions on the Internet and a particu-
lar niche in services. A couple companies were mentioned
that generated SEVERAL MILLION dollars in credit card
transactions a week! I decided to go exploring and got
into their sites. The article was right! However, I need
to explore the sites for a little while to establish firm
control and locate machine extractable data. I think it
is worth it. SMAK
```

On May 5, the cooperating witness (under the direction of the FBI) asked, "How many of the credit card numbers are valid?" The cooperating witness bought 710 of them for $1 each. SMAK sent the database as an encrypted e-mail attachment. The numbers were determined to be valid credit card numbers with credit limits from $5,000 to $12,000. The cooperating witness paid SMAK the $710 via anonymous Western Union wire transfer.

On May 13, the cooperating witness purchased 580 more credit card numbers for $5 each. Another small sample of the cards was researched with the issuing bank and found to be valid. The purchase limits on these cards ranged from $2,000 to $25,000. SMAK received the $2,900 again via anonymous Western Union wire transfer. Fifteen numbers were chosen at random for verification.

The meet was arranged for May 21 at 11:15 a.m., in the smoking room at gates 60–67 in the American Airlines Terminal at SFO. Salgado brought an encrypted CD-ROM containing approximately 100,000 credit card numbers and a paperback copy of Mario Puzo's *The Last Don*. The code to decrypt the CD-ROM was composed of the first letter of each sentence in the first paragraph on page 128. Salgado was arrested and advised of his constitutional rights. He waived his rights and spoke to the FBI.

On May 27, he was released on $100,000 bail.

On June 6, Salgado was indicted on five counts: three counts of computer crime under 18 U.S.C. Section 1030, and two counts of tracking in stolen credit cards under 18 U.S.C. Section 1029.

Counts one and two cited 18 U.S.C. §1030 (a) (4) and related to "unauthorized access of computer in furtherance of fraud." They call for penalties of up to five years in custody; $250,000 in fines; three years supervised release; and $100 penalty assessment. Count three cited 18 U.S.C. §1030 (a) (5) (B) and related to "unauthorized access of computer causing damages."

It calls for penalties up to five years in custody; $250,000 in fines; three years supervised release; and $100 penalty assessment.

Count four cited 18 U.S.C. §1029 (a) (2) and relates to "trafficking in stolen credit card numbers." It calls for penalties of up to five years in custody; $250,000 in fines; three years supervised release; and $100 penalty assessment.

Count five cites 18 U.S.C. §1029 (a) (3) and relates to "possessing more than fifteen stolen credit card numbers." It calls for penalties of up to five years in custody; $250,000 in fines; three years supervised release; and $100 penalty assessment.

On August 25, Salgado pleaded guilty on four of the five counts. He was sentenced to two and a half years in prison and five years of probation during which he is prohibited from having access to any computers.

Don't Underestimate Internet-Based Credit Card Theft

FBI sources stress the important role that Visa USA's Fraud Control team played in helping keep the investigation on track and moving swiftly, particularly by providing vital figures on the scope of financial losses.

The operation involved 86,326 compromised credit card accounts affecting 1,214 different financial institutions.

Forty-five of them had more than 100 accounts at risk.

Considering average credit card fraud losses (for example, $616 for mail order/telephone order fraud, $1,335 for credit card counterfeiting, and $1,836 for fraudulent credit applications), the potential impact could have been a staggering $1 billion. The average $125 cost for card reissue alone adds up to over $10 million dollars ($125 × 86,326 = $10,790,750).

The next time you hear a high-tech industry sycophant on TV telling consumers that it is "perfectly safe" to send your credit card numbers over the Internet, remember these figures. The real security concern for information security practitioners and law-enforcement agents has never been the risk to just one consumer doing a single credit card transaction over the Web. The real security concern centers on the vulnerability of front-line commerce servers doing millions of dollars worth of transactions and the back-end database servers brimming with credit card information. The encryption of a single transaction doesn't guarantee the confidentiality of the networked computer on which it is stored, just as a properly administered firewall doesn't ensure that there are no other points of entry into the network it guards.

The Crest of an Electronic Commerce Crime Wave?

The significance of the Salgado case should not be lost. It showed that there is a market for databases of credit card information purloined from commercial Web sites. Salgado thought it was plausible that someone would offer him big money for the data. It also shows that such data is not very difficult to obtain. No one has suggested that Salgado was an "elite hacker." Indeed, one writer close to the underground described him to me as "a bottom feeder." But he was standing in SFO with an encrypted database containing more than 80,000 credit card records stolen from the on-line sites of three commercial enterprises, wasn't he? There were firewalls in place, and Secure Socket Layer (SSL) was used, but Salgado got around them. He is brighter than some observers have characterized him, but it is also easier to accomplish such hacks than many have been led to believe.

The Salgado case also offers a glimpse into the modus operandi of electronic commerce criminals. He launched his attacks from a compromised account of an innocent individual, he conducted on-line negotiations using encrypted e-mail, and he received initial payments via anonymous Western Union wire transfer.

Information Age crime will be different in many ways from Industrial Age crime.

In the twenty-first century, bank vaults, armored cars, closed circuit video cameras, and silent alarms will still be used; but firewalls, intrusion detection, encryption, digital signatures, and other sophisticated technologies will grow in importance. However, as the Salgado case shows, technologies like firewalls and encryption alone aren't enough. For the dream of the electronic commerce gold rush to come true, corporations are going to need adequately staffed and trained information security teams, and they will inevitably have to turn to competent law enforcement agencies to capture and convict those who rob them.

The Salgado case, like the Citibank and Phonemasters sagas that follow, illustrates the emerging nature of electronic commerce crime. For a list of controls for conducting secure electronic commerce, see Chapter 18.

Citibank

The newspaper clipping from September 19, 1997, is rather yellowed now. The headline reads, "Security on trial in case of on-line Citibank heist." The piece was written for *USA Today* by Michael J. Zuckerman. "Zuck" is one of the few journalists working the cybercrime beat in a real way at the national level. He is also perhaps the best and most tenacious.

> After a 30-month extradition battle with U.S. authorities, the Russian accused of being the mastermind of the biggest bank heist in the brief history of cyberspace is in a federal prison in New York City awaiting trial.
>
> Vladimir Levin, 30, has attained folklore status as the hacker who engineered the 1994 theft of $10 million from Citibank. It is the only documented case of on-line bank robbery.
>
> The thin, bespectacled Levin faces charges of funneling millions in cash from Citibank branches worldwide to his accomplices' accounts in California, Israel, Finland, Germany, the Netherlands and Switzerland, all without ever leaving his computer keyboard in St. Petersburg, Russia.
>
> The case is extraordinary not only for the amount stolen and the method by which it was accomplished but also for the furor it has stirred within the financial community and the Internet security community.

I had kept the article tucked away for three years, waiting for the opportunity to dig into the story. The Citibank case drives a lot of people crazy.

The bankers want the story to go away. They want the story to seem like less than it really is. E-commerce proponents in dot-com startups want the story to go away, too. It's bad for business, it makes customers and investors nervous, it draws attention to the dual Achilles' heels of on-line business: the frail and porous state of the infrastructure itself and the problem of weak user authentication.

Reporters, on the other hand, want it to be more than it is or at least different than it is. They want it to be about a state-of-the-art twenty-first century cyber bank heist. They want it to be an Internet crime story. Well, it was neither. Nevertheless, it is a very significant story, not only because of what we know about it, but because of the questions that still remain unanswered.

Fortuitously, as I began the process of putting this book together, Edward Stroz, formerly the head of the FBI's Computer Intrusion Squad in New York City, left government service and started his own private investigations firm, Stroz and Associates.

I was fortunate enough to debrief Ed on the Citibank case after he left the Bureau. During our discussions, he was able to set some of the record straight.

Where Did It All Begin? How Did It Happen?

According to Stroz, one of Levin's transfers caught the eye of a Citibank employee in Finland. It just looked unusual: the amount, the time, what he had seen before and after the transfer, what he knew about what that customer was doing at the time. It didn't add up. It wasn't something he expected to see. He didn't label it a hack or fraud right away, but it stuck in his head. It set off an alarm.

Meanwhile, one of Citibank's customers in South America had the habit of doing his on-line banking activity at night. Perhaps he was an insomniac. (Of course, that was one of the virtues of the system: You could do your transactions wherever and whenever you liked.) Well, as a result of this customer's insomnia, he was looking at the displayed transaction activities at a period of time that Levin and his friends were counting on people *not* looking.

It was a well-thought-out attack plan. They had thought no one would be up at that hour of the night in South America, but they hadn't factored in the risk of running into an insomniac. Someone was up doing business in the middle of the night and saw something that Levin and others weren't counting on being seen, and then made a call that they weren't counting on anyone making.

Misconceptions Dispelled

How did Levin do it? How could it happen?

Three misconceptions need to be cleared up right at the beginning. First, the Citibank caper wasn't an Internet crime; the Customer Cash Management Account (CCMA) system that Levin attacked was a dialup, telecom-based product, not an Internet, TCP/IP-based product. Second, the Citibank caper says at least as much about the telecommunications industry as it does about the banking industry. There is usually a big tradeoff between ease of use and security. And there was one in this instance. Third, there was no indication or evidence of insider collusion.

"If you really want to get it right," Stroz elucidates, "if you really want to stratify what does it take for something like that to get done, you have to distinguish between the phone system and the banking system. The phone system was never put together with expectation that they would be streaming quantities of money across it. So you can't really blame the phone company either.

"You have this convergence of technologies," he continues. "Along with it, consequently, you have a convergence of risk. Those who are going to be first in this arena are going to stub their toes once in a while. This is an example of how it can happen. It says less about the banking industry than it does about the way this kind of communications protocol is subject to new risks.

"You have to break it down into two components," Stroz says. "There are the bank mechanisms in place to make the product available, and then there is the telecommunications system that the world uses to transmit any kind of circuit-switched networks. What Levin did was not so much attack the bank, but attack the telecommunications network, which gave him the information he needed to work with the bank product.

"The bank does not control the public switch network," Stroz asserts, "but it had to use it to provide its customers with this new product. What Levin did, as far as I can tell, was to exploit what he knew about telecom traffic to get the kind of information he needed to execute the bank transfers. Levin got the information he needed about the CCMA on-line; that's what all the evidence points to."

If you're having trouble getting your mind around what we're talking about, consider the following example as one possible scenario. Pull out your ATM card. Turn it over. There's a 1-800 number on the back. If you dial that number, you will probably follow a series of prompts, asking you for your bank account number, your social security number, and, perhaps, your PIN.

How are you supplying your bank with these pieces of authentication? Well, you are punching them into your telephone. The authenticating information is really only a series of tones or pulses being transmitted over the phone lines, isn't it? If someone could intercept your phone call, which is not that difficult, he or she could pretty easily figure out your account number, PIN, etc. On-line banking really isn't much different if all you are using to log in is a reusable password.

Many people, both in the banking industry and in the computer security field, insist that an insider was involved. Why do these rumors persist? Well, if you are the banking industry, you send a much better message about yourself to your customers if you are able to say, "Oh, well, there was a bad apple. There was nothing wrong with the system. It was a human failure. There is no defense against that. We got rid of that person. You can't criticize us for that. An insider could victimize anybody. Our system is rock-solid." But according to Stroz, there is "not a shred of documented evidence that there was an insider."

Was Levin really that good? If he was so good, how come he got caught? How was the case cracked? Stroz provides some insights.

"It was remarkable that these guys pulled off something like this with poor computer processing power in a third-world country with third-world infrastructure," he says. "They were able to carefully select which accounts to withdraw from and in what denominations the money should be carefully moved among the many transfers. That was what impressed everybody: how well that they had done this and how far they had gotten.

"They targeted many accounts," Stroz explains. "They looked for accounts that denominated their transactions at a size and at a time that they did not think would be detected, which is very shrewd. They moved it all around to multiple locations. I think that's good money laundering. Was it good enough not to be detected? No.

"Remember, insomnia plays a role in the story," he continues. "Now does that mean that their technique was bad? I don't think so. It just points out that the type of scheme that they tried to pull was dangerous. It did get noticed. And once it did get noticed, the response by Citibank, the FBI, and the Russians was of a quality that they were able to grab the guy. The scheme wasn't really flawed. They just ran risks."

What It Took To Take Levin Down

"You have to give Citibank a pat on the back for doing the right thing," Stroz remarks. "They found it; they worked on it. They could just have filled out a suspicious activity report a month after they heard about it. They are obligated to do that by law. But they called the Bureau before they even filled out the form. They worked together with the FBI and the U.S. Attorney's Office to get this guy."

Stroz also stressed the contributions of the lead investigator, FBI Special Agent Steve Garfinkel, and the lead prosecutor, Dietrich Snell, then an assistant U.S. attorney, now with the New York State Attorney General's Office.

"It was a tiny, tight team," Stroz explains. "They brought the kind of judgment and support to each other that allowed a case like this to get done.

"It isn't like a checklist you could hand to somebody," he says. "It takes a talented ball player to pull off some of these plays. You can tell somebody else what to do, 'Run over there, turn, spin, and catch the ball.' But there's only a handful of people who can actually do it well. People don't appreciate or respect the kind of judgment that goes into this kind of case."

That authorities managed to apprehend Levin in London "is a part of the puzzle that can't be laid out in great detail," Stroz explains. "They were able to persuade Levin to travel to London. And once he was there, they were able to apprehend him. It took a combination of some finesse, some fact, and some cooperation. There were cooperators involved in this case. People who have access to other people and who are cooperating with law enforcement either out of the goodness of their hearts or because they are jammed up big time.

"You put all that on the table and try to come up with a plan of action that's going to work," Stroz continues. "When Levin went to London, people wondered, 'Well, gee, did the Russians put a gun to his head? Did they strap him in and tell him he was going to go into obligatory military service?' None of that was in play. It was actually something that required a lot more judgment skill and finesse."

Suffice it to say that Levin was very surprised when he was arrested.

There is some irony in regard to the technological challenges involved in the Citibank case. You might imagine that the investigation required some world-class, cutting-edge cybercrime expertise. Well, as Stroz explains, the reality was quite the opposite.

"As we trailed back through the telecommunications systems in order to find out where the origination point for this trouble was," Stroz explains, "we wound up snaking from the U.S. into Russia. In these high-tech cases, the first thing people think they need is the country's best brains and most up-to-date minds in terms of optical switching, etc. But when we really got into the devil's territory in this case, we were looking at mechanical switches, twisted pair, labels written in the Cyrillic alphabet, all kinds of wacky stuff."

Stroz says that "the skill set needed to find the originating point for these transmissions was not going to be aided by bringing in the top experts in the current state of the technology. Nor was banking expertise what we needed to track Levin down. What we needed were telecommunications experts, and quite specifically we needed telecom experts who were relevant to the technology in place over there, which was decades old. We needed blueprint analysis in another language. It was really a telecommunications chore more than anything else. It wasn't one that demanded cutting-edge understanding. Indeed, using a primitive network in some ways aided Levin, not that he had a choice."

Sprint was the telecommunications service that Citibank was using at the time, so Sprint was able to answer a lot of questions. "Here is a data stream that came in via telephone lines," Citibank asked, "what can you tell me about who initiated it?" Sprint didn't build the Russian telecommunications infrastructure. Sprint technicians followed the trail through the telephone lines on a trap-and-trace basis, working an antiquated technology, with technicians who speak a different language and use a different alphabet. Consequently, they depended heavily on the Russian police to talk with the people who run the telecom system.

The fraudulent transactions were traced all the way to the phone in the house where Levin lived in St. Petersburg. Table 7.1 details the transactions in counts 3–21 against Levin.

Table 7.1   Timeline of Vladimir Levin's Citibank Cyber-Heists

Date	Wire Transmission
6/30/94	Transfer of $143,800 from an account held by PNB at Citibank in New York, New York, to the Carmane account
7/15/94	Transfer of $384,000 from an account held by CFI at Citibank in New York, New York, to the Carmane account
8/5/94	Transfer of $218,000 from an account held by Artha Graha at Citibank in New York, New York, to an account held by Primorye (USA) Corp. at Bank of America in San Francisco, California
8/5/94	Transfer of $304,000 from an account held by SUD at Citibank in New York, New York, to an account held by Shore Co. at Bank of America in San Francisco, California
8/23/94	Transfer of $983,770 from an account held by Alberta at Citibank in New York, New York, to an account held by Auto Rik Import-Export at ABN-AMRO Bank in the Netherlands
8/23/94	Transfer of $73,215 from the BCO account to an account held by Oy Finn Enterprise Ltd. at KOP in Finland
8/23/94	Transfer of $208,600 from the BCO account to an account held by Damir Chadaev at the Deutsche Bank in Germany

Table 7.1 continued

Date	Wire Transmission
8/23/94	Transfer of $194,511 from the BCO account to an account held by Serguei Vassiliev at KOP in Finland
8/24/94	Transfer of $191,300 from an account held by Toepffer at Citibank in New York, New York, to an account held by Damir Chadaev at the Union Bank of Finland in Finland
8/24/94	Transfer of $31,200 from the Invest Capital account to an account held by Ekaterina Korolkova at Sumitomo Bank in San Francisco, California
8/24/94	Transfer of $49,300 from the Invest Capital account to an account held by Ekaterina Korolkova at Wells Fargo Bank in San Francisco, California
8/24/94	Transfer of $26,800 from the Invest Capital account to an account held by Ekaterina Korolkova at Union Bank in San Francisco, California
8/24/94	Transfer of $53,200 from the Invest Capital account to an account held by Ekaterina Korolkova at Great Western Bank in San Francisco, California
8/24/94	Transfer of $32,800 from the Invest Capital account to an account held by Ekaterina Korolkova at Pacific Bank in San Francisco, California
8/24/94	Transfer of $197,630 from the LAIB account to an account held by Alexios Palmidis at American Israel Bank Ltd. in Tel Aviv
8/24/94	Transfer of $181,000 from the LAIB account to an account held by Alexios Palmidis at Union Bank of Israel in Tel Aviv
8/24/94	Transfer of $198,900 from the LAIB account to an account held by Alexios Palmidis at First International Bank of Israel in Tel Aviv
8/24/94	Transfer of $174,000 from the LAIB account to an account held by Alexios Palmidis at Israel Discount Bank Ltd. in Tel Aviv
8/24/94	Transfer of $188,300 from the LAIB account to an account held by Alexios Palmidis at Israel Continental Bank Ltd. in Tel Aviv

Source: United States of America v. Vladimir Leonidovich Levin, a.k.a. Vova, U.S. District Court, Southern District of New York.

You Don't Know How Lucky You Are, Boys…Back in the USSR: Unanswered Questions About Megazoid and the Russian Mafia

Was Levin really the mastermind or was he working for organized crime? Was there another hacker besides Levin? What was his relationship to the people who withdrew the stolen funds in various places around the world? Who really orchestrated the caper?

Stroz offers some comment: "There is still some mystery surrounding this aspect of the case. If you are wondering was there another guy, yes, it is very possible. The Russians are very difficult people to deal with.

"Even Levin, when we had him in our office interviewing him, was trying to bullshit us. In the United States, when you find one of these people, at some point the likelihood is that they give it up, it is no longer worthwhile for them to deny it. He finally came around to plead, but he was denying it up to a point I would not have expected. He was denying forensic evidence that we had, and we had to stick it in his face.

"Given that mindset," Stroz continues, "if there were other people involved what is the likelihood that he would have given them up? Unless you brought them in and sat them in front of him, he is probably going to continue to deny, at the point where you would want additional leverage on Levin.

"Everybody involved in the case knew that the amount of time Levin had already been incarcerated, just on bail issues and everything else, was going to be equal and greater than the final sentence was going to be. So Levin knew that the authorities really couldn't do too much more to him. He was kept in jail in London because of the extradition process. When he arrived in New York, he was a flight risk and so he was detained there as well. Thus, every day that went by, until he pled guilty or a trial actually occurred, he was earning time in detention."

According to Stroz, there are allusions and references in the interviews to indicate that there were others involved. "No one ever said that it had to be Levin and Levin alone," Stroz comments. "It is very plausible that there was someone else in Russia at the time on the granular level doing these things with Levin. Levin would never admit to that, so there wasn't a lot of traction you could get to prove it. However, journalists who have gone onsite have identified human beings who have come forth on camera."

Stroz is referring to Megazoid, a hacker and an unemployed university graduate living in St. Petersburg.

In 1996, Megazoid was interviewed by British TV's Channel Four. He told the British TV reporters that *he* broke into Citibank, not Levin. For three months, he had access to Citibank. He built backdoors into password-protected programs to allow access to his fellow hackers.

But Megazoid and his friends were hacking purists. They were not roaming around inside Citibank's networks for profit, Megazoid claimed, they were only exploring.

According to Megazoid, one of his hacker colleagues got drunk in a bar and bragged of the Citibank hack to a member of the Russian Mafia. For two bottles of vodka and US$100, the friend disclosed the secrets of the Citibank hack to the mobster.

"Russia *is* organized crime," Stroz concludes. "It would be amazing to have an event in which organized crime wasn't involved in some way. When you look at the people that Levin associated with and the businesses he was in, there were organized crime identities that surfaced in this case. That is not to say it was an organized crime operation, but it is not to be denied either. Levin never really came around on this, as Russians rarely do. And maybe he's fearful."

Whether Levin was the mastermind or just a superstar cracker for some shadowy Russian Mafia, the Citibank caper was certainly a gang operation.

Consider the fate of the "mules," as the cash couriers are referred to in the money laundering world.

From Russia With Love: The Sad Tale of Ekaterina and Evygeny

FBI Special Agent Andrew Black of the San Francisco Computer Intrusion Squad was instructing out on the firearms range when he was paged from his supervisor on the White Collar Crime squad. He was informed that Citibank had been hacked and that approximately $10 million had been wired out of its cash management network during the course of several weeks.

Black was tasked to coordinate the investigation between the New York and San Francisco field offices. Money had gone out from Citibank to accounts all over the world: Israel, Belgium, Germany, Britain, etc. There was only one location where any money came back into the United States and that was in San Francisco. The money, $250,000, was wired into five accounts in the Financial District.

Working with the bank personnel, Black identified the account holders, Evygeny Korolkov and Ekaterina Korolkova, a Russian couple with green cards, apparently in S.F. for the summer. He was a retired bus driver from St. Petersburg. She was much younger. They had opened the five accounts shortly before the wire transfers arrived.

Korolkov had quite a plan. He got on a plane to St. Petersburg, and once he was safely back in Russia, he called Ekaterina and instructed her to withdraw the money and meet him back in St. Petersburg. "Brilliant plan," Black observed, "for him."

Ekaterina attempted to withdraw money from one of the accounts. She was informed that her account had been frozen. She feigned indignation and said she would return the next day to argue it with bank officials.

Meanwhile, Black had obtained an arrest warrant. "I went to her residence," he says, "a two bedroom apartment in the Marina District. I had a Russian-speaking agent as my interpreter. She had all her bags packed in the foyer. She had a one-way ticket leaving for St. Petersburg the next morning. She had several cases of toilet paper packed in her bags, which was perhaps the most incriminating evidence of the intent to flee the jurisdiction. Toilet paper is quite a commodity in Russia."

Ekaterina didn't speak any English, but Black had an excellent interpreter.

"Ekaterina was advised of her rights both in Russian and in English," Black explains. "She agreed to talk with me. We spoke with her for three hours. She was very angry at her husband for leaving her. She claimed that she didn't ask any questions, that her husband just told her to withdraw the money, and that she didn't knew what the source of the money was.

"We gave her a phone and had her call her husband in St. Petersburg," Black continues, "and over the course of a couple of days she shamed him into returning to the United States. She really chewed him out over the phone in Russian."

He flew to New York and began cooperating with the investigation. They got relatively light sentences. They were cooperating and they were seen as low-end mules.

And what happened to Evygeny and Ekaterina?

"Ekaterina had a talent we were unaware of," Black informs me. "She was an exotic dancer. She began to perform in New York. She earned a comfortable living. Evygeny stayed at home and looked after their child."

Authorities made two other arrests of ring members. Vladimir Voronin was nabbed at a bank in Rotterdam as he tried to withdraw $1 million. Alexei Lachmanov, a Georgian national carrying a fake Greek passport, was arrested trying to withdraw almost $1 million from a bank in Tel Aviv. The Voronin and Lachmanov busts underscore the probability that the Citibank caper was far more than a scheme hatched by a few St. Petersburg hackers with too much time on their hands.

Levin was sentenced to three years (remember, the time he spent in detention is counted against that) and ordered to make restitution of $240,015 to Citibank. He is currently fighting extradition. It seems the Russians want him back, and Levin doesn't want to go.

The Phonemasters Case

In October 1999, I glanced at the front page of the *Wall Street Journal*. The headline read "Audacious 'Phonemasters' Stole Numbers, Pulled Scams, Tweaked Police."

> [Calvin Cantrell and the "Phonemasters"] had gained access to telephone networks of companies including AT&T Corp., British Telecommunications Inc., GTE Corp., MCI WorldCom (then MCI Communications Corp.), Southwestern Bell, and Sprint Corp. They broke into credit-reporting databases belonging to Equifax Inc. and TRW Inc. They entered Nexis/Lexis databases and systems of Dun & Bradstreet, court records show.
>
> The breadth of their monkey-wrenching was staggering; at various times, they could eavesdrop on phone calls, compromise secure databases, and redirect communications at will. They had access to portions of the national power grid, air-traffic-control systems and had hacked their way into a digital cache of unpublished telephone numbers at the White House. ...Their customers included private investigators, so-called information brokers, and—by way of middlemen—the Sicilian Mafia. According to FBI estimates, the gang accounted for about $1.85 million in business losses.
>
> ...[They had] a price list: personal credit reports were $75; state motor-vehicle records, $25; records from the FBI's Crime Information Center, $100. On the menu for $500: the address or phone number of any "celebrity/important person."
>
> ...[Cantrell and two others] agreed to plead guilty to federal charges of one count of theft and possession of unauthorized calling-card numbers and one count of unauthorized access to computer systems.[1]

In 1995, I had done some digging around about something called Blacknet.

Supposedly, those involved in the scheme were "super information brokers" dealing in everything from trade secrets, product designs, and manufacturing methods to personal medical records, merger activity, and lascivious e-mail. If you wanted to buy or sell any information, you would just use their public key to send an encrypted message to any one of several locations in cyberspace. They would check you out and if they thought you were okay, they would contact you.

Some sources said Blacknet was a cyberpunk hoax. Other sources said it was an FBI sting.

---

1. "Phone Hex: How a Cyber Sleuth, Using a 'Data Tap,' Busted a Hacker Ring; Audacious 'Phonemasters' Stole Numbers, Pulled Scams, Tweaked Police; A Sex-Line Prank on the FBI," by John Simons, The Wall Street Journal, October 1, 1999.

The computer security "old guard" told me I shouldn't dignify the rumor by putting it in print, but I ran with it anyway. I just wanted to raise the question. The concept seemed plausible to me. Whether "Blacknet" itself existed wasn't important. What *was* important was that similar criminal activity was probably already underway.

Indeed, "Blacknet" turned out to be a hoax propagated by Tim May.[2]

Scott Charney, then head of the U.S. Department of Justice's Computer Crime and Intellectual Property (CCIP) section, wouldn't confirm or deny the existence of Blacknet itself, but did say that he saw such activity as an emerging threat.

"We're getting more and more evidence of organizations being put together to traffic in information," Charney says. "That's almost a natural progression, considering the environment we're dealing with.

"Even within the stereotypical 'hacker 'category," he continues, "the so-called hacker ethic is changing. There used to be the notion that hackers meant to do no harm. But now some hackers have said, 'Hey, I want get out of my parents' house. I need money. If there's something I can sell, I'm going to sell it.' We've seen hackers selling credit cards."

What Charney couldn't talk about at that time was a criminal investigation that had commenced down in Dallas, Texas.

In August 1994, FBI Special Agent Mike Morris got a tip from a private investigator (PI) that two hackers in Dallas, Calvin Cantrell and Brian Jaynes, were selling information to other less scrupulous PIs. Indeed, two PIs, William "Trace" Carpenter and Paul Crute, were arrested and convicted for succumbing to the enticements of Cantrell and Jaynes.

But there turned out to be much more to what came to be known as the Phonemasters case, as former U.S. Prosecutor Matt Yarbrough explains.

"It all started off as an information-selling business," he says. "They were hacking Equifax; they were hacking Southwestern Bell. They were getting into the files and selling the unlisted telephone numbers of celebrities, etc. They were not only selling to PIs, but to whoever was interested. Their price list was posted on a BBS. That was the basis for the wiretap application."

Blacknet was, indeed, a reality. The gang included Corey Lindsly (a.k.a. Tabbis, the acknowledged ringleader) in Philadelphia and John Bosanac (a.k.a. G) in San Diego, as well as Cantrell and Jaynes in Dallas.

---

2. "Introduction to BlackNet," May, Timothy C. from High Noon on the Electronic Frontier: Conceptual Issues in Cyberspace, Peter Ludlow (ed.), MIT Press, 1996, pp. 241-243.

The FBI got its wiretap approved and then set up the United States' first-ever Title III data interception on a high-speed analog telephone line on Cantrell's home phone. The FBI was doing real-time interception of both voice and data (i.e., keystroking) and was recording both conspiratorial conversations and actual hacking activity on-line.

According to Yarbrough, when FBI agents started to listen, they were "just blown away." It turned out that Cantrell and Jaynes were involved in a larger group.

"They were stealing information and selling it," he says. "They were getting into every major database. They were creating scripts to automate the downloading of 1-800 numbers, 14-digit international numbers, 7-digit domestic calling numbers, etc.

"They were breaking and entering. They broke into a Southwestern Bell office in Arkansas and stole a bunch of switching manuals. They were very aggressive dumpster divers. They did great intel on people. They went so far as to break in and steal machines. They were also phenomenal at social engineering. They were so knowledgeable from their dumpster diving that they could call in and pretend to be somebody else and get root access over the phone. They did it all.

"They even stole an STU phone and another machine from SWB [Southwestern Bell] and then began to do their own wiretaps," Yarbrough continues. "So at one point we were tapping them, and they were tapping SWB employees. We were getting a download image of what they were downloading, capturing all of the wiretap that they were doing. We were tapping a tapper."

One of the Phonemasters (not identified and not charged for this particular crime) even hacked into the FBI's National Crime Information Center (NCIC) computer. The NCIC computer houses all the criminal records for federal, state, and local law enforcement agencies.

Usually, a standalone system (i.e., one not connected to any network) is used to dial in and access the NCIC computer. But a local police chief had wanted access to the NCIC from his desktop, so it was connected up to the local area network (LAN) in the office of the police department. The problem was that a modem was connected to that LAN to service it remotely.

One of the Phonemasters worked as a technician for the service company. He would call the secretary and say, "Hey, we have to do maintenance on the LAN over the weekend, so leave it up and running." And the Phonemasters would have access to the NCIC database throughout the weekend.

How the Phonemasters Almost Blunder into Discovering the FBI's Surveillance

The Phonemasters investigation came very close to being blown at least twice.

According to Yarbrough, Cantrell and Jaynes decided to look into the file that contains all the court-ordered wiretaps for one of the phone companies. The telephone companies can't share that information because if they did, they would be guilty of obstruction of justice.

Yarbrough explains: "What Corey Lindsly did then is that he sent out a page and said, 'Hey, you've got a wiretap on your phone.' A lot of these crooks and drug dealers would say, 'Why are you calling me and telling me this?' And Corey would say, 'Oh, I work for the phone company and I'm ready to quit and I just thought I would let you know.' Well, the Drug Enforcement Agency executed a search warrant on a drug dealer and actually recovered a phone recorder with voice mail from Corey Lindsly on it telling the suspect that his phone was being tapped.

"They were going to Southwestern Bell switches," Yarbrough tells me. "They were looking up stuff on people. They never bothered to check on it for their own phones."

The FBI's surveillance of the Phonemasters was almost discovered in another way as well, Yarbrough recalls. "Quantico had come up with the magic black box for the tap, which was placed in a ditch down in the ground outside Cantrell's house," Yarbrough explains. "Rain got in there and killed the box with the taps in it. That killed the phone lines.

"Calvin called SWB and asked, 'Why is my phone down and why is my phone the only phone that is down in this area?' He had gotten a hold of some SWB engineer walking through SWB's switch facility. Mike Morris heard that call. They had to rush to get someone in SWB to intercept this SWB employee before he looked at the switch and said, 'Wow, there's something funny on your line,' which would have tipped Cantrell off that he was being tapped."

A "Dream Wiretap" Results in an Enormous Challenge

"It was a dream wiretap," Yarbrough concludes. "It was golden. We didn't have to worry about it coming through an ISP. Unlike in the Global Hell investigation, for example, in which we had to deal with the nightmare of Global Hell members who were also sysadmins sticking their exploits and downloads into innocent third-party ISP customer files."

(Years later, in 2000, when federal investigators wanted to do the wiretap on Mafia Boy in the DDoS case, they actually referred to the Phonemasters case as a model.)

Although the FBI was first tipped off in 1994, were up on the tap by December 1994, and did the takedown in February 1995, the case wasn't resolved in court until 1999.

Yarbrough explains, "We had this massive amount of data that we had to reassemble to determine what was going on. It wasn't like we were capturing IRC chat. There were a lot of UNIX commands. There were also downloads of customer files, credit card numbers, and account numbers. It was zeros and ones that translated into other numbers. That was an enormous problem. We weren't Sprint, we weren't AT&T."

This problem led the feds to another groundbreaking move.

Yarbrough says that they had to go to court for an exception to the Grand Jury secrecy rule and the wiretap rule. "[The exception said that] we could not figure out what the hell we had unless we showed it to the victims (GTE, Sprint, Southwestern Bell). We actually made them sign confidentiality agreements against each other so that they would feel comfortable. Let's all get into a room. No one has to worry about trade secrets. We're all going to sit down and go through this stuff together. That's what took so long. Getting into a forum so that they could read it in, and then once we got it figuring out how we are going to use it and having to do something special that we had never done before to accomplish that.

"The problem wasn't just the keystroke either," Yarbrough continues. "Sometimes their conference calls would last for 10 hours. Sometimes they were up to 15 or 20 people on the conference call. They would go into great deal on technical subjects. For example, how to get around SecureID, how to pull sniffers out, how to install backdoors. It was just like going to a daily lecture on hacking. Furthermore, it was all on tape. The tapes had to be transcribed. Well, transcribers didn't know what these things are or even how to spell the terms that were being used. It sounded like a foreign language to them."

Investigators had still more problems to overcome. Yes, wiretaps are the best evidence in the world, but if you have a faster way to do it, you should do it. Wiretaps are too costly and too time-consuming.

How do you present this huge, complex body of evidence? Morris and the other FBI agents involved in the case realized that there was no way they could move forward with it in a typewritten form. They decided to put into a special, searchable database with a Boolean index.

Quantifying the Financial Losses Proved Essential in Court

The work that Morris and the other FBI agents put into indexing the wiretap evidence turned out to be a brilliant move because the sentencing hearing became kind of a mini-trial, as Yarbrough recalls.

"Corey Lindsly was the ringleader. He was the smartest of them all. He knew the entire systems of these telecom companies. He worked for Bell Atlantic at one point, near where their backbone was in Pennsylvania. When you listen to the conversations, you realize he was that mastermind. He always made Calvin do the downloads. He always insulated himself. In the transcripts, Calvin often questions whether or not they should be doing it. 'Should we really take this whole database? Should we really do it?' And Corey is always insistent, 'No, that's the plan!' He would be demanding about it.

"But Corey Lindsly said, 'I will plead straight up with no plea agreement or anything. I won't agree to a single fact. You will have to prove it all.' That's why we essentially had to put our entire case on.

"We would have gotten our butts handed to us in that sentencing hearing." Yarbrough observes, "We would never have been able to prove the losses of $1.85 million, if we hadn't been able to pull a hacker in by their neck and look for specific things."

Yarbrough says all parties agreed to the loss amount except Corey Lindsly. "He wanted to say only $25,000 in losses and wanted to take us to the mat on it. His lawyer was a very difficult former prosecutor out of Philadelphia. She said he was a 'White Hat' and that he never had any intention nor did he know that this information was being sold. Lindsly's argument was, 'I'll plead to a felony for unauthorized access under Title 18 Section 1030, but you can only go after Cantrell for $1.85 million. He is the one that transferred the information across the bulletin board and made a profit on it. I didn't actually put any of that money in my pocket. I didn't transfer the information, so you can't do that to me.' Well, the sentencing guidelines say that when it is a conspiracy and when it was reasonably foreseeable that he knew that his coconspirators were doing that then you can hold him responsible also. With that database, we were able to pull out conversation after conversation to prove that Corey was always aware that Cantrell was selling information.

"My bottom line argument to the judge," Yarbrough explains, "was that without Corey Lindsly these guys never would have done this or done it so extensively. Nor did Cantrell have the skill set to do or download the information but for his association with Lindsly. Lindsly opened the barn door. Every time Cantrell or Bosanac tried to close it, Lindsly would open it wider."

"Corey goes to Denver," Yarbrough tells me. "He calls Calvin, and says, 'Can you send me some TOBES (the gang's slang for credit card numbers)?' Why should I send you some? Go in there and get them yourself. No, no, I am here in Denver. I don't have it in my stuff."

Cantrell sent 860 TOBES.

"We captured that," Yarbrough says. "We saw that being sent. We used just that download and one other. We took just those numbers. We sent them to Sprint. They ran it against their fraud database; there is $1.5 million in reported fraud. That's not counting the people who never knew that Lindsly charged them $10 for a phone call. That's why you download so many, so that you can rotate them (with so many you can go a long time before you have to try the same one again). Of that $1.5 million reported in that database, $950,000 related to the card numbers they had downloaded."

Yarbrough tells me that they tallied $40,000 in direct damages to Southwestern Bell, plus $600,000 because they had to go to a smart card system for stronger authentication. "Charney told me no one had ever gotten credit for smart cards before. But I told my attorney to go for it, and the judge bought it. I don't think it would normally work. We argued that they weren't going out to get the latest, greatest alarm system or something, but that they had to go to smart cards to return to the system's original point of integrity on the day that the Phonemasters broke in.... [T]he sniffers and backdoors were so pervasive that SWB couldn't find them all. What the judge bought on I think is that I argued, 'Look, this isn't IBM or some other company doing this for its own executives and employees. This is a public service provider with legal duty to ensure the integrity of its system.'"

GTE losses were all straight calling card fraud.

Transcript of an FBI Wiretap on the Phonemasters[2]

Calvin Cantrell: No, no, no, hold on.

Corey Lindsly: I'm there now.

John Bosanac: No, don't, don't, don't, don't.

CC: Get out!

CL: Two more, two more, two more numbers. What are you doing?

CC: I'm looking up (800) numbers.

2. Source: Matt Yarbrough, NetSec 2000 General Session Presentation

[Unintelligible]

CL: What are you doing, pulling tones so you can trade them for Nintendo games?

CC: I wouldn't pull any of those, because I'm gonna write a program tomorrow or the next day.

CL: Man, I'm, I'm just laughing, here we go.

CC: [Unintelligible] kind of natural, like, publication.

CL: No, it's a terminal electronic.

CC: Are you off there now?

CL: Okay.

CC: All right, wait, wait, termination, confirmation, I'm off. But if you're not registered like track is, is it?

CL: Not to my knowledge, but I would have to check to be certain.

CC: You know, while we're at it, we, you, you ought, we ought to just do it for the whole fucking…

M: Hello?

CC: We ought just do every switch.

[Unintelligible]

CC: Why the hell not?

CL: That is the plan, that is what we are gonna do.

CC: It won't take it, what…

CL: That's a…

JB: I think he's running a 7D puller and a 14D puller.

CL: Oh, really?

JB: Uh-hmm.

CC: A 14D puller is gonna, is gonna [unintelligible] gonna go ahead and do it.

CL: Zero, zero, zero.

JB: I told you how to do it.

CL: For x = 000.

JB: Well, the problem is [unintelligible] pulled my account number.

[unintelligible]

JB: The account number still occurs sequentially. I mean, there's like big gaps.

[unintelligible]

CC: Actually, account numbers do...

CL: Any kind of accounting on the inquiries?

JB: Right.

CC: There obviously isn't.

CL: Yeah, at this point, I think it's, it's obvious that there isn't. Because I mean, the way we, yeah, I, at this point [unintelligible] the way we've been pulling things [unintelligible]

[unintelligible]

CC: Fucking butt FM (another hacker) called me tonight, and he was fucking inquiring about it, asking [unintelligible]

CL: That's not good.

CC: Yeah, I think, I think that's why he's talking to Nokes (another hacker), because Nokes is very interesting.

[unintelligible]

CC: Yeah, extremely.

CL: Well, let's not give it to Nokes yet.

CC: Well, we aren't gonna give it to Nokes.

JB: Oh, guess who's been working with Nokes?

[unintelligible]

JB: No, no, no, I was telling, I was telling...

CC: I know. I know.

JB: I was telling Fat Boy (Cantrell).

[unintelligible]

CL: No, who's been working with Nokes?

[unintelligible]

CL: Nothing's happened yet.

CC: Nothing's happened yet.

JB: It wouldn't be anything that I got off Nokes just patch.

CL: It is.

JB: Yeah. And that's all I have on it.

CL: I don't know if he put the limp thing in there or not.

JB: He put it somewhere big. And it's holding water, so...

CL: Well, we got to take that thing completely.

JB: Yeah.

CL: Because we got to be in there by the time they cut over secure ID.

JB: Yep.

CC: Yeah. I mean, everything, you gotta have like finger shit in there and stuff. So like you [unintelligible]

CL: Trust me, we know what we're doing.

JB: How's that gonna bypass security?

[unintelligible]

JB: Come on, are you really kidding me when you say that?

CL: If you have the machine, you can easily bypass it. Yeah, if the machine is already patched, it's not gonna be a problem to bypass security that you put on top of the patches.

CC: Well, okay, I didn't, I didn't know.

JB: Actually, I don't read on that.

CL: What has to be done if it can't be relied on the log in patch, though, because you have to assume they're gonna upgrade log in when they go to security.

CC: Right.

JB: Right.

CL: Exactly. That's why you're gonna have [unintelligible]

[unintelligible] sticking wood patches in there, either, because [unintelligible]

JB: You're gonna have to have, basically have something on a high numbered port.

CL: Yeah, yeah, I mean, that's not gonna be a problem.

JB: Okay.

CL: Trust me, they'll have more modifying areas to fucking...

CC: So what, so you already have access, you already have a Bell Atlantic code or something?

CL: Yeah. One on the Internet, and we don't know if that's next to anything. We don't know anything about it.

CC: And that came from Nokes.

JB: Is Nokes like, uh, cautious?

CL: Is he what?

JB: Cautious?

CL: Yeah, yeah. He's certainly not any less cautious than you are.

JB: Fuck you! I don't talk to FM.

CC: Well, no...

CL: Yeah, okay. Applehead and FM call you on your parents' line and you fucking talk to them.

CC: They fucking call me up, what am I supposed to say, uh, Bye?

CL: I don't do that shit anymore. Leave me again.

CC: Well, I didn't say I'm gonna do anything.

JB: I'm in a vise now.

CL: Whatever, it doesn't fucking matter. We're all gonna get busted anyway. I mean, I, I can just see if they, if they figure out who all is going, and I'm...

[unintelligible]

CL: It would be ugly.

JB: Yeah.

CL: Certainly. Just remember, nobody fucking rats anybody else. No deals.

> JB: Good company, [unintelligible]
>
> CL: Yeah.
>
> CC: Well, I'll them
>
> JB: Yeah, no deals is right.
>
> CL: No deals. I'm serious. I don't care what your fucking lawyers tell you: "Oooie, you're gonna have to make a deal, you're facing serious time." Fuck that.

Well, "Fat Boy" did talk. Corey Lindsly did not. He had no comment to the court; he did not apologize for anything that he had done. Consequently, he got a sentence of over 41 months, which is one of the longest sentences for a hacker in U.S. history.

Cantrell got 24 months. Bosanac got 18 months.

"The Number You Have Reached Has Been Disconnected..."

The Phonemasters case took years to lay to rest.

It was a multiple-district case involving Texas, Pennsylvania, Ohio, Colorado, California, Oregon, New York, Florida, Canada, Switzerland, and Italy.

It required the execution of 11 simultaneous search warrants in 1995 as well as 11 independent plea negotiations wrapped up by 1999.

It was, indeed, an international investigation.

For example, Calvin Cantrell in Dallas passed stolen credit card information to Rudy Lombardi (a.k.a. "Bro") in Canada. Lombardi then sent it back into the United States to Thomas Gurtler in Ohio. Gurtler then sent it on to Samir Gherbi in Switzerland. Gherbi then passed it on to organized crime in Italy.

But as Mike Morris, the FBI Special Agent who worked the case with Stu Robinson, Matt Yarbrough, and the others, observes, perhaps the most significant issue in the Phonemasters case really has nothing at all to do with electronic commerce.

"Frankly, the reason so much time and energy were spent on the Phonemasters was that they were inside phone companies and they had 'root.' In some of the phone companies they had hacked, they just 'owned' switches. But in others, they actually 'owned' every system that the phone company had. If someone owns the phone switch outside your place of business, they can listen to your phone calls, reroute your phone calls, or make sure you don't get any phone calls at all. If you own a telecommunications system, you can just knock out so much. That was the greatest concern. Some of the phone switches they owned were outside of missile bases."

Hacktivists and Cybervandals

Perhaps the most romantic image of the hacker is one borrowed from the Old Testament: the young David slaying the huge tyrant Goliath with his slingshot. Indeed, many see "hacktivism"— for example, the defacement of a corporation's Web site because of its environmental abuses or a government Web site because of human rights violation—as a noble calling.

On December 10, 1999, Dr. Dorothy Denning of Georgetown University (a true cyberhero like Parker, Christy, Rhodes, and some of the others mentioned in this book), gave an important address to the World Affairs Council on "Activism, Hacktivism and Cyberterrorism."

Denning broke the phenomena down into three broad classes of activity: activism, hacktivism, and cyberterrorism.

Activism is the normal, non-disruptive use of the Internet in support of an agenda or cause. Operations in this area include browsing the Web for information; constructing Web sites and posting materials on them; transmitting electronic publications and letters through e-mail; and using the Net to discuss issues, form coalitions, and plan and coordinate activities.

Hacktivism is the marriage of hacking and activism. It covers operations that use hacking techniques against a target Internet site with the intent of disrupting normal operations but not causing serious damage. Examples are Web sit-ins and virtual blockades, automated e-mail bombs, Web hacks, computer break-ins, and computer viruses and worms.

CHAPTER 8

Cyberterrorism is the convergence of cyberspace and terrorism. It covers politically motivated hacking operations intended to cause grave harm such as loss of life or severe economic damage. An example would be penetrating an air traffic control system and causing two planes to collide.

Denning elaborated on the nuances:

> There is a general progression toward greater damage and disruption from the first to the third category, although that does not imply an increase of political effectiveness. An electronic petition with a million signatures may influence policy more than an attack that disrupts emergency 911 services. Although the three categories of activity are treated separately, the boundaries between them are somewhat fuzzy. For example, an e-mail bomb may be considered hacktivism by some and cyberterrorism by others. Also, any given actor may conduct operations across the spectrum. For example, a terrorist might launch viruses as part of a larger campaign of cyberterrorism, all the while using the Internet to collect information about targets, coordinate action with fellow conspirators, and publish propaganda on Web sites.[1]

Well, the relative merits of hacktivism are debatable. In many cases, right or wrong might not correspond to legal or illegal. For example, lying down on the highway to obstruct the flow of rush hour traffic as an act of civil disobedience in protest against acts of genocide is quite different than lying down on the highway to obstruct rush-hour traffic for some petty, personal grievance. The difference is the difference between a hacktivist and a cybervandal.

The following two tales involve acts of cybervandalism rather than "hacktivism."

Hackers Run Amok in "Cesspool of Greed"

On Thanksgiving Day weekend in 1994, hackers broke into systems at GE, IBM, NBC, Sprint, and Pipeline (an ISP). The hackers gained root access and launched a program that fired off an e-mail message every few seconds. The message contained the following manifesto:

```
GREETINGS FROM THE INTERNET LIBERATION FRONT

Once upon a time, there was a wide area network called
the Internet.

A network unscathed by capitalistic Fortune 500 companies
and the like.

Then someone decided to do-regulate the Internet and hand
it over to the "big boys in the telecommunications indus-
try. "Big boys" like SprintNet, MCI, AT&T, and the like.
Now we all know how this story ends - Capitalist Pig
```

---

1. *Computer Security Journal*, Vol. XVI, Number 3, Summer 2000.

```
Corporation takes control of a good thing, and in the
ever-so-important-money-making-general-scheme-of-things,
the good thing turns into another overflowing cesspool of
greed.

So, we got pissed.

The ILF is a small, underground organization of computer
security experts. We are capable of penetrating virtually
any network linked to the Internet - ANY network.

so read this VERY carefully.

The ILF has now declared war on any company suspected of
contributing to the f inal demise of the Internet'. If
you f it into any of the above mentioned categories of
disgust, FEAR US.

Better-yet, take an axe to your petty fucking firewall
machine before WE do.

Just a friendly warning Corporate America; we have
already stolen your proprietary source code. We have
already pillaged your million dollar research data. And
if you would like to avoid financial ruin, then heed our
warning and get the fuck out of dodge.

Happy Thanksgiving Day Turkeys, — ILF

(pipeline, sprint, ibm, .and at&t have felt our wrath,
more to come)

PS: If you would like to drop us a line, post a plaintext
message encrypted with the enclosed PGP public key to one
of the following newagroups: Alt.security or any security
sub.

The Pretty Good Privacy encryption package is available
via anon ftp soda.borkelay.edu.....
```

In a related incident, Josh Quittner, a journalist who wrote a tome on the exploits of the infamous Legion of Doom (LOD) and Masters of Deception (MOD) discovered that his Internet mailbox was jammed with unwanted e-mail and that his telephone had been reprogrammed to reach a recorded greeting that spewed obscenities.

The *Wall Street Journal*, *Time*, and *Information Week* all gave prominent coverage to the attack, but the articles revealed very little. No one was talking much, as usual. Many questions were left unanswered.

For example, what was the Internet Liberation Front (ILF)?

I called Jeff Moss (a.k.a. Dark Tangent), the young entrepreneur behind the annual DEFCON convention of hackers and phreakers held in Las Vegas, for his perspective.

"The ILF is going to be a nightmare," he tells me. "It's not MOD; it's some ex-members of MOD. It's some people who were doing some stuff before, and now they've created this smoke screen, and it is really convenient to hide behind. Now anyone that does anything bad will just claim they're ILF, and it will just confuse the issue as to who is really doing what. It's just a diversion."

Moss said published accounts on the Thanksgiving weekend hacks didn't tell the whole story. He asserted a major telecommunications company (he wouldn't say which one) had been seriously compromised.

"They have a history of very poor security," Moss says. "Someone is always breaking into them and doing something. This time they just got taken to the cleaners. Every router password was changed and then all the routers were crashed, so they couldn't reboot.

"They had to go in to manually power down and power up each router," he continues. "All the hubs were being sniffed. There was an incredible amount of compromise. They could not monitor customer activity; they had no idea what was going on with the network. It got to the point where they had no control over anything. They've had problems in the past, but this was the biggest and baddest."

Well, the ILF didn't turn out to be a nightmare. (Except perhaps for Southwestern Bell and a young man named Christopher Schanot.) The commercialization of the Internet went on unabated.

In the Spring 1995 issue of *Gray Areas*,[2] Netta Gilboa, *Gray Areas'* publisher and a fascinating woman in her own right, conducted an interview with anonymous member of the ILF. Here are excerpts from her interview:

Gilboa: Why was Thanksgiving picked?

ILF: It was picked for [its] historical significance.

Gilboa: Do you plan to strike only on holidays?

ILF: We plan to strike only when we feel it necessary, holidays are picked because admins are away so our fun lasts longer.

Gilboa: Why was [Quittner] picked?

ILF: Quittner had nothing to do with the Net fun, he is the epitome of inaccurate journalism and overall stupidity, anything that happens to him in the future he deserves....

---

2. "Getting Gray With The Internet Liberation Front," By Netta Gilboa *Gray Areas* (Vol. 4, No. 1), Spring 1995

Gilboa: You mentioned power as your motive for this. Please expand on this. Do you lack power in real life and so you compensate for it by attacking on the Net? How much fun is the power to wield when you can get caught by revealing you were the one who did it?

ILF: I suppose I have as much power as anyone else in real life, I could just go out and kill someone instead of hacking their system or turning off their phone, but that does seem to lack finesse.

Gilboa: People are saying mail bombs are lame and these were easy hacks. Please comment as to how easy the places you chose were to enter. Also, do you plan to attempt anything super difficult to prove your skill to them?

ILF: I don't need to prove my skill to anyone. They don't talk shit when I am around because they are too scared. As for the difficulty of the hacks...none of those idiots could get it.

Gilboa: Any regrets about ILF so far?

ILF: I am not the regretting type, what was done was done, no turning back.

Gilboa: Did everyone you initially asked to join ILF agree? Do you plan to add members? As your media attention grows, some hackers are going to want to be linked to you for their fifteen minutes of fame.

ILF: Nobody was "asked" to be in ILF. It was just for Thanksgiving, and I suppose for any other time when we decide it's necessary.

Gilboa: What haven't you been able to hack?

ILF: Nothing.

Gilboa: Of all the places you've "owned," what has interested you the most and why?

ILF: Many places I have been in were, and are very interesting, but this is not the place to discuss them.

Gilboa: There have been many hacks and hoaxes this holiday season. Did ILF do any of these?

ILF: No, we did nothing to Primenet. It was just some lame ass kids trying to annoy us. All I [am] willing to admit to is what was done on Thanksgiving, which was of course just a joke, and also a small way of getting a point across that nobody is safe from us.

The statement of purpose for *Gray Areas*, Gilboa's magazine, says that it "exists to explore the gray areas of life," particularly the "illegal, immoral, and controversial."

Other features that ran in the Spring 1995 issue included an article on a male "adult film star" and a "Jethro Tull bootleg video list."

Gilboa's exploration of life's "gray areas" would lead her to play a larger role in the ensuing saga.

Schanot Goes Underground

Shortly after the *Gray Areas* article appeared, a teenager named Christopher Schanot fled his St. Louis home by train, with a ticket left for him by Netta Gilboa at the St. Louis train station.

Schanot did not notify his parents of his plans to depart. Schanot's father, fearful for his son's safety, first notified local authorities and then the FBI.

Within three weeks of Schanot's departure, his father turned over to the FBI his son's personal computer (which was missing a hard drive) and several pages of notes in the young Schanot's handwriting.

Trish McGarry, the U.S. DoJ prosecutor in St. Louis who worked the case, recalls, "His father wanted our help in locating him. He contacted the FBI. He said, 'I think my son has been abducted or lured away.' He said that one day he dropped his son off at school to work on the yearbook, and his son never came home. At the same time, Southwestern Bell had contacted the FBI about intrusions it had detected and traced to a phone line in Schanot's home. So we started working it. The father brought the PC to the Grand Jury and said, 'Here you can have it.' He thought the boy was in trouble. He was concerned that the boy had engaged in some intrusion activities. He believed that some people had him in their clutches and were making him do some of these illegal things."

The FBI retrieved files from another hard drive in Schanot's computer, which included a typewritten message headed "Greetings from the Internet Liberation Front" saved to his computer on November 24, 1994, the day of the ILF Thanksgiving break-in and mailbombing (the text of the message corresponds to the ILF message Gilboa published in her magazine) and a typewritten list of questions and answers that correspond to the Gilboa's ILF interview. (This list was saved to Schanot's computer on January 22, 1995, at least three months before the issue of *Gray Areas* containing the interview was released.) The papers Schanot's father turned over also contained a list of numbered answers that correspond with the answers to Gilboa's ILF interview.

According to Schanot's father, those answers were in his son's handwriting.

Based on the evidence uncovered, the DoJ believed that Schanot was responsible for the Thanksgiving 1994 break-ins and mailbombings. But no charges were ever filed in that investigation.

Forensic analysis of Schanot's computer disclosed that Schanot had been keystroke-logging all his hacking activities. According to McGarry, these "fabulous logs" contained evidence that Schanot had hacked Bellcore (a research-and-development company for Bell companies throughout the United States and a federal contractor) and SRI International (a research-and-development contractor that does information security consulting and has top-secret contracts with the U.S. government).

Bellcore and SRI were subsequently contacted.

Schanot's computer also contained a file of hundreds of passwords to various multinational corporations, universities, governmental organizations, military contractors, and credit reporting agencies as well as a file of hundreds of credit card numbers and AT&T calling card numbers.

David Ippolito, the friend who drove Schanot to the train station, told FBI Special Agent Scott Skinner that Schanot admitted having recently hacked into several large companies and governmental organizations and was fearful of arrest. Schanot told Ippolito that he was going to Philadelphia to "lay low." Ippolito also saw a computer hard drive in Schanot's possession on the day he drove his friend to the train station.

In June 1995, Schanot's father had a telephone conversation with Netta Gilboa that was consensually monitored and tape-recorded. In the conversation, Gilboa said that she did not know where Schanot was, that she thought Schanot had gone to a place where he did not want to be found, that she had sent copies of her magazine to Schanot's friend's house because Schanot originally did not want her to know where he was or even who he was, that Schanot was planning to take off long before he knew her, that Schanot could get into any computer system that he wanted to, and that if Schanot were caught, it would be on the front page of every newspaper.

Schanot's Indictment and Capture

In Fall 1995, Schanot turned 18. Shortly thereafter, he went back into one of the Southwestern Bell systems to retrieve the password file that had been produced by the sniffer.

McGarry explains the significance of Schanot's blunder. "That action triggered my ability to charge him. Most of what he had done was done before he turned 18. If he had not gone back in to get that file, I would not have been able to charge him as an adult."

Schanot was indicted by a federal grand jury in Missouri on charges of hacking into systems at Southwestern Bell, Bellcore, SRI International, and Sprint.

He was charged with invading those companies' computer systems, installing sophisticated computer codes in those systems that allowed him access to all the information on the systems, and installing other computer codes that allowed him to gather user IDs and passwords to other computer systems through the "hacked" companies.

In March 1996, in an effort to locate Schanot, Agent Skinner ran a check in the Transnational database using Schanot's Social Security number. The database links Social Security number usage to addresses listed by the person reporting the Social Security number. It indicated that Schanot had used his Social Security number in February 1996 and reported his address as 291 Hastings in Broomall, Pennsylvania. FBI Special Agent John Treadwell checked the address reported and found that it did not exist. The FBI staked out the post office box and arrested Schanot when he showed up with Gilboa to pick up the mail.

As a result of Schanot's conduct, security of these computers had been completely compromised, resulting in Schanot's access to confidential data and the discontinuation of service. Southwestern Bell, for one, reported that Schanot's actions have cost the company more than $500,000 in damages and repairs.

How Schanot Rang Southwestern's Bell

Sometime during the summer of 1994, James G. McBride, the son of William S. McBride, a SWB employee, provided Schanot with the user ID and password for a Southwestern Bell computer system known as rappal.sbc.com. Rappal is a computer system located in St. Louis, Missouri, which Southwestern Bell uses in interstate commerce and communications. The elder McBride had let his son use his user ID and password to access the rappal system for e-mail and Internet purposes.

Of course, Southwestern Bell had not authorized McBride's son to access the rappal system or to share his father's user ID and password with any other individual. And of course, Southwestern Bell had not authorized the younger McBride to provide his user ID and password to his son or anyone else. (Such breakdowns in security awareness happen in corporate cultures where security—and employee responsibility for it—is not taken seriously enough.)

After receiving the rappal user ID and password from McBride, Schanot accessed rappal and through rappal eventually located a Southwestern Bell Telephone Sun machine on which he installed an Ethernet sniffer program to gather additional user IDs and passwords.

The sniffer program was installed on the Ethernet, which is the protocol used to allow a user to log in from one machine to another machine or to download or transfer data from one computer to another. From its placement on the Ethernet, the sniffer program gathered and stored the following login information: the name or address of the machine where a transaction was originating, the machine where the user was directing a transmission, the login ID and the password, and the 4,096 keystroke characters following the login ID and password.

The information gathered from the sniffer program (the output) was recorded in a log file that Schanot could access. The information contained in the log file gave Schanot the addresses and names of other Southwestern Bell Telephone computer systems as well as valid user IDs and passwords that allowed him to access those computer systems.

Schanot installed the sniffer program on at least one Southwestern Bell Sun computer prior to October 23, 1994. The records of Southwestern Bell Telephone reveal that during October 1994 Schanot's sniffer was residing on the Sun computer known as elros.sbc.com.

The elros system was used in interstate commerce and communications to run a Southwestern Bell Telephone application and software known as Customer Network Access (CNA).

On October 23, 1994, Schanot transferred the elros.sbc.com sniffer program to another Southwestern Bell computer system used in interstate commerce and communications and known as bigbird.sbc.com, a Unix computer system that ran an application for access to engineering records for special circuits. By use of commands transmitted to the bigbird system, Schanot installed his own source code to gain root authority on bigbird.sbc.com and to install the sniffer program on bigbird.

This source code intentionally installed by Schanot increased the root users to include him, damaged the integrity and security of the bigbird computer system, and allowed Schanot to gain unauthorized complete control of the computer. Schanot intended to damage the security firewall of the bigbird.sbc.com system by installing the program to allow him root access.

On November 28, 1994, Schanot entered the bigbird.sbc.com computer by use of the deslogin program he had installed. This access to bigbird was without the authorization of Southwestern Bell Telephone. When he entered bigbird on November 28,

Schanot activated the sniffer program. The sniffer ran until December 7, 1994, when Schanot deactivated it. At the time it was deactivated, the bigbird sniffer log file contained approximately 1,700 different login IDs and passwords that the sniffer program had captured.

During March 1995, Schanot began to access two computers in Morristown, New Jersey, owned by Bellcore and known as bell.bellcore.com and irisdn.bellcore.com. Bellcore uses both these computer systems in either interstate commerce or communications. Bellcore is owned by the seven regional phone companies and provides interstate investigative and research support to these seven companies. Between March 11, 1995 and April 2, 1995, Schanot, while working from his home in the St. Louis area, entered the irisdn.bellcore.com system in Morristown, New Jersey.

Schanot installed a hidden source code (deslogin) that allowed him to bypass the irisdn firewall and gain access to the irisdn computer system. Bellcore did not authorize Schanot to place the deslogin source code into its irisdn system. Schanot intended to damage and alter the operations of the irisdn computer by installing this source code. The deslogin program installed by Schanot allowed him to gain root access to irisdn.bellcore.com. Once having root access, Schanot had complete control over the computer system and was able to remove, view, and alter files.

Schanot did not have authorization from either Southwestern Bell Telephone or Bellcore to install deslogin source code into the various computer systems mentioned earlier. Nor was he authorized by Southwestern Bell Telephone or Bellcore to install sniffer programs to capture the electronic or wire data being transmitted over the computer lines.

Southwestern Bell claimed in court that the cost for the investigation, clean up, and recovery of its computer systems was $46,766. Bellcore claimed that the cost for the investigation, clean up, and recovery of its two computer systems was $40,000.

Attack of the Zombies

The Distributed Denial of Service (DDoS) attack that rocked Yahoo!, eBay, Amazon.com, and other icons of the Internet in February 2000 was an extraordinary and historic event.

We can learn many lessons from the tale.

Once Upon A Time, An Eerie Calm Descended on Cyberspace...

The Y2K rollover had been very tense. Many good men and women had spent Christmas and New Year's in fortified command centers, instead of at home with their loved ones. But the hundreds of billions of dollars spent on the Millennium Bug weren't wasted.

Of course, some high-profile glitches occurred. A U.S. spy satellite failed over the Middle East. A computer that tracks nuclear weapons materials went down at the Oak Ridge National Laboratory. Several Japanese nuclear power plants had Y2K-related problems. The thermostats failed in a South Korean housing complex. Some British retailers couldn't process credit card purchases for a couple of days.

But the digital world did not come to an end. Those who had been in a high state of readiness began to stand down. After a while, everything went back to normal.

My colleague Rik Farrow and I had kept in close touch for several weeks. We had been waiting for the other shoe to drop. We hadn't been expecting anything catastrophic in regard to the Y2K rollover itself. We had been expecting something very different.

Rik and I had been discussing the possibility of a large-scale Distributed Denial of Service (DDoS) attack. There had been intimations, rumblings from the underground. We had even endeavored to get people ready.

On February 1, 2000, CSI members received the February issue of the *Computer Security Alert*, my monthly newsletter, via snail mail. The front page headline read, "Stop Living in Denial about Denial of Service Attacks." Yes, something was in the wind.

We had seen warnings from credible sources.

On November 18, 1999, Carnegie Mellon's Computer Emergency Response Team (CERT) issued *CERT Incident Note IN-99-07* alerting anyone who was paying attention that two DDoS tools, Trinoo and Tribe Flood Network (TFN), had been installed on unwilling, unwitting hosts by intruders exploiting known vulnerabilities to gain access.

On December 30, 1999, the FBI's National Infrastructure Protection Center (NIPC) posted a similar warning on its Web site (www.nipc.gov). It also offered a free software application (developed by NIPC) that system administrators could use to scan for evidence of Trinoo and TFN. NIPC urged anyone who was paying attention to download the software, run it on their systems, and report any evidence of DDoS preparations to their local FBI office or to NIPC itself.

Some of the United State's largest financial institutions received detailed warnings of impending threats through something called the Financial Services Information Sharing and Analysis Center run by Global Integrity Corporation. According to the Associated Press, the urgent alerts, by e-mail and pager, began fully four days before Yahoo! fell under electronic assault. The Center cautioned that dangerous attack software had been discovered implanted on powerful computers nationwide. The messages ultimately identified specific Internet addresses of attacking machines. Participating banks weren't allowed to share the warnings with government investigators under the rules of an unusual $1.5 million private security network created in recent months for the financial industry.

A week or so after the February issue of the *Computer Security Alert* hit the inboxes of corporate America, the other shoe finally dropped.

Blow by Blow

On Monday February 7, Yahoo! took the first hit.

Yahoo! is one of the best performing sites on the Internet. It is normally accessible 99.3 percent of the time, according to Keynote Systems, an Internet performance analysis service. But during the DDoS onslaught, the Yahoo! portal was rendered inaccessible for three hours. Availability during that span of time ranged from zero to 10 percent.

The *New York Times on the Web* offered perspective:

> In December Yahoo! said it was serving up to 465 million Web pages each day, meaning it may have lost as many as 100 million page views during the failure, said Jordan E. Rohan of the Wit Capital Group in New York. He said the cost to Yahoo! in lost advertising and e-commerce revenue would possibly reach the range of $500,000.[3]

On Tuesday February 8, Buy.com, eBay, CNN, and Amazon.com took hits. Although Buy.com never closed down, it hit a low of 9.4 percent availability. The company had issued its initial public offering (IPO) that morning. eBay was almost entirely incapacitated for hours.

Less than 5 percent of CNN's normal flow of users could reach its site between the hours of 4:45 and 5:30 p.m. Amazon.com was besieged from 5 p.m. to 5:30 p.m. During the attack, accessing Amazon's home page took up to five minutes.

On Wednesday February 9, ZDNet.com was unreachable between the hours of 4:15 and 6:15 a.m. E*Trade activity slowed to a crawl between 5:00 a.m. and 7:00 a.m.

---

3. "Yahoo Attributes a Lengthy Service Failure to an Attack," by Matt Richtel, *The New York Times*, February 8, 2000.

One E*Trade customer who was "on hold" for half an hour while the stock he wanted to sell dropped six points told the *Washington Post* that he would "never place an order online again."

On Wednesday evening, Excite was hit. Its home page was slowed for two hours between 7:15 p.m. and 9:15 p.m. approximately. Excite's availability slipped to 42.9 percent.

It seemed as if someone was just running a finger down the NASDAQ ticker, launching attacks on icon after icon of the Internet economy.

An unprecedented media frenzy ensued. Numerous news organizations, including *NBC Nightly News*, CNN, ZDTV, National Public Radio, the *Los Angeles Times*, *USA Today*, and the *New York Daily News*, sought me out during the three days of the attack as well as in the aftermath. "What's going on? What is a DDoS? Who is doing it and why?"

Here are some answers to those questions.

How DDoS Works

Denial of service tools have been around in some form or another for quite awhile.

The goal of a denial of service attack is to render the target system inoperable. Some denial of service attacks are designed to crash the targeted system; others are designed simply to make the targeted system so busy that it can't handle its normal workload.

In a distributed denial of service, one attacker can control tens or even hundreds of servers and aim the cumulative firepower of all these systems against a single target. Instead of launching an attack from a single system, the attacker breaks into numerous sites, installs the denial of service attack script on each one, and then orchestrates a coordinated attack to magnify the intensity of the onslaught.

Who Launched the Attacks and Why

Everyone wanted to know, "Who's doing this and why?"

Well, it could have been "hacktivists" angered by the commercialization of the Internet's pristine wilderness and wanting to strike a blow against the Empire.

It could have been a nasty little experiment in dot-com stock manipulation. For example, someone might have said, "If we create a massive disruption on the Net, maybe the price for stock shares in this Internet security start-up will really take off."

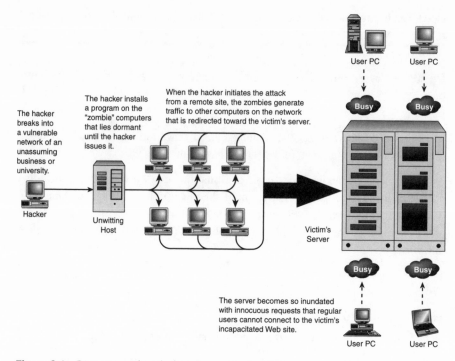

The hacker breaks into a vulnerable network of an unassuming business or university.

Hacker

The hacker installs a program on the "zombie" computers that lies dormant until the hacker issues it.

Unwitting Host

When the hacker initiates the attack from a remote site, the zombies generate traffic to other computers on the network that is redirected toward the victim's server.

Victim's Server

User PC   User PC

Busy   Busy

The server becomes so inundated with innocuous requests that regular users cannot connect to the victim's incapacitated Web site.

Busy   Busy

User PC   User PC

Figure 8.1   Dissecting a denial of service attack.

It could have been related to some as-yet-unreported extortion attempt. For example, someone might have said, "Look, what happened to Yahoo! and the others was just a demo. If you don't wire $500,000 into this Cayman Islands bank account, we're going to bring your e-commerce site to its knees." (Think this scenario is implausible? Remember that numerous sites are doing hundreds of thousands of dollars an hour in on-line sales.)

It could have been simply an act of vandalism—albeit a rather extravagant one.

It could have been precocious "script kiddies" who were just carried away with the power the DDoS tools put at their fingertips.

Whatever the motivation, the fallout was pretty bad. Even the hacker establishment wanted to distance itself from the attacks. On February 9, *2600: The Hacker Quarterly* (www.2600.com) posted a fascinating disclaimer:

> We feel sorry for the major Internet commerce sites that have been inconve-
> nienced by the Denial of Service attacks. Really, we do. But we cannot permit
> them or anyone else to lay the blame on hackers. So far, the corporate media
> has done a very bad job covering this story, blaming hackers and in the next
> sentence admitting they have no idea who's behind it. Since the ability to run

a program (which is all this is) does not require any hacking skills, claiming that hackers are behind it indicates some sort of knowledge of the motives and people involved. This could be the work of someone who lost their life savings to electronic commerce. Or maybe it's the work of communists. It could even be corporate America itself! After all, who would be better served by a further denigration of the hacker image with more restrictions on individual liberties?[4]

Aftermath

On Thursday, February 10, U.S. Attorney General Janet Reno announced an FBI investigation. "We are committed in every possible way," Reno declared, "to tracking down those responsible."

On Friday, February 11, the *San Francisco Examiner* reported that the attack on CNN's Web site had been tracked to the University of California, Santa Barbara (UCSB).

On the same day, Reuters reported that NetCologne, a German ISP, had traced an attack back to a German university, which in turn took one of its servers off-line after it had been found to be running TFN "zombie" code.

On Saturday, February 12, Stanford and the University of California, Los Angeles (UCLA) were added to the list of launching pads (at least for the assault on CNN).

On Sunday, February 13, someone identifying himself as Coolio vandalized a Web site belonging to RSA Data Security. Numerous Internet postings attributed to Coolio led some investigators to believe the 17-year-old New Hampshire resident to be a suspect in the DDoS attacks on Yahoo!, eBay, etc. The FBI questioned him.

But apparently there are no forthcoming charges involving this particular Coolio, at least related to the DDoS attack. Coolio is allegedly responsible for several unrelated crimes, including vandalizing Web sites for the Drug Abuse Resistance Education (DARE) program, a Chemical Weapons Convention site maintained by the U. S. Commerce Department, and the RSA site.

On March 9, Dennis Moran, a.k.a. Coolio, a 17-year-old hacker questioned by the FBI about the DDoS attacks, was charged with vandalizing the DARE Web site. He was charged with two counts of unauthorized access to a computer system. Each charge is punishable by up to 15 years in prison. Moran allegedly hacked into the Los Angeles Police Department Web site DARE.com twice in November and defaced it with two pro-drug slogans and images, including one depicting Donald Duck with a hypodermic syringe in his arm.

Several other Coolios are under investigation.

---

4. "Hackers to Blame? Doubtful." *2600: The Hacker Quarterly*, February 9, 2000.

On February 15, U.S. President Bill Clinton held a White House summit on the implications of the attack. Invited attendees included Rich Pethia of CERT; Vinton Cerf of MCI Worldcom; Stephen Kent of BBN Technologies (GTE); Mudge from @stake (of L0pht fame); representatives from Yahoo!, eBay, Excite, and E*Trade; and yes, Eugene Spafford of CERIAS. Several of CERIAS's sponsors also participated in the meeting (e.g., AT&T, Veridian/Trident, Microsoft, Sun, HP, Intel, and Cisco).

Government participants included President Clinton himself, as well as Attorney General Reno, Secretary of Commerce William Daley, and Richard Clarke of the National Security Council.

Spafford posted an eyewitness report to his friends.

> I came away from the meeting with the feeling that a small, positive step had been made. Most importantly, the President had made it clear that information security is an area of national importance and that it is taken seriously by him and his administration. By having Dave Farber of University of Pennsylvania and myself there, he had also made a statement to the industry people present that his administration takes the academic community seriously in this area. (Whether many of the industry people got that message—or care—remains to be seen.)

Meanwhile, on the same day as the White House summit, the *Washington Post* reported that 26-year-old Robert Heath Kashbohm was arrested for allegedly launching a denial of service attack against the Virginia Department of Motor Vehicles (DMV) Web site. The site was shut down for approximately 45 minutes on Sunday February 13. Investigators took less than an hour to trace the source of the attack. The suspect was apprehended about 24 hours later.

Why did I include this sad little news item? Well, it is a good reminder that those who launched the attack against Yahoo! and others were competent.

It has become conventional wisdom that nowadays, due to the widespread availability of automated attacks, just about anybody could do something similar.

Yes, it is true that hackers could download the software and figure out how to launch the attack. But how many novices would remain untraceable and avoid arrest for even this long? Whoever went after the icons of the Internet with the hammer of DDoS didn't do it from his or her home PC.

On Thursday, February 17, the Associated Press reported that federal investigators had "fast-breaking leads" but that the perpetrator(s) disguised themselves well.

FBI Director Louis Freeh said that Bureau field offices in five cities (Los Angeles, San Francisco, Atlanta, Boston, and Seattle) had opened investigations. Freeh confirmed that agents in other cities and overseas were involved as well.

On February 20, 2000, CNN provided its viewers with a rare glimpse into the forensic investigation:

> The bureau is better equipped now to handle the investigation than it has been in the past. In this search, investigators are using specialized filtering software to isolate suspicious computer traffic. By systematically removing normal message traffic, the FBI can focus on the far fewer strands of unusual traffic, which have odd signatures.
>
> But once the sinister traffic is located, the game of connect-the-dots has just begun.
>
> While the FBI has located some of the computers used in the attack, they are still trying to find those computers directing them. The trigger computer has been directed through dozens of others, masking the origin.
>
> In a tedious process, investigators work backward, going to each site and looking for logs that provide directions to the previous site, each time getting one step closer to the original attacker.[5]

The cybercops were looking for a single needle in several hundred haystacks.

In April, law enforcement uncovered at least one of the needles hidden under one of the haystacks.

On April 18, 2000, CNN reported that a Canadian juvenile had been arrested and charged in connection with the DDoS attacks.

> Sources familiar with the investigation said the arrest involves a Canadian juvenile who goes by the computer name "mafiaboy." The individual is believed to have played a role in the attack against CNN.com, and investigators are continuing to examine whether he played a role in other attacks.
>
> The Royal Canadian Mounted Police (RCMP) said in a written statement that charges were brought "against a person stemming from cyber-attacks that were launched in the beginning of the month of February 2000 in the United States against many Internet sites, namely CNN.com, Yahoo!, eBay, Amazon.com, Excite and Etrade."
>
> In mid-February, Internet Direct, a Canadian Internet Service Provider, was interviewed by the RCMP, which took a lead role in the overall investigation. Mafiaboy had two accounts on an ISP acquired by Internet Direct. A representative for Internet Direct said the accounts were canceled for terms of service violations.
>
> Mafiaboy will be charged under the Computer Fraud and Abuse Act, which was expanded in 1996 to cover all computers used in commerce. It prohibits the unauthorized access to obtain information, the transmission of anything that causes damage, fraud and extortion. Penalties can include up to 6 months in jail or 10 years for a repeat offender and twice the gross monetary loss to the victim.[6]

---

5. CNN, February 20, 2000

6. "Canadian juvenile charged in connection with February 'denial of service' attacks," by Pierre Thomas and D. Ian Hopper, CNN, April 18, 2000

I would be very surprised if "mafiaboy" was the sole perpetrator of these attacks. I would not be surprised if he was the only one ever charged with the crime.

Calculating the Financial Impact

In that fateful February issue of the *Computer Security Alert*, the one with the front page headline that screamed "Stop Living In Denial About Denial of Service," I had asked Rik Farrow to comment on whether DDoS attacks pose a real threat to e-commerce.

> There is a very real potential for devastating DoS attacks against e-commerce sites. While the number of people who actively go out and break into hundreds of sites is small (in comparison to the earth's total population), this still leaves us with hundreds or thousands of potential attackers. The difficulty in backtracing these attacks, the enormous leverage by using many attack servers, makes this very scary indeed.
>
> Amazon claims to have lost $600,000 while being down for 10 hours. This is small potatoes compared to Charles Schwab, which does $2 billion a week in on-line trading. We might get to see people jumping out of windows if their e-trade connection suddenly stopped working just as the market suffered a dramatic downward turn. And a widescale, distributed DoS attack might contribute to such a downward turn.[7]

Well, that "widescale" attack came all-too-soon. And watching some of those involved try to put a price tag on the event underscored the difficulty of quantifying financial losses in the aftermath of digital crimes.

On February 11, the Yankee Group, a market research firm, suggested that the DDoS attacks that had just subsided could result in $1.2 billion in financial losses to businesses.

How did these "industry analysts" get to that figure?

They estimated revenue lost to the Web sites that were actually attacked ($100 million of lost revenues in sales and advertising). Then they added in the losses in market capitalization resulting from the diminution in share prices of some "Internet-sensitive" companies ($1 billion) and the money that companies will spend to upgrade the security of their on-line systems ($100–$200 million).

Although it is admirable that the Yankee Group took the "soft costs" of cybercrime into account, the $1.2 billion figure is far too speculative. It isn't the one we need to successfully argue the case for more robust corporate information security postures.

Indeed, according to Dr. Gene Spafford of CERIAS (www.cerias.purdue.edu), such outlandish numbers might actually hurt that noble cause.

---

7. "Stop Living In Denial About Denial of Service," by Rik Farrow. *Computer Security Alert*, February 2000

"First of all," he tells me, "security upgrades shouldn't be considered a loss. Even if they were considered a loss, what security upgrades could cost $100 million? Are they gold-plating all the wires at the ISPs?

"I have almost no confidence in that $1.2 billion figure," Spafford continues. "Furthermore, it is damaging to publish figures like that. It overinflates expectations. It is counterproductive. It harks back to the hysteria leading up to the Michelangelo virus."

"Look at how much business they would normally do in an equivalent period of time," he remarks, "then compare that to how much business they did during the time of the attack and in its immediate aftermath. Add to that staffing and other recovery costs related to the incident. You might also want to include a marginal loss for future business from customers who got turned off. That's about it."

For example, according to APB News, a Web-based crime news service, Amazon.com did $676 million in sales in the fourth quarter of 1999. Amazon is projected to reap $528 million in sales for the first quarter of 2000. Based on the projected sales figures for 1Q00, APB News surmised that Amazon could have lost $244,000 for every hour of service that was interrupted.

Spafford concurred that a far more plausible figure for the total financial losses in this particular three-day DDoS attack against multiple sites would fall in the range of tens of millions of dollars.

However, the Yankee Group's puzzling calculations pale in contrast to eBay's statement on Thursday, February 24, that they incurred only $80,000 in "new expenses" and absolutely no "lost revenues."

Can you imagine any brick-and-mortar business making such an assertion if all foot traffic had been cut off for several hours? No. They would say that they had lost business during those hours, even if business resumed at a normal pace after the disruption.

The Moral of the Tale

A week after the flashpoint, some astute commentary started to bubble up on the Internet.

Consider the remarks of Lauren Weinstein of People for Internet Responsibility (www.pfir.org), posted to Dr. Peter Neumann's Risks Forum:

> It seems apparent that the rush to move all manner of important or even critical commercial, medical, government, and other applications onto the Internet and the Web has far outstripped the underlying reality of the existing Internet infrastructure.

Compared with the overall robustness of the U.S. telephone system, the Internet is a second-class citizen when it comes to these kinds of vulnerabilities.[8]

Bruce Schneier of Counterpane Systems (www.counterpane.com) weighed in through his electronic newsletter, *Crypto-Gram*:

> The real problem is that there are hundreds of thousands, possibly millions, of innocent naive users who are vulnerable to attack. They're using DSL or cable modems, they're always on the Internet with static IP addresses, and they can be taken over and used as launching pads for these (and other) attacks. The media is focusing on the mega e-corporations that are under attack, but the real story is the individual systems.

> Similarly, the real solutions are of the "civic hygiene" variety. Just as malaria was defeated in Washington, D.C. by draining all the swamps, the only real way to prevent these attacks is to protect those millions of individual computers on the Internet. Unfortunately, we are building swampland at an incredible rate, and securing everything is impractical.[9]

Very little can be done about Internet security unless enterprises and individuals take their own on-line security postures more seriously.

The most compelling aspect of the DDoS attack against Yahoo!, Amazon.com, and the like wasn't how it was done (DDoS attack tools are well-documented and readily available throughout cyberspace). Nor was it that such high-profile sites were targeted and successfully attacked. Nor was it the mystery surrounding the motivation of the attackers. The most compelling aspect of the tale isn't even the financial impact of the attack itself or its long-term implications for the growth of e-commerce. The most compelling aspect of the "Attack of the Zombies" is that hundreds of systems throughout cyberspace were hacked into and used as launching pads without detection.

If those responsible for the security of the sites used as launching pads had paid the slightest bit of attention, or heeded the warnings from CERT and NIPC, the evidence of the DDoS preparations would have been uncovered, and the attack itself could have been thwarted or at least minimized. And certainly, if such diligence had been exercised, authorities would have a much better chance of apprehending the perpetrators.

---

8. "PFIR Statement on Recent Internet Denial of Service Attacks," by Lauren Weinstein, *The Risks Digest* Volume 20, Issue 79, February 15,2000

9. "Distributed Denial-of-Service Attacks," by Bruce Schneier, *Crypto-Gram*, February 15, 2000

What Should You do About DDoS?

Here are the views of three subject matter experts in response to some practical questions I posed about what you should be trying to accomplish in the aftermath of the DDoS attack on Yahoo!, eBay, Amazon.com, etc.

Power: What should organizations be doing to help mitigate the risk that they will be used as a launching pad?

Erin Kenneally, Pacific Institute for Computer Security, San Diego Supercomputer Center: Despite the fact that there are no industry standards, per se, regarding computer security, it can be agreed that there exists an informal, albeit somewhat discrepant, body of "best practices." "Mitigating the risk" means having security policies and accompanying procedures to help achieve some modicum of security: things like knowing what's on one's machines, keeping abreast with patches and widely disseminated news of OS vulnerabilities, scanning one's network for vulnerabilities and conducting code reviews, installing filters (i.e., egress filters to prevent outgoing source address spoofing), using routers to block incoming spoofed packets, monitoring bandwidth and type of packets coming across one's network, having an awareness of attack signatures, etc.

Rik Farrow, www.spirit.com: Use firewalls. A properly configured firewall severely limits the massive scanning for vulnerable systems and also makes breaking into these vulnerable systems more difficult. For sites that cannot use firewalls (universities and research institutes), use an ID system that can detect scans while they are in process, as well as detecting the use of rcp (remote copy) commands made from internal systems to remote sites. According to both Dave Dittrich (University of Washington) and David Brumley (Stanford University), remote copies were used during the installation of daemon software (used to send floods). A remote system should never trust one of your internal systems enough to permit the copy to succeed…except if the remote system has already been hacked. Finally, patch your systems! Although this is not easy simply because of the logistics involved, you must install security patches on all systems. Today, all major operating systems vendors provide security patches to their operating systems free of charge from their Web sites or FTP servers. Old, unpatched, vulnerabilities offer the easiest means for exploiting systems on a massive scale.

Marcus Ranum, Network Flight Recorder (www.nfr.net): Install a firewall. Install virus scanning software on any Windows desktop that is connected to the Internet. Audit your network periodically to notice when you're being used as a launching pad. A large number of the sites that were used for launching-off points have, basically, no security. From what I hear, they were a mix of commercial, academic, and government sites—most of which have no firewalls or other traffic control/monitoring in place. That's simply amazingly lame, isn't it? A site should be able to tell whether it has been broadly penetrated and is running hundreds of zombie machines. That would be a huge step in the right direction. Many PCs that are being controlled by Trojan horses are not running virus scanning software.

Beyond these basic steps, ISPs need to start looking at ingress and egress filtering, to cut down on spoofing. They also should be detecting it automatically and notifying the upstream source. Those are harder to implement but would go a long way, too.

In order to really deal with DoS (and hacking in general) we're going to need to raise the level of accountability for Internet traffic by a few orders of magnitude. Unfortunately, a few bad apples are going to ruin anonymity for the rest of us in the barrel.

Power: What should organizations do to detect whether they have been hacked and set up as a launching pad?

Kenneally: Having a detection plan should go hand-in-hand with having a good security plan. For example, if one has a solid handle of what is running on one's machines, "abnormalities/anomalies" can be more easily observed and given appropriate attention. If detection is not part of security, going in after the fact will be much harder. Trying to detect a hack is hard enough, but trying to detect that there hasn't been a hack…well, you would be better off inserting a sharp stick in your frontal lobe.

Farrow: You can detect that you have been attacked in several ways. If your ID system notices unusual network activity (the remote copies mentioned above as an example), you can assume that the internal systems involved have been successfully attacked. If the attack had not been successful, you would not have detected the remote copies. Also, a group of security professionals have written a C program that scans networks for daemons that have been installed. You can also use commercial software, from companies such as Axent, Cisco, or NAI, to scan networks for the daemons. These scans will only be successful if the daemons have not been modified so that they listen to different ports or use different commands and/or encryption keys. Systems themselves can be scanned for the daemons. A version of trinoo designed to run on Windows 98 systems has appeared, and virus scanning software (if recently updated) can detect the installation of trinoo. Tools like Tripwire and Axent ESM can detect modifications made to Unix systems.

Ranum: Well, obviously, this is what intrusion detection systems are useful for.

Power: What should they do once they have detected such a hack?

Kenneally: This will vary somewhat depending on the nature of the hack, what assets were available or could have been the target of the intruder, what is the pattern of the attack (this will indicate whether there is an ongoing threat and also the sophistication of the attacker), the nature of the site affected, and the nature of the potential damage.

For those who lack the analysis capabilities and know nothing more than that their system has been compromised, it would be best to take the system offline, collect any and all logs of activity, do a forensic autopsy of the machine (if possible), and notify others who might have been affected.

Farrow: If you do detect that a system has been hacked, your first step should be to remove it from the network (disconnect the network cable). Then, make a complete backup of the system so that your investigation will not disturb any evidence left behind by the attackers. In particular, you are looking at the date stamps left on the files installed by the attackers and at logs created during the time period when those files were installed. You will hopefully also have other, external, methods for logging network activity (such as Argus, Shadow, NIDS, an ID system or some other method for monitoring your network), as local logs can be modified, and date stamps changed as well. You use your network logs to confirm what you find locally, as well as possibly discovering the same pattern of connections in a similar timeframe that indicate that other systems have been compromised.

You might also discover that one or more of your systems has been hacked because you detect the flood of packets on your own network. Track this down, disconnect the system, and proceed to preserve and examine evidence. If you do not have the capability to unravel potential evidence yourself, contact CERT, FIRST, or law enforcement (if serious financial damage has occurred), and let them decide what to do with the evidence. Once you have acted to preserve the evidence, return the system to service after cleaning it up. System recovery may require complete reinstallation of system and other software from trusted backups or installation media. But do not put a system back online without installing all security patches (unless you really want to go through this drill again).

Ranum: Record whatever information you can about the source of the traffic that is controlling the zombie. A sniffer or an intrusion detection system will help with this. Then, contact the administrator of record for the source domain and let him or her know that someone is abusing the system.

Power: What should an organization do once it has been informed that DDoS is being launched from its site?

Kenneally: Initiate basic, common-sense investigatory measures: Determine what machines were affected, shut down the zombied machines or find another way to "stop the blood flow," and collect and analyze traffic logs to try and trace back to the perpetrator.

Farrow: You do want to determine that you are not being fooled, but be polite. It is very likely the case that your site is at fault, not the caller. Don't shoot the messenger.

Ranum: Contact your lawyer and pray the victim site doesn't think you've been negligent enough to sue you. Just kidding. For now. In five years, I predict that my joke won't be a joke anymore. Obviously, if you're informed that you have zombies that are being used against a victim site, you should immediately begin cleaning up the affected machines. Try to capture the control traffic and backtrack it. Provide that information to the victim.

Power: What should a site (e-commerce or otherwise) do once it has been launched against, i.e., once it is already under attack? What steps, technical and non-technical, should it take? What should it do vis-à-vis forensic data?

Kenneally: Depends on what type of site you're dealing with. For an e-commerce or content site, it would help to have alternative plans in place. For example, sites with a vast array of resources (money) can make the decision to notify their provider to stop all traffic originating from the zombied machines, and then reroute traffic. In essence, have features in place that will mitigate damages once a compromise of this nature has occurred, such as redundant systems, fast response capabilities, and large amounts of bandwidth. Also, it would be helpful to have some good old-fashioned mechanisms in place, such as telephone capabilities so that business-related transaction interruption is minimized.

Farrow: For forensic trace-back purposes and possible legal recourse, it would be helpful to maintain a secure log traffic log of such malfeasance. For evidentiary integrity, this system should be in place before the intrusion (i.e., logging records should be kept within the normal course of business) and there should be documented accountability for the capture, handling, processing, and storage of this information. Targets of DDoS should start by contacting their ISP. They need to be able to tell their ISP as much as possible about the nature of the attack. Is the attack composed only of a flood of UDP packets? ICMP packets? TCP SYN packets? Or are they seeing a mixture of all of the above? As far as forensics go, having a method for capturing information about the attacks (type of packets, source and destination IP addresses and ports, data length) would be useful. Doing this requires having either an ID system or a network monitor listening to the network leading to the public servers.

Ranum: Record sources and as much as possible about the traffic. In general, large amounts of it will be spoofed anyhow. The main thing to do is to make sure you've filtered off as much of the hostile traffic as possible and have hardened your systems by keeping them at the latest software revisions. A number of sites have been affected by DDoS attacks that are easily blocked with filtering.

Power: Much has been said of "filtering." How can it be used to prevent attacks? How can it be use to blunt an attack in progress? What's possible? What does it get you?

Kenneally: It is possible to employ egress filters to prevent outgoing source address spoofing, as well as to use routers to block incoming spoofed packets. Depending on the size and configuration of the network, various levels of monitoring bandwidth and type of packets coming across one's network are possible. Also, information freely and widely available on newsgroups, mailing lists, and incident-monitoring sites enable IS/IT managers to become aware of attack signatures, how attack signatures can be altered, and how packets can be spoofed, for example.

One problem here is that attack signatures can be disguised in various ways and if you're not familiar with those tricks, you're no better off. Also, aside from the knowledge problem, many companies lack the technology to decode signatures and packets as fast as they flood the network. So it's like sleeping in a house that's filling up with CO_2 and having no detectors to alert you to the danger.

Farrow: There are two types of filtering involved: preventative and mitigative. The preventative filtering is what was described in RFC 2267 as "ingress filtering," although many networks can do egress filtering as well. In either case, the concept is to prevent packets with spoofed source addresses from leaving your networks. Most firewalls will do this by default. Cisco routers, when using newer versions of the Cisco operating system (IOS 12 or later), can do this simply by using the command

```
ip verify unicast reverse-path
```

Linux and BSD systems have a similar capability built into the operating system and can do this if they are being used as routers. What these mechanisms do is check the routing of an arriving packet to see whether it was received on the correct interface. Routers always compute the correct interface for sending out a packet; that is what routers do. But routers and systems acting as routers can also compute the network interface that a packet should have arrived on by examining the source address and checking the route for that source address. If the arrival interface is incorrect, the source address may be spoofed.

I must say "may be" because some networks support "best" path routing, in which case there may be more than one source route. But, if your network does not support alternative routes (say, you have just one connection to the Internet), then this is not a problem.

Small ISPs can program their terminal servers to reject packets leaving their terminal servers with spoofed source addresses. This takes very little in terms of processing power and is a feature of any recent terminal server. I have asked the security personnel involved at three of the sites involved as sources of attacks, and all of these sites do filter out spoofed source addresses (which means that the attacks that came from these sites where easy to track back). Sites that do *not* filter out spoofed source addresses will be more difficult to identify...but not impossible.

Someday, perhaps, it will be illegal to permit packets with spoofed source addresses to leave your network, just like it is illegal to drive a car without brakes or airplanes with mechanical problems. When a site is under attack, its ISP may be able to filter out all or some of the attacking packets. For example, if a Web server farm is being flooded by UDP packets, the ISP that provides the connection to those Web servers could block all unnecessary UDP packets (which would usually be all of them). If the attack involved both UDP and ICMP floods, most of these packets could be blocked as well. But if a SYN flood was launched against ports 80 and 443, the ISP could block these packets only if these packets use consistent source addresses. Keep in mind that the attackers have had access to a wide array of attack servers (daemons), and that tools other than trinoo can launch four different attacks or combinations of attacks.

Ranum: Some of the DDoS attacks rely on ICMP traffic—this is traffic that can often be easily blocked using a router filter. Other things are harder to filter. Suppose you're an e-commerce site. Your customers need to reach your http server; there's no sensible way to filter that. If someone launches an overload attack against your http server then if you filter it, you'll be filtering your customers, which is unacceptable. In that case, you need to react to the addresses from which the traffic is coming and filter based on those, which is nightmarishly complicated and unpleasant.

The $80 Million Lap Dance and the $10 Billion Love Letter

I n 1999, a wave of *malware* (malicious software), including Melissa, CIH/Chernobyl, Happy99, and ExploreZip, hit corporations, government agencies, and individual users very hard—and some of them hit hard in a new way.

There was nothing new about the malicious nature of the programs. Many nasty bits of code, from Michelangelo to Form, have chewed up hard disks, corrupted files, and disrupted operations throughout the years. Nor was there anything new about malware being spread over the Internet. Several years had already gone by since spreading malware via diskettes and BBSs was eclipsed by distribution over the information superhighway (the Internet, of course, is faster, more direct, more far-reaching).

What *was* new was that some of these programs were exploiting features of popular e-mail applications to propagate themselves throughout cyberspace.

The Melissa virus (CA-99-04) spreads mainly as Microsoft Word 97 and Word 2000 attachments in e-mail. Because Melissa propagates by automatically e-mailing copies of infected files to other users, it caused severe problems across the Internet. In addition to its ability to cause denial of service by overloading mail systems, the virus could also cause confidential documents to be leaked without the user's knowledge.

When the Happy99.exe Trojan horse (CERT IN-99-03) is executed for the first time, a fireworks display saying "Happy 99" appears on the computer screen. At the same time, it modifies system files to e-mail itself to other people.

I remember talking someone very close to me through recovery from Happy99.exe. It had written over vital system files and rendered her laptop unable to boot up.

The ExploreZip Trojan horse (CERT CA-99-06) affects Windows 95, 98, and NT systems. It modifies system files and destroys files. For ExploreZip to work, a person must open or run an infected e-mail attachment, which allows the program to install a copy of itself on the victim's computer and enables further propagation. ExploreZip can also behave as a worm, propagating to other network machines without human interaction.

CIH (CERT IN-99-02), a.k.a. Chernobyl, the other major malware event of 1999, is also a nasty piece of work. When it is triggered, it overwrites the first 2,048 sectors of each hard drive in the computer with random data. This area of the hard drive contains important information about the files on the computer. Without this file information, the computer thinks the hard drive is empty. The virus also writes one byte of data to the BIOS boot block that is critical for booting a computer.

But unlike the other malware mentioned here, CIH/Chernobyl is more classic in how it spreads: It simply infects executable files (i.e., those with .exe file extensions) and is spread by executing an infected file. Because many files are executed during normal use of a computer, the CIH virus can infect many files quickly, but it wasn't designed to exploit any of the features of popular e-mail applications.

Consequently, although very destructive, CIH had far less of an impact than Melissa, for example, which didn't carry a destructive payload at all.

Let's take a look at the stories behind the headlines involving Melissa (the biggest malware story since the Morris Worm) and Love Letter (the malware story that would dwarf both Melissa and the Morris Worm).

Table 9.1   Viruses Spread Faster, Infect More Systems, and Exact a Higher Cost as Time Goes By

Virus	Year	Type	Time to Reach "Most Prevalent"	Damages
Jerusalem, Cascade, Form...	1990	.exe file, boot sector	3 years	$50 million for all viruses over 5 years
Concept	1995	Word macro	4 months	$50 million
Melissa	1999	E-mail enabled, Word macro	4 days	$93–385 million
Love Bug	2000	E-mail and enabled, VBS	5 hours	>$700 million

Source: ICSA.net

The $80 Million Lap Dance

On Friday, March 26, 1999, the Melissa virus was launched.

On Saturday, March 27, CERT issued an advisory (CA-99-04).

Within 48 hours, high-tech giants Intel and Microsoft had to shut down some of their e-mail servers. Indeed, according to Network Associates, a leading anti-virus software developer, at least 20 large corporations were seriously impaired in the initial hours. Other major corporations mentioned in initial news reports included Lucent Technologies, Motorola, DuPont, and Compaq. One company reported that 60,000 users had been infected. By Monday, March 26, Melissa had reached at least 100,000 computers at more than 300 organizations.

The spread of the virus captured the headlines that weekend. Much hyperbole and misinformation abounded. For the sake of the record, I have included the CERT Advisory on Melissa. During big, hysteria-generating events such as Melissa and Love Letter, it is good to reference the relevant CERT advisories to keep everything in perspective.

(Of course, CERT advisories can be spoofed—but that's another story...)

On Monday, March 29, Christopher Bubb, head of the Computer Analysis and Technology unit of the New Jersey State Division of Criminal Justice received a call from John Ryan, associate general counsel for America Online (AOL).

Ryan told Bubb that over the weekend AOL had received some indications through its own internal investigation that the company might have been the conduit for the initial release of the virus. The earliest evidence of Melissa, according to Ryan, was in a posting on the alt.sex site,through one of AOL's servers.

People at AOL had found a file called list.zip, which was a download that promised a list of sexually oriented Web sites and user ID and password combinations for accessing them. That was the lure. Many people downloaded list.zip and ran the program it contained; as they did so, they executed the virus and spread it to others.

According to Bubb, AOL's investigators had done an excellent job in documenting events. They were very good at record keeping. They tagged individual messages— even in newsgroups such as alt.sex—very well.

Their tagging provided information on the message itself and also information on the equipment the message came through.

That's how AOL could feel confident that one of its systems had been the point of origin. AOL knew Melissa had been created on AOL systems and could tell from the tagging that it had not come in from outside.

So the investigators knew that the posting had originated in an AOL-hosted news-group. They knew that an AOL user account had initiated the posting. But was this AOL account a fraudulent one or was it a legitimate one that someone had hacked into?

They had a West Coast AOL user account and an East Coast access via TCP/IP from Monmouth Internet, a local New Jersey ISP. That raised an eyebrow. It could have been a user with mobile access from a laptop on the road, or it could be someone trying to hide his tracks. It turned out that someone had indeed misappropriated the user account.

After hearing a brief outline from Ryan, Bubb contacted the New Jersey State Police, who, in turn, contacted AOL to join in the investigation.

On Tuesday morning, Bubb received a fax from AOL saying, "Here's what we have. It's pointing your way...." Moving quickly, Bubb obtained warrants for the whole panoply of information that AOL as well as Monmouth Internet could provide. When he mentioned his actions were in regard to the Melissa virus, everyone along the way expedited the process.

Don't mistake the purpose of the warrants. AOL had already been cooperating under the law from the beginning because what it brought to Bubb and the New Jersey State investigators was what AOL had observed in the course of doing business.

Bubb obtained warrants legally authorizing AOL to provide the information that it could beyond what investigators had observed initially.

The next breakthrough came when the New Jersey State sleuths went to Monmouth Internet to see what they could contribute to the investigation. They happened to have Automatic Number Indexing (ANI, a form of caller ID) capability that provided data which took investigators to the actual telephone that made the call. Some systems have it; some systems don't. The ANI information led investigators to the suspect's house.

The suspect also used a computer at his workplace to check on the progress of Melissa. By logging on from work, he had put another fingerprint on the crime, which helped investigators triangulate who the perpetrator was.

They now had evidence of two Melissa-related accesses from two different locations: one the suspect's home, the other the suspect's place of work.

Based on this information, Bubb obtained a search warrant for the residence in Aberdeen, New Jersey. But the suspect had fled. He had also removed his computers before he left. (They have never been recovered.)

Investigators then resorted to "good old gumshoe detective work to track him down," according to Bubb. They tracked him to his brother's house in neighboring Eatontown, New Jersey.

Bubb had received the initial call from AOL at 9 a.m. Monday, and by 9 p.m. Thursday, a suspect had been apprehended.

If AOL had not kept very good records of newsgroup postings or if Monmouth Internet had not had ANI, the suspect might have gotten away with his crimes, or at the very least been much harder to identify as the perpetrator.

After his arrest, David L. Smith, 30 years old at the time, boasted that he had named the virus after an exotic dancer he had met in Florida where he went to school.

Ironically, Smith, a contract programmer for AT&T, ran the Help Desk for Microsoft products. Indeed, he had written VBS code to automate users' e-mail systems.

Smith was charged under both State and Federal laws. In August 1999, he admitted his guilt in court, as he had to law enforcement at the time of his arrest.

He also agreed to causing $80 million in damages.

Why $80 million? Well, it's simply the upper end of the scale for damages used in the federal sentencing guidelines. The actual losses related to Melissa were reported to be hundreds of millions of dollars, but once the toll reached $80 million, those prosecuting the case had all they could want or even use in order to impress the court. The Melissa case had reached the outer limits of what was even conceived of in the federal sentencing guidelines.

Melissa was the first incident since the Morris Worm in 1988 (see Chapter 5) to seriously disrupt operations on so many systems throughout cyberspace in such a short time. It was also the first serious incident of its kind since the Internet had become commercialized in the mid-1990s.

Unfortunately, another 12 years didn't pass before the next malware crime of such sweeping impact. The Love Letter worm would hit a little over one year later.

CERT® Advisory
CA-99-04-Melissa-Macro-Virus

March 27, 1999 (Last revised: March 31, 1999)

Systems Affected

- Machines with Microsoft Word 97 or Word 2000
- Any mail handling system could experience performance problems or a denial of service as a result of the propagation of this macro virus.

Overview

At approximately 2:00 PM GMT-5 on Friday March 26 1999 we began receiving reports of a Microsoft Word 97 and Word 2000 macro virus which is propagating via email attachments. The number and variety of reports we have received indicate that this is a widespread attack affecting a variety of sites.

Our analysis of this macro virus indicates that human action (in the form of a user opening an infected Word document) is required for this virus to propagate. It is possible that under some mailer configurations, a user might automatically open an infected document received in the form of an email attachment. This macro virus is not known to exploit any new vulnerabilities. While the primary transport mechanism of this virus is via email, any way of transferring files can also propagate the virus.

Anti-virus software vendors have called this macro virus the Melissa macro or W97M_Melissa virus.

I. Description

The Melissa macro virus propagates in the form of an email message containing an infected Word document as an attachment. The transport message has most frequently been reported to contain the following Subject header

```
Subject: Important Message From <name>
```

Where <name> is the full name of the user sending the message.

The body of the message is a multipart MIME message containing two sections. The first section of the message (Content-Type: text/plain) contains the following text:

```
Here is that document you asked for ... don't show anyone else ;-)
```

The next section (Content-Type: application/msword) was initially reported to be a document called "list.doc". This document contains references to pornographic web sites. As this macro virus spreads we are likely to see documents with other names. In fact, under certain conditions the virus may generate attachments with documents created by the victim.

When a user opens an infected .doc file with Microsoft Word97 or Word2000, the macro virus is immediately executed if macros are enabled.

Upon execution, the virus first lowers the macro security settings to permit all macros to run when documents are opened in the future. Therefore, the user will not be notified when the virus is executed in the future.

The macro then checks to see if the registry key

```
"HKEY_Current_User\Software\Microsoft\Office\Melissa?"
```

has a value of "... **by Kwyjibo**". If that registry key does not exist or does not have a value of "... **by Kwyjibo**", the virus proceeds to propagate itself by sending an email message in the format described above to the first 50 entries in every Microsoft Outlook MAPI address book readable by the user executing the macro. Keep in mind that if any of these email addresses are mailing lists, the message will be delivered to everyone on the mailing lists. In order to successfully propagate, the affected machine must have Microsoft Outlook installed; however, Outlook does not need to be the mailer used to read the message.

This virus can not send mail on systems running MacOS; however, the virus can be stored on MacOS.

Next, the macro virus sets the value of the registry key to "... **by Kwyjibo**". Setting this registry key causes the virus to only propagate once per session. If the registry key does not persist through sessions, the virus will propagate as described above once per every session when a user opens an infected document. If the registry key persists through sessions, the virus will no longer attempt to propagate even if the affected user opens an infected document.

The macro then infects the Normal.dot template file. By default, all Word documents utilize the Normal.dot template; thus, any newly created Word document will be infected. Because unpatched versions of Word97 may trust macros in templates the virus may execute without warning. For more information please see:

http://www.microsoft.com/security/bulletins/ms99-002.asp

Finally, if the minute of the hour matches the day of the month at this point, the macro inserts into the current document the message "Twenty-two points, plus triple-word-score, plus fifty points for using all my letters. Game's over. I'm outta here."

Note that if you open an infected document with macros disabled and look at the list of macros in this document, neither Word97 nor Word2000 list the macro. The code is actually VBA (Visual Basic for Applications) code associated with the "document.open" method. You can see the code by going into the Visual Basic editor.

If you receive one of these messages, keep in mind that the message came from someone who is affected by this virus and they are not necessarily targeting you. We encourage you to contact any users from which you have received such a message. Also, we are interested in understanding the scope of this activity; therefore, we would appreciate if you would report any instance of this activity to us according to our Incident Reporting Guidelines document available at:

http://www.cert.org/tech_tips/incident_reporting.html

II. Impact

- Users who open an infected document in Word97 or Word2000 with macros enabled will infect the Normal.dot template causing any documents referencing this template to be infected with this macro virus. If the infected document is opened by another user, the document, including the macro virus, will propagate. Note that this could cause the user's document to be propagated instead of the original document, and thereby leak sensitive information.

- Indirectly, this virus could cause a denial of service on mail servers. Many large sites have reported performance problems with their mail servers as a result of the propagation of this virus.

"My Baby, She Wrote Me a Letter..."

Written in VBScript, the Love Letter worm propagates in a variety of ways, including sending copies of itself to everyone in your Microsoft Outlook address book, overwriting certain file types (e.g., .jpeg and mp2) so that it executes when you double-click those files, and even exploiting IRC chats to infect other participants.

In its original "Love Letter Worm" advisory (CA-2000-04), released on Thursday, May 4, 2000, CERT reported more than 250 individual sites and more than 300,000 individual systems had been affected. Several sites had suffered "considerable network degradation as a result of the mail, file and Web traffic generated by the malicious program."

Spreading westward from the Philippines, Love Letter did an estimated $10 billion in damages. Eighty percent of U.S. Federal Government agencies were infected. Thirty percent of British e-mail systems were infected. Seventy percent of German systems were infected. Eighty percent of all Swedish systems were infected.

Even ATM systems in Belgium were shut down.

According to initial news reports on May 4, Vodafone AirTouch, Time Warner, Seagram, Silicon Graphics, the British House of Commons, the U.S. Department of Defense, the Federal Reserve, Cox Cable, DaimlerChrysler, the Motion Picture Association of America (MPAA), the Buenos Aires newspaper *La Nacion*, and the Colombian Finance Ministry were among the many large or prominent organizations hit hard.

Some industry analysts estimated that 43 million users were infected within the first 24 hours and that 1.9 million of them opened the attachment to release the worm.

In subsequent reports, on Friday May 5, Ford Motor Company acknowledged that 125,000 of its e-mail users worldwide had been affected. Nextel—like Vodafone, a wireless phone company—shut down e-mail for all its 13,000 employees.

Other organizations mentioned on the second day of the crisis included AT&T, Merrill Lynch, Delta Air Lines, Northwest Airlines, National Public Radio, Lucent, the *Philadelphia Inquirer*, the U.S. Department of Transportation, and the Florida State Lottery.

On Saturday May 6, the third day of the crisis, New Zealand Telecom's Xtra Internet service deleted 17,000 messages containing the Love Letter.

Clearly, many organizations did not learn the lessons of the Melissa outbreak.

Organizations that did learn the lessons had filters (i.e., they blocked all messages with the subject line "I Love You") in place within 15 minutes. They had updated DAT files from the anti-virus vendors within one hour. Their user populations could not even pick up their phones without hearing about what was expected of them in the crisis. These organizations were ready because those responsible were prepared, vigilant, and empowered.

I placed a call to Padgett Peterson of Lockheed Martin (Orlando, Florida). After all, Padgett had been, like John the Baptist, a voice in the wilderness, warning of such attacks both before and after Melissa.

Peterson lays much of the blame on Microsoft's door.

"Move the clock back to March 1998," he begins. "Do you remember what I was talking about? I said that we were in a lull. I said that VB scripting, particularly Microsoft's inclusion of 'create object to get object' was going to be a problem. No one knew what I was talking about. Well, guess what 'I Love You' used?

"If Microsoft were split up so that you had Office on one side and the Windows OS on the other side," he continues, "there would have to be open publishing of the standards used to communicate between the two. People wouldn't be surprised when I said things like, 'Common Data Objects (CDO) is going to hurt us.' All these vulnerabilities would be open for examination."

Meanwhile, unlike the Melissa manhunt or some of the other cases documented in *Tangled Web*, the investigation soon fell apart.

On May 6, Reuters reported that Philippine police were awaiting a judge's warrant to arrest a man suspected of creating the Love Letter worm. The suspect was described to the press as a "23-year-old man living in Pandacan, a crowded suburb of Manila."

"Our operatives are out in the field for surveillance," Nelson Bartoleme, head of the National Bureau of Investigation's (NBI) anti-fraud and computer crimes division told the wire service. *"Gosh darn it, we're ready to go. We just have to find a judge."*

Are you following this twist in the story? Can you imagine it?

Let's say you are responsible for releasing the most devastating malware attack in the short but poignant history of cyberspace. Let's say you are—strictly for argument's sake—"a 23-year-old man living in Pandacan, a crowded suburb of Manila."

You read on the Internet about a suspect who matches your description and is believed to be in a location that matches yours.

Surveillance is supposed to be in place. Look out the window. If you cannot detect the undercover officers, maybe the CNN cameras will tip you off.

On May 8, an arrest was made. Filipino authorities took Reomel Ramones, 27, into custody. Irene de Guzman, Ramones' 23-year-old girlfriend, was also sought. Investigators believed her computer was used to launch the worm.

Of course, by the time the NBI found the judge to sign the papers, fought their way through the CNN cameras, and went inside the suspects' apartment, both the young woman and her computer were gone.

The Reuters story described Ramones and de Guzman as "bank employees" and "a quiet, unassuming couple."

On May 9, the Associated Press reported that Ramones' relatives claimed he was innocent. They pointed accusing fingers at de Guzman's brother, a 23-year-old man named Onel de Guzman, who also lived in the apartment.

The NBI termed Onel de Guzman as "a person subject to investigation."

On May 10, ZDNet Asia reported that while a student at AMA Computer College (AMACC) in Manila, the young man had submitted a thesis titled "Trojan Horse." In the paper, he proposed writing a program so that "people, specifically Internet users, can get Windows passwords, such as Internet accounts, to spend more time on the Internet without paying." The thesis was rejected.

Meanwhile, Ramones was freed due to lack of evidence.

On June 15, the *Washington Post* reported that the NBI was preparing to go ahead with criminal charges.

> "After a month-long investigation, authorities have concluded that the student, Onel de Guzman, who lived in a dilapidated Manila apartment from which the virus was released and whose thesis proposal was similar to portions of the bug, was responsible for sending out the electronic plague in an ill-fated effort to steal Internet-access passwords from people in the Philippines.
>
> But de Guzman will be charged only with fraud and malicious mischief, crimes that have relatively light penalties in the Philippines because the country does not have laws that specifically forbid the dissemination of computer viruses, officials said."[1]

On June 29, CNN reported that the NBI had, indeed, used a credit-card fraud law to charge de Guzman.

> NBI officials said they had charged de Guzman with violation of the Access Device Act which covers illegal use of passwords for credit cards and other bank transactions.
>
> The Philippine Justice Department will make the decision whether to proceed based on the evidence the NBI has said it has gathered
>
> The NBI said that among the evidence it has compiled are de Guzman's computer school thesis proposal in which he described a Love Bug-type program he wanted to write for the project. Investigators said they had also compiled interviews and other computer evidence pointing to de Guzman.[2]

Well, "case closed" doesn't really apply here. After all, a suspect who is allegedly responsible for financial losses in the billions of dollars around the world is being charged under an ill-fitting statute in the Philippines.

There is an ominous warning that echoes through the Melissa and Love Letter outbreaks. It could have been a lot worse, as Peterson observed.

"A professional could have written the Love Letter code so that the first thing it did was run some test commands to see which board set the system used," Peterson explains, "then it would have flashed the system's BIOS. You would have ended up with a non-bootable system that would have required a hardware change to make it usable again. There isn't a single enterprise in this country that couldn't be taken out in about 30 minutes by a dedicated professional."

---

1. "'Love Bug' Charges to Be Filed" by Rajiv Chandrasekaran, *Washington Post* June 15, 2000

2. "Philippine officials charge alleged 'Love Bug' virus creator," CNN June 29, 2000

CERT® Advisory
CA-2000-04 Love Letter Worm

May 4, 2000

Systems Affected

- Systems running Microsoft Windows with Windows Scripting Host enabled

Overview

The "Love Letter" worm is a malicious VBScript program which spreads in a variety of ways. As of 5:00 pm EDT(GMT-4) May 8, 2000, the CERT Coordination Center has received reports from more than 650 individual sites indicating more than 500,000 individual systems are affected. In addition, we have several reports of sites suffering considerable network degradation as a result of mail, file, and web traffic generated by the "Love Letter" worm.

I. Description

You can be infected with the "Love Letter" worm in a variety of ways, including electronic mail, Windows file sharing, IRC, USENET news, and possibly via webpages. Once the worm has executed on your system, it will take the actions described in the Impact section.

Electronic Mail

When the worm executes, it attempts to send copies of itself using Microsoft Outlook to all the entries in all the address books. The mail it sends has the following characteristics:

- An attachment named "LOVE-LETTER-FOR-YOU.TXT.VBS"
- A subject of "ILOVEYOU"
- The body of the message reads "kindly check the attached LOVELETTER coming from me."

People who receive copies of the worm via electronic mail will most likely recognize the sender. We encourage people to avoid executing code, including VBScripts, received through electronic mail regardless of the sender without first-hand prior knowledge of the origin of the code.

Internet Relay Chat

When the worm executes, it will attempt to create a file named *script.ini* in any directory that contains certain files associated with the popular IRC client mIRC.

The script file will attempt to send a copy of the worm via DCC to other people in any IRC channel joined by the victim. We encourage people to disable automatic reception of files via DCC in any IRC client.

Executing Files on Shared File Systems

When the worm executes, it will search for certain types of files and replace them with a copy of the worm (see the Impact section for more details). Executing (double clicking) files modified by other infected users will result in executing the worm. Files modified by the worm may also be started automatically, for example from a startup script.

Reading USENET News

There have been reports of the worm appearing in USENET newsgroups. The suggestions above should be applied to users reading messages in USENET newsgroups.

II. Impact

When the worm is executed, it takes the following steps:

Replaces Files with Copies of the Worm

When the worm executes, it will search for certain types of files and make changes to those files depending on the type of file. For files on fixed or network drives, it will take the following steps:

- For files whose extension is *vbs* or *vbe* it will replace those files with a copy of itself.

- For files whose extensions are *js*, *jse*, *css*, *wsh*, *sct*, or *hta*, it will replace those files with a copy of itself and change the extension to *vbs*. For example, a file named *x.css* will be replaced with a file named *x.vbs* containing a copy of the worm.

- For files whose extension is *jpg* or *jpeg*, it will replace those files with a copy of the worm and add a *vbs* extension. For example, a file named *x.jpg* will be replaced by a file called *x.jpg.vbs* containing a copy of the worm.

- For files whose extension is *mp3* or *mp2*, it will create a copy of itself in a file named with a *vbs* extension in the same manner as for a *jpg* file. The original file is preserved, but its attributes are changed to hidden.

Since the modified files are overwritten by the worm code rather than being deleted, file recovery is difficult and may be impossible.

Users executing files that have been modified in this step will cause the worm to begin executing again. If these files are on a filesystem shared over a local area network, new users may be affected.

Creates an mIRC Script

While the worm is examining files as described in the previous section, it may take additional steps to create a mIRC script file. If the file name being examined is *mirc32.exe*, *mlink32.exe*, *mirc.ini*, *script.ini*, or *mirc.hlp*, the worm will create a file named *script.ini* in the same folder. The *script.ini* file will contain:

```
[script]

n0=on 1:JOIN:#:{
n1=  /if ( $nick == $me ) { halt }
n2=  /.dcc send $nick DIRSYSTEM\LOVE-LETTER-FOR-YOU.HTM
n3=}
```

where DIRSYSTEM varies based on the platform where the worm is executed. If the file *script.ini* already exists, no changes occur.

This code defines an mIRC script so that when a new user joins an IRC channel the infected user has previously joined, a copy of the worm will be sent to the new user via DCC. The *script.ini* file is created only once per folder processed by the worm.

Modifies the Internet Explorer Start Page

If the file *<DIRSYSTEM>\WinFAT32.exe* does not exist, the worm sets the Internet Explorer Start page to one of four randomly selected URLs. These URLs all refer to a file named *WIN-BUGSFIX.exe*, which presumably contains malicious code. The worm checks for this file in the Internet Explorer *downloads* directory, and if found, the file is added to the list of programs to run at reboot. The Internet Explorer Start page is then reset to "about:blank". Information about the impact of running *WIN-BUGSFIX.exe* will be added to this document as soon as it is available.

Sends Copies of Itself via Email

The worm attempts to use Microsoft Outlook to send copies of itself to all entries in all address books as described in the Description section.

Modifies Other Registry Keys

In addition to other changes, the worm updates the following registry keys:

```
HKLM\Software\Microsoft\Windows\CurrentVersion\Run\MSKernel32
HKLM\Software\Microsoft\Windows\CurrentVersion\RunServices\Win32DLL
HKLM\Software\Microsoft\Windows\CurrentVersion\Run\WIN-BUGSFIX
HKCU\Software\Microsoft\Windows Scripting Host\Settings\Timeout
HKCU\Software\Microsoft\Internet Explorer\Main\Start Page
HKCU\Software\Microsoft\WAB\*
```

Note that when the worm is sending email, it updates the last entry each time it sends a message. If a large number of messages are sent, the size of the registry may grow significantly, possibly introducing additional problems.

Spies and Saboteurs

PART III

Corporate Spies: Trade Secret Theft in Cyberspace

O nce upon a time, a small engineering firm invested a fortune in the research and development of a new product. Its employees toiled ceaselessly for 14 months. They were way ahead of their leading competitor in the race to market. The project was going so smoothly that the CEO even went on a vacation.

One bright sunny morning, while the CEO was far away, a consultant showed up and said he had been hired to conduct a study for that absent executive. He had an expensive briefcase and wore a Rolex watch.

The consultant handed out his business card and buttered up some of the people in key positions. He said, "The CEO told me that you were one of the people that I should be working with." He said, "I understand you're next in line for that promotion. Oh, maybe I wasn't supposed to tell you."

Eager to please the CEO's charming new consultant, the firm's employees provided an empty conference room for the stranger to work.

During a tour of the facility, the consultant was introduced to some of the engineers working on the new product. They offered him a copy of the blueprints to review. He tucked them under his arm.

He took everybody out to lunch. He talked to marketing about when they were going to roll out the product and what it was going to look like. He talked with finance about how much it cost to develop it and who their suppliers were. He thanked everybody, shook their hands, and left.

The consultant, it turned out, was actually working for their number-one competitor. He handed the plans over to the competitor lock, stock, and barrel. With the proprietary information gathered by the phony "consultant," that unscrupulous competitor beat the small firm to the punch and brought its product out first.

Yes, the small firm was victimized by an adept, audacious corporate spy, using social engineering techniques. It is just one of many ways that trade secret theft is carried out.

The Corporate World's Dirty, Little, Secret War

One of the most intriguing results of the CSI/FBI survey over the last four years concerns the entities that respondents perceive as likely sources of attack. Each year, more than 80% of respondents see disgruntled employees as a likely source of attack. Each year, more than 70% see hackers as a likely source of attack. There is nothing surprising in either of these results. They track with the "conventional wisdom" that the greatest threat comes from disgruntled employees and juvenile hackers.

What is surprising is that each year between 44% and 53% of respondents see their U.S.-based corporate competitors as a likely source of attack, and that between 20% to 30% see their foreign competitors and foreign governments as likely sources of attack. Most people deny that such activity occurs.

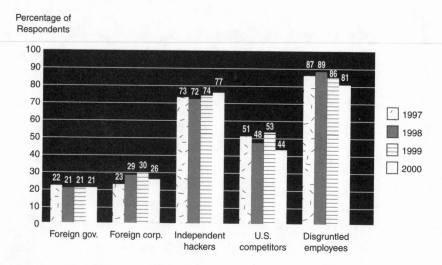

Figure 10.1 Likely sources of attack.

Source: 2000 CSI/FBI Computer Crime and Security Survey
2000: 583 Respondents/90%
1999: 460 Respondents/88%
1998: 428 Respondents/83%
1997: 503 Respondents/89%

Consider the following conversation with a senior information security practitioner at a Fortune 50 corporation.

"I was looking at that survey you did with the FBI," he said. "I don't believe it."

"What don't you believe?" I asked.

"I don't believe that 50% of corporations are attacked by other corporations."

"Why not?"

"Well, we don't do that," he stated. "In our industry, there are only four or five companies. We compete, but we also work together. We couldn't do that and still work together."

"Okay. What do you do?"

"Well, we will put someone outside their factory to count trucks."

"Okay," I answered. "Nothing illegal about counting trucks. What else?"

"Well, we also check out the color of the smoke from their factory smokestacks."

"Okay. Nothing illegal about looking at smokestacks," I said. "What else?"

"Well, we pay close attention to executive travel. You can find out a lot from monitoring the travel of corporate executives."

"Hmm. That's a gray area. How do you do it?"

"Oh, there are ways. But we don't hack into each other's systems. It just doesn't happen. Except, of course, for the time that the Israelis hacked into our network, stole some data, and sold it to the French. But that sort of thing just doesn't happen."

After he dropped that little bombshell, the senior information security practitioner just winked at me and walked away without further comment. And that's the way it is when you're dealing with the high-grade threat, whether the topic is information warfare or economic espionage: official denial and off-the-record confirmation.

Theft of proprietary information is perhaps the greatest threat to U.S. economic competitiveness in the global marketplace. Consider the financial losses involved.

The number of CSI/FBI Computer Crime and Security Survey respondents that reported theft of proprietary information hasn't increased significantly over the years. Nor has the number of those willing or able to quantify their losses. But the total financial losses reported by the handful that could quantify them has risen every year.

Table 10.1   Respondents Reporting Theft of Proprietary Information

Year	Incidents	Quantified Losses	Losses Reported
1997	101	21	$20,048,000
1998	82	20	$33,545,000
1999	104	23	$42,496,000
2000	118	22	$66,708,000

Source: CSI/FBI Computer Crime and Security Survey

The American Society for Industrial Security (ASIS) 1997 "Special Report on Trends in Intellectual Property Loss" estimated that U.S.-based companies suffer in excess of $250 billion in losses annually.

According to a subsequent study that ASIS conducted in collaboration with PriceWaterhouse Coopers LLP in 1999, Fortune 1000 companies sustained losses of more than $45 billion from thefts of their proprietary information. Forty-four companies of the total 97 that responded reported a total of more than 1,000 incidents of thefts. Of these, 579 incidents were valued with a total estimated loss of nearly $1 billion. The average company responding reported 2.45 incidents with estimated losses per incident of more than $500,000. The vast majority of the reported incidents were in high technology (530) and services organizations (356). Although manufacturing reported only 96 incidents, the acknowledged losses of manufacturing companies accounted for the majority of losses reported in the survey and averaged almost $50 million per incident.

These financial losses can be devastating. The stakes are very high.

For example, Igene Biotechnology launched a lawsuit to recover $300 million in damages from Archer Daniels Midland for theft of trade secrets involving an enzyme product that gives farm-raised trout and salmon a pinkish hue like that of wild fish.

Furthermore, as the global economy heats up, national security and corporate security dovetail. Consider the case of Ellery Systems, which had done very sophisticated work for NASA and the European Space Agency. Liaosheng Wang, a Chinese national who worked for the firm, allegedly transferred more than 122 proprietary source-code files to someone in the People's Republic of China. Ellery sustained serious financial losses as well as the loss of hundreds of jobs, but charges against Wang were dropped because they had failed to obtain a signed non-disclosure agreement from him.

If an enzyme to give farm-bred salmon the same pinkish hue of wild fish could be valued at $300 million, what could the research and development secrets of the U.S. and EU space programs be worth?

Theft of proprietary information has been accomplished primarily through insiders utilizing their direct access—whether authorized or unauthorized—to misappropriate vital data for competitors.

Increasingly, however, due to the extraordinary growth in both Internet connectivity and intranet/extranet deployment, freelancers in the hire of your corporate competitors are simply going to hack into your networks and take what they want.

Indeed, ASIS's 1997 "Special Report on Trends in Intellectual Property Loss" cites "computer penetration" as one of the "top three external methods" of stealing proprietary information. And even in more traditional trade secret theft cases where insiders are involved, computers are used.

Consider the following news item from the *Wall Street Journal*:

> Security experts agree that "netspionage," or computer-based espionage, is the most pressing risk for companies. About 80% of trade secrets are stored in digital form, says William Boni, Los Angeles-based director of corporate investigations at PricewaterhouseCoopers.
>
> Hackers are especially dangerous because they can copy data without leaving a trace that they broke into a computer. Alan Brill, senior managing director of Kroll-O'Gara Co., a New York-based corporate investigation firm, says, "You could have all your documents stolen, and never know it."[1]

Table 10.2 Highest Rated Threat Groups

Aggregate		Score	%
Trusted	Current Employees	169	98
	Former Employees Working Elsewhere	163	94
	Temporaries/On-site Contractors	163	94
External	Computer Penetrations	155	90
	Domestic Competitors	150	87
	Foreign Competitors	142	82

High-Tech		Score	%
Trusted	Current Employees	39	100
	Former Employees Working Elsewhere	35	92
	Vendors/Suppliers	34	89
External	Domestic Competitors	36	95
	Computer Penetrations	35	92
	Foreign Competitors	34	89

1. "Trade & Commerce: Stop, Thief! Business espionage has been common for as long as there have been secrets worth stealing" by Rachel Emma Silverman, *Wall Street Journal*, January 11, 1999

Table 10.2 continued

	Services	Score	%
Trusted	Current Employees	73	96
	Former Employees Working Elsewhere	71	93
	Temporaries/On-site Contractors	70	92
External	Computer Penetrations	67	88
	Domestic Competitors	60	79
	Competitive Intelligence Professionals	59	78

	Manufacturing	Score	%
Trusted	Current Employees	57	98
	Temporaries/On-site Contractors	56	97
	Former Employees Working Elsewhere	56	97
External	Domestic Competitors	54	93
	Competitive Intelligence Professionals	53	91
	Computer Penetrations	53	91

Source: 1997 "Special Report on Trends in Intellectual Property Loss," American Society for Industrial Security (ASIS)[2]

Table 10.3 Impact of Intellectual Property Losses on Companies by Industry Category

Industry Category	No Impact	%	Reporting Impact	%
Loss of Competitive Advantage				
High Tech	9	24	21	55
Services	39	51	25	33
Manufacturing	24	41	20	34
Loss of Market Share				
High Tech	12	32	19	50
Services	40	53	24	32
Manufacturing	25	43	20	32

2. Polled security directors in Fortune 1,000 and 300 Fastest Growing corporations with 172 respondents.

Industry Category	No Impact	%	Reporting Impact	%
Loss of Revenue				
High Tech	10	26	21	55
Services	32	42	30	39
Manufacturing	20	34	29	50
Increased R&D Costs				
High Tech	11	29	19	50
Services	42	55	21	28
Manufacturing	27	47	21	36
Embarrassment/Loss of Image				
High Tech	17	45	14	37
Services	39	51	25	33
Manufacturing	26	45	23	40
Increased Legal Costs				
High Tech	15	39	16	42
Services	41	54	22	29
Manufacturing	25	43	25	43
Legal Cost Associated with Loss of Third-Party Information				
High Tech	20	53	11	29
Services	40	53	22	29
Manufacturing	29	50	19	33
Increased Insurance Costs				
High Tech	23	61	7	18
Services	42	55	21	28
Manufacturing	33	57	16	28

Source: 1997 "Special Report on Trends in Intellectual Property Loss," American Society for Industrial Security (ASIS)[2]

Some Real-World Tales of Economic Espionage

The following examples of economic espionage are culled from news items. They illustrate the broad range of perpetrators, the diverse methods used, and the many types of companies and proprietary information involved in economic espionage.

In 1994, Northwest Airlines hired away an employee of American Airlines by dangling a pay raise of $16,000 a year. But the real target, according to American, was their "yield management system." This intricate system helps carriers set fares based on various pricing strategies and flight schedules. Well, just before the employee jumped ship, she dropped a diskette with American's "spill tables" (a critical component of the yield management computations) into a FedEx overnight letter to her new boss.

In September 1995, William Gaede, a software engineer, was arrested for stealing $10 to $20 million worth of computer industry secrets from the Intel Corporation and offering them to competitors and foreign governments. The charges included the possible breach of national security and other criminal activities involving high-tech espionage.

Working as an Intel subcontractor, Gaede had downloaded voluminous data on the Pentium microprocessor to his home computer, videotaped the data displayed on the computer monitor, and planned to sell the tapes to foreign governments.

William Gaede pleaded guilty to federal charges of mail fraud and interstate transportation of stolen information. His plea bargain allowed him to remain in the United States after serving a 33-month sentence and ensured that his wife would avoid prosecution.

In 1996, Johnson & Johnson's diabetes products subsidiary encouraged workers to illegally spy on rivals and gave "Inspector Clouseau" and "Columbo" awards for those who obtained the most information, a competitor charged. Boehringer Mannheim Corp., a German-owned drug and medical device company, made the allegations in a federal court lawsuit against Johnson & Johnson and LifeScan Inc. subsidiary. Boehringer, which was acquired by The Roche Group in 1997, has U.S. offices in Indianapolis.

According to the suit, awards were presented at meetings, with prizes to members of the sales force who obtained the best information about their competitors and their plans. The suit also claims a LifeScan employee stole a prototype of a diabetes monitoring system and took it to a LifeScan lab in California.

In January 1997, Johnson & Johnson and Boehringer Mannheim settled out-of-court and the terms were kept confidential.

In January 1997, Volkswagen (VW) and General Motors (GM) also settled their trade secret theft battle out-of-court. VW agreed to pay General Motors $100 million and buy at least $1 billion worth of GM parts to settle the U.S. automobile manufacturer's lawsuit alleging VW stole trade secrets.

In March 1997, Masanori Uekihara, a Japanese citizen and former executive of a Silicon Valley computer chip manufacturer, was ordered held without bail following his arrest in an alleged scheme to steal a competitor's secrets. According to court papers, Uekihara showed up on a loading dock impersonating an official of Toshiba and asked for data and samples of a chip that was being developed.

In July 1997, a New York judge ruled that KPMG, one of the nation's largest accounting firms, had abused its relationship with one of its audit clients. The suit, brought by the consulting firm Stern Stewart and Company, accused KPMG of using its position as the firm's long-term auditor and tax accountant to create a rival business.

In August 1997, Harold C. Worden, a former employee of Eastman Kodak, agreed to serve 15 months in prison and pay a fine of about $30,000 for transporting stolen property across state lines (thousands of pages on the design of a multimillion-dollar machine for the plastic base used in consumer film).

Worden agreed that the company suffered damages of $26,700 related to the loss of information, or roughly half the income earned by Worden's consulting firm that allegedly provided trade secrets to Kodak competitors.

In December 1997, Eastman Kodak sued Minnesota Mining and Manufacturing (3M) for allegedly using the trade secrets that Worden had sold them.

In September 1997, David Biehl of Redwood City, California, was sentenced to two years and seven months in federal prison for his part in an industrial espionage ring that victimized several semiconductor companies. Biehl and his cohorts illegally obtained proprietary drawings from three firms and used them to manufacture and sell similar parts through another company.

In February 1998, federal prosecutors obtained more than 100 written communications between a U.S. subsidiary of Reuters Holdings PLC and a consulting company that investigators believed was hired to steal information from the computers of a competitor, Bloomberg LP. The communications from the subsidiary, Reuters Analytics, Inc., included memos and other records requesting detailed information about technical programs for analyzing investments. The consultant was then said to have electronically broken into Bloomberg's corporate computers and obtained the information.

In April 1998, Wells Fargo's brokerage unit sued Merrill Lynch & Co., accusing Merrill of a campaign to recruit its top producers and learn the names of clients with billions of dollars in investment accounts. The company claims Catherine Miller, who left Wells Fargo for Merrill, took confidential information on as many as 1,000 clients with $175 million in investments.

In September 1998, PeopleSoft sued Harris Group LLC, a Chicago recruiting firm, for unfair competition and misappropriation of trade secrets, accusing the startup of using secret data about PeopleSoft employees' salaries and skills to try to hire them.

In February 1999, citing federal wiretap law, a Pennsylvania district judge ordered Sladekutter, a Web design firm, to stop hacking into the computer systems of its competitor, Labwerks. "This is corporate espionage by a competitor aimed at putting us out of business," said Labwerks's John Kuntz.

In May 2000, a jury in Santa Clara County (California) Superior Court convicted David Hawkins, a former employee of Cisco Systems, of stealing information from the company estimated to be worth billions of dollars. Hawkins was found guilty of stealing the source code for a Cisco product called Private Internet Exchange (PIX) sometime before leaving the firm in August 1996, said Deputy District Attorney Frank Berry, Jr.

Hawkins had joined Cisco about a year before when the company acquired Translation Network, Inc. (TNI). He had been working for the smaller TNI for a little more than a week when the acquisition took place.

The defendant, Berry said, stayed on with Cisco for about nine months before starting his own business. Thereafter, Hawkins began promoting a product to rival PIX, called Aegis, which went on exhibit in May 1997 at a huge industry trade show. One of those in attendance at the show was TNI's founder, John Mays. Hawkins's demonstration aroused suspicion because of the unusual similarity of Aegis and the software owned by Cisco. Cisco estimated that its product was worth $2 billion.

Cisco launched an internal investigation and came up with enough evidence to turn the case over to the district attorney's office.

Two months later, officers served a search warrant on Hawkins's business, which he operated out of his home. They found two versions of the original PIX source code on the hard drives of two computers in his office.

Hawkins faces a maximum of three years in state prison.

Tit for Tat? State-Sponsored Economic Espionage

In 1999, the U.S. National Counterintelligence Center (NACIC), which operates under the auspices of the National Security Council, reported that U.S. economic data, trade secrets, and vital technology are sought most actively by eight nations. The eight nations are not identified, but likely include France, Russia, China, Taiwan, Israel, Germany, and Iran.

Ah, *vive la France*. The French are so much fun to tease.

In April 1997, the *Fraud Bulletin* reported that French intelligence agents routinely conduct a formal program of "bag operations" against foreign corporate businessmen. Ten to fifteen times a day, according to the story, French operatives break into hotel rooms of visiting businessmen to gather information.

In late 1999, London's *Sunday Times* corroborated that story when it reported that British Aerospace (BAe) executives were burglarized at a Toulouse hotel by French secret service agents involved in industrial espionage. The raid was allegedly conducted by a Direction et Surveillance du Territoire (DST) unit called Protection du Patrimoine Economique, which is said to operate specialized break-in operations targeting foreign companies. The agents allegedly searched through briefcases and stole documents from BAe officials while they were meeting with officials from the French aviation company Airbus Industrie.

In June 1998, *Le Point*, a French magazine, reported that France systematically listens to telephone conversations and cable traffic of many businesses in the United States and other nations. The Germans who bought into the French 1A spy satellite system are being given access to political and economic secrets as part of a Franco-German commercial information agreement similar to one between the United States and Britain.

In January 2000, London's *Sunday Times*, corroborating the *Le Point* report, declared that French intelligence was indeed intercepting British businessmen's calls after investing millions in satellite technology for its listening stations.

Since the French government upgraded signals intelligence last year, secret service elements are now using it to tap into commercial secrets. At least eight centers scattered across France are being "aimed" at British defense firms, petroleum companies, and other commercial targets. Targets include executives at British Aerospace (BAe), British Petroleum, and British Airways, according to French sources.

Senior executives have been told not to discuss sensitive issues on mobile phones, and BAe staff have been told to be "especially careful" during campaigns for new business, such as the current battle to supply Eurofighter missiles.

An executive within one British defense firm said, "Top people use the same mobile telephones as anyone else, without any sort of high-tech security equipment. There is an understanding that we need to be careful. People never say anything that they would not want heard elsewhere, especially at sensitive times and during projects when other people may have an interest in listening."

Over the past year or so, you might have read about Echelon, a vast secret network of listening posts and supercomputers built during the Cold War.

Echelon, the rumor goes, searches worldwide communications, including phone conversations, e-mails, and faxes, scanning for key words of interest to the English-speaking nations: i.e. the United States, the United Kingdom, Canada, Australia, and New Zealand. In the post–Cold War era, critics allege, its big, sensitive ears have been turned to economic espionage.

The NSA's interception of 1994 phone calls between a French firm and Brazilian officials about a $1.4 billion satellite system for the Amazon has been offered as an example of Echelon activity. Bribes were allegedly made during these phone conversations. The U.S. government informed the Brazilian government, and Raytheon, a U.S. corporation, won the contract instead.

It is also claimed that the U.S. used Echelon intel to help Seattle-based Boeing beat European Airbus to a lucrative airplane deal with Saudi Arabia.

Of course, Echelon has received far more mainstream media attention on both sides of the Atlantic than the well-documented activities of French intelligence.

In March 2000, the European Parliament announced that it would set up an investigation into allegations that the United States uses Echelon for economic espionage. In July 2000, it formed a committee to investigate allegations. The committee will have one year to establish whether the Echelon system actually exists and whether European industry has been hurt by its interception of communications.

In a March 2000 op-ed piece in the *Wall Street Journal*, James Woolsey, a Washington lawyer and former director of the Central Intelligence Agency, offered insightful commentary on the Echelon flap:

> Yes, my European friends, we have spied on you. And it's true that we use computers to sort through data by using keywords. Have you stopped to ask yourself what we're looking for?
>
> The European Parliament's recent report on Echelon, written by British journalist Duncan Campbell, has sparked angry accusations from continental Europe that U.S. intelligence is stealing advanced technology from European companies so that we can—get this—give it to American companies and help them compete. My European friends, get real. True, in a handful of areas

European technology surpasses American, but to say this as gently as I can, the number of areas is very, very, very small. Most European technology just isn't worth our stealing.

Why, then, have we spied on you? The answer is quite apparent from the Campbell report—in the discussion of the only two cases in which European companies have allegedly been the targets of American secret intelligence collection…That's right, my continental friends, we have spied on you because you bribe.[3]

In March 2000, *Intelligence Newsletter* highlighted perhaps the most ironic twist in the entire Echelon tale.

Details of the Echelon affair that spilled from a debate in the European Parliament stirred a lot of anti-U.S. sentiment in Europe, and singularly among the French public who accused Washington of being behind all of the spy network's eavesdropping exploits. But in the hullabaloo the French government remained strangely silent despite strident calls by many leading public figures for Paris to denounce the existence of Echelon. In truth, officials concerned with such matters in Paris were ill-at-ease, either at the defense ministry or in the French prime minister's office.

Intelligence Newsletter has received information confirming that the French foreign intelligence agency, DGSE [Direction Générale de la Sécurité], has long worked closely with the U.S. NSA in the eavesdropping field. According to a retired officer who worked for DGSE until 1991, the transfer of know-how enabled the French secret service to build up an effective interception network of its own between 1985 and 1990.[4]

Everyone is getting very upset.

According to the president of the European Police Trade Unions and the chairman of the Association of Security Consultants, the annual damage caused by industrial espionage in German industry alone is about 20 billion deutsche marks (US$120 billion).

According to Vienna's International Chamber of Commerce (ICC), the Austrian industry suffers losses of 8–14 billion schillings ($682 million to $1.7 billion) per year from espionage activities.

Even the head of Belgium's Surete d'Etat said in 1997 that he would like to see his service step into the business intelligence fray. So the service hired 100 new inspectors to be assigned specifically to helping businesses and universities protect Belgium's economic, industrial, and scientific secrets.

Of course, economic espionage is a worldwide problem, it isn't just a post–Cold War squabble between the industrialized democracies of the West.

---

3. "Why We Spy on Our Allies," by R. James Woolsey, *Wall Street Journal*, March 17, 2000.

4. "French Secretly Embarrassed over Echelon," *Intelligence Newsletter #378*, March 16, 2000.

Indeed, the growth of the global economy means that you have competitors on other continents, not just in other cities. And the commercialization of the Internet means that those competitors, wherever they are, can reach your internal information systems.

Here are some other examples of the international glut in economic espionage.

The Japanese and the Koreans are both perceived as being extremely aggressive in the field of economic espionage. But as you can see by the following incidents, they too have been targeted, by the Russians and the Taiwanese.

In February 1998, the Japanese government disclosed that Russian intelligence agents had hired a 59-year-old Japanese freelance translator with a technical background to render the internal documents of high-tech companies into English.

The translator soon gained access to classified information.

Four Russian intelligence agents, using false Japanese names and tradecraft, met with him more than 60 times. The man would hand off the translated documents to his contacts as he passed them in a narrow lane in a residential area. They paid him about eight million yen (US $66,000) and gifts, including a watch.

In 1998, South Korean authorities arrested 19 people for stealing secret semiconductor technology from the Samsung Electronics Company, the world's largest memory-chip maker, and selling it to Nanya Technology Corporation, a Taiwanese company, for $100,000 a month.

In 1995, the Canadian Security Intelligence Service (CSIS) reported that a number of Canadian companies operating in vital sectors had been targeted by foreign governments to obtain economic or commercial advantage.

The damage to Canadian interests takes the form of lost contracts, jobs, and markets, and, overall, a diminished competitive advantage. Information and technology that have been the target of economic espionage include trade and pricing information, investment strategy, contract details, supplier lists, planning documents, research and development data, technical drawings, and computer databases.

Two incidents among many serve as examples:

A Canadian company's technology was compromised when the company, hoping to secure a lucrative contract from a foreign government, allowed a national of that country to work on a sensitive, leading-edge technology project. The foreign government then proceeded to duplicate the technology based on the information obtained through the direct access their representative agent had to this project.

A foreign government is believed to have tasked its intelligence service to gather specific information. The intelligence service in turn contracted with computer hackers to help meet the objective, in the course of which the hackers penetrated databases of two Canadian companies. These activities resulted in the compromise of the companies' numerous computer systems, passwords, personnel, and research files.

Yes, your eyes are getting sore, and we haven't even looked yet at the activities of the People's Republic of China.

EEA Sinks Its Teeth In

In October 1996, U.S. President Bill Clinton signed the Economic Espionage Act (EEA) into law. The EEA makes it a federal crime to take, download, receive, or possess trade secret data without consent.

The following is a summary of the bill's criminal provisions:

(a) Imposes up to a $500,000 fine and a 15-year prison sentence on any person that steals or misappropriates a trade secret in order to advantage a foreign government, instrumentality, or agent.

(b) Imposes up to a $10 million fine on any organization that commits an offense described in (a).

(c) Imposes a fine and up to a 10-year prison sentence on any person who steals a trade secret in order to benefit any party, including a foreign corporation, other than the owner.

(d) Imposes up to a $5 million fine on any organization that commits an offense described in (c).

(See Appendix A for the full text of the EEA.)

As of the end of 1998, five cases had been prosecuted under the Economic Espionage Act (EEA) of 1996. Three cases involved domestic espionage activity: For example, two brothers were arrested for trying to sell information on Pittsburgh Plate Glass to an FBI agent posing as a representative of Dow Corning. The two cases in which foreign interests were revealed involved an attempt to steal an anti-cancer drug formula from Bristol-Myers Squibb and theft of proprietary manufacturing information from Avery Dennison Corp. Taiwanese companies were implicated in both cases. The Avery Dennison case alone is estimated to have resulted in economic losses of $50–60 million.

As of the end of 1999, 18 cases had been engaged in under the EEA.

Let's take a closer look at a few of these cases.

In April 1998, Steven L. Davis, 47, was sentenced to 27 months in prison for five counts of trade secret theft under the EEA. He was also ordered to pay $1,271,171.00

to Gillette and Wright Industries, a subcontractor of Gillette. (The loss figure was stip-ulated in the plea agreement to be between $1 million and $5 million.)

Davis was employed as a process controls engineer for Wright Industries, Inc., a Tennessee designer of fabrication equipment, which had been hired by Gillette to assist in the development of a new shaving system.

In February and March 1997, Davis made technical drawings of the new system avail-able to Gillette's competitors in the razor market, Warner-Lambert Co., Bic, and American Safety Razor Company. He delivered the drawings to Gillette's competitors by fax and e-mail.

In January 2000, a Youngstown, Ohio, federal judge sentenced P. Y. Yang, chief exec-utive of the Taiwan-based Four Pillars Ltd., to two-years probation along with six months of home detention for violating the 1996 Economic Espionage Act. Mr. Yang's daughter, Hwei Chang Yang, was sentenced to one-year probation on the same charge. The Yangs each faced a maximum penalty of 10 years in prison and $250,000 in fines for violating the espionage law.

In April 1999, the Yangs were convicted of paying Ten Hong Lee, a senior research engineer at Avery Dennison, $160,000 over an eight-year period to obtain adhesive formulas and other innovations developed by the company, which is based in Pasadena, California. Four Pillars and Avery Dennison compete in the Asian adhesive-label market.

Four Pillars itself also was convicted on the espionage charges and fined $5 million by a U.S. District Judge for accepting the pilfered secrets. According to the court papers, Avery Dennison estimates a loss of at least $30 million because of the theft.

The Yangs' lawyers countered that Four Pillars never used any of the information it obtained from Avery Dennison to gain a competitive advantage and that the execu-tives have already served two years home detention waiting for a trial.

In February 2000, in a separate trial, a federal jury in Cleveland, Ohio, awarded Avery Dennison $40 million in damages from Four Pillars for stealing Avery's trade secrets by bribing a senior Avery Dennison engineer to get access to confidential information about adhesive formulas and label technology.

Lee supplied Four Pillars with some of Avery's most closely held secrets, prosecutors said, including chemical formulations for Avery's diaper tape and a battery-label lam-inate the company was developing for Duracell's PowerCheck battery. Payment for Lee's services was allegedly laundered through members of his family in Taiwan.

Avery first learned of a possible leak when the company tried to hire a Four Pillars sci-entist. The scientist turned down the job but allegedly told Avery officials that some-one was leaking secrets to Four Pillars.

Avery hired a private investigator and in October 1996 went to the FBI.

In January 1997, Lee and other Avery officials were invited to a meeting and told of a file containing secret details of the company's business plans in Asia. A video camera later captured Lee going through the file.

In March 1997, FBI agents confronted Lee, and he subsequently pleaded guilty to one count of wire fraud and agreed to cooperate with federal investigators.

In September 1997, with Lee's cooperation, the FBI set up a second sting at a hotel near Cleveland. There, Lee met with the Yangs in a room monitored by a concealed video camera and provided them with a secret Avery patent application and other proprietary documents. The video recorded the Yangs using a knife to slice out portions of the documents, reportedly portions that contained the Avery logo and wording that indicated the documents were privileged and confidential. The Yangs were arrested several hours later at the Cleveland airport as they were about to leave the country.

In 1999, 53% of CSI/FBI respondents considered their U.S. corporate competitors as a likely source of attack. In 2000, the number of respondents who viewed their competitors as a likely source of attack dropped to 44%. Could the increase in EEA cases be a contributing factor? Hopefully, and quite possibly.

Naomi Fine of Pro-Tec Data (www.pro-tecdata.com), one of the world's leading authorities on economic espionage and how to thwart it, explains, "There has been a greater perception of the value of proprietary information over the last few years. Look at some of the indictments under the Economic Espionage Act. You can see that there are greater claims for the cost of the trade secret, greater claims for the value of the trade secret and for the consequences of the loss. This heightened awareness of value may contribute to the increase in size of the losses that the survey results reflect.

"In the hyper-competitive business environment," she says, "there is a perceived increase in the value of information in general. People have a better understanding of how much information is needed in order to compete effectively. People are realizing, 'We own it. We have every right to protect it. We are not out there just trying to be litigious. This is serious business.'

"The whole environment has changed," she continues, "and because it has changed, people are more inclined to report to legal counsel and law enforcement. They don't just slough it off. They don't see it as 'just information,' they see it as the life-blood of what they're doing."

Fine feels that the EEA has not only contributed to respondents' ability to quantify their financial losses, but also to their willingness to report such incidents to both legal counsel and law enforcement.

"The EEA actually has benefited the business community both because it provides heightened visibility and awareness and because it demonstrates that law enforcement is serious and that there are Federal resources available to help U.S. companies to combat such activity."

The stakes are getting very high in EEA-related criminal investigations.

In March 2000, a federal grand jury in San Jose, California indicted a former engineer at Intel Corp., Say Lye Ow, a 29-year-old Malaysian, under the Economic Espionage Act.

Investigators accuse Ow of stealing Intel secrets before he left the company in 1998, and particularly documents concerning a microprocessor twice as powerful as those developed up to now. The new microprocessor, which Intel has been developing for the past six years under the name Itanium, is due to be released summer 2000.

The indictment says that Intel's information was found during a search of Ow's office in May 1998 after he had taken a job at Sun Microsystems.

Intel isn't accusing Sun itself of unfair practices…yet.

Seven Steps to EEA Compliance

What should you do to ensure that your enterprise is EEA-compliant?

Naomi Fine offers some practical advice.

First, find out about some of those corporate cultures or subcultures in your organization so that you understand what your company's true risk tolerance is and what your company's standard is for addressing these gray areas. Second, put in place an Economic Espionage Act compliance program.

The EEA provides a specific road map for developing and implementing a compliance program because the federal sentencing guidelines provide a very clear seven-step program for complying with any federal crime.

According to Fine, the following seven steps will help you avoid committing a crime and reduce your culpability:

1. Compliance standards and procedures: "The organization must have established compliance standards and procedures to be followed by its employees and other agents that are reasonably capable of reducing the prospect of criminal conduct."

2. Responsibility to oversee compliance: "Specific individual(s) within high-level personnel of the organization must have been assigned overall responsibility to oversee compliance with such standards and procedures."

3. Delegation of discretion: "The organization must have used due care not to delegate substantial discretionary authority to individuals whom the organization knew or should have known through the exercise of due diligence had a propensity to engage in illegal activities."

4. Communications and training: "The organization must have taken steps to communicate effectively its standards and procedures to all employees and other agents, e.g. by requiring participation in training programs or by disseminating publications that explain in a practical manner what is required."

5. Monitoring and reporting: "The organization must have taken reasonable steps to achieve compliance with its standards by utilizing, monitoring, and auditing systems designed to detect criminal conduct by its employees and other agents and by having in place and publicizing a reporting system whereby employees and other agents could report criminal conduct by others within the organization without fear of retribution."

6. Enforcement and discipline: "Standards must have been consistently enforced, through appropriate disciplinary mechanisms, including, as appropriate, discipline of individuals responsible for the failure to detect an offense. Adequate discipline of individuals responsible for an offense is a necessary component of enforcement; however, the form of discipline that will be appropriate will be case specific."

7. Continuous improvement: "After an offense has been detected, the organization must have taken all reasonable steps to respond appropriately to the offense and to prevent further similar offenses including any necessary modification to its program to prevent and detect violations of law."

Fine also suggests that you revise relevant documentation.

"One of the things that a court would be looking at is all the documentation that reflects your company's intent," she explains, "for example, a statement that says it is our company's policy not to use the information that may be a trade secret of another company without the consent of the other company." Fine says you can include this language in employment applications and employment offer letters, your code of conduct or your ethics statement, information protection policies, employee and management reference materials such as handbooks and procedure manuals, and employee and management training that you already have in place. "You should also include it in your contractor or vendor rules."

Fine highlights some of the EEA's profound implication for information protection professionals.

"You should have a greater interest in monitoring the information that's accessed or stored on your computing resources," she counsels. "Knowing that you will have personal liability in the event that someone takes trade secret information from another company without their consent and stores it in and uses it on your computing resources, you should have a greater personal concern as to what information resides on your computing resources.

"You should also have an increased concern about sharing information within your computing resources," she continues. "Access controls are now more important than ever. Without access controls, trade secret information from another company could infect your entire network and could spread the liability and the culpability of your company.

"You should also exercise increased vigilance in computer security," Fine concludes. "It will help your company take advantage of the EEA: By taking reasonable steps to protect your own information, you are putting your company in a better position to help you pursue enemies who take your information and use it for their benefit."

Insiders: The Wrath of the Disgruntled Employee

E ach year, the *CSI/FBI Computer Crime and Security Survey* asks the respondents (large Fortune 500–type corporations and big government agencies) to rate the likely sources of cyberattack. Invariably, for five years now, disgruntled and dishonest employees have topped the list, with more than 80% of respondents citing them as a likely source, and for good reason.

While the external threat from hackers and trade secret thieves has increased, the danger from insider attacks has remained constant. The internal threat has not diminished. It is as palpable and immediate as ever.

The danger is reflected in other survey results as well. For example, in the 2000 CSI/FBI survey, reports of unauthorized access by insiders rose for the fourth straight year: In 1999, 55% of respondents reported incidents, but in 2000 it jumped to 71%.

There are numerous, published reports of high-profile incidents of insider crimes, misdemeanors, and abuses. And for every published report I could cite you, dozens more occur and are hushed up.

Types of Cyberattack by Insiders

What types of cyberattacks are perpetrated from the inside?

Financial fraud has been a serious white-collar crime problem for a very long time. But in the Information Age, it is also a computer crime.

In the 2000 CSI/FBI Survey, financial fraud was reported by 11% of the huge organizations that responded. Only 13 of the 68 organizations that had reported financial fraud could quantify the dollar losses involved. But the total dollar loss for those 13 organizations amounted to $55,996,000. And the aggregate loss for financial fraud reported by respondents over the last four years amounts to $131,903,00.

Most incidents of computer-based financial fraud are the work of insiders.

For example, Nikita Rose, a 26-year-old woman, was sentenced to eight months in prison along with three years of supervised release afterward for accessing a computer to defraud Salomon Brothers Investors Fund of $538,325 in shareholder funds.

In November 1999 Tania Ventura, a 26-year-old cashier at Bloomingdale's, the swank East Side department store in New York City, was placed under investigation for credit card theft. After swiping the credit cards through the store's credit device, Ventura allegedly swiped them through a second time, but in a credit card scanner attached to her Palm Pilot.

Of course, it is important to note that as Internet-based electronic commerce has increased, financial fraud conducted by outsiders will also increase. (See Chapter 7.)

Other serious cyberattacks perpetrated by disgruntled or dishonest employees, temporary workers, and contractors include theft of proprietary information for sale to competitors (see Chapter 10) and sabotage of data and networks for the sake of revenge.

An information-security program, no matter how sophisticated or comprehensive, cannot be airtight. There is no such state as 100% security. If you could create such an environment, you would not be able to conduct business in it. The aim of information security is always to minimize the risks: make financial fraud, theft of proprietary information, sabotage of data and network, and other serious cyberattacks less likely.

To understand the growing problem of unauthorized access by insiders, according to Rebecca Herold, formerly of The Principal Financial Group and now of the Netigy Corporation, you must understand the context under which it is increasing.

Unauthorized access by insiders is increasing because of the expanding use of intranets and extranets. These types of networks are usually not implemented with comprehensive access controls. By definition, they are meant to be open.

Furthermore, for the sake of convenience, sensitive information is often placed on these networks and is made more accessible to disgruntled or dishonest insiders. With the increased technological capabilities and savvy, far too many people still assume that ignorance is a good control. The attitude prevails that "if people don't know I'm putting something out on this site, they will not know to look."

The increasing use of remote access technology also lends itself to unauthorized access. Sometimes dial-in systems are implemented without mirroring the access controls that are present for people who have to log in to the network within corporate facilities.

In an environment dependent on intranets, extranets, and remote access, the potential threat from the three types of cyberattack mentioned increases.

Insiders could use information to engage in financial fraud resulting from their access to customer and employee credit information, Social Security numbers, account information, etc. Dishonest employees or non-employee insiders could use unauthorized access to gather information to provide your competitors with advantages. The sabotage perpetrated by insiders could compromise network availability or completely shut a network down.

To get a handle on the situation, Herold suggests organizations must develop a body of policies and back them up with access control technologies.

Organizations definitely need to implement policies to allow insiders minimal access: for example, deny everything except for that which is explicitly needed to fulfill job requirements. They need to observe additional policies to remove insider access to certain resources as soon as insiders are transferred to new job responsibilities and to completely remove access as soon as insiders are terminated. System access controls should be configured to ensure compliance with these policies.

It is also advisable to determine where the critical systems or sensitive information reside on the internal networks and consider deploying internal firewalls, which can guard the gateways to these vital points, just as a firewall is deployed at the Internet gateway.

Here are two stories that epitomize different aspects of the insider threat.

Oracle Scorned: The Unauthorized Access of Adelyn Lee

What is unauthorized access by insiders? Well, it can take many forms. Consider the case of Adelyn Lee.

Adelyn Lee was either a marketing coordinator or an executive assistant (depending on whom you ask) at Oracle Corporation.

The news media reported that Lee allegedly had an office romance with Oracle's CEO, Larry Ellison from November 1991 until April 1993. (Ellison is one of the richest people in the country, with a net worth of $1.6 billion, according to *Forbes* magazine.)

Five days after their last date, her employment was terminated.

Lee sued Oracle for wrongful dismissal, claiming that Ellison had ordered her to be fired because she wouldn't have sex with him. She also alleged that he had warned her that she would lose her job if she ended the relationship.

Craig Ramsey, an Oracle vice president and Lee's direct supervisor, said the company let her go because she lacked sensitivity to business issues and was incapable of interacting with other employees.

Many pages of e-mail messages exchanged between Lee and Ellison during their affair were central to the civil case. One vital piece of evidence was a message supposedly sent to Ellison by Ramsey after Lee's dismissal. The message read "I have terminated Adelyn per your request."

Ellison had responded: "Are you out of your mind! I did not request that you terminate Adelyn. I did not want to get involved in the decision for obvious reasons."

Lee won a $100,000 settlement in the civil case.

But Lee's triumph unraveled on her.

San Mateo County Deputy District Attorney Paul Wasserman concluded that Ramsey could not have sent the e-mail because his cell phone records indicated that he was driving in his car at the time that the alleged e-mail had been sent. As Ramsey's executive assistant, Lee knew his passwords (and indeed had been responsible for changing them for him periodically). Lee was then charged with felony perjury for lying and sending false e-mail.

The prosecutor said Lee sent the message herself by conducting unauthorized access into Ramsey's account on Oracle's e-mail system. He sought to portray Lee as a greedy and conniving woman who had tried to use her torrid affair with Ellison to solicit gifts and favors. E-mail messages in which Lee asked for an Acura NSX, a loan, and a Rolex watch were submitted as evidence.

On January 28, 1997, Lee was found guilty of felony perjury and the falsification of evidence. She was handcuffed and taken to jail. Her friends withdrew $100,000 from her bank account and tried to bail her out. But a judge ruled that the bail money was "tainted" because it had been won as a result of the forged e-mail evidence.

The judge ordered Lee's account frozen pending a sentencing determination that she might have to pay the $100,000 back to Oracle.

In July 1999, Adelyn Lee lost an appeal on her perjury conviction.

Posting to Risks Forum back in April 1996, Peter G. Neumann of SRI International enumerated some of the lessons to be learned from the sordid affair.

1. Don't believe that e-mail FROM: headers accurately represent the sender.
2. Don't believe the content of e-mail, whether or not the headers are correct.
3. Don't share your passwords overtly with anyone or let someone else be responsible for your passwords.
4. Don't use covertly compromisible reusable fixed passwords;1 how often you change them is more or less irrelevant.
5. Use one-time nonreusable authentication tokens instead of fixed passwords.
6. Even if you use PEM, PGP, stronger-crypto e-mail, or whatever, you cannot ensure authenticity because of untrustworthy operating systems and untrustworthy users.
7. Beware of trying to use e-mail as nonrepudiatable court evidence.
8. However, don't believe that cell-phone records are valid as court evidence. They too could be bogus or altered. If someone drags you into court, find someone who can demonstrate how easily those records could have been altered!

Omega Man: The Implosion of Tim Lloyd

In the 2000 CSI/FBI survey, 28 respondents were able to quantify financial losses from incidents involving sabotage of data or networks for a total of $27,148,000. Here are some news items that illustrate the impact of such insider attacks.

In 1996, a Hong Kong computer operator crashed Reuters computer network, disrupting financial trading to five banks for 36 hours.

In November 1997, a temporary staff computer technician was charged with breaking into the computer system of Forbes, Inc., publisher of *Forbes* magazine, and causing a computer crash that cost the company more than $100,000. According to the complaint against George Mario Parente, the sabotage left hundreds of Forbes employees unable to perform server-related functions for a full day and caused many employees to lose a

---

1. For example, clear text passwords—passwords that are not encrypted—can be intercepted during transmission; passwords that are easily guessed can be broken in seconds by password cracking software; passwords can also be gleaned from the naive user through hackers with social engineering skills.

day's worth of data.

In July 1998, the first woman convicted of computer hacking in the United States was sentenced for trashing a U.S. Coast Guard personnel database.

Shakuntla Devi Singla, 43, a former Coast Guard employee, was sentenced to five months in jail plus five months of house arrest and was ordered to pay $35,000 restitution for destroying information and crashing the system. It took 115 Coast Guard employees, including network administrators, more than 1,800 hours to restore the lost data. The recovery effort cost $40,000.

In October 1999, a former Federal Aviation Administration (FAA) engineer was charged with stealing the only copy of a computer code for software used to direct jetliners at O'Hare International Airport. A federal grand jury charged Thomas Varlotta, 42, with damaging and stealing government property. He faces up to 25 years in prison. Prosecutors say he erased the code from a hard drive and quit the next day. The code was later recovered in a search of his home, although it had been encrypted and required six months to unscramble.

In March 2000, Abdelkader Smires, 31, a database engineer angry at his employer, was arrested on charges of using codes to disable computers in a three-day cyberattack on his company, Internet Trading Technologies. The attacks were traced to a computer at Queens College and authorities determined that Smires, who had once taught computer science there, had been using that computer.

But none of these real-world incidents of sabotage by disgruntled insiders rivals the case of the Omega Man, Tim Allen Lloyd of New Castle, Delaware.

In May 2000, Lloyd, a 37-year old former network administrator for Omega Engineering Corp. of Bridgeport, New Jersey, was convicted in the first federal prosecution of a computer sabotage case. The jury, which deliberated for more than three days, decided Lloyd was guilty of planting a timebomb that deleted more than a thousand programs vital to the company's high-tech measurement and control instruments manufacturing operation.

According to Omega, which serves NASA and the U.S. Navy as well as customers in the private sector, Lloyd's sabotage resulted in damages, lost contracts, and lost productivity that totaled more than $10 million.

Lloyd had worked for Omega for 11 years. He had hustled his way up from a lowly machinist to file system administrator. On July 10, 1996, Lloyd was terminated.

Sharon Gaudin, a *Network World* correspondent who covered the trial from start to finish and immersed herself thoroughly in the details of this fascinating case, provides some insight into Lloyd's downward spiral.

"About a year earlier," she recounts, "Lloyd went from being a star employee to an angry man who lashed out, verbally and physically, at his co-workers, bottlenecked projects simply because he wasn't in charge of them, and even knowingly loaded faulty programs to make co-workers look bad, according to Omega executives. In that year, he had received verbal warnings, was written up twice, and demoted.

"Lloyd was lashing out at his co-workers because his ego was bruised," Gaudin observes. "He was the genesis of the network, and suddenly his status and clout were slipping away from him. And a team player he did not want to be. Lloyd, who had started interviewing for a new job early in June of 1996, had started planning to leave Omega months before he was fired. Either way he was going out the door, he was planning on leaving a parting gift for the company that had 'disrespected' him."

On July 30, 1996, two weeks after Lloyd was terminated, his timebomb was activated just as he had planned. It deleted more than one thousand programs and purged them irretrievably. The programs that Lloyd's timebomb destroyed had enabled Omega to manufacture 25,000 products and customize them into 500,000 different designs.

Lloyd had worked late on February 21, April 21, and May 30, 1996. During those off-hours, he had free reign over Omega's file server. He had tested his timebomb successfully, deleting the data and then restoring it. It worked flawlessly.

Those at Omega struggling to recover from the serious crash that occurred on July 30 started to scramble around looking for the backup tapes. After all, when all else fails, you just have to restore from the backups. But what if the backups have disappeared?

Lloyd had been in charge of doing the backups to the system that had crashed.

As Gaudin explains, Jim Ferguson, Omega's plant manager, put in a call to Lloyd.

"Ferguson says Lloyd told him he didn't have the backup tape," Gaudin says. "Lloyd, according to testimony, says he left them in the upper left-hand corner drawer of his desk at Omega. But Ferguson himself had helped clean out Lloyd's desk. There was no backup tape there.

"Ferguson called Lloyd again and again," Gaudin adds. "Once, Lloyd said he would check around his house but never called back. Ferguson called again and Lloyd said he hadn't had a chance to check. Ferguson called again and Lloyd told him he had some tapes but not Omega's tapes. Ferguson then recorded one of his calls and went to Lloyd's house to plead in person. While he was there, Lloyd handed over a pneumatic pump, a computer case, and a power cord. No backup tape.

"The plant manager says even while he was pleading with Lloyd for information about the tape, he still was having a hard time imagining that Lloyd would have damaged the system. Ferguson had held on to that kind of trust even when Lloyd had become a problem employee."

On August 12, 1996, Omega placed a call to the U.S. Secret Service, which assigned Special Agent William Hoffman and launched a four-year criminal investigation. (For more on the role of the U.S. Secret Service in the battle for law and order in cyberspace, see Chapter 17.)

As Gaudin explains, Lloyd was the focus of the investigation from the beginning.

Lloyd had Novell certification training, he had complete access to the system, he was the last one with the backup tape, and he had a motive.

Hoffman, along with several other Secret Service agents, conducted a search on Lloyd's home Aug. 21, 1996. The agents seized about 700 pieces of potential evidence. That haul included computers, motherboards, keyboards, more than 500 disks, CD-ROMs, 12 hard drives, and tapes.

"What immediately stuck out from that haul were two backup tapes, which had both been erased," Gaudin says. "One was labeled *Backup* with the dates 5/14/96 and 7/1/96 and the words *Tim Lloyd*. July 1, 1996 was the date that Lloyd had asked for and been given Omega's backup tape. Both had been reformatted, which erases the tapes, the day before Ferguson visited Lloyd's house asking about the tapes."

Meanwhile, at Ontrack Data International in Eden Prairie, Minnesota, Greg Olson, director of Ontrack's Worldwide Data Recovery Services, was examining forensic evidence to determine what caused the devastating crash.

According to Gaudin, Olson searched the wreckage of the Omega file server for common commands or phrases used in deletion processes until he had pieced together six lines that looked like they could do some real damage.

Gaudin says that to test the code, Olson took an exact copy of the Omega file server and set up a test environment with an attached workstation. He then configured the system for various dates prior to the July 30, 1996 date at the beginning of the code string. Olson configured the system for January 1, 1996 and logged in. Nothing unusual happened. Then he configured the system for April 30, 1996 and logged in. Nothing unusual happened. He then tried July 29, 1996. Nothing unusual happened. Olson then tested July 30, 1996, matching the configuration date up with the date in the code. Nothing.

Then he configured the system for July 31, 1996, one day after the date in the code and the exact date of the crash at Omega. "I logged on and everything on the system was deleted," he told the jury. "On the screen, it was saying it was fixing an area of the system, but actually it was deleting everything.... Everything was gone."

"And Olson says some planning went into this," Gaudin says. "Along with the six lines of code that did the damage, Olson also found three similar test programs. Those three programs, each similar to the six lines of code in the damaging program, were dated Feb. 21, 1996; April 21, 1996; and May 30, 1996. The first two programs had only one line that was dissimilar from the damaging code. That one line substituted a simple test folder, which could have held as little as one word, for the line in the damaging code that called for everything on the server to be deleted. The third test program dated for May 30 was set up exactly as the code that brought down the system."

"This tells everyone that we're capable," Assistant U.S. Attorney V. Grady O'Malley, who prosecuted the case for four weeks in Newark District Court, told Gaudin. "There are people out there who believe they can't be caught. This shows them that we can track down the evidence, understand it, and logically present it to a jury."

Six Lines of Code = $10 Million in Financial Losses

`7/30/96`

The date is the triggering point in the code string, executing the rest of the commands as long as it is after July 30, 1996.

`F:`

This line of the code gives access to the server.

`F:\LOGIN\LOGIN 12345`

This automatically piggybacks User 12345, which has supervisory rights and no password security, with whichever user first logs in on the file server.

`CD \PUBLIC`

This line gives access to the public directory, a common storage area on the file server.

`FIX.EXE /Y F:\*.*`

FIX.EXE is a DOS-based executable file that served as the deletion command but

showed the word *fixing* on the screen instead of *deleting*. This is a slightly modified version of the MS-DOS program Deltree.exe.

/Y answers *yes* to the implied question of "Do you want to delete these files?"

F:*.* refers to all files and folders on the entire server volume

```
PURGE F:\ /ALL
```

This line calls for all the deleted information to be immediately purged.

The Lloyd and Lee cases underscore the difference between a comprehensive information protection program that incorporates personnel security policies and procedures and security awareness training for users as well as firewalls, encryption, and
passwords.

Consider the Lee case. Oracle could have deployed the strongest firewalls in Silicon
Valley. Oracle could have used the toughest encryption available in its Internet communications. But neither technology would have thwarted Lee's e-mail forgery and
saved Oracle the ensuing legal imbroglio. Co-workers shouldn't share passwords.
(Well, authentication shouldn't rely solely on passwords anyway, but that's a bigger
issue.) Having a corporate policy that says you shouldn't share your passwords with
co-workers is one of the most basic concepts in information security.

Of course, Oracle could have had such a policy in place. Perhaps it was ignored.
That's one of the weaknesses of relying too much on policy: Just because you have a
policy doesn't mean employees adhere to it. There must be consequences for violation of such policies. And users, particularly executive-level users, must be impressed
with the risks that the policy is intended to mitigate. Security awareness training for
users at all levels of your organization is vital. (See Chapter 19.)

However, in the Lee case, Ellison was already endangering himself and his corporation by breaking even more fundamental corporate taboos about becoming involved
with subordinates. It is hard to imagine that an e-mail password protection policy
would have impressed him very much.

Nevertheless, a corporation drawn into court in some case that hinges on e-mail evidence is a lot better off if it can show that it at least has a such a policy in place. In
court, you must be able to show a standard of due care. You must be able to demonstrate that you have taken reasonable measures to protect your information and educate your users about inappropriate activity and its consequences.

Instituting personnel policies regarding information protection also helps to mitigate your risk from a wide range of insider abuses and attacks.

Consider the Lloyd case. Lloyd had been a troubled employee for quite a while before he trashed Omega's computer operations. There had been serious problems. He was known to be disgruntled. He had been involved in altercations. He had voiced his dissatisfaction. He was going to be fired. And yet, he had unrestricted and unmonitored access to Omega's internal networks. He had control of the backup tapes.

In an organization that takes information protection seriously and has instituted a comprehensive program, if someone like a Lloyd comes to the attention of the personnel department, it is a matter of policy and procedure that information security is notified. (Well, that's based on the assumption that there is an information security department to notify. See Chapter 15.)

If personnel and information security are working on the problem together, a lot can be done to mitigate the risk of sabotage from a disgruntled and soon-to-be-exiting employee.

Having a body of personnel policies regarding information protection will also mean that you will pay more attention to whom you are hiring in the first place. In this way, through background checks, etc., you can mitigate the risk of bringing in people who will develop into problems later on.

Infowar and Cyberterror: The Sky Is Not Falling, But...

On September 20, 1999, *Newsweek* ran the following story with a headline that read "We're in the middle of a cyberwar":

> It's being called "Moonlight Maze," an appropriately cryptic name for one of the most potentially damaging breaches of American computer security ever....
>
> ...The suspects: crack cyberspooks from the Russian Academy of Sciences, a government-supported organization that interacts with Russia's top military labs. The targets: computer systems at the Department of Defense and Energy, military contractors and leading civilian universities. The haul: vast quantities of data that, intelligence sources familiar with the case tell *Newsweek*, could include classified naval codes and information on missile-guidance systems. This was, Pentagon officials say flatly, "a state-sponsored Russian intelligence effort to get U.S. technology...."
>
> ...As a federal interagency task force begins its damage assessment, a key question is whether or not the Russians managed to jump from the unclassified (although non-public) systems where they made their initial penetration into the classified Department of Defense network that contains the most sensitive data.

> ...Besides, one intelligence official admitted, classified data often lurk in unclassified databases. With enough time and computer power, the Russians could not sift through their mountains of pilfered information and deduce those secrets they didn't directly steal.[1]

Well, September 20 is my birthday. When I read this story, I wondered if the Gods of Cloak and Dagger had given me a lovely present to unwrap. If this much of the story had made it to the pages of *Newsweek*, someone wanted it to get out.

"What can you tell me about 'Moonlight Maze?'" I asked my unimpeachable source at the DoD.

"All I say is that everything in that story is true."

If the *Newsweek* piece had been inaccurate or exaggerated, my source wouldn't have hesitated to say so.

There may or may not ever be a definitive statement made about "Moonlight Maze." But it was, indeed, the real deal.

Indeed, one Russian "leader" couldn't keep from boasting.

On December 19, 1999, Reuters reported that Russia's "maverick politician," Vladimir Zhirinovsky, was asked if he would have a drink to celebrate the results of the parliamentary elections. "No. No way, we Russians don't drink anymore." he replied.

"We now use computers to send viruses to the West, and then we poach your money. We have the best hackers in the world."

Information warfare (IW), or information operations as it is also referred to, is a very difficult beat to cover.

If you cover it, you are going to be filing your stories from a realm of smoke and mirrors. The more truth there is to some tale of infowar, at least at this juncture in history, the less will be said about it by official sources.

But having spent several years in that realm of smoke and mirrors, I can tell you, unequivocally, there are large powerful bodies moving in the shadows.

If you cover it honestly, you're going to get heat from both sides. The naysayers will accuse you of banging the war drum for the Pentagon. "The DoD is just looking for new threats to use as an excuse for more budget dollars," doubters will argue. But the Chicken Littles clucking "the sky is falling, the sky is falling" and tearing out their feathers over dire predictions of some "electronic Pearl Harbor" will accuse you of underestimating the severity of the threat.

---

1. "We're in the middle of a cyberwar," by Gregory Vistica, *Newsweek*, September 20, 1999

But having spent several years in that zone of responsibility between the extremes of denial and bombast, I tell you it is just where you want to be on this particular subject. Despite garbled, tabloid-style news items about impending "electronic Pearl Harbors" and "cyberspace Chernobyls," there is justifiable concern over potentially devastating attacks against critical, national infrastructures such as the power grid, the telecommunications network, and the air traffic control system. (Remember, as of 1998, an estimated 20,000 people have already died due to the catastrophe at Chernobyl. Those who invoke its name should be more circumspect.)

The term *information warfare* has been used in different ways by different people with different motives, as Martin Libicki of National Defense University explains.

"Coming to grips with information warfare is like the effort of the blind men to discover the nature of the elephant: The one who touched its leg called it a tree, another who touched its tail called it a rope, and so on. Is a good definition possible? Does having one matter? Perhaps there is no elephant: only trees and ropes that aspire to become one. One aspect of information warfare, perhaps championed by a single constituency, assumes the role of the entire concept, thus becoming grossly inflated in importance."

For example, the military and intelligence professionals who formulated the aggregate of concepts that fall under the term *information warfare* had a very clear, precise understanding of what they meant by it. In military parlance, IW connotes things like command and control warfare (C2W), electronic warfare (EW), psychological operations (PsyOps), etc.

But there are two "information warfare" arenas.

One is the domain of those actually involved in national security. The other is a three-ring circus of pulp fiction, hyperbole, and shameless self-promotion. It is important to distinguish one from the other.

Within the arena of genuine "information warfare," the hardcore national security issues (such as the risk of serious attacks on vital infrastructure) first raised by military and intelligence professionals are being addressed at the highest levels of government and industry.

Libicki has characterized much of what is offered up in the other IW arena as being of the "bogeyman variety," and focused mostly on "hacker warfare." He has even devised a table on "Information Warfare: What's New and What's Effective," which serves as a useful tool for separating the fantasy from the reality.

Table 12.1   Information Warfare: What It Is and What It Isn't

Form	Subtype	Is It New	Effectiveness
C2W	Antihead	Command systems, rather than commanders, are the target	New technologies of dispersion and replication suggest that tomorrow's command centers can be protected.
	Antineck	Hard-wire communication links matter	New techniques (e.g., redundancy, efficient error coding) permit operations under reduced bit flow.
IBW		The cheaper the silicon the more can be thrown into the system that looks for targets	The United States will build the first system of seeking systems, but, stealth aside, pays too little attention to hiding.
EW	Antiradar	Around since WWII	Dispersed generators and collectors will survive attack better than monolithic systems.
	Anticomms	Around since WWII	Spread spectrum, frequency hopping, and directional antennas all suggest communications will get through.
	Crypotography	Digital code making is now easy	New codemaking technologies (DES, PKE) favor code makers over code breakers.

Form	Subtype	Is It New	Effectiveness
Psychological Warfare	Antiwill	No	Propaganda must adapt first to CNN, then to Me-TV.
	Antitroop	No	Propaganda must adapt first to DBS, then to Me-TV.
	Anticommander	No	The basic calculus of deception will still be difficult.
Hacker Warfare		Yes	All societies are becoming potentially more vulnerable, but good housekeeping can secure systems.
Economic Information Warfare	Economic Blockade	Yes	Very few countries are yet that dependent on big-bandwidth information flows.
Cyberwarfare	Techno-Imperialism	Since the 1970s	Trade and war involve competition, but trade is not war.
	Info-Terrorism	Dirty linen is dirty linen whether paper or computer files	The threat may be a good reason for tough privacy laws. Too soon to tell.
	Semantic	Yes	
	Simula-warfare	Approaching virtual reality	If both sides are civilized enough to simulate warfare, why would they fight at all?
	Gibson-warfare	Yes	The stuff of science fiction.

Source: Martin Libicki, National Defense University, Current and Future Danger: A CSI Primer on Computer Crime & Information Warfare.

Consider the following excerpts from the testimony of John Deutch, who was at that time the Director of the Central Intelligence Agency, during the U.S. Senate's "Security in Cyberspace" hearings in 1996.

> Our government, business and citizens have become increasingly dependent on an interconnected network of telecommunications and computer-based information systems. The National Intelligence Council, with help from a number of intelligence community agencies, produced a classified report compiling our knowledge of foreign information warfare plans and programs. While the details are classified and cannot be discussed here, we have evidence that a number of countries around the world are developing the doctrine, strategies and tools to conduct information attacks. At present, most of these efforts are limited to information dominance on the battlefield; crippling an enemy's military command and control centers, or disabling an air defense network prior to launching an air attack. However, I am convinced that there is a growing awareness around the world that advanced societies, especially the U.S., are increasingly dependent on open, and potentially vulnerable information systems.

Indeed, during the "Security in Cyberspace" hearings, it was revealed that, according to the National Security Agency (NSA), at least 100 nations are preparing for information warfare in the twenty-first century.

Here are some examples of the ways in which infowar and cyberterror have already altered the delicate balance between war and peace in the Information Age.

Cyberwar in Kosovo?

In 1999, the North Atlantic Treaty Organization (NATO) launched "Operation Allied Force," a military action to thwart the Serbian campaign of ethnic cleansing against the Albanians of Kosovo. It was a successful endeavor. Millions of Albanian Kosovar refugees returned to their homes.

The war in Kosovo was also a cyberwar laboratory. It has been referred to as the first war of the Internet age.

Of course, there was a lot of digital rocks and bottles hurled across cyberspace.

For example, during the military action itself, NATO announced that its Web server in Brussels had been under a ping-of-death attack from somewhere within Serbia. In retaliation, various Internet denizens sent half a million e-mail bombs to www.gov.yu, the main Yugoslav Web site.

There were also reports of a U.S. group called Team Spl0it and European and Albanian hackers altering Serbian Web sites, as well Russian hackers going after U.S. Navy Web sites.

Hackers with Chinese Internet addresses mounted a cyberblitz against United States and allied forces after NATO bombed Beijing's embassy in Belgrade in May, a top Air Force official said. But the blitz emanating from China was "not terribly sophisticated" and consisted mostly of spam meant to clog networks.

But these events, although captivating to the public imagination and the mainstream media, were merely sideshows.

According to one high-level draft briefing paper, a group of information warriors, or what the DoD refers to as an *information operations cell*, was one of the "great successes" of the 78-day war. The briefing also said that IO has "an incredible potential" and that "properly executed, IO could have halved the length of the campaign."

U.S. President Bill Clinton issued an intelligence "finding" allowing the Central Intelligence Agency to find "ways to get at Milosevic." It was a top-secret plan to destabilize Yugoslav leader Slobodan Milosevic and included using computer hackers to attack the foreign bank accounts of Milosevic and his cronies in Russia, Greece, and Cyprus where they had stashed their loot.

But did America go through with its attack on Milosevic's foreign bank accounts?

According to Bruce Berkowitz of the Rand Corporation, writing in the May/June 2000 issue of *Foreign Affairs*, "officials thought they could steal the money electronically and thereby pressure Serbian leaders." But Berkowitz says the plan was scrapped because other officials called it "half-baked."

"After all, banks keep backup records," Berkowitz observed, "so the scam would have failed and, in the process, exposed America's ability to penetrate computer systems."

U.S. commanders also reportedly took a look at attacking the computer systems that controlled public utilities in Serbia. But they decided to hold back. Why?

In November 1999, the *Washington Post* ran a fascinating story entitled "U.S. sees potential and peril in hacking enemy" that highlighted the legal and ethical issues involved in preparing for infowar.

> During last spring's conflict with Yugoslavia, the Pentagon considered hacking into Serbian computer networks to disrupt military operations and basic civilian services.
>
> But it refrained from doing so, according to senior defense officials, because of uncertainties and limitations surrounding the emerging field of cyber warfare.
>
> Midway through the war with Yugoslavia, the Defense Department's top legal office issued guidelines warning that misuse of computer network attacks could subject U.S. authorities to war crimes charges. It advised commanders to apply the same "law of war" principles to computer attack that they do to the use of bombs and missiles. These call for hitting targets that are of military necessity only, minimizing collateral damage and avoiding indiscriminate attacks.

Military officials said concern about legalities was only one of the reasons U.S. authorities resisted the temptation to, say, raid the bank accounts of Slobodan Milosevic. Other reasons included the untested or embryonic state of the U.S. cyber arsenal and the rudimentary or decentralized nature of some Yugoslav systems, which officials said did not lend themselves to computer assault.

U.S. forces did attack some computers that controlled the Yugoslav air defense system, the officials said. But the attacks were launched from electronic jamming aircraft rather than over computer networks.[2]

What really happened in that cyberwar laboratory during Operation Allied Force? It is unlikely you will ever know.

Consider these comments of Berkowitz in *Foreign Affairs*.

Discussing computer warfare policy is even harder because such operations often require secrecy and sometimes require hiding the U.S. government's role. Victory in information warfare depends on knowing something that your adversaries do not and using this advantage to confound, coerce, or kill them. Lose the secrecy and you lose your advantage.

Moreover, such secrecy is often fragile.

Knowing that U.S. forces can penetrate a particular computer system will ensure that America's enemies avoid using it. Simply realizing that the United States is involved in such activities will encourage our foes to protect themselves.[3]

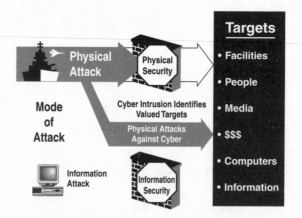

Figure 12.1 Interdependencies: new risks and vulnerabilities.

Source: PCCIP

Of course, information warfare doesn't just consist of hacking. Information itself can be used as a tool: Disinformation and propaganda can be spread very effectively over the Internet. PsyOps is an aspect of infowar.

---

2. "U.S. sees potential and peril in hacking enemy," *Washington Post*, November 8, 1999

3. "War Logs On," by Bruce Berkowitz, Foreign Affairs, Volume 79, Number 3, May/June 2000.

Dismayed by anti-American propaganda worldwide during the conflict, the Clinton Administration struck back with an information offensive of its own: a State Department unit to control the flow of government news overseas, especially during crises. President Clinton signed the directive during the thick of the Kosovo war.

In "Activism, Hacktivism, and Cyberterrorism," the paper I mentioned in Chapter 8, Dr. Dorothy Denning of Georgetown University provides some context for Clinton's directive.

During the Kosovo conflict, people in Yugoslavia had full access to the Internet, including Western news sites. In April 1999, the *Washington Post* reported that, according to U.S. and British officials, the government controlled all four Internet access providers in Yugoslavia and kept them open for the purpose of spreading disinformation and propaganda. The *Post* also said that Belgrade, with a population of 1.5 million, had about 100,000 Internet connections. Individuals without their own connections could get access at Internet cafes.

Even though Serbs had access to Western news reports, both through the Internet and through satellite and cable television, many did not believe what they saw and heard from Western media. They considered coverage on Western television stations such as CNN and Sky News to be as biased as that on the Yugoslav state-run station, citing instances when Western reports of Serbian atrocities turned out to be wrong.

Government Web sites on Kosovo tended to feature propaganda and materials that supported their official policies. An exception was the U.S. Information Agency Web site, which presented a survey of news stories from around the world, some of which were critical of NATO actions. Jonathan Spalter, USIA Chief Information Officer, commented that "The measure of our success is the extent to which we are perceived not as propaganda but anti-propaganda."

The British government's Foreign Office used its Web site, in part, to counter Serb propaganda. Concerned that the Yugoslav public was getting a highly distorted view of the war, Foreign Secretary Robin Cook posted a message on its Web site intended for the Serbs. The message said that Britain has nothing against the Serbs but was forced to act by the scale of Yugoslav President Slobodan Milosevic's brutality.

The Serbs used e-mail distribution lists to reach tens of thousands of users, mostly in the United States, with messages attacking the NATO bombing campaign. One message read

```
In the last nine days, NATO barbarians have bombed our
schools, hospitals, bridges, killed our people but that
was not enough for them now they have started to destroy
our culture monuments which represents the core of exis-
tence of our nation.
```

Most recipients were annoyed by this unwanted e-mail, which the *Wall Street Journal* dubbed "Yugospam."

In a conversation in July 1999, Dennis Longley, a professor in the Information Security Research Centre at Australia's Queensland University of Technology, told me the Centre had received a suspicious e-mail from Serbia. The message had two paragraphs. The first was the usual friendly greetings, whereas the second was a rant about NATO that read like pure propaganda, characterizing NATO as a "terrorist organization that brought nothing but a gigantic humanitarian disaster to Kosovo," while attributing the cause of the problem to "Albanian terrorist and separatist actions." The second paragraph exhibited a style unlike the first and a standard of English well below that of the sender, leading them to speculate that Serb authorities had modified the e-mail. If that is so, one is left wondering how much other anti-NATO talk hitting the Net was the work of the Serbian government.

Even though the Yugoslav government did not prohibit Internet activity, fear of government reprisals led some to post their messages through anonymous remailers so they could not be identified. Microsoft Corp. initiated a section called "Secret Dispatches from Belgrade" on the Web site of its online magazine *Slate*. An anonymous correspondent gave daily reports of both alleged Serb atrocities and civilian suffering inflicted by NATO bombs.

After human rights organizations expressed concern that the Yugoslav government might be monitoring Internet activity and cracking down on anyone expressing dissenting views, Anonymizer Inc., a provider of anonymous Web browsing and e-mail services, launched the Kosovo Privacy Project Web site. The site, which went on-line in April 1999, offered surfers anonymous e-mail and instant, anonymous access to Voice of America, Radio Free Europe, and about 20 other Web sites.

China, U.S., and Taiwan: Has Code War Replaced Cold War?

The future of U.S./China relations is uncertain. After the collapse of the Soviet Union brought an end to the Cold War, the Nixon/Kissinger policy of "triangulation" become obsolete. Are we headed for a new Cold War or will it be a Code War instead? There is ample evidence that the Chinese understand the potential of cyberwar.

Consider the following June 1998 Reuters news item regarding the activities of the People's Republic of China:

> "An adversary wishing to destroy the United States only has to mess up the
> computer systems of its banks by high-tech means," [CIA director George]
> Tenet quoted an article in China's official "People's Liberation Daily" as saying.

> ...According to [the National Defense University's (NDU)] "Strategic Trends in China," ...Chinese military officials believe that the United States relies on satellites for 90 percent of its combat information and communications. Targeting these satellites "could cripple the United States at a low cost to China."
>
> ...[An NDU research fellow] who wrote a Pentagon study of China's interest in information warfare, said Beijing had the world's largest program of its type.[4]

In November 1998, *Wired*, also citing a Pentagon study, reported that the People's Liberation Army of China was building lasers and other weapons designed to destroy satellites and interfere with U.S. intelligence and commercial communications networks. The anti-satellite weapons, called Asats, are designed to damage sensors on space-based reconnaissance and intelligence systems. The report said the lasers could also be used to jam Global Positioning Systems (GPS), commonly used in commercial communications and navigation systems.

In August 1999, a person claiming to be from mainland China hacked into several Taiwan government Internet sites to insert pro-China messages amid a heated row between the two sides over Taiwan's political status.

In September 1999, Agence France-Presse reported that Taiwan had stepped up military training to thwart any electronic warfare by rival China. War games held in China focused on using electronic equipment to paralyze or destroy enemy computer and communications systems.

In November 1999, the *New York Review of Books* reported that China and Taiwan were already at war.

> The battles are not being fought on land or sea, or even, strictly speaking, in the air; they take place in cyberspace. The soldiers in this war are invisible figures buried deep inside government offices, 'hacking' their way into computers on enemy territory.
>
> In August alone, 72,000 cyberspace attacks were launched from mainland computers, 165 times with success.[5]

In January 2000, Agence France-Presse reported that Taiwan's military was preparing for cyberwar with China and had developed 1,000 computer viruses just for that purpose. One scenario that was considered at that time by Taiwan's Defense Ministry was that China might well invade Taiwan's computer systems and alter the outcome of the March 2000 presidential election.

In June 2000, *Intelligence Newsletter* reported that the Pentagon's "Annual Report on the Military Power of the People's Republic of China" shed light on the existence of

---

4. "China, others spot U.S. computer weaknesses: CIA," Reuters, June 24, 1998.

5. Ian Buruma, "China in Cyberspace," in *New York Review of Books* (November 4, 1999).

information warfare systems in China. It also stated that Chinese capability in that sphere had increased greatly over the past 12 months.

The report said the Communication Command Academy in Wuhan had emerged as one of the Chinese Army's major infowar research centers. In December 1998, the Academy staged the first infowar simulation exercise while a task force of 20 instructors at the academy wrote a book entitled *Command and Control in Information Warfare and Technology in Information Warfare*.

Additionally, the report said the Academy had laid on 31 courses in information warfare for military personnel. With regard to methods, the Chinese military appears keen on computer network attacks and in researching methods to insert computer viruses into foreign networks.[6]

But China is only *preparing* for cyberwar with the United States and Taiwan; it is already engaged in cyberwar with digital dissidents within China itself as well as hacktivists from the outside world.

In June 1998, police in the People's Republic of China charged 20 Taiwanese businesses with spying for Taiwan. The counterespionage section of the Public Security Ministry accused them of "intercepting confidential information regarding China's defenses on the Internet." The affair followed the arrest of two Chinese with New Zealand citizenship for installing a fax system via the Internet that can be used in China.

In July 1998, China arrested a software engineer for subversion after supplying e-mail addresses to an American-based pro-reform magazine, said a spokesman for the Center for Human Rights and Democratic Movement in China. The spokesman said a 150-member strong police squad in the Chinese city are monitoring Internet usage, blocking the access of some users, and confiscating the computers of others.

In October 1998, *Nando Times* ran the following story:

> China's cyber-police partially blocked access to Web site of the government-backed "Chinese Society for Human Rights" to prevent China's own on-line population from catching a glimpse at the critical messages left by a hacker identified only as Bronc Buster.
>
> "I simply cannot believe the total b-s-propaganda of this Web site," the hacker wrote. "China's people have no rights at all, never mind 'human rights.' I really can't believe our government deals with them. They censor, murder, torture, maim, and do everything we thought left the Earth with the middle ages."
>
> Chinese cyber-police use firewall technology to routinely block access to Web sites of scores of foreign and Hong Kong-based human rights groups as well as those advocating Tibetan autonomy and Taiwan independence.

---

6. "Infowar, Chinese-style," *Intelligence Newsletter*, June 29, 2000.

> Bronc Buster wrote that it took less than 10 minutes to access and alter the Chinese Web site. "Your security is a total joke," he mocked.[7]

In May 1999, Shanghai ordered local paging stations and computer information vendors to stop providing news reports. Information suppliers, including telephone and computer-based services, must stop disseminating political news temporarily, including news downloaded from the Internet.

In June 1999, Shanghai punished 278 unregistered Internet cafes in a crackdown on uncontrolled forays into cyberspace.

In July 1999, a Chinese engineer was arrested on charges of posting secrets about a new warplane to an Internet bulletin board. Authorities tracked down the engineer after the article posted in May 1999 spread to other Internet sites.

In the same month, Chinese authorities took their crackdown on the Falun Gong meditation group to Web sites in the United States and elsewhere, with at least one "hacking" attempt that appeared to trace back to Chinese national police in Beijing.

Perhaps the day of reckoning for information warriors in the U.S. military and intelligence agencies will come out there where the shadow-side of cyberspace intersects the Taiwan Straits. Perhaps not. Either way, those empowered to steward the national security must be prepared.

Storming the Digital Bastille

Furthermore, such activities, as former CIA Director Deutsch observed, are not limited to nation-states, but also include would-be nation-states and revolutionaries bent on righting wrongs and overturning the power structures within their countries.

Here are a few examples. In many instances, çthese activities blur the distinctions between hacktivism and infowar.

In 1997, Mexican hackers affiliated with the Zapatista guerillas had declared cyberwar on the government. They plastered the image of Emiliano Zapata on the Finance Ministry's Web site. They claimed to have monitored electronic visits by Mexican senators to X-rated Internet salons. They vowed to search official databases for incriminating numbers and publicize government bank account activity, cellular phone conversations, and e-mail communications.

In 1998, *Wired* reported the following:

---

7. *Nando Times*, October 28, 1998.

The Pentagon struck back against Internet activists who attempted to hold an "on-line sit-in" Wednesday at the Defense Department's main Web site. The attack…also targeted sites for the Frankfurt Stock Exchange and the president of Mexico.

…The group, who call themselves Electronic Disturbance Theater, support the Zapatista rebels in Chiapas, fighting against the Mexican government. To draw attention to their cause, they attempted to temporarily disable certain Web sites by asking demonstrators to load a hostile Web-based program called FloodNet.

…Participants in the FloodNet protest needed only to load the FloodNet Web page. The page contained a Java applet configured to request and load the three target Web sites every three seconds. The Electronic Disturbance Theater estimated that up to 10,000 people took part in the demonstration, delivering 600,000 hits to each of the three Web sites per minute.

The Pentagon's Web site support team apparently struck back with a Java applet of its own. That applet sensed requests from the FloodNet servers and loaded—and re-loaded—an empty browser window on the attacker's desktop. The move forced protesters to reboot their computers.[8]

In 1997, hackers affiliated with Tamil guerillas deluged the e-mail servers of Sri Lankan embassies throughout Europe, North America, and Asia with up to 800 messages a day for two weeks, paralyzing the entire network. "We are the Internet Black Tigers," the messages read, "and we're doing this to disrupt your communications."

In 1997, Portuguese hackers capped a two-month protest over the treatment of East Timor by breaking into the Indonesian military's home page and altering it.

In 1999, José Ramos-Horta, 1996 Nobel Peace Prize laureate, warned that an international squad of computer hackers would wreak havoc on Indonesia if the country hampered voting in East Timor's independence referendum. "A dozen special viruses are being designed to infect the Indonesian electronic communications system, including aviation," said Ramos-Horta.

Violence was encouraged and allowed by the Indonesian military. Despite the effort to intimidate them before the voting and the rampage and terror that descended on them after the voting, the East Timorese opted for independence.

The United Nations, the United States, and others intervened. The Australians landed on East Timor. But no cyberwar materialized.

Helter Skelter in Cyberspace

The deranged too have entered the Information Age. And they are not simply using the Net as a cheap, confidential (à la PGP) means of global communications. They are also using it to gather information to build deadlier weapons and strike with more effectiveness. And soon, perhaps, they will use it as a delivery system.

---

8. "Pentagon Deflects Web Assault," by Niall McKay, Wired News, September 10, 1998.

Law enforcement and intelligence community officials have been speaking out on this threat for a while now; their warnings are too often discounted.

Consider Aum Shinri Kyo, the Japanese doomsday cult responsible for a sarin nerve gas attack on the Tokyo subway in 1995. Twelve people were killed and 5,000 more were injured. When the authorities cracked down on Aum Shinri Kyo, they revealed that the group was in the process of making both chemical and biological weapons.

Aum Shinri Kyo also had a "Ministry of Intelligence" dedicated to pilfering high-tech secrets from Japanese and American corporations and research institutions. With 40,000 members worldwide and more than $1 billion in assets, the cult procured much of what it needed legally or on the black market.

When it needed information that it could not acquire through either of these channels, it resorted to hacking.

For example, a five-man commando team of Aum cult members repeatedly broke into the Mitsubishi Heavy Industries (MHI) compound in Hiroshima. They logged on to the MHI mainframe and downloaded megabytes of restricted files onto laptop computers as part of their effort to build a laser weapon.

Remarkably, despite a crackdown by Japanese law enforcement, the cult is growing again.

I have kept tracking the Aum cult over the years, playing a hunch that there would be more to the story.

In March 2000, the BBC reported that Japan's Defense Agency had delayed the introduction of a new computer system after discovering that it used software developed by members of the Aum Shinri Kyo cult. The discovery has prompted fears that the cult could use the software to infiltrate government computers and gain access to vital defense information. Tokyo police said the Defense Agency was one of 90 government bodies and private firms that had ordered software produced by the cult. "We had been expecting to introduce the system today but halted the plan for the time being as it is too dangerous," a Defense Agency spokesman said. "Nobody knows what they have done to the system. We need to check it thoroughly."

What is the significance of this story?

Consider the following news items.

In August 1998, a computer glitch in Lewiston, Maine, shut down the chlorination system and caused the chlorine content of the city water to drop below the safety threshold, affecting 40,000 residents. This occurred during the night and was not discovered until a routine check 14 hours later. Notices were then sent out to 9,000 homes advising people to boil water before drinking. It took 30 hours to solve the problem. The city has now installed an automatic system to notify an on-call supervisor in case this recurs.

In the same month, air traffic controllers had to resort to handwritten notes to keep track of hundreds of planes over New England and upstate New York when a computer failed.

In October 1998, telecommunications services relying on analog leased lines were severely disrupted in Osaka and parts of western Japan after a power failure at an exchange operated by Nippon Telegraph and Telephone Corp. A spokeswoman confirmed that 110 and 119 emergency service numbers were disrupted. Among other systems affected, most bank and post office automated teller machines were left off-line. Cellular phone service was cut in several areas of central Japan. Flights to and from western Japan were delayed as the failure cut links between air traffic control centers.

Some Y2K tests conducted by Australian government agencies produced some alarming results. In one of them, the Reserve Bank's vaults flew open. In another, at Coffs Harbor, a coastal town about 300 miles north of Sydney, microprocessors at the water-storage facility were tuned to 2000 dates, and the entire chemical holdings (normally used in regulated amounts to purify water) were dumped into the water. Experts say this could have killed the town's entire population.

The stock exchange in Brussels, Belgium shut down for two hours in 1997 because of a Y2K-related software problem. Estimated lost commissions equaled US$1 million.

On December 30, 1996, an aluminum plant in New Zealand shut down with molten aluminum still in the runs.

According to the *World Review*, in 1998 there had already been 10,000 reported instances of Y2K-related problems, according to U.S. figures. By the end of 2000, there will have been more than 50,000 reported computer failures due to Y2K problems. Even if when the clock ticks over, that figure rises only tenfold, that is still 500,000 computer failures.

What's my point? Well, the danger of cyberattacks against infrastructure targets (for example, the air traffic control system, the power grid, the stock exchanges, the water supply, etc.) is one of the primary concerns of those officials preparing the U.S. and its allies for the potential infowars of the twenty-first century.

The unrelated and unintentional incidents listed above were all computer-related. Consider just for a moment what havoc and mayhem a skilled cadre of Aum-like cultists could accomplish with the kind of access they were unwittingly allowed to applications destined for the internal networks of the Japanese Defense Agency. What if such cyberterrorists became involved in developing application software for the air traffic control system or the power grid?

The U.S. Government might have held back against Milosevic in Kosovo, in part because of questions involving ethics and international law, but I doubt that Aum cult or its equivalents would feel the same pangs of conscience.

In September 1999, the U.S. National Infrastructure Protection Center (NIPC) hosted its "International Computer Crime Conference" in New Orleans. Representatives from law enforcement agencies in more than 20 countries attended sessions on topics ranging from "Computer Crime and Critical Infrastructure Protection in the United Kingdom" to "Techniques in Computer Forensics, Searches, Data Handling and Processing and the Identification, Acquisition and Protection of Evidence in Computer Investigations."

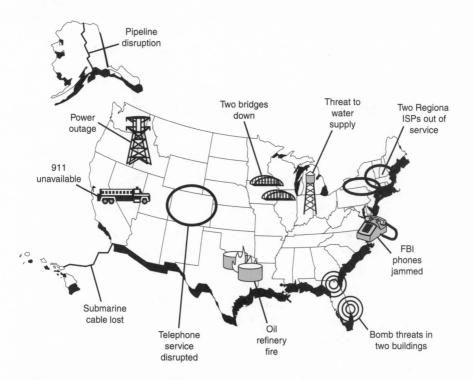

Figure 12.2 Coincidence or attack?

Source: PCCIP

To provide a journalist's overview, I delivered my presentation, "Current and Future Danger: Executive Briefing on Computer Crime and Information Warfare," as I already had in São Paulo, Brazil; Johannesburg, South Africa; Kyoto, Japan; and Calgary, Canada.

An NIPC staffer, Brian Dastur of the Special Technologies Applications Unit, took the attendees on a keystroke-by-keystroke guide to bringing down an inadequately secured infrastructure target (in his example, a power grid). Using an ISP account paid for by cash, with a false name, he wove his way through universities, corporations, and ISPs that he had already hacked, to attack the final target, a small power company. He performed a reconnaissance scan for live systems. He scanned for the likely target. He used tcpdump to grab all the data on the network segment it was attached to, including both user and superuser passwords. He then used telnet to get on the system he had selected as his target, and moved some tools to it. Using a homemade script, undetectable to many intrusion detection systems, he ran a buffer overflow that caused the system to hiccup. The hiccup, in turn, allowed him to gain superuser access and "own" the system. He then issued the command to shut down the power grid. "Imagine a company that has a backup system on the same network as the primary system with all the same passwords," Dastur mused. "If you don't believe this could happen, think again. It does."

Digital Dirty Tricks and Cyber Plumbers

Information warfare has also begun to play a part in domestic politics around the world.

In a Cabinet meeting, the Sri Lankan Science and Technology Minister, Batty Weerakoon, read out an e-mail meant for former Prime Minister, Ranil Wickremesinghe, now the leader of the opposition. Wickremesinghe accused Weerakoon of screening telephone calls, fax messages, and e-mails of journalists, politicians, and businessmen.

Prior to a national vote on whether Australia should continue as a member of the British Commonwealth, acknowledging the Queen of England as its sovereign, a 20-page fax threatening the Australian Republican Movement (ARM) was sent at 7:10 a.m. "We have declared infowar on you. Every item in your office will be working against you," the fax read. Within 20 minutes, ARM's national telephone call center was disabled, e-mail facilities were jammed, and the office's computer system was shut down. A group calling itself the Australian Underground and Empire Loyalist Movement sent the fax.

Dabbling in U.S. domestic politics, hackers have made their presence felt. In the early days of her campaign, some Web surfers found it impossible to reach Hillary Clinton's Web site (www.hillary2000.org). Their browsers would go automatically to a rival site (www.hillaryno.com), maintained by Friends of Giuliani (her former potential rival for a New York Senate seat) instead.

In the early months of the George W. Bush presidential campaign, Zack Exley, a 29-year-old Sommerville, Massachusetts resident, put up a site satirizing a Bush presidential bid, grabbing the unused domain name, www.gwbush.com.

Bush complained about the Web site during a news conference, saying "there ought to be limits to freedom" and calling Exley a "garbage man." Bush also filed a complaint with the Federal Election Commission.

The parody Web site received 6,451,466 hits during the first 25 days of May, thanks in part to the story's front-page treatment by the *New York Times* on-line edition.

Of course, cyberattacks and digital disinformation are not aimed solely at candidates and officials.

In September 1998, *TechWeb* posted a news item about David Talbot, editor of *Salon* magazine. *Salon* is the WWW publication that broke the story detailing the adultery of Rep. Henry Hyde (R-Ill.), one of President Bill Clinton's most powerful congressional critics.

> Already Talbot has received death threats as a result of his article. Threats have also been issued against other top editors. Their fax machine was shut down by a series of "black faxes"—a tactic in which the sender repeatedly faxes an all-black piece of paper in a deliberate attempt to break the recipient's machine. The magazine stopped accepting incoming e-mail after an avalanche of hate mail and spam clogged their servers.
>
> ...The concerted attacks against the site are unlikely to disappear quickly, Talbot said. "There is a hard-core conservative information infrastructure in this country, and they've been using it against Salon for some time now," he said.[9]

Defensive Information Warfare

In the United States, preparation for defensive information warfare is well under way. (Well, defensive information warfare is the only aspect of the emerging field that anyone will acknowledge, for the record, that they're working in.)

The National Security Agency (NSA) and the National Institute of Standards and Technology (NIST) held their annual National Information Systems Security Conference (NISSC) in Crystal City, Virginia in October 1999.

Of course, information warfare (IW) and cybercrime were among the major themes of the conference. Several leading authorities on both subjects held forth.

Dr. Dorothy Denning of Georgetown University and author of *Information Warfare and Security* chaired a panel, "Focusing on the Criminal Threat," that included Pat Gallagher, former Director of National Computer Security Center and Chair of the Global Organized Crime Information Warfare/Information Assurance Task Force; Special Agent Jim Christy (AFOSI), Law Enforcement and Counterintelligence Coordinator for the Defense-Wide Information Assurance Program (DIAP); and Mark Pollitt, Unit Chief for the Computer Analysis Response Team (CART) of the FBI (Washington, D.C.).

---

9. "Salon Hyde Exposé Spurs Death Threats, Hacks," by John Borland, TechWeb News, September 17, 1998

Gallagher stated that the U.S. faces a real and imminent IW threat from diverse groups that are "competent, connected, well-funded, and angry." Reminding attendees that "information is the commodity," he urged them to reflect on life before the OPEC oil embargo in the 1970s. OPEC's aim, Gallagher observed, was not just to increase profit, but to achieve a new balance of power.

Although he cited the work of the President's Commission on Critical Infrastructure Protection (PCCIP) and Presidential Decision Directive 63 (PDD63) as a good beginning, Gallagher said more must be done. Recalling Teddy Roosevelt's show of strength in sending the "great white fleet" around the world, Gallagher asked, "How do you project information power globally?"

The DoD's Jim Christy spoke on DIAP's effort to integrate law enforcement, intelligence, and IT security within the huge agency. Christy and his colleagues have been charged to establish a means for DoD-wide awareness of cyberattacks within four hours of detection by the end of the year. The task is formidable; the activities of 35 organizations within DoD alone must be coordinated. Indeed, it is a struggle to even understand who is doing what.

Acknowledging that the DoD is not there yet, Christy enumerated some of the obstacles:

- Insufficient IDS
- Insufficient analysis capability
- Insufficient notification system
- Insufficient training

The presentation contained many valuable lessons for information security practitioners whether in sprawling government agencies or huge corporations.

Christy listed some vital decision-maker questions:

- Who is attacking?
- Who will be attacked?
- Who is directing the attacks?
- What happened?
- What systems are targeted?
- What systems have already been attacked?
- What is the operational impact of the attacks?
- What is the objective of the attackers?
- Where are the attacks physically initiated?

- When did the attacks occur?
- When are the next attacks coming?
- Why are specific systems targeted?
- Why is this organization targeted?
- How are they getting access?

He also offered a list of recommendations for organizations under attack from whatever foe:

- Contact law enforcement
- Turn on audit trails and logs
- Use keystroke monitoring
- Designate an incident management team
- Designate evidence custodian
- Record dollar losses associated with incident
- Make back-ups, print out logs
- Document activity
- Theorize (e.g., law enforcement will need to know where to start, they will ask how the attacker got in, etc.)

Denning also participated in a panel on "Lessons Learned Teaching Information Warfare," chaired by Prof. Lance Hoffman of George Washington University.

In Denning's course at Georgetown University, students sign on for extensive readings, weekly papers of 600 words in answer to a set of questions (many of these relate to the ethical issues involved in IW), and a term paper of 5,000 words. Guest lecturers—for example, someone from the CIA's Office of the General Counsel—provide diverse perspectives. The content of the course ranges from IW methods and incidents to discussion of the national and international security issues that IW raises.

The class consists of both graduate and undergraduate students with diverse majors such as economics, Russian, and chemistry; many students come from the Science and Technology in International Affairs and National Security Studies programs. The class is limited to 30 students per term, and students have to be turned away. Of course, hacking intrigues the students.

Denning warns them, "If you land in jail, I won't bail you out."

Muggers and Molesters in Cyberspace

? login

Identity Theft

Most of *Tangled Web* focuses on cybercrimes that target corporations, government agencies, and infrastructure, but this chapter and the following one explore two truly odious cybercrimes: identity theft and on-line traffic in child pornography.

What is identity theft?

Consider the sad tale of Adelaide Andrews, a thirty-something investment researcher living in San Diego. In 1995, Andrews started receiving disturbing phone calls from money-lenders and collection agencies looking for payments she had no idea that she owed. The situation got worse very quickly. Her application for refinancing on her home mortgage was rejected. The bank said she was a bad credit risk. To add insult to injury, the Internal Revenue Service (IRS) informed her that she owed taxes on income she had never received. Someone, using her identity, had established credit lines of up to $10,000, rented apartments, set up utilities, and took in income. There was even a Nevada arrest warrant for domestic battery issued against her.

Andrews hired a private investigator to track down the identity thief. She suspected that a medical office employee had taken her name and Social Security number (that's all you really need!) from her file. It took her two years to get her credit history straightened out. Law enforcement would not pursue the case. None of the financial institutions or credit bureaus involved would pursue the case. In frustration, Andrews filed a civil suit against Trans Union and Experian (formerly TRW).

Stephen Shaw, a Washington-based journalist, also had his finances savaged by an identity thief. A car salesman named Steven Shaw in Florida ran some random credit checks looking for someone with a name similar to his own and an excellent credit history. He came up with everything he needed to operate as Stephen Shaw: Social Security number, current and previous addresses, and his mother's maiden name (easily obtainable through running such a credit check). Steven opened 35 credit card and charge accounts and racked up $100,000 worth of car loans, personal loans, stereo equipment purchases, airplane tickets, clothing, and appliances all in Stephen's name.

It took Stephen Shaw more than four years to clean up his credit history.

In March 2000, Jerry Orbach, a star on the television show *Law and Order*, filed a lawsuit against eBay, the Internet auction site. According to Orbach, eBay was responsible for the "identity theft" that hurt his credit rating and caused him personal and professional embarrassment. It seems that eBay allowed someone to advertise two of his 1958 acting contracts for sale. They included his Social Security number. Someone subsequently used it to commit credit card fraud in his name.

Of course, you don't have to troll eBay auction offerings for Social Security numbers.

According to the U.S. Social Security Administration, 81% of SSN misuse involves identity theft. I have included a table on the evolution of authorized uses of Social Security numbers (SSNs) from Simson Garfinkel's gripping tome, *Database Nation*, the definitive work on privacy-related issues in the Internet age.

Table 13.1   Pervasive Use of Social Security Numbers Is Dangerous to Your Privacy[1]

Year	Authorized Uses of Social Security Numbers
1943	Federal agencies use SSN exclusively for employees.
1961	Civil Service Commission uses SSN as an employee identifier.
1962	Internal Revenue Service uses SSN as taxpayer identification.
1967	Department of Defense uses SSN as an Armed Forces identifier.
1972	United States begins issuing SSNs to legally admitted aliens at U.S. entry and to anyone receiving or applying for federal benefits.
1975	AFDC (Aid for Families with Dependent Children) uses SSN for eligibility.
1976	States use SSN for tax and general public assistance identification and for driver's licenses.

---

1. Database Nation: The Death of Privacy in the 21st Century by Simson Garfinkel (ISBN 1-56592-653-6).

Year	Authorized Uses of Social Security Numbers
1977	Food stamp program uses SSN for household member eligibility.
1981	School lunch program uses SSN for adult household member eligibility.
1981	Selective Service System uses SSN for draft registrants.
1982	Federal loan program uses SSN for applicants.
1983	SSN required for all holders of interest-bearing accounts.
1984	States authorized to require SSN for AFDC, Medicaid, unemployment compensation, food stamp programs, and state programs established under a plan approved under Title I, X., XIV, or XVI of the Social Security Act.
1986	SSN may be used as proof of unemployment eligibility.
1986	SSN required for taxpayer identification for tax dependents age five and over (effective for 1988 returns).
1986	Secretary of Transportation authorizes use of SSN for commercial motor vehicle operator's licenses.
1988	SSN required for taxpayer identification for tax dependents age two and over (effective for 1990 returns).
1988	States use parents' SSNs to issue birth certificates.
1988	States and/or blood donation facilities use SSN for blood donor identification.
1988	All Title II beneficiaries required to have SSN for eligibility.
1989	National Student Loan Data System includes SSN of borrowers.
1990	SSN required for taxpayer identification for tax dependents age one and over (effective for 1991 returns).
1990	SSN required for eligibility for all Department of Veterans Affairs payments.
1990	SSN required for officers of food and retail stores that redeem food stamps.
1994	Use of SSN authorized for jury selection.
1994	Use of SSN authorized by Department of Labor for claim identification numbers for worker's compensation claims.
1994	SSN required for taxpayer identification for tax dependents regardless of age (effective for 1996 returns).

Table 13.1 continued

Year	Authorized Uses of Social Security Numbers
1996	SSN required for any applicant for a professional license, commercial driver's license, occupational license, or marriage license (must be recorded on the application). The SSN of any person subject to a divorce decree, support order, or paternity determination or acknowledgement would have to be placed in the pertinent records. SSNs are required on the death certificates.
1996	The Attorney General authorized to require any noncitizen to provide his or her SSN for inclusion in Immigration and Naturalization Service (INS) records.
1996	Driver's licenses required to display an SSN.

In September 1999, Image Data LLC, an identity-fraud prevention service (Nashua, New Hampshire) released a study that suggests that one out of every five U.S. citizens or one of their relations have been a victim of identity theft.

In March 2000, the National Fraud Center released *Identity Theft: Authentication as a Solution*, a report that showed that incidents of identity theft are expanding with a rapidity that rivals the growth of the Internet itself. For example, consumer inquiries to the fraud-victim assistance department of Trans Union rose from 35,235 in 1992 to 522,922 in 1997. Furthermore, according to the U.S. General Accounting Office (GAO), arrests for identity fraud rose from 8,806 in 1995 to 9,455 in 1997. The GAO also stated that financial losses due to identity theft over that period rose from $442 million to $745 million.

The report declared that "the Internet takes the shadowy form of the identity thief and provides him or her with the shelter of its anonymity, and the speed of its electronic transmissions." It also underscored the fact that "the potential harm caused by an identity thief using the Internet is exponential."

Identity theft is a crime perpetrated both by individuals and organized groups. It is also a global phenomenon. Indeed, U.S. Secret Service Special Agent Gregory Regan testified before the Senate Judiciary Subcommittee on Technology that organized Chinese fraud rings both on the mainland and overseas are more likely to hack into databases to compromise credit cards and identity details, whereas their Nigerian counterparts are more likely to follow the more traditional route of bribing bank employees.

The National Fraud Center's report recommended increased reliance on stronger authentication technologies (for example, digital certificates, digital signatures, and biometrics) to thwart such attacks on individuals. However, I would be leery of any technological solution based on digital certificates, digital signatures, and biometrics that did not also incorporate a smart card. Of course, since authentication solutions incorporating smart cards are going to cost more than those without them, we probably won't see them until there is a lot more financial institution blood in the water.

Meanwhile, you can take simple steps to at least limit your risk in regard to identity theft. Here are some examples.

Place a phone call to 1-888-567-8688 to request that your name be removed from marketing lists to reduce the number of those preapproved credit card applications that you receive via snail mail.

Protect your SSN as much as possible. Do not be so agreeable when businesses ask you for your SSN. Ask them if they could use some other form of identification. In many cases, the businesses ask for it simply for their own convenience and if pressed will accept some viable alternative.

Check your credit report yearly by calling and ordering your report from each of the three credit bureaus to ensure no irregular or unauthorized activity has occurred.

If someone really wants to take your identity, they will, at least electronically. The best you can hope to do until the financial institutions start handing out smart cards is limit your risk as much as possible and be as alert as you can so that the theft doesn't go too far before you detect it.

The United States Secret Service (www.treas.gov/usss/) provides some excellent tips on what to do if you suspect that you have become a victim of identity theft:

> If you have been the victim of credit card fraud or identity theft, the following tips will assist you:

- Report the crime to the police immediately. Get a copy of your police report or case number. Credit card companies, your bank, and the insurance company may ask you to reference the report to verify the crime.

- Immediately contact your credit card issuers. Get replacement cards with new account numbers and ask that the old account be processed as "account closed at consumer's request" for credit record purposes. You should also follow up this telephone conversation with a letter to the credit card company that summarizes your request in writing.

- Call the fraud units of the three credit reporting bureaus. Report the theft of your credit cards and/or numbers. Ask that your accounts be flagged. Also, add a victim's statement to your report that requests that they contact you to verify future credit applications. The following is a list of addresses and numbers to the three credit bureaus:

Equifax Credit Information Services—Consumer Fraud Div.
P.O. Box 105496
Atlanta, Georgia 30348-5496
Tel: (800) 997-2493
URL: www.equifax.com

Experian
P.O. Box 2104
Allen, Texas 75013-2104
Tel: (888) EXPERIAN (397-3742)
URL: www.experian.com

Trans Union Fraud Victim Assistance Dept.
P.O. Box 390
Springfield, PA 19064-0390
Tel: (800) 680-7289
URL: www.transunion.com

- Keep a log of all conversations with authorities and financial entities.

- As with any personal information, only provide your credit card number to merchants you know. Also, remember to protect your social security number. You have to give your social security number for employment and tax purposes, but it is not necessary for many businesses. Notify the Social Security Administration's Office of Inspector General if your social security number has been used fraudulently.

- The Federal Trade Commission (FTC) is the federal clearinghouse for complaints by victims of identity theft. Although the FTC does not have the authority to bring criminal cases, the Commission assists victims of identity theft by providing them with information to help them resolve the financial and other problems that can result from identity theft. The FTC also may refer victim complaints to other appropriate government agencies and private organizations for further action. If you have been a victim of identity theft, you can file a complaint with the FTC by contacting the FTC's Consumer Response Center.

By Phone:
Toll-free 877-FTC-HELP (382-4357)
TDD 202-326-2502

By Mail:
Consumer Response Center
Federal Trade Commission
600 Pennsylvania Ave, NW
Washington, DC 20580
URL: www.ftc.gov/ftc/complaint.htm

Child Pornography on the Internet

Detective Inspector Anders Persson of the Swedish National Police stood tall, with strength and quiet dignity, displaying digital evidence of hell on earth and in cyberspace.

Mouse click by mouse click, horrific, graphic images of the sexual intercourse between adults and young children filled the screen. The gathering of two hundred law enforcement officers from around the world fell utterly silent.

Persson was demonstrating the Swedish Digital Reference Library, a central image bank of digital child pornography. Most of the amassed picture files were captured during raids or downloaded from the Internet.

The project's objective is to learn more about the origin and distribution of the pornographic material and be able to assist in cracking down on the producers of the images and stopping the abuse of the children.

In the course of his presentation, Persson shared the history of the project.

In 1997, the Swedish National Crime Intelligence Division was tasked with establishing and maintaining the library. The Swedish child protection unit started up the project. This unit was responsible for supervising the operational value and technical development of an image library and mapping the distribution of the material. The library is able to handle both photographs and video film, which are translated into digitized images for ease of storage and search. Initially, the image bank contained 56,000 pictures, all from Sweden. Currently the library contains more than 300,000 images from all over the world.

The unit's biggest problem once it set up the library was that it still could not compare images found with those of other forces. There was no search facility for the different images, and therefore there was still a requirement for police officers who knew from experience where the different images were stored and all the background information surrounding each picture. The problems were compounded when new officers joined the team, as it was impossible for them to find images matching seized videos or stills.

The unit tried looking at various search solutions, such as text searching of the images. Text searching is a very good way of finding the right pictures, but the problem is that you must keep a large number of staff just describing the different images.

Remember that one CD can contain up to 12,000 images and in most cases the investigators are handling hard disks with the capacity of up to 10GB and sometimes more. If the investigators had to describe each picture in detail before they were operationally available for searching, it would take far too much time and opportunities would be lost. The Swedish child abuse unit decided that the future of a search tool for images could not be based on any textual pre-work of the images.

Persson came across Excalibur Visual RetrievalWare (www.excalib.com), software that recognizes images without requiring any preparation of the image.

Using the Excalibur software, Persson and his colleagues could search the database for matches to a particular image based on different qualities such as brightness and texture. They could search through hundreds of thousands of images to find ones taken in the same room at the same time. They could search the image database for tattoos, furniture, rugs, and other clues that could lead to the identification of a perpetrator or a location. They could take an image in which the face of the perpetrator had been disguised, and then search the database for a similar image and find another image taken in the place at the same time and put a face on the original one.

For example, the unit interviewed some children who said that they were taken to a certain Danish hotel. The investigators took photos of the bed and other objects in the rooms of that hotel and then searched the database for similar images as well as indexing the hotel room photos against any incoming images.

In 1998, Persson's unit made a request for images from other European countries to add to its burgeoning database. It received child pornography from law enforcement in Portugal, Switzerland, the United Kingdom, Norway, Denmark, Finland, the Netherlands, and Germany. In 1999, the Swedes hosted a seminar to evaluate the library project with 50 delegates from numerous countries (Belgium, Denmark, Finland, France, Germany, Luxembourg, Russia, Spain, Switzerland, the United Kingdom, Norway, the Netherlands, and the United States), as well as Europol and Interpol.

They started off with a 400 megahertz Pentium PC with 128MB RAM and 18GB hard drive running Windows 95, and then they upgraded to Windows NT Server 4.0 with 256MB RAM, 32GB hard drive, six workstations, a color laser printer, and a LAN.

The Swedish Child Protection Unit (CPU), which is responsible for the library, consists of three law enforcement officers on permanent assignment and one on temporary assignment. Currently, it has 360,000 images in the database, including copies and series. As a result of its efforts, 50 children have been identified, and the unit has begun to receive many queries from other countries. Although its caseload has increased 200%, its staffing has not been increased.

At the end of Persson's presentation, someone asked why Interpol had not done at least as much as what his small unit had done?

Persson politely answered that Interpol was looking into it.

It was a poignant tale.

Consider how much Persson and his handful of colleagues had accomplished and how little they had to work with in terms of personnel and equipment.

Consider how much money (trillions of dollars, according to some estimates) is being poured into the Internet. Dot-com mania has captured the public imagination. It is a digital gold rush. There are fortunes to be made. Everyone is in a big hurry to cash in.

Something is way out of whack.

Do You Have Your Priorities Straight?

For several years, throughout the mid-1990s, a fierce debate raged over the U.S. government's ban on the export of encryption technology.

On one side, the FBI, Justice Department, NSA, CIA, and National Security Council argued that the unfettered, global sale of strong encryption technology would make the task of tracking down drug traffickers, terrorists (whether foreign or domestic), child pornographers, and other dangerous elements more difficult than ever.

With powerful encryption for cell phones and Internet e-mail, hard-core criminals (whether cyber or traditional) would gain a profound advantage. The spread of such products had to be slowed down. The only way to do that was to dam the flow of U.S. crypto technology (some of the world's best) by squeezing hard and resisting the market's pressure for liberalization (fueled as it was by the global drive toward e-commerce over the Internet).

On the other side, Netizens of all stripes, from privacy advocates, like the Electronic Frontier Foundation (EFF) and Electronic Privacy Information Center (EPIC), to technology vendors, like Microsoft and RSA Data Security, howled a great, collective "NO!" "Lift the export restrictions," they demanded. "We, the free and unregulated citizens of the Internet will secure ourselves."

The technology vendors wanted the restrictions lifted because they limited their profits. The privacy advocates wanted them lifted because they saw the export controls as a way for "Big Brother" to pry into the on-line communications of individuals and groups.

The Netizens saw no credibility at all in the argument that law enforcement would be placed at a serious disadvantage in its efforts to put bad guys out of business.

I recall hearing more than one privacy advocate say, "If I hear one more word about child pornography I am going to scream!"

Well, in 1999, after a long, valiant, and perhaps misguided battle, which included numerous attempts at compromises such as key escrow plans, the Clinton Administration moved decisively to give the Netizens what they wanted and remove the export controls.

Meanwhile, the problem of child pornography on the Internet is growing.

During testimony before the Senate Appropriations Subcommittee for the Departments of Commerce, Justice, and State, the Judiciary, and Related Agencies in March 1998, FBI Director Louis Freeh confirmed it.

> When I testified last week before the Subcommittee on the FBI's 1999 budget request, I outlined for the Subcommittee a number of challenges facing the FBI as it moves toward the 21st century. One of these challenges is the growing use of encryption by criminals to conceal their illegal activities. The 'Innocent Images' initiative has uncovered sexual predators who use encryption in their communication with each other and in the storage of their child pornography computer files. This encryption is extremely difficult, and often impossible, to defeat.
>
> It is essential that law enforcement agencies at all levels of government maintain the ability, through court order, to access encrypted communications and data relating to illegal activity.[1]

The Internet industry showed its muscle in fighting the U.S. government tooth and nail over the crypto export ban. It continues to show its muscle fighting software piracy on a global scale through the Business Software Alliance. But it has done nothing on any similar scale in regard to eradicating or even mitigating this scourge.

---

1. "Statement for the Record of Louis J. Freeh, Director, Federal Bureau of Investigation on Child Pornography on the Internet and the Sexual Exploitation of Children Before the Senate Appropriations Subcommittee for the Departments of Commerce, Justice, and State, the Judiciary, and Related Agencies," March 10, 1998

Anders Persson battles on undaunted.

In the United States, the FBI launched a serious undertaking, Operation Innocent Images, in 1994.

I vividly recall a powerful presentation on Operation Innocent Images done by Doris Gardner, a dedicated FBI Special Agent, who worked on-line and undercover with the handle of "Young and Sassy." Gardner is now a Supervisory Special Agent in the FBI's Charlotte office.

By March 1997, Innocent Images had generated 200 search warrants, 40 consensual searches, 81 indictments, 91 arrests, and 83 felony convictions. By 1999, 1,497 cases had been opened, and 532 arrests had been made. (For more information on "Innocent Images," refer to www.fbi.gov/.)

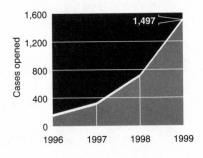

Figure 14.1 FBI crackdown on child pornography.[2]

Source: FBI

Even the hacker underground takes the problem seriously.

Consider the following story posted on the *Wired* Web site in February 2000:

> Kent Browne used to spend most of his free time hacking Web sites, erasing hard drives, disabling servers, and knocking folks out of chat rooms.
>
> Like many hackers, he subscribed to the classic Machiavellian argument, that the end justifies the means—especially when the end was eradicating child pornography on the Internet.
>
> In early December, he and some fellow hackers from New York to Australia started a group called Condemned, and announced their intention to take down child pornographers by any means necessary.
>
> But when Browne, 41, talked to Parry Aftab, an attorney who heads the biggest and most well-known of the anti-child pornography groups—Cyber Angels—he had a sudden change of heart.

2. "Net entices, then traps pedophiles," by M.J. Zuckerman, *USA Today*, June 7, 2000

"She said that the one problem we would have would be with law enforcement. If they knew we were doing illegal stuff, they wouldn't touch us with a 10-foot pole," he said. "Quite frankly, I'm an older guy. I've got two kids. And I don't want to take any chances."

So now he and the rest of Condemned's loosely organized volunteers use specially designed software and good old-fashioned Internet search engines to ferret out the bad stuff and tip off federal agents in the U.S. Customs Service and the FBI.

They're not alone. Natasha Grigori and her volunteer staff at antichildporn.org (ACPO) have also decided to hang up their hacking shoes. At her old organization, Anti Child Porn Militia, Grigori was dedicated to the use of hacking to disable child pornography Web sites. "We started out very angry, we started out very militant," she said.

But a trip to Def Con in Las Vegas made her change her mind.

She started talking with people on the right side of the law, and they told her they supported her cause, but not her means.

"You can't stop a felony with a felony," she says now.

But the decision to go "legal" was a difficult one, and she lost most of her volunteer hackers. "Less than a dozen out of 250 stuck with us," she said. "They didn't like the idea. They just thought we could rip and tear."

Browne also says he had a hard time leaving the hacking behind, mostly because he thought it was right.

"Which is more illegal? Having children's pictures on the Internet or hacking down the servers?" he asked. "Morally, I felt I was right."[3]

Law enforcement agencies—well, at least the Swedes and the FBI—are serious.

The hacker community is serious. (Remember Kuji, one of the Rome Labs hackers from Chapter 6? Kuji is the UK representative for ACPO. His Web site, www.bogus.net/kuji, carries the following message: "Please help out…it is for the future of our children. I am the UK [liaison] for these guys. If you want to help get in touch."

But the moguls of cyberspace are still mum on the problem of child pornography on-line. What's the problem? The U.S. export ban on crypto has been lifted; the problem of child pornography is no longer being used as "an excuse" to keep the ban in place.

But the Internet industry has yet to do anything to deal with this problem.

Indeed, the only recent headline-grabbing story about child pornography on-line that involved a high-tech industry executive sent a very different message. Patrick J. Naughton, a former Infoseek and Disney executive, was arrested in 1999 for crossing state lines with the intent of having sex with a "minor" he met in an Internet chat room. The "minor" turned out to be an FBI undercover agent.

---

3. "Hackers' New Tack on Kid Porn," by Lynn Burke, Wired News, Feb. 3, 2000.

The Defense of Cyberspace

PART V

Inside Fortune 500 Corporations

Ziff-Davis TV has a weekly half-hour show called *Cybercrime*. I am an occasional contributor on breaking news stories. The show also has a weekly one-minute feature called "Chaos Theory," in which industry experts are invited to rant and rave for 60 seconds on a topic of their own choosing. Well, I said "yes." And I took the opportunity to address some of the fundamental information security issues that are widely misunderstood and neglected in both corporations and government agencies.

If you ask a dot-com CEO or Fortune 500 CIO whether their organizations take Internet security seriously, they're going to say, "Yes, indeed, we take it very seriously."

Some of them are just telling you what you want to hear. They don't really believe their organizations are at risk. Others actually believe that their organizations really do take Internet security seriously. They have succumbed to the hype of industry analysts, vendors, and even their own IT people.

Both are deluded.

Here is a spot quiz to test their organization's level of commitment:

- Is there an actual information security department within the organization? The problem isn't just Internet security; it's information security enterprise-wide. You have to address everything from Web sites and database serves to fax machines and hard copies, inside as well as outside.

- Where does the head of this information security department report? If he or she doesn't report directly to the CIO—in other words, on the same level as the head of IT—information security won't be involved in decisions about deployment of applications, etc.

- What kind of budget does this information security department have? The rule of thumb used to be 1–3% of the total IT budget, but that was before organizations starting doing millions of dollars a day in e-commerce. Today at least 3–5% would be more realistic.

- Finally, how many people work on information security directly? The average among those orgs that have any at all is one information security professional for every 1,000 users. That antiquated notion stems from the mainframe world, but most organizations don't even have that many information security professionals on the job.

If you are a stockholder, an investment banker, a business partner, a client, a customer, or even a corporate council, you might want to spring this spot quiz on the CEO or the CIO.

Most of them won't even know the answers to these questions. Most of those who do know the answers will fail the test. They are just playing Russian roulette with your money. No firewall, no encryption product, no IDS, no PKI will save you or them from such negligence.

Perhaps you should sell your stock or take your business elsewhere.

It was a very successful "Chaos Theory" segment. It elicited a strong response from the viewership. Where did that diatribe come from? Well, it came from spending long hours talking to the best and the brightest information security professionals in Fortune 500 corporations and other successful enterprises and getting them to share their frustrations and insights.

Here are two glimpses into their thinking processes.

First, a group of subject matter experts (SMEs) answer a CSI Hotline question on "How Your Information Security Unit Should Be Structured." (CSI members call into the Hotline with their burning questions, then I canvass some of the SMEs to get a few different perspectives on the query.)

Second, a CSI Advisory Council meeting turns into a roundtable on "Where Information Security Should Report." (The CSI Advisory Council meets twice a year to discuss industry issues.)

How to Structure Your Information Security Unit

The following query from a CSI member is typical of numerous Hotline calls over the years. Hopefully, the insights of the experienced practitioners from Fortune 500 corporations and other large, successful enterprises will help you formulate your approach to this perennial question.

I am director of security for a large state agency. I have one person performing mainframe security on both IBM and DEC systems and one person performing physical security and supervising numerous security guards. The department has over 1,000 permanent employees (most of them at headquarters and a few hundred located in dozens of field offices throughout the state, including over 30 interstate auditors located throughout the country). Our IBM mainframe at the state computing center is separate; we also have our own separate WAN utilizing encrypted links.

We do not allow employees to be connected to external networks, such as the Internet, while they are connected to our tax systems. (We collected over $10 billion last year.) We desire to begin using electronic commerce. We have to begin collecting sales tax this way by July 1 of next year and will also probably begin collecting individual income taxes this way as well in another year.

A consulting firm recommended that we install a firewall and accompanying perimeter detection systems. It also recommended that we centralize all security. We are not performing Novell, UNIX, and Windows NT security. The firm further recommended that we have one unit in computer security (possibly two people) to do day-to-day security administration (such as creating and modifying accounts, resetting passwords, etc.) and another unit with security consultants. This would include possibly three people who would set the policies and rules for the firewall and monitor our WAN for attacks. This unit would also set policy and direction for the mainframe, UNIX, Novell, individual workstations, etc. and perform other security analysis duties, such as evaluate exposures and threats, participate in the application development process, develop formal alert processes and organize a CERT, investigate security incidents, provide consulting, and compliance checks and audits.

While my organization does some of these things today, it certainly is not staffed to perform any of them in a comprehensive manner that will be required. Before we proceed defining and staffing this organization, agency management has asked me to determine how other organizations' security functions are staffed to meet the challenge of electronic commerce as well as perform the duties I have mentioned above. (I should mention that I am fortunate to be reporting directly to the deputy secretary of the agency.)

Ernest Hernandez, CISSP, Sprint Paranet, CSI Advisory Council comments, "I have attached a high-level org chart of a typical security organization in this day and age."

"Most (non-government) security organizations report to a CIO, or to the director of IT.

"Most organizations that I have seen have a 'separate' physical security group that reports to a Risk Management group," Hernandez says. "However, the physical security group could report to the CIO; it just seems to make more sense reporting in a different area. Plus, physical security usually takes more bodies so the security group has a better chance of 'adding' bodies if they are not also part of the physical security group.

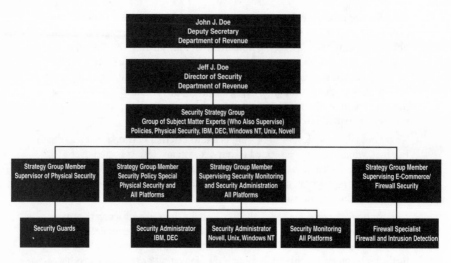

Figure 15.1 Information security organization chart.

Source: Ernest Hernandez, Sprint Paranet

"The sample org chart I have provided here," Hernandez continues, "would be for a consultant-level group of people with high skills in at least one or two areas (policies, UNIX security, Windows NT security, etc). Members of that same group would serve as 'supervisors' (with technical responsibility only) over the departmental functions below them."

Dr. Eugene Schultz, CISSP, of Global Integrity/SAIC, also offers some insights.

"My first reaction is that although intelligent structuring of an InfoSec function is important, I fear that the consultancy which made the recommendations may have placed too much emphasis on structure. Structure is, of course, important, but regardless of the structure, effective InfoSec functions get their job done anyway.

"A lot of the effectiveness of an InfoSec function depends on the communication and persuasive abilities of the InfoSec manager and his or her staff," Schultz says. "An effective InfoSec function develops leverage by being able to understand and relate to the business case of the organization they serve. If InfoSec staff preach security for security's sake, the InfoSec function will fail. If InfoSec staff understand the business needs of the organization and sell what they do accordingly, they are likely to succeed.

"All that said," Schultz continues, "sometimes it is best to have a highly centralized InfoSec function. Sometimes it is better to have a decentralized function. A centralized function (especially one that reports directly to a CIO) is likely to have more leverage in terms of influencing policy, standards, etc. It is, at the same time, more likely to be out of touch with the business units.

"A decentralized function is advantageous in that it is more likely to understand the needs of business units and to be able to work with them. But achieving centralized standards, having a centralized enforcement capability, and so on are more difficult," he cautions. "A possible general rule of thumb is that the higher the security-related risk, the greater need there is for a centralized function.

"I should add that staffing level is always a battle," Schultz says. "The best way to obtain the needed level of staffing is to communicate and promote the business case for security, whatever that may be."

Chris Grillo of Minnesota Power and Light, another CSI Advisory Council member, has some recommendations:

- "The installation of a firewall is a must and should be considered a cost of providing the electronic commerce. The firewall enables you to provide the electronic commerce service. Without it, you would not provide the service.

- "The centralization of security monitoring for the LAN environment and possibly the mainframe environment is the way to go. There should be a centralized focal point in security so nothing falls through the cracks.

- "If limited resources is an issue for the security department, decentralize the 'administration' of the user accounts (creating, deleting, resetting passwords, etc.) to the help desk or system administrators."

Grillo recommends that the security department should then have responsibility in three major areas:

1. IT security strategy and planning:
   - Architecture
   - Policy and guidelines
   - Risk assessment
   - Incident investigation
   - Consulting
   - Audit interface
   - Project management interface
   - Industry interface
   - Others...

2. IT security monitoring:
   - NT platform
   - UNIX platform

- Novell
- Workstations
- Firewalls (intrusion detection monitoring, not administration)
- Email (virus and Trojan horse prevention)
- Applications/databases (Oracle, etc.)
- Telecomm (modems)
- Others…

3. IT security awareness:

- Security department Web development and update (if applicable) security presentations
- Monthly article coordination
- Security primers/consulting
- Others…

Grillo says, "With the right tools and people you would be able to provide adequate security monitoring in the three areas above with three to four people given your user base and the complexity of your environment (medium)."

Donn B. Parker, CISSP, of Atomic Tangerine comments, "The specific answer would be very complex. However, a useful approach would be to contact many of the other 50 state departments, find those that are similar, and get input from them on their organizations. This would go a long way in making sure you are in an acceptable range of due diligence, and you can learn from other similar organizations about what works best—best practices. Many of the others will have a long history and experience to rely on, and many will be more advanced, providing good direction."

Bob McKee, CISSP, of The Hartford Group wraps it up.

"My answer could take many pages. However, I would summarize by offering the following: I would agree with the recommendations made by the consulting firm that the CSI member referred to in your message.

"I would emphasize the importance of establishing a central organization," McKee says, "and also for the separation of the security administration and consulting functions within it. Both of these functions have become multidimensional. For example, the administrative function would typically include ongoing support of IDs and passwords and a hotline to support the user. It may also include administration of a corporate security-awareness program and responsibility for policy development and compliance monitoring. The responsibilities of a consulting group could consist of firewall configuration support, intrusion detection software deployment, evaluating emerging technologies and concepts such as VPNs, and strong authentication techniques and offering expertise to management and project teams.

"Regardless of the structure of the security organization, a highly motivated and well-trained staff is necessary to provide adequate information protection," he continues. "Whether the organization is large or small, providing each individual with the opportunity to upgrade their skills and knowledge as they go about doing their jobs is a critical success factor, as is adequate compensation. Perhaps even more important is offering a challenging work environment with room for individual growth. This takes a good deal of work. However, if it can be accomplished, attracting and retaining qualified people will be easier.

"The number of people required to adequately support security requirements is a function of the size and scope of the business and the technical environment that must be supported," McKee explains. "Among the factors to be considered would be the willingness of management to fund staff for this purpose, the number of users to support, their geographic location, operating system diversity, and the degree to which the Internet, intranets, and extranets are used. The introduction of e-commerce will complicate matters, adding expense and potential exposures.

"Determining an adequate staffing level and developing expertise is an extremely formidable task for any security organization and may not be possible without outside assistance," McKee advises. "That assistance can range from simply making use of the advice and expertise of the research groups, to asking a professional services organization for an assessment and/or ongoing support, to the outsourcing of specific security functions. In this particular situation, it is probably a good investment to hire a third party to assess current capabilities against future needs and to provide a set of findings that can be used to strengthen the capabilities of the organization."

Well, what do the world-class organizations do?

At CSI's 26th Annual Computer Security Conference and Exhibition, held in Washington, D.C. (November, 1999), Peter Schelstraete and Dan Erwin of the Dow Chemical Company accepted the annual Information Program of the Year award. The Dow Chemical Company is a global science and technology company that develops and manufactures a portfolio of chemical, plastic, and agricultural products and services for customers in 168 countries. With annual sales of more than $18 billion, Dow conducts its operations through 15 global businesses employing 39,000 people. It has 123 manufacturing sites in 32 countries and supplies more than 3,500 products.

In a general session, Erwin highlighted Dow's program.

"Our information security program at Dow has grown from what was a hobby for a select few in the 1970s to a scattered, site-administered program in the 1980s to a cohesive, proactive, global function that adds value to Dow's bottom line today.

"Our approach has been to divide security into a series of manageable elements and then manage them in a professional way. We assign appropriate, risk-based controls using Value Based Management analysis, taking into account all pertinent business and technology constraints."

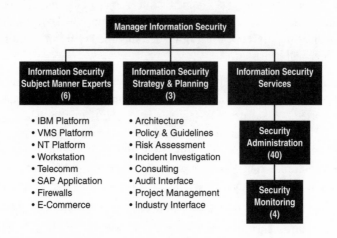

Figure 15.2 Information security organization chart.

Source: Dow Chemical Company

Where Should Your Information Security Unit Report?

Where information security should report is one of the perennial questions that concerned information security practitioners have been grappling with for a long time.

Reporting structure is an important issue for information-security practitioners in government as well as the private sector. Consider the comments of the DoD's Jim Christy.

"One of the things that we've found is that information security is in the wrong logical place in the organization. It is always buried down in the IT section. It doesn't have the ear of the CEO or the Commander. The CEO or Commander is saying 'Connect, connect, connect.' And the guy who is in charge of the IT section is going do what his or her boss says. Down below them is the information security person saying, 'Hey, if you do that these are the ramifications.' But the big boy doesn't get to hear that. So we recommend you change the organizational structure so that the two of them have an equal voice and the CEO or Commander hears both sides and can make a risk management decision."

So where should information security report? Of course, the safe answer is, "It depends."

But to help your formulate your own view, I held a roundtable on the subject with members of the CSI Advisory Council.

In the course of their freewheeling discussion, our panel of experts examined various reporting structures, tackled a real-world query from the CSI Hotline, and offered some insightful questions to ask yourself when evaluating where information security rightfully belongs in your organization's reporting structure. Hopefully, some of the practical wisdom and debating points thrown out by the CSI Advisory Council will help you prepare for the next battle royal.

Richard Power, CSI: Where should information security report?

Gerald W. Grindler, ASK Consulting: Normally, information security should report to the chief information officer (CIO). Most of the alternatives are unappealing at best. The relationship between corporate security—we call them the guards, guns, dogs, and locks guys—and information security is usually a very strained relationship. All of the big ticket items (headline stories, senior management's awareness, etc.) are falling in the information security arena right now.

As the info security people get more actively involved, this causes problems with the corporate security people who feel that they are the only ones qualified to handle investigations. Traditionally, the corporate security people are not on the information systems side; hence, the "battle over turf" begins.

I certainly don't think information security belongs anywhere close to internal audit. The internal audit folks are auditing the policies and procedures developed by info security, so there would be a conflict of interest. Now I would not be a good ex-information-security manager if I didn't put my two cents in to wish that corporate information security should report on a dotted line somehow to the Audit Committee of the Board of Directors.

I know that is really wishing for the stars, but information security deals with the protection of information assets of the company. I used to tell people that in most cases the computer-based information was equal to the total asset value of the company: for example, a $20 billion company equals $20 billion worth of information assets. It's a stretch I know, but it is not a bad place to start.

Dan Erwin, Dow Chemical: "Where should information security report?" is the wrong question. The question that needs to be asked is "What should the security department look like?" We reengineered our whole company. During that process we went through function decomposition of the information security group. Basically we decided we had three elements in our group. The elements broke down into administration and monitoring. That was the lowest level element, and those people basically were lower skill sets. They tend to give out profiles; they handle the "I forgot my password" and "I need access to something for an extra 24 hours" requests. They cover the desk 24 hours a day and are attached to the help desk organization. That's where they report. And that, as it turns out, is being outsourced.

The level up from that is what we call "Design and Configuration." These are the people that design profiles, set up domains in NT, do the firewall work. Also, they design all the tools that the admin and monitor people use, and they design user-friendly administration front-ends, they design the reports from the back-end, e-mail interfaces. They also do investigative work. They monitor reports. That's a fairly techie group. I don't like where they report in our company. I think they should report to an operations manager; they report to Research and Development.

We have another group at the top we call "Strategy and Planning." Strategy and Planning is a combination of consultants. They report to a function called strategy and planning; a fairly high-placed function. We do risk assessment. Everybody has a special task. We all jump around. We work mostly with project teams. All new projects have a computer security person assigned to them.

We are all 25-year people. There's nobody in that group with under 22 to 25 years. We report to senior management and require no supervision. When we start talking about where we report, what usually happens is you get people at the administration level who want to report to someone at the executive level, and they don't have the skill sets to report there and there is no support structure for them. They need somebody that can help them figure out how to advance in their career. These are junior people who need supervision and training.

Hal Tipton, currently independent consultant, formerly Rockwell International: You work in a unique environment where you have good security skills all the way through top management.

Fred Trickey, formerly Columbia University, currently The Netigy Corporation: That structure, which seems very suited to your corporate culture, evolved out of a mature information security program. How many people are you talking about in total?

Erwin: We have about 14 to 17 people in Admin/Monitor; about 7 to 8 in Design/Configure.

Tipton: Are they full-time security people?

Erwin: Full-time.

Trickey: If someone asks, "How do I start a security program?" and you hand them that, they are going to commit ritual *hari-kari*.

Erwin: This answers the question where you report, not how to start a program. In the function decomposition we tried to figure out what the functions were. We decided the major functions we needed were risk assessment specialists, security architecture specialists, security admin. That was one cut at it. Another cut was the roles. We said we need somebody that creates strategy, somebody that defines partner needs, we need somebody that defines technical needs, we need somebody that creates solutions, somebody that delivers solutions. And we said we need somebody to manage the group. That's probably the smartest thing we've done in the many years.

Power: Is there anything good about information security reporting to audit?

Everyone: No.

Power: And what's wrong about it is…?

Grindler: Conflict of interest. You have the lawmakers and the judicial system in the same organization.

Power: And that would be true for a company of any size?

Trickey: Absolutely.

Grindler: Although medium- and small-sized companies tend to put it under audit.

Power: What if the auditors have a lot of clout?

Erwin: You use that clout.

Tipton: Find out who the auditor reports to…usually it's the controller.

Cheri Jacoby, Price Waterhouse: What if the internal audit function has been outsourced?

Trickey: The biggest problem with audit is that it's a conflict of interest.

Tipton: If you have to be related to audit, you should be a parallel organization reporting to the same chief.

Power: Usually internal audit reports to…?

Will Ozier, independent consultant: The audit committee and the board of directors.

Tipton: The external auditors report to the audit committee and the board, but internal auditors usually report to the controller.

Power: What about reporting somewhere in Information Systems (IS)?

Everyone: No.

Power: So let's lay out the arguments for not reporting to IS.

Trickey: You don't want to report to IS because your goals are different. IS goals are to get the systems developed and out. I've had a lot of battles with IS and IS people who say, "We've got to get this system running. We're going to bring it up without security and we'll put security in later." Later never happens.

Jacoby: IS is functionality and productivity, period. And they view security as inhibitors.

Trickey: The only way it can work in IS is if you can completely shift the perception of information security to make it enabling rather than disabling and that's a major cultural shift.

Ozier: It's also not totally true.

Tipton: And it's very dangerous.

Jacoby: But another good reason to have it under the CIO but parallel to IS is the CIO is also over IS and he can tell them, "You will have security involved." You need somebody that has authority over IS.

Grindler: We used to say security is not a technical issue, but that's not so true anymore. The reason you want it under the CIO is that you need technologists that can satisfy, i.e., produce security solutions. And then we can rotate those people in and out of our group once they've shown that they're the top of top.

Power: What about reporting to the CIO? That's supposedly the trend.

Tipton: I like the CIO because this is the guy in charge of the information and we're all information security folks. If you can report to the CIO in parallel with IS, that's fine. CIO is a high profile person.

Trickey: If there *is* a CIO…

Grindler: To be successful, you have to be on the same level as the people that are running the data center.

Ozier: I still have a problem with the CIO. Yes, he's responsible for getting information out, but it again goes to a budgetary conflict. He could still say "I need to get this information function going, and I need to save bucks, and I'm going to save bucks with security."

Tipton: Part of his responsibility is security enforcement....

Ozier: There is still the issue of "my watch." I'm going to be in this job for three or four years. I can afford to take the chance because odds-wise it's a good risk. For the individual making the decision, it's a good risk. I hate to say that, but it's true. If business owns the information, I don't think information security should be under the CIO.

Tipton: I do, because the CIO is in charge of the IS group. The CIO in parallel to the information security group could be part of IS, in parallel to IS under the CIO, and I think it would work fine.

Ozier: Okay, it's conceivable. But my thinking on it would be to report to chief operations officer or chief financial officer.

Power: Okay, what about reporting to the chief financial officer (CFO)?

Tipton: We had a lot of experience with that. The problem is that you're financially oriented and your operations and engineering people don't believe that you're in charge of them. And so you have a problem getting to them.

Jacoby: The bottom line is...it depends. The CFO is a very visible position. He has a lot of clout, assuming he's a guy who doesn't think of information security as just another cost center. Otherwise, when they look for places to cut, watch out!

Trickey: For a large organization that makes a lot a sense: banks, insurance, large manufacturing sector. For a small warehouse and distribution firm in East Texas, they don't have that kind of corporate structure, but they still may have a need for information security.

Jacoby: It's all about risk. What are the risks to the organization?

Trickey: It's all risk-based. We're seeing more and more distribution. We've got computing centers all over the organization. Central IS was a bottleneck in certain ways, and there are many gains to be made by distributing the function but central IS also provided some very critical corporate functions—security, integrity, control—that we're losing. We're distributing them out, too. And I've been arguing to pull back some of the control and integrity functions and decentralize them. Let all these people do their own development, but let them do it under established standards. That's why I think it's critical that information security be seen as central, and I would argue that it's a staff function not a line function.

Tipton: I don't think it makes any difference whether it's staff or line, in the final analysis. There was a discussion about putting it under the chief financial officer, and that's where we were, and that was a mistake. That was a mistake because we would write our policies and procedures and implement those within the financial organization and the engineering groups and all the people that you want to have following these things didn't believe that they needed to follow financial policy. You run into that type of thing. So you move it to operations and that's better.

Power: What about reporting to the chief operating officer (COO)?

Erwin: I can think of specific industries where that would work.

Ozier: COO is very line oriented. It's a logical place.

Trickey: I again think you have a slight conflict of interest. The COO's job is to keep things moving. And if the InfoSec officer comes along and says, "Look, you've got to something about this." No matter, it's working. It ain't broke, don't fix it. It depends on the organization.

Erwin: If you're running a nuclear power plant, security is probably a big part of the organization.

Jacoby: I've got to believe that there are industries that don't have COOs. Is this true?

Trickey: I don't think service industries have COOs.

Tipton: Maybe where information security reports to in an organization depends on where the information security needs are. It's risk analysis once again. If the greatest risks are financial, then maybe the CFO might be the right place. If the greatest risks are operational, maybe COO. Normally it's information, so the CIO would make the most sense, particularly in the growing service sector. Information is their product. Certainly in my industry information is the product.

Power: What about corporate security?

Erwin: It's a really bad fit. But as I said before, if you go to that group, it depends what kind of industry you're in—for example, in manufacturing it's tightly tied to loss control, trying to prevent something from happening.

Tipton: Too far down the food chain.

Erwin: In our situation, corporate security reports directly to the vice president. They have a very high profile.

Trickey: I don't think it's a problem because of where it reports; it's a perception problem. I have never seen any organization where security was the most popular kid on the block. You don't want to be associated with them. It throws you back into the cop mode instead of the enabling mode.

Power: Any other places to report that we haven't considered?

Erwin: There's another organization starting to grow up in big companies, and probably other people have them, and that's risk assessment. I've been working with them a bit lately. They're still wrestling with insurance policies and stuff like that. But they're quickly starting to talk about what if this kind of information made it into the press. They're starting to drift over into our world. They're highly placed guys, both politically and structurally. In our organization they're guys at the executive level.

Jacoby: Another area is quality management. That's not a bad fit—if quality is something seen as very necessary in your particular business. The downside to that is sometimes quality is seen as the topic *du jour*.

Trickey: The danger there is that it might wind up being ephemeral. Today's buzz term. But basically, when you think about it, information security is a quality function.

Jacoby: Not only that, if you talk to the quality professionals, quality is a way of life. That's kind of what we're preaching, too. And they're an easy win as far as getting support for security. They're not a hard sell at all.

Trickey: We've run a few quality improvement programs, and I have been in on all of them. I have been brought in on all of them because our quality people do recognize information security is...

Tipton: That could be a good organization but once again, their goals are a little different than information security.

Trickey: I would say that, like audit, they're good partners but I'm not sure that's the right organizational place to be.

Tipton: Quality management is more related to audit itself. They're compliance-oriented.

Power: Are there any other places that information security should definitely not report to?

Erwin: Another place you shouldn't be is in software. But that's the way it is in lot of organizations that are just starting. Because they have to install a product, all of a sudden, software guys are coming into the security group.

Trickey: That is where it absolutely should not be.

Ozier: I agree. That's totally wrong.

Erwin: But if you talk to small companies, that's where you'll often find it.

Ozier: Then the information security technologist needs to be really cognizant of the problems inherent in it and be able to communicate them effectively to management.

Trickey: I work extraordinarily closely with the software people. I work directly with the manager of operations and technology services and with his system support software people. But I also restrict them highly because they're the people who can do the most damage.

Ozier: Systems programmers, the guys who manage the operating systems and systems utilities, are by far the most dangerous potentially. Interesting enough, they are also the weirdest people in the entire operation.

Trickey: And they work at 0:dark thirty, in the middle of the night, when nobody knows what they are doing.

Erwin: And they get really bored with the administration portion of it, so they give everybody access all.

Tipton: A close second would probably be finance because the controllers are responsible for the internal controls, and actually security is a part of internal controls. And so oftentimes, controllers at a financial organization are a real problem.

Trickey: Emergency management, if by that you mean disaster recovery (DR), is appropriate, to be in the same organization as information security. It depends on staff and budgets. But it should not just be included as an add-on responsibility. I could see an argument for emergency management or disaster recovery and information security being together. I don't see physical security and information security together.

Jacoby: He's got a bigger problem: They've got to get away from audit first.

Trickey: I can't imagine anyone even contemplating putting physical security under audit.

Ozier: Information security certainly has an interest in how effectively physical security is managed.

Trickey: Physical control of access to servers and hosts, and prevention of theft of equipment, is certainly an interest of information security, but I think it is really a separate organizational function.

Power: So what about leaving DR and IP together and physical security separate?

Trickey: That would work. You see that a lot.

Power: What about putting physical security and disaster recovery together?

Ozier: Physical security is not cognizant of information protection.

Power: What about each having its own area with its own reporting structure?

Trickey: That's probably best. In this scenario, they are three separate organizations reporting to a security manager. Parallel is maybe better way to put it than "separate."

Tipton: That would be good, that would work.

Trickey: And then the question is, "Where does that central security manager hang?" And the answer there is, "Not audit!"

Power: And they would come together under a corporate security officer. And he or she would report to...?

Tipton: Depends on the organization.

Trickey: Yes, it depends. Maybe the CIO. Some executive-level person.

Ozier: You got to be careful when you call it a "corporate security officer."

Power: Because it sounds like physical security?

Ozier: Yes. The corporate security officer usually comes from the physical security side and doesn't care about information security. So it always winds up getting leftovers.

Power: But the guy asking the question is the head of information protection...

Trickey: Well, then perhaps they should be three parallel organizations under him and he should report not to audit. Depending on the organization, it could be the CIO or CFO.

Tipton: Because the physical security guys are not necessarily oriented toward information protection, they've got all kinds of other assets to protect, including people.

Trickey: But having them under the information protection officer would facilitate what we were talking about earlier, the protection of information resources in a distributed environment. Because you could heighten the physical security guys awareness about information security issues.

Tipton: Yeah, I think that would be good.

Power: How should information security practitioners determine where they would even want to report if anyone would listen?

Jacoby: Ask yourself some questions. What area of your organization has the highest visibility? Do you have a CIO? What does your organization look like?

Tipton: You really need to get a copy of the organizational chart and study it.

Ozier: How mature is the organization structure?

Erwin: How flat is your organizational structure?

Jacoby: What industry are you in? How valuable is information to your organization? In what way is it an asset of the organization?

Trickey: What is the risk on information being released? Who would get hurt if the information is released? Whose ox is going to get gored if it's lost?

Erwin: I like your idea of a series of questions. The only thing we've agreed upon here is that it shouldn't report to audit and it shouldn't report down in the bowels of the IS organization. Everything else depends on who you are and what you are.

Jacoby: And that it's very much risk-based. I think we've all agreed on that too.

Erwin: There's another whole thing to consider here. Alan Krull, a great philosopher in my opinion, always said you had to have a gorilla in your corner. Wherever you report to, go find somebody up at that level that actually cares about security. Go find yourself a champion, a gorilla that can make something happen. That's more important than the set of letters you pick, pick a guy that cares.

Trickey: And the champion may not be who you report to.

Inside Global Law Enforcement

I n early May 2000, in response to a request from a U.S. government agency, I met with a bright young man who had just been entrusted with developing a cyberdefense strategy for a very small European country. That earnest patriot and I "talked shop" for a while. To divulge the nature of the conversation would be irresponsible, but one moment early on in the interchange was quite poignant.

He said, "We border on three countries: X, Y, and Z."

"Actually, you have four borders: X, Y, Z, and the Internet."

"Yes," he said, after pausing for a moment. "That's the problem, isn't it?"

In the physical world, passports are inspected, visas are issued, customs forms are reviewed. In cyberspace, with a click of your mouse, you can access a server in Lithuania, with your next click a few seconds later you can access a server in Fiji with no paperwork at all. That's one of the extraordinary advantages of the Internet, and it can be exploited for good or ill. Over the Internet, someone can commit a crime in one country while sitting at a computer in another country where the act is not considered a crime at all.

In the physical world, when crimes are investigated, physical evidence is collected: for example, fingerprints, DNA, marked bills, video footage, and smoking guns. In cyberspace, the very definition of evidence is shaken up. What is really provable in the digital world? Most of the crimes detailed in *Tangled Web* were resolved with plea-bargaining and admissions of guilt. Someday soon a well-heeled cybercriminal's lawyers will challenge the veracity of forensic evidence (a la Barry Scheck in the O.J. Simpson trial). It will be a fascinating court case.

Twenty-first century law enforcement faces numerous problems in regard to crime on the Internet, including jurisdiction and forensics. These are both national and global problems. They demand both national and global solutions. You can't shut out the Internet. Who would want to, anyway? Information crime demands information age law enforcement.

Here is a glimpse at some of the work that has been undertaken so far.

National Infrastructure Protection Center (NIPC)

In 1995, U.S. President Bill Clinton issued Presidential Decision Directive 39 (PDD 39) instructing Attorney General Janet Reno and a Cabinet-level committee to evaluate vulnerabilities in the nation's critical infrastructure and recommend countermeasures.

In response to PDD 39, Reno organized the Critical Infrastructure Working Group (CIWG). In January 1996, CIWG recommended the creation of a full-blown commission to develop a national strategy for the protection of critical infrastructure in the long-term as well as an interim task force to pull together existing resources with which to meet potential infrastructure attacks in the short-term.

Acting on CIWG's recommendations, President Clinton issued Executive Order 13010, which established the President's Commission on Critical Infrastructure Protection (PCCIP) and the Infrastructure Protection Task Force (IPTF).

In June 1997, the Department of Defense (DoD) conducted Eligible Receiver, a no-notice joint staff exercise to test how well it would respond if its information infrastructure were the target of a serious campaign of cyberattacks. A DoD "red team" of experts exploited known vulnerabilities using tools and techniques researched from open sources over the Internet. They succeeded in breaking into networks, launching denial of service attacks, and disrupting phone systems. They succeeded in reading, altering, and destroying e-mail messages. They succeeded in gaining superuser access to more than 36 computers (i.e., they could create or delete user accounts, they could shut the systems down, they could reformat hard disks).

In October 1997, the PCCIP issued its report to the President. The PCCIP made numerous recommendations, including the creation of a national warning center, under the control of the FBI, to alert the country to infrastructure attacks.

In early February 1998, the Solar Sunrise case dominated the headlines. (For details of the Solar Sunrise case, see Chapter 6.)

In late February 1998, against the backdrop of Solar Sunrise and Eligible Receiver, Attorney General Reno and FBI Director Louis Freeh acted on the advice of the PCCIP and announced the formation of the National Infrastructure Protection Center (NIPC), located at FBI Headquarters in Washington, D.C.

In April 1998, President Clinton issued Presidential Decision Directive 63, a sweeping mandate that, among other things, formally recognized NIPC's central role and instructed other agencies to participate in and support NIPC's work.

In June 1998, Michael A. Vatis, Deputy Assistant FBI Director and Chief of NIPC, testified before the Senate Judiciary Subcommittee on Technology, Terrorism, and Government Information on NIPC's role in confronting the range of cyberthreats to infrastructure.

> The NIPC's mission is to detect, deter, warn of, respond to, and investigate unlawful acts involving computer intrusions and unlawful acts, both physical and cyber, that threaten or target our critical infrastructures. This means we do not simply investigate and respond to attacks after they occur, but we try to learn about them and prevent them beforehand. To accomplish this mission, the NIPC relies on the assistance of, and information gathered by, the FBI's 56 Field Offices; other Federal agencies; state and local law enforcement agencies; and perhaps most importantly, the private sector.

> In recognition of the vital roles all of these entities must play, I want to emphasize that the NIPC is founded on the notion of a partnership. We are building this partnership first through inclusive representation. Our intent is that the Center be staffed with professionals from other Federal agencies, from state and local law enforcement, and from private industry.

> Equally important is the need to build a two-way street for the flow of information and incident data between the government and the private sector. The government, with unique access to national intelligence and law enforcement information, can develop a threat picture that no entity in the private sector could develop on its own. We need to share this with the industry. At the same time, we need to learn from industry about the intrusion attempts and vulnerabilities that it is experiencing. This will help us paint the vulnerability and threat picture more completely and will give us a head start on preventing or containing a nascent attack.

> We are not the nation's super-systems administrator or security officer, responsible for securing everyone's infrastructures or systems against intruders or advising on the latest security software or patches to fix vulnerabilities. That role clearly must be filled by systems administrators in each company, by chief information officers in government agencies, and by industry groups and other entities (such as computer emergency response teams) with expertise in reducing vulnerabilities and restoring service.

Rather, our role is to help prevent intrusions and attacks by gathering information about threats from sources that are uniquely available to the Government (such as from law enforcement and intelligence sources), combining it with information voluntarily provided by the private sector or obtained from open sources, conducting analysis, and disseminating our analyses and warnings to all relevant consumers. And, if an attack does occur, our role is to serve as the Federal Government's focal point for crisis response and investigation.[1]

NIPC was organized into three sections:

- "**NIPC's Computer Investigations and Operations Section (CIOS)** manages computer intrusion investigations conducted by FBI Field Offices throughout the country; provides subject matter experts, equipment, and technical support to cyberinvestigators in federal, state, and local government agencies involved in critical infrastructure protection; and provides a cyberemergency response capability to help resolve a cyberincident.

- "**NIPC's Analysis and Warning Section (AWS)** provides analytical support during computer intrusion investigations and long-term analyses of vulnerability and threat trends. When appropriate, it distributes tactical warnings and analyses to all the relevant partners, informing them of potential vulnerabilities and threats and long-term trends. It also reviews numerous government and private sector databases, media, and other sources daily to gather information that may be relevant to any aspect of our mission, including the gathering of indications of a possible attack.

- "**NIPC's Training, Administration, and Outreach Section (TAOS)** coordinates the training and education of cyberinvestigators within the FBI Field Offices, state and local law enforcement agencies, and private sector organizations. It also coordinates the outreach to private sector companies, state and local governments, other government agencies, and the FBI's field offices. In addition, this section manages the collection and cataloguing of information concerning "key assets" across the country. Finally, it provides the entire Center with administrative support, handling matters involving personnel, budget, contractors, and equipment."[2]

The Role of Computer Analysis Response Team (CART)

Another essential element of the U.S. Federal Government's response to cybercrime and infrastructure attacks is the FBI's Computer Analysis Response Team (CART).

---

1. U.S. Senate Committee on the Judiciary. Infrastructure Protection: Hearing before the Subcommittee on Technology, Terrorism, and Government Information, June 10, 1998.

2. Source: NIPC Web site www.nipc.gov/organization.htm

CART came into existence in 1991. Thirty CART personnel are headquartered in the FBI building in Washington, D.C. and others are located in regional offices throughout the country.

NIPC is one of CART's several "clients" within the FBI.

Mark Pollitt, CART's Unit Chief, explains its role.

"One of CART's missions is to go out to electronic crime scenes—residences, businesses, wherever—to identify, seize, and protect the latent evidence. The other mission is similar to that of fingerprint examiners or the DNA examiners: We try to extract information from the latent evidence that will assist in the investigation of the case."

What kinds of crimes does CART get involved in?

According to Pollitt, CART collects and examines evidence in regard to every single violation that the FBI investigates.

"Well over half of our work falls into two categories: traditional white-collar crime (for example, financial fraud) and child pornography. Everything else makes up something like 35 percent of our work load."

Computer intrusion cases, Pollitt observes, are still a relatively small part of CART's work load—less than 7 percent.

"Certainly, the number of cases reported and followed up on is a factor. Remember, CART doesn't get involved until there is a crime scene. But you also have to realize that computer intrusions are still rare occurrences relative to some of the more traditional crimes. There are far more people dealing in child pornography than there are breaking into computers. There are far more criminal enterprises out there making money in white collar fraud schemes than there are breaking into computers."

What does computer crime evidence look like?

For the most part, Pollitt remarks, the largest single category are still PCs in either standalone or LAN environments. Enterprise servers, large file servers, applications servers, and Web servers are becoming more common in two areas—white collar crime and Internet-related crimes (whether involving intrusions or Internet fraud).

"Whenever possible we take the entire PC. That's our preference. Our second choice is to remove the media. That is a relatively rare occasion. The third and least desirable option is to create an image on site of every computer. You can only do very directed seizures of particular files if you know with absolute certainty what you're looking for and where it actually resides. We prefer to seize the boxes if we can. Of course, when you're talking about large network servers, etc. our preference is not to take all of it unless it is essential. In such cases, what we like to have is a full logical backup of whatever part of it is determined to be pertinent. That depends on the circumstances. If the entire enterprise is criminal, or you're trying to prove some transactional aspect, you might take the whole thing, or you might not be able to depending upon who owns it. You may have to take a full backup or in some cases even an image. But trying to restore images from RAIDs or storage arrays is not an easy thing to do, so we try to avoid that."

The sad fact is that most corporations don't have policies or procedures in place for preserving evidence. Pollitt offers some practical tips on where people should begin.

"In this day and age, if you don't have a data security plan, you're nuts. You better plan for the possibility that you might have to collect evidence—whether it's for a civil or criminal matter—while you're at it. Preserving evidence is not your number-one priority, but staying in business surely is. If you don't have an effective data backup and storage program, you're already behind the power curve in respect to any potential digital crime evidence that you want to collect.

"If we have both the machine in its current state and incremental backups of what happened over the last several hours, days, weeks, or months—we may be able to produce crucial evidence down the road.

"If you think anything may be important to making a case or determining the facts of a circumstance, you should treat it as evidence. Preserve it immediately. Do not do anything to alter, damage, or destroy that information."

A provable chain of custody is also important, as Pollitt explains.

"The courts, of course, are far more stringent about those of us in law enforcement who are trained to do that as a matter of course than they would be with a corporation. Having a chain of custody is certainly going to make it easier to get it entered as evidence and make it more powerful evidence when you do. Establishing a chain of custody is a very good thing to do for a lot of reasons—only some of which are legal. Not only could the evidence have been changed, it could be lost. There is nothing quite as embarrassing as getting all through a case and not having a key piece of evidence your case was based on."

What goes into being able to show a strong chain of custody?

A chain of custody is a physical restriction of access coupled with a documentation that demonstrates what happened. A chain of custody is not simply a piece of paper with people's signatures on it; it is the fact that those people can testify that these things happened at those dates and times. You have to preserve the physical integrity of the evidence; for example, putting it in a cardboard box with sealing tape and your initials over it. But if you don't have a concurrent document that says what date and time you sealed it up, you have only accomplished half of what you need to do.

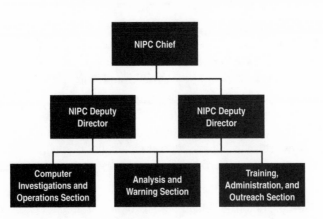

Figure 16.1 NIPC organizational structure.[3]

"Isn't It Good, Norwegian Wood..."

Over the last several years, I have delivered "Current and Future Danger," CSI's executive briefing on computer crime and information warfare, at conferences around the world, including São Paolo, Brazil; Johannesburg, South Africa; Tokyo; Calgary, Canada; and Lisbon. In May 2000, at the invitation of the Norwegian government, I had the pleasure of delivering it in the mysterious northern twilight that inspired Henrik Ibsen's *Peer Gynt* and Edvard Munch's *Madonna*.

The venue was "The Internet as the Scene of the Crime," an international computer crime conference held in May. Participants from more than 30 countries—from China to Denmark, from Chile to Cameroon—gathered for three days of talks in Oslo. The event was hosted by Økokrim (www.okokrim.no).

The origin and evolution of Økokrim is indicative of a process that is going on at a national level in countries great and small throughout the world. Without competence and courage in places as far away from Washington, D.C. as Oslo, Tel Aviv, and Singapore, the cybercrime deterrent (however formidable at the U.S. end) will be ineffective.

Let's take a look at a success story.

Established in 1989, Økokrim, the "national authority for the investigation and prosecution of economic and environmental crime in Norway" investigates and prosecutes a broad range of illegal activity from embezzlement to the dumping of hazardous wastes. Økokrim also provides assistance for local police and prosecutors, collects intelligence on criminal activity, and cultivates international cooperation.

---

3. Ibid.

Established in 1994, Økokrim's computer crime team, led by Senior Public Prosecutor Inger Marie Sunde, consists of two prosecutors and seven special investigators. Four of the investigators have computer science educations. Two are top candidates straight from university. They bring the attitudes and skills of the "hacker" generation. Two are accomplished computer engineers (one in his mid-40s, one in his 50s). They bring experience and stability and work to build bridges to scientific institutions. The three other special investigators have traditional law enforcement backgrounds. Traditional investigative techniques, of course, are just as important as ever. Indeed, as we have seen in the United States, many hacking crimes are solved outside of cyberspace.

Sunde explains the rationale behind her mix of investigators. "Økokrim is based on the principle of multidisciplinary competence," she tells me, "which means a lot of cooperation between the investigators. We give the computer engineers limited police powers after half a year with Økokrim (with consent from the Ministry of Justice). As a result they have formal powers to take statements from suspects and witnesses, but they do not have coercive powers, meaning that house searches and arrests have to be led by the ordinary police investigators, but the computer engineers can participate and assist during these actions. It is easier to make computer engineers part policemen than to create computer engineers out of policemen."

Each Økokrim computer crime case has two investigators assigned to it: one with a traditional law enforcement background and one with a computer engineering background. They work with one of the prosecutors who defines the legally relevant investigative issues, generates warrants, and communicates with the courts.

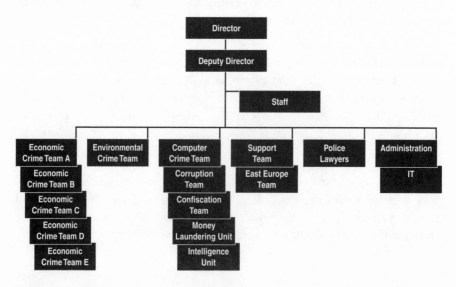

Figure 16.2 Økokrim organizational structure.

Case Study in the Struggle Over Subscriber Data

Sunde organized and moderated "The Internet as the Scene of the Crime." She also gave a presentation on a landmark cybercrime-related ruling she recently won at the bar of the Norwegian Supreme Court.

The details of the court battle and how similar issues have been handled under U.S. law should give you a feel for some of the legal obstacles that must be overcome during the investigation and prosecution of cybercrimes.

In January 1997, an ftp site of child pornography files had been reported to the local police. (Both distribution and possession of child pornography are crimes according to the Norwegian Civil Criminal Code.) The police tried to get the relevant subscriber data from Telenor Nextel (TN), the largest Norwegian ISP (later known as Nextra), but TN refused. The local police submitted the case to Sunde at Økokrim, who offered assistance and turned to the Supreme Court for a ruling.

The question put before the Norwegian Supreme Court was whether the police were entitled to subscriber data pertaining to a specified Internet connection, based on the IP address and the exact time of the connection.

Sunde explains, "In such cases, during the initial phase of the investigation, there is seldom any information other than the IP address, the time, and the date. Therefore, the police are totally dependant on the ISP for subscriber information. (Of course, there are exceptions: For example, in 1999, we caught three hackers on basis of information from Internet Relay Chat [IRC] and an address list from a cell phone. But in the majority of cases, we have to rely on the IP address, the time, and the date the initial phase of the investigation.) Once the ISP provides the subscriber information, we are in the position to collect a lot more data before we strike."

Sunde and Økokrim were asking for subscriber data to both the Internet account and the telephone number used in the dial-up connection. In criminal cases, subscriber data associated with Internet accounts is often fake or reveals a legitimate Internet account that has been hacked or misappropriated in some other way. The only reliable information relates to the telephone number used to dial in to the account. Indeed, the telephone number used may not even belong to one of its own customers. (The ISP sells only Internet connections. It doesn't sell telephone access.)

Unfortunately, the investigation could not go forward until the Supreme Court made a decision. Consequently, the investigation was stalled from July 1998 until January 2000. The legal argument revolved around interpretations of the Norwegian Telecommunications Act of 1995 (article 9-3), which says information about use and content transmitted by telecom services (including ISPs) shall be privileged.

But an exception is allowed under the Telecommunications Act: The police, prosecution, and judiciary are entitled to subscriber data in the course of an investigation without having to resort to a court order. For example, personal phone numbers are publicly available in the telephone directory in Norway, and individuals have the right to request that their numbers be unlisted (secret). But the legal exception was included in the Telecommunications Act to make it clear that even unlisted phone numbers should be made directly available to the police because "the subscriber has no legitimate reason to be kept anonymous from the police, and because the police have a strong need for such data in the course of their work." The lawmakers, however, had not given the Internet any thought at all, so the legal territory in this case was unmapped.

TN argued that it was not unwilling to give subscriber data to the police, but the ISP asserted that the police had to produce a court order in each case. It also asserted that the data was traffic, not subscriber data, and that it was therefore against the European Union's Data Protection Directive to give the information directly to the police. And TN argued, above all, that the police could not get data that related to a dial-up connection with a dynamic IP address.

Sunde argued that the use of dynamic IP addresses is due only to the limitations of the IP resources (TN had 300,000 customers and only 60,000 IP addresses at its disposal). Consequently, it allocated a portion as fixed addresses (used for organizations) and a portion as dynamic addresses (used for individual subscriber accounts).

"Due to technical limitations," Sunde contends, "the subscriber/user was getting a type of anonymity which was unintentional and without any foundation in their contract with TN.

"I did not see the point in a legal safeguard requiring the police to get a court order in every case," she continues, "as the court has no real data to control at this point in an investigation, since the data only consisted of an IP address and a time. The court was in no position to control the accuracy of the log and would regularly have to endorse the police request. Therefore, I argued, it was a waste of time and resources.

"Finally, I made it a point that giving subscriber data to the police in these cases does not jeopardize the safeguards of the individual. At later stages of the investigation, we still need court orders to carry out searches."

In December 1999, after a two-day trial, the Norwegian Supreme Court ruled in favor of Sunde, Økokrim, and the police. The investigation could proceed, and the legal precedent was established for the future.

Sunde extols the verdict: "Vital data can now be obtained and exchanged efficiently and expeditiously at the police level during the early stages of an investigation. It also enables law enforcement to quickly exclude computers used as intermediaries, which is of great importance in transcontinental cases."

Sunde, however, points out other problems: "Of course, this solution is only of value to the police if the ISP has maintained traffic logs. Currently, they have no duty to maintain logs. Furthermore, the EU's Data Protection Directive tries to impose strict limitations on their rights to do so. It seems to me that the European Union has created a supernational state without police."

U.S. Law Versus Norwegian Law

How does Økokrim's legal victory in Norway relate to similar challenges faced by U.S. law enforcement?

Susan Brenner, Associate Dean of the University of Dayton School of Law, who is responsible for an excellent Internet site on cybercrime and law (www.cybercrimes. net), offers some insights.

"Norway does not have constitutional protection equivalent to the Fourth Amendment," Brenner explains. "All their constitution says is 'search of private homes shall not be made except in criminal cases.' So, more can be done there than in the United States. They don't have an exclusionary rule, so even if the police goof up and do something they're not supposed to, you can still use it. The same is true in many other countries.

"The Fourth Amendment to the U.S. Constitution creates a right to be free from 'unreasonable searches and seizures,'" Brenner explains. "If the police engage in a search or seizure, it must be reasonable, and it can be reasonable in one of two ways: (1) conducted pursuant to a search (and seizure) warrant issued on probable cause and meeting other procedural requirements; or (2) conducted pursuant to an exception to the warrant requirement. The exceptions that are most likely to apply to computer/data searches are: (a) consent ('go ahead and search officer, I don't mind, I surrender my rights'); or (b) exigent circumstances (the police search because if they took the time to get a warrant someone might be harmed or evidence might be destroyed).

"For example, applying the Fourth Amendment, the Supreme Court held that it was a search for police to attach a bugging device to a phone booth, because the person's conversation was meant to be private. (*Katz* v. *U.S.*) The court said the search was unreasonable because they didn't obtain a warrant.

"But the Court has also held that it was not a search for police to install a pen register, which merely recorded the numbers someone dials because the phone company automatically has access to that. Since the phone company has access to it, it is not private and getting that information is not a search, so police did not need a warrant to do that. (*Smith* v. *Maryland*)"

"On the one hand," Brenner tells me, "subscriber data would seem to fall under the cases I mentioned: i.e., that there is no Fourth Amendment right to privacy in it, and therefore no 'search' if police get it, because it belongs to the entity that generates the records. (And you could, of course, go even further and use the pen register case and argue you could get other things, as well.) But Congress adopted a statute, which changes things, which gives people more privacy than they have under the Fourth Amendment."

18 U.S. Code section 2703(c)(1)(C) says that "a provider of electronic communication service or remote computing service shall disclose to a governmental entity the name, address, local and long distance telephone toll billing records, telephone number or other subscriber number or identity and length of service to a subscriber." The service can disclose the kinds of services provided to the subscriber only if the government uses a grand jury subpoena, an administrative subpoena authorized by a federal or state statute, or the options under 18 U.S. Code section 2703(c)(1)(B). This statute lets a service disclose other kinds of subscriber information if the government gets a search warrant, if the subscriber consents to the disclosure (which is an exception to the warrant requirement), or if the government submits a formal request, pursuant to another part of the statute, seeking information relevant to telemarketing fraud.

"The bottom line," Brenner asserts, "is that an ISP might well be able to provide the information under the U.S. Constitution, but the U.S. Congress has enacted a statute that makes it impossible to do so without getting a warrant or a subpoena."

Council of Europe Floats a Cybercrime Treaty

Of course, the case that Sunde of Økokrim argued successfully before the Norwegian Supreme Court involved Norwegian law enforcement, a Norwegian ISP, and a Norwegian subscriber. In many such cases, whether network intrusions or child pornography, the issue involves multiple law enforcement agencies and multiple ISPs in multiple countries under diverse rules of law.

The problem is one of the many pressing reasons that the world needs a treaty for cyberspace. The Council of Europe (COE) has been working on one for several years. It would be the first international treaty addressing such issues.

In May, the Group of Eight (the United States, the United Kingdom, France, Germany, Japan, Canada, Italy, and Russia) held a three-day conference on cybercrime.

The G-8 made a plea for private businesses to cooperate with governments in combating cybercrimes and for governments to harmonize Internet-related law, speed up judicial procedures, and reduce the numerous barriers (for example, language and cultural differences) between law enforcement agencies in different countries.

In conjunction with the G-8 cybercrime conference, the COE unveiled the first draft of the Council of Europe Convention on Cybercrime.

At Økokrim's "Internet as the Scene of the Crime," Peter Csonka of the Council of Europe gave the second public presentation of the draft treaty.

The 41-nation Council of Europe issued two prior recommendations, one in 1989 and another in 1995, encouraging governments to adapt laws to deal with Information Age crimes, prior to the release of the draft treaty.

Because of the importance of the treaty, non-member states Canada, South Africa, Japan, and the United States actively participate in the negotiations.

The draft Convention is expected to be finalized by December 2000. Then it would be adopted by the Committee of Ministers and open for signature by September 2001.

In "Chapter II: Measures to be taken at the national level," the Convention describes the substantive criminal law that governments should enact in regard to four distinct types of criminal activity in cyberspace:

- Offenses against the confidentiality, integrity, and availability of computer data and systems (for example, network intrusions or denial of service)
- Computer-related offenses (for example, financial fraud)
- Content-related offenses (for example, child pornography)
- Copyright-related offenses

In the course of Csonka's talk on the draft document, however, I realized that economic espionage had been excised from the text. Previously, it had been included along with forgery and fraud as a "computer-related offence," (i.e., use of computers as tools to commit a traditional crime).

I asked him why economic espionage had been taken out of the text. He smiled wryly and acknowledged that "one large member nation, and one large non-member nation" had problems with it being in the treaty.

The COE Convention on Cybercrime is an important step forward. Leaving economic espionage out of it is unfortunate. But in spite of that glaring omission, the document will accomplish a great deal.

For the full text of the treaty, see Appendix A.

Inside the U.S. Federal Government

The U.S. government (USG) has a big problem. It has millions of users on millions of computers (not even counting contractors sitting on .gov networks). It has hundreds of thousands of networks. It has an IT budget of $20–$80 billion (that's only counting office systems, not the computers you need to fly a jet fighter or steer an aircraft carrier). Yes, indeed, the digital world of the USG is a vast expanse of cyberspace, and it is under siege.

Consider the size of the Pentagon's computing environment alone: 2.1 million computers; 10,000 local area networks (LANs); 100 long-distance networks; 200 command centers; and 16 central computer processing facilities (i.e., MegaCenters).

One fascinating DoD-related news item from the *Federal Computer Week* (FCW) should give you a feel for the immensity of the task at hand:

> DoD Web-watchers find war plans on-line
>
> A new reserve unit that monitors the Defense Department's presence on the World Wide Web has found an astonishing amount of classified or sensitive material on public sites.
>
> The Web Risk Assessment Team, established by the Joint Task Force for Computer Network Defense, is made up of reservists who spend one weekend each month scanning DoD Web sites.
>
> A survey of 800 major DoD sites on the Internet recently revealed as many as 1,300 "discrepancies," some of them involving highly classified information. The team uncovered more than 10 instances where information on Pentagon war plans was posted.

Also among the discoveries has been information on computer system vulnerabilities and more than 20 detailed maps of DoD facilities.

Some of the maps and photographs included detailed plans for a facility
known as "Site R," which serves as the alternate Joint Communications Center
for U.S. nuclear forces. The overhead photo of "Site R" showed the location of
underground tunnel entryways and a detailed floor plan of the facility.

Likewise, the Web site for an annual exercise known as "Cobra Gold" included
an entire list of participating units, communications frequencies and call signs
for aircraft and data on Identification Friend or Foe squawks, which are signals
used by pilots to determine if a plane is friendly or enemy.

In another instance, the team found a classified excerpt in a policy on coun-
terterrorism.[1]

Incredible, isn't it?

There was no need to hack through firewalls or break cryptographic algorithms to get
to the sensitive data uncovered by the Web Risk Assessment Team. It was just hanging
out there on .gov servers, like ripe, juicy fruit on a heavy-laden vine. No ill-intent
involved, only a huge and far-flung organization's desire to communicate with itself.

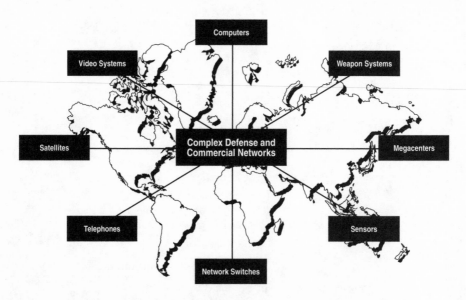

Figure 17.1   The Department of Defense information infrastructure.

Source: GAO/AIMD-96-84 Defense Information Security Report.

1. "DoD Web-watchers find war plans on-line," by Dan Verton, Federal Computer Week, 4/26/00

Table 17.1   Areas of Information Security Weakness Reported for the 24 Largest U.S. Government Agencies[2]

General Control Area	Significant Weakness Identified	No Significant Weakness Identified	Area Not Reviewed
	Number of Agencies		
Entitywide security program planning and management	17	0	7
Access controls	23	0	1
Application software development and change controls	14	4	6
Segregation of duties	16	1	7
System software controls	9	0	15
Service continuity controls	20	0	4

Source: GAO/AIMD-98-92 Federal Information Security Report.

Inside the Pentagon

The significance of the Rome Labs case, documented in Chapter 6, was not lost on the likes of Air Force's Jim Christy or the GAO's Keith Rhodes. If two teenage hackers on a digital joy ride could penetrate the computer systems of high-risk sites, certainly a disciplined cadre of professionals could do it for sinister reasons.

In May 1996, one month prior to the Nunn hearings on "Security in Cyberspace," the U.S. GAO released a report entitled *Computer Attacks at Department of Defense Pose Increasing Risks* (GAO/AIMD-96-84). The GAO report stated that attacks on Defense computer systems had become "a serious and growing threat." The report continues:

> Although no one knows the exact number, the Defense Information Systems Agency (DISA) estimates show that Defense may have experienced about 250,000 attacks last year and that the number of attacks is increasing.

---

2. Most of the audits used to develop this table were performed as part of financial statement audits. At some agencies with primarily financial-related missions, such as the Department of the Treasury and the Social Security Administration, these audits covered the bulk of mission-related operations. However, at other agencies whose missions are primarily nonfinancial, such as the Departments of Defense and Justice, the audits used to develop this table may provide a less complete picture of the agency's overall security posture because the audit objectives focused on the financial statements and did not include evaluating systems supporting nonfinancial operations. Nevertheless, at agencies where computer-based controls over nonfinancial operations have been audited, similar weaknesses have been identified.

Establishing an exact count of attacks is difficult since some attackers take measures to avoid detection. In addition, the Department does not detect or react to most attacks, according to DISA, and does not report the majority of attacks it does detect.

Estimates of the number of computer attacks are based on DISA's Vulnerability Analysis and Assessment Program. Under this program, DISA personnel attempt to penetrate computer systems at various military service and Defense agency sites via the Internet. Since the program's inception in 1992, DISA has conducted 38,000 attacks on Defense computer systems to test how well they were protected. DISA successfully gained access 65 percent of the time.

Of these successful attacks, only 988 or about 4 percent were detected by the target organizations. Of those detected, only 267 attacks or roughly 27 percent were reported to DISA. Therefore, only about 1 in 150 successful attacks drew an active defensive response from the organizations being tested.[3]

The GAO report concluded that DoD policies on information security were outdated and incomplete. According to the GAO, DoD policies did not require certain vital information security activities, including

- No specific Defense-wide policy requiring vulnerability assessments or criteria for prioritizing who should be targeted first.

- No DoD policy requirement for correcting identified deficiencies and vulnerabilities.

- No DoD policy requiring internal reporting of attacks or guidance on how to respond to attacks. (System and network administrators need to know when and to whom attacks should be reported and what response is appropriate for reacting to attacks and ensuring systems availability, confidentiality, and integrity.)

- No policy for DoD organizations to assess damage to their systems after an attack has been detected. (As a result, these assessments are not usually done. However, these assessments are essential to ensure the integrity of the data in those systems and to make sure that no malicious code was inserted that could cause severe problems later.)

- DoD users lacked sufficient security awareness.

- Many users did not understand the technology they were using, the vulnerabilities of the network environment they were working in, or even their own responsibilities for protecting critical information.

- DoD network and system administrators lacked sufficient technical training.

---

3. Computer Attacks at Department of Defense Pose Increasing Risks (GAO/AIMD-96-84).

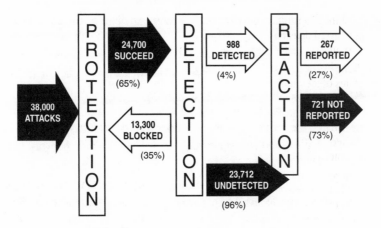

Figure 17.2   Results of DISA vulnerability assessments.

Source: Defense Information Systems Agency as depicted in the GAO/AIMD-96-84 Defense Information Security Report.

The GAO interviewed 24 individuals responsible for managing and securing systems at four military installations. Sixteen stated that they did not have enough time, experience, or training to do their jobs properly. In addition, eight stated that system administration was not their full-time job, but rather an ancillary duty.

Furthermore, the GAO's findings were confirmed by an Air Force survey of system administrators. It found that 325 of 709 respondents were unaware of procedures for reporting vulnerabilities and incidents, 249 of 515 respondents had not received any network security training, and 377 of 706 respondents reported that their security responsibilities were ancillary duties.

Many installations lacked a full-time, trained, experienced information systems security officer. Without a full-time security official, important security activities were usually done in an ad hoc manner or not done at all. According to DoD officials, installation commanders give a low priority to security duties, which explains the lack of full-time, trained, experienced security officers.

The GAO made some recommendations on what the DoD should do, including

- Develop department-wide policies for preventing, detecting, and responding to attacks on DoD information systems. This includes a mandate that all security incidents be reported within DoD, that risk assessments be performed routinely to determine vulnerability to attacks and intrusions, that vulnerabilities and deficiencies be expeditiously corrected as they are identified, and that damage from intrusions be expeditiously assessed to ensure the integrity of data and systems compromised.

- Require the military services and Defense agencies to use training and other mechanisms to increase awareness and accountability among installation commanders and all personnel as to the security risks of computer systems connected to the Internet and their responsibility for securing their systems.

- Require information system security officers at all installations and set specific standards for ensuring that these as well as system and network managers are given sufficient time and training to perform their duties appropriately; continually develop and cost-effectively use department-wide network monitoring and protection technologies.

- Evaluate the incident-response capabilities within DISA, the military services, and the Defense agencies to ensure that they are sufficient to handle the projected threat.

This is just one aspect of a sustained and exhaustive effort.

What's Going On in the Murky Waters at Foggy Bottom?

In January 2000, a laptop computer containing highly classified data on weapons proliferation vanished from a conference room in the State Department's Bureau of Intelligence and Research. The investigation of the missing laptop led to the revelation that some systems used to work with classified data were not equipped with password protection, encryption, or any other cybersafeguards. Why?

Well, the "thinking" was that the area in which the systems were used was secured, so the systems themselves didn't need to be secured. But guess what? Physical security had broken down. During a subsequent inventory, two more laptops were proved to be missing. One of them had been checked out to Assistant Secretary of State Morton Halperin.

It wasn't the first time that Foggy Bottom security breaches had led to bad PR.

In December, 1999, a Russian listening device was discovered in the conference room of the Bureau of Oceans, located on the same floor as Secretary of State Madeleine Albright's office (the seventh), but at the opposite end of the building.

In March 1998, an unidentified man strolled into an office on the executive floor of the U.S. State Department building (at the height of tensions over impending military action in the Persian Gulf) and walked off with some documents as two secretaries looked on. According to initial news reports the papers were top-secret.

"Computer Security: Pervasive, Serious Weaknesses Jeopardize State Department Operations" (GAO/AIMD-98-145), a GAO study conducted at the request of the U.S. Senate Government Affairs Committee, articulated numerous problems.

State's lapses in physical security were just the tip of the iceberg.

The GAO study demonstrated that the State Department had serious problems in regard to dial-in security and internal network security as well as physical security.

The GAO's penetration tests demonstrated that State's sensitive but unclassified information systems could be "easily accessed by unauthorized users who in turn can read, delete, modify, or steal sensitive information on State's operations."

The GAO team simulated outsiders to demonstrate unauthorized access to State's systems via dial-up modem connections. They could have "modified or deleted important data, shut down services, downloaded data, and monitored network traffic such as e-mail." They also simulated insiders to demonstrate that they could misappropriate administrator access to host systems on multiple operating system environments, including UNIX and Windows NT. They were able to view "international financial data, travel arrangements, detailed network diagrams, a listing of valid users on local area networks, e-mail, and performance appraisals, among other sensitive data."

GAO penetration testers were able to get into a State facility without the necessary identification. Once inside, they explored an unlocked work area and came across unattended computers that had been left logged on to the LAN. They even discovered a user ID and password taped to one of these computers. With the access provided by these systems, they were able to download a password file. In another unlocked area, they were able to access the LAN server and gain supervisor-level access to a system. With supervisor-level access, they could have added or deleted users, implemented unauthorized programs, and eliminated audit trails.

(In May 2000, the GAO released a study showing that physical security lapses were pervasive throughout the U.S. Federal Government, even in the most sensitive agencies. Using fake law enforcement ID badges and declaring they were armed, GAO investigators got through security checks at the DoJ, the Pentagon, the CIA, and the FBI as well as the State Department.)

Just as they did with the DoD two years earlier, the GAO elucidated many glaring weaknesses in the State Department's information security posture, including

- Lack of a comprehensive information security program
- Insufficient senior-management commitment to information security
- Lack of accountability due to State's decentralized organization

- Lack of risk analysis to determine appropriate controls
- Incomplete information security policies
- Inadequate efforts to heighten security awareness among users
- No regular evaluation of controls to gauge effectiveness

What is really at risk? The GAO report explained:

> The potential consequences of misuse of this information are of major concern. For example, unauthorized deletion or alteration of data could enable known criminals, terrorists, and other dangerous individuals to enter the United States. Personnel information concerning approximately 35,000 State employees could be useful to foreign governments wishing to build personality profiles on selected employees. Manipulation of financial data could result in overpayments or underpayments to vendors, banks, and individuals, and inaccurate information being provided to agency managers and the Congress. Furthermore, the overseas activities of other federal agencies may be jeopardized to the extent they are supported by State systems.[4]

Indeed, there are other risks as well. The information-security vulnerabilities highlighted in the GAO's security assessment of the State Department could lead to anything from the collapse of a peace agreement or the death of a hostage.

FAA Secured on a Wing and a Prayer?

In May 1998, the GAO also released *Air Traffic Control: Weak Computer Security Practices Jeopardize Flight Safety* (GAO/AIMD-98-155), its study of computer security at the Federal Aviation Administration (FAA).

In testimony delivered to the U.S. House of Representatives' Subcommittee on Technology in August 1998, Joel C. Willemssen of the U.S. General Accounting Office (GAO) warned of serious problems in the Federal Aviation Administration (FAA), involving both Y2K and computer security issues.

> FAA cannot provide assurance that the air traffic control systems on which it depends are sufficiently resistant to intrusion. FAA's weak computer security practices were detailed in the classified version of a report we made available in May to key congressional committees and appropriate agency officials. An unclassified version of the report is available to the public.
>
> Underlying weaknesses in FAA's management have allowed the agency's Y2K, computer security, and other information technology problems to persist. Our work over the last two years has identified some of the root causes of, and pinpointed solutions to, these long-standing problems—including an incomplete

4. GAO/AIMD-98-145, page 3

systems architecture, weak software acquisition capabilities, unreliable cost information, and a problematic organizational culture. Although FAA has initiated efforts in response to some of our recommendations on these issues, most of them have not been fully implemented.[5]

Willemssen's testimony on the FAA's computer security problems offers many sobering lessons. Consider the following remarks, and ask yourself how well your organization would measure up under such scrutiny:

> In assessing the adequacy of computer security at FAA earlier this year, we found significant weaknesses that compromise the integrity of FAA's air traffic control (ATC) operations. This review resulted in a number of findings too sensitive to discuss in open hearings. FAA's ATC network is an enormous collection of interrelated systems that reside at or are associated with hundreds of ATC facilities. These systems and facilities are linked together by complex communications networks that transmit both voice and digital data.

> It is essential that FAA's approach to computer security be comprehensive and include the following three elements: physical security of the facilities that house ATC systems (e.g., locks, guards, fences and surveillance), information security of the systems (e.g., safeguards incorporated into computer hardware and software) and telecommunications security of the networks linking the systems and facilities (e.g., secure gateways, firewalls and communications-protection devices).[6]

FAA had significant weakness in every area of computer security that the GAO investigated: for example, physical security, operational systems security, development of new systems, management structure, and implementation of computer security policy. ATC physical security management and controls were ineffective.

"The agency's management of physical security at its ATC facilities has been ineffective," Willemssen testified. "Known physical weaknesses exist at many facilities."

ATC operation systems security is ineffective and systems were vulnerable.

"According to FAA's latest information, less than 10 percent of its operational systems (seven out of 90) have undergone risk assessments," Willemssen assessed. "As a result, FAA does not know how vulnerable these operational systems are and consequently has no basis for determining how to best protect them."

FAA was not effectively incorporating security features into new ATC systems.

---

5. U.S. House Committee on Science. Serious Challenges Remain in Resolving Year 2000 and Computer Security Problems: Hearing before the Subcommittee on Technology. August 6, 1998.

6. Ibid.

"FAA has no security architecture, concept of operations or standards," he reported. "As a result, implementation of security requirements across ATC development is sporadic and ad hoc. With no security requirements specified during systems design, any attempt to retrofit such features later will be increasingly costly and technically challenging."

FAA's management structure was not effectively implementing or enforcing computer security policy.

"Civil Aviation Security has not adequately enforced security policies it has formulated, Air Traffic Services has not adequately implemented security policy for operational ATC systems, and Research and Acquisitions has not adequately implemented policy for new ATC system development."

Furthermore, problems persisted because FAA's management of its information technology was ineffective.

"Our recent reviews have identified some of the root causes," Willemssen said. "ATC systems architecture is incomplete, ATC software acquisition capabilities are weak, ATC cost information is unreliable and FAA's organizational culture is problematic."

Lessons Learned from the NASA Probe

In May 1999, the GAO released *Information Security: Many NASA Mission-Critical Systems Face Serious Risks* (GAO/AIMD-99-47), a security assessment the state cyberdefenses for the National Aeronautics and Space Administration (NASA).

Using nothing more than publicly available Internet access, the GAO penetration testing team even succeeded in gaining access to NASA systems responsible for supporting command and control for earth-orbiting spacecraft and processing and distributing data received from these spacecraft.

The vulnerabilities encountered during the tests fell into four major categories:

- Poorly chosen passwords
- Inadequate data access controls
- System software patches not kept up to date
- Unnecessarily broad trust relationships among networked systems

For example, the GAO team found passwords like "guest," "admin," and "jjones." They also found old, unpatched versions of sendmail running on NASA computers. When they ran a war dialer, they found potentially active modem connections. NASA officials could not identify which systems these connections went to. Oh yes, they had a written policy restricting the connection of modems to mission-critical systems, but they had no procedures for registering them or tracking them down.

Sound familiar? There aren't many information security programs in the private sector that have dealt adequately with these problems. Of course, countermeasures for weak passwords, compromised system software, rogue modems, etc. are reiterated *ad nauseam* in PowerPoint presentations and enshrined in written policies. But unless there is both vigilant compliance-monitoring and management commitment (i.e., budget dollars), policies and checklists are hollow.

Consider the vulnerabilities cited in these studies of the DoD, State, the FAA, and NASA. Compare them to the problems that exist in your enterprise. Review the recommendations that the GAO made to the departments and agencies they scrutinized. Ask yourself what is left undone for your organization.

Maybe government isn't really all that more inefficient than the private sector; maybe it's just more honest.

Is Something Nasty Floating in Your Alphabet Soup?

I doubt the GAO will issue a report on information security at the Central Intelligence Agency (CIA) or the National Security Agency (NSA) for us to peruse any time soon. But culling through recent news items, it is evident that there have been problems at both Langley and Fort Meade, at least with disgruntled and dishonest insiders.

Harold Nicholson, Traitor

Treason, like trade secret theft and financial fraud, is increasingly a computer-aided crime. Consider the case of Harold Nicholson.

The criminal complaint filed against ex-CIA official Harold J. Nicholson stated that he spied for Russian intelligence from around June 1994 through November 16, 1996. It is also alleged that he received approximately $180,000 from the SVR for his espionage activities. During his career, Nicholson held a top-secret clearance.

A CIA audit revealed that Nicholson was doing keyword searches on "Russia" and "Chechnya" and tried to access databases for which he wasn't authorized.

His notebook computer's hard drive contained numerous classified CIA documents relating to Russia. The files were deleted, but the FBI was able to recover some of the files and fragments of others. Investigators also found a 3.5-inch floppy disk that contained summary reports on CIA human assets.

Although the Nicholson affair was strictly a national security matter, there is an important lesson to be learned for information security practitioners in both public and private sectors: In the Information Age, most espionage will target digital data stored on computers and will therefore be an information-security problem. And that's going to hold true whether the espionage is economic, industrial, or military, whether it's directed by rival governments or corporate competitors, whether it involves troop movements or sales leads. So perhaps you should sit everyone down and ask some questions.

How good are your audit trails and logs? Are they reviewed regularly? How is your data classification scheme holding up? Is your workforce savvy to its responsibilities vis-a-vis proprietary information? When was your most recent enterprise-wide security assessment performed? How well has the organization done in following up on whatever recommendations were made?

Douglas Groat, Would-Be Traitor

The case of Douglas Fred Groat also offers a glimpse into the information security problems that intelligence agencies face.

In July 1998, Groat, a former CIA operative, pleaded guilty to trying to extort $1 million from the agency in return for his silence about CIA eavesdropping operations.

Groat, who was divorced and living in a Winnebago at the time of his arrest, had worked for the CIA's Science and Technology Directorate before he was fired. Groat's job had been to break into diplomatic missions and steal the crypto keys used for secret communications.

According to the U.S. Justice Department indictment, the disgruntled ex-operative had told two foreign governments how the agency had cracked the "cryptographics systems" they used to scramble their communications from diplomatic missions.

By pleading guilty to extortion, Groat avoided being tried for espionage: a far more serious offense. Of course, the CIA also avoided a potentially embarrassing trial.

Like the Nicholson affair, the Groat case offers practical lessons to be learned whether you're concerned with national security or corporate security. The damage that disgruntled, dishonest employees can inflict on your organization should not be underestimated in your risk analysis or overlooked during the exit process. Strong crypto is useless if the crypto keys or other vital elements of the crypto system itself are vulnerable to physical or electronic theft.

John Deutch: A Good Man Blunders

John Deutch did not betray his country. He made a mistake, but it was a big one with repercussions that rocked the agency.

In December 1996, Deutch stepped down as Director of Central Intelligence (DCI). No problem. CIA directors come and go. But when CIA technicians found 31 secret files in an unsecured personal computer at Deutch's home, trouble ensued.

The CIA turned the case over to the DoJ, which investigated for a year before deciding not to file charges in April 1999. DoJ turned the case back over to the CIA.

In early February 2000, CNN broke the news that a classified report from the CIA's inspector general contained a bombshell.

> Former CIA Director John Deutch used a home computer that contained sensitive information to access the Internet, a CIA report concluded, raising fears that secrets stored on the machine could have been stolen.
>
> Officials say Deutch had an account with America Online that he used to access the Internet. Informed officials told CNN that he once received an unsolicited e-mail from a former Russian scientist on the computer, which was crammed with top-secret materials.[7]

Later that month, the Senate Intelligence Committee released an unclassified version of the report on Deutch's indiscretion.

> Throughout his tenure as DCI, Deutch intentionally processed on home computers large volumes of highly classified information to include top secret code word material.... Whether any of the information was stolen or compromised remains unknown.[8]

In August 1999, Deutch was stripped of his security clearances.

In May 2000, the CIA "punished" six current and former employers for their mishandling of the initial investigation. Formal reprimands were issued to two former senior officials and to one current one. Another former employee and one current official were admonished in writing, and one other current employee was orally admonished.

Meanwhile, DoJ has come back into the mess and opened a criminal investigation.

Lessons to be learned?

Certainly, the Deutch case illustrates why security awareness training for users is of paramount importance. If the DCI had realized the potential vulnerabilities of accessing the Internet on a system that also contained highly classified documents, he probably would not have violated the rules concerning the proper handling of such information.

---

7. "Ex-CIA chief surfed Web on home computer with top-secret data" CNN, February 3, 2000

8. U.S. Congress. Senate. Select Committee on Intelligence. *Report of Investigation: Improper Handling of Classified Information by John M. Deutch* (1998-0028-IG). *Report prepared by* Daniel S. Seikaly. Released February 18, 2000.

Furthermore, if it had been very clear that there would be severe consequences for ignoring established policies and procedures in regard to the use of top-secret materials on computers, Deutch would have had even more incentive to play it by the book.

King and Lipka, Traitors

That other alphabet soup agency, the NSA, has had its own problems with disgruntled, dishonest insiders (i.e., traitors).

First Class Petty Officer Daniel King, a 40-year-old cryptologist working for the NSA, admitted to downloading confidential NSA documents onto CD-ROM and mailing the disc to the Russian embassy in Washington, D.C.

The espionage was detected during a routine polygraph test. The information sent to the Russians is alleged to relate to the use of U.S. submarines in signal intelligence (SIGINT), particularly the tapping of Russian undersea communications cables.

Robert Lipka worked for the NSA at Fort Meade from 1965 to 1967. He photographed top-secret documents and sold them to the KGB for a measly $27,000. Lipka wrote a letter to the NSA Director threatening to place classified information on the Internet if his case was not resolved in 45 days.

In September 1997, Robert Lipka, 51, pleaded guilty and was sentenced to 18 years in jail.

Conclusion

Yes, the U.S. federal government has a very big problem—a sweeping problem. It will never be eliminated. Indeed, even mitigating it will prove difficult. But at least the executive branch (under the Clinton administration) is hip to the problem.

Consider Presidential Decision Directive 63 (PDD-63).

With a stroke of the pen, U.S. President Bill Clinton ordered a governmentwide initiative to reorganize its own cyberdefenses and work with the private sector to build digital bulwarks for critical elements of the national infrastructure (e.g., the power grid, the air traffic control system, and the telecommunications network).[9]

---

9. There is also a White Paper on PDD-63 available at http://www.whitehouse.gov/WH/EOP/NSC/html/documents/NSCDoc3.html.

On May 22, 1998, the office of the White House Press Secretary issued the following details:

PROTECTING AMERICA'S CRITICAL INFRASTRUCTURES: PPD-63

This Presidential Directive builds on the recommendations of the President's Commission on Critical Infrastructure Protection. In October 1997, the Commission issued its report calling for a national effort to assure the security of the United States' increasingly vulnerable and interconnected infrastructures, such as telecommunications, banking and finance, energy, transportation, and essential government services.

Presidential Decision Directive 63 is the culmination of an intense, interagency effort to evaluate those recommendations and produce a workable and innovative framework for critical infrastructure protection.

The President's policy sets a goal of a reliable, interconnected, and secure information system infrastructure by the year 2003, and significantly increased security to government systems by the year 2000, by:

- Immediately establishing a national center to warn of and respond to attacks.
- Ensuring the capability to protect critical infrastructures from intentional acts by 2003.

Addresses the cyber and physical infrastructure vulnerabilities of the Federal government by requiring each department and agency to work to reduce its exposure to new threats;

Requires the Federal government to serve as a model to the rest of the country for how infrastructure protection is to be attained;

Seeks the voluntary participation of private industry to meet common goals for protecting our critical systems through public-private partnerships;

Protects privacy rights and seeks to utilize market forces. It is meant to strengthen and protect the nation's economic power, not to stifle it.

Seeks full participation and input from the Congress.

PDD-63 sets up a new structure to deal with this important challenge, including:

- A National Coordinator whose scope will include not only critical infrastructure but also foreign terrorism and threats of domestic mass destruction (including biological weapons) because attacks on the US may not come labeled in neat jurisdictional boxes;
- The National Infrastructure Protection Center (NIPC) at the FBI which will fuse representatives from FBI, DOD, USSS, Energy, Transportation, the Intelligence Community, and the private sector in an unprecedented attempt at information sharing among agencies in collaboration with the private sector. The NIPC will also provide the principal means of facilitating and coordinating the Federal Government's response to an incident, mitigating attacks, investigating threats and monitoring reconstitution efforts;

- Information Sharing and Analysis Centers (ISACs) are encouraged to be set up by the private sector in cooperation with the Federal government and modeled on the Centers for Disease Control and Prevention;

- A National Infrastructure Assurance Council drawn from private sector leaders and state/local officials to provide guidance to the policy formulation of a National Plan;

- The Critical Infrastructure Assurance Office will provide support to the National Coordinator's work with government agencies and the private sector in developing a national plan. The office will also help coordinate a national education and awareness program, and legislative and public affairs.

Some have knocked PDD-63 as simply not enough. Others have criticized PDD-63 as a smoke screen for some sinister Orwellian plot. But I suggest that it is simply a sign that, at least in the U.S. Federal government, the single most important element of a successful information protection program—management mandate back up by dedicated resources—is in place (at least until January 2001).

Ask yourself these questions: Would your CEO sign the corporate equivalent of PDD-63 for the scale of your enterprise? Would your CEO even understand these dangers? And if your CEO understood these dangers, would your CEO admit they were real? Even if your CEO acknoweldges the dangers, would you receive the kind of management mandate that PDD-63 illustrates?

Countermeasures

I n Chapter 15, I underscored the importance of how your enterprise's information security entity is organized, to whom the group's head reports, what its budget is, and whether it is adequately staffed. I include these exhortations again here because a list of countermeasures that does not take these fundamental structural issues into account is a useless exercise.

Organizational Issues

Does your organization have an information protection unit? If it doesn't, you have not taken the first step. Does the head of your information protection unit report directly to the CIO or some other corporate officer (for example, CFO)? If not, you are not going to have the clout to get the job done. Does your information protection unit have a budget that is at least 3–5% of the total IS budget? If not, you are not going to have the bullets. Is your information protection unit adequately staffed? Staffing levels will, of course, vary from environment to environment. But as a rule of thumb, the average among Fortune 500 companies is at least one information protection professional for every 1,000 employees. If an organization doesn't have at least one IP professional for every thousand users, it just won't get the job done. (Remember, I said "at least." Indeed, a dot-com business doing heavy e-commerce may have only a few hundred employees and yet need a very robust IP staff.)

These aren't the only questions to raise. Here are some others. How is your information protection unit itself organized? What do your information protection job descriptions look like? What is the information protection unit's mission statement? I have even been asked "What should we call our unit? Data Security, Information Security, or Information Protection?"

That last one is not as ridiculous as it might sound to you. Perhaps you have noticed that throughout *Tangled Web*, I have used the terms *information security* and *information protection* interchangeably?

Bob Cartwright, CISSP, formerly of the Chevron Corp. and currently with the Netigy Corporation, elucidates the issue.

"*Information protection* signals a department that is proactive in protecting the second most valuable resource of the company (the first being their employees). The name does not imply the 'gun and badge' that *security* invokes. People are more receptive to working with Information Protection personnel and feel less anxiety or threatened by the title, which leads them to being more honest and helpful. In the client/server world, the Information Protection department is responsible for more than just the 'data' on the mainframe.

"*Data security*," he continues, "is an outdated term that invokes memories of the department that was responsible for determining who could enter the data center, etc. This was the title when all the 'data' was kept in the central repository.

"*Information security* implies more responsibilities than does *data security*. No longer is the department only responsible for the mainframe data but they are concerned with LANs, WANs, Internet, intranet, extranet, etc. Both of the titles with *security* implies a sense of the police. I have found that by using the Information Protection title, there is not the fear associated with security and the fear that 'Big Brother is watching.' Information Protection is thought of more as a team member."

Risk Analysis

Five elements are involved in risk analysis: assets, threats, vulnerabilities, impact, and safeguards.

Risk analysis refers to any one of several methodologies used to come to an informed decision about most cost-effective controls to limit the risks to your assets across the spectrum of threats.

For example, let's say you have a wad of cash (asset) hidden under your mattress, but your housemate is a thief (threat) and there is no lock on your bedroom door (vulnerability). If you don't do something to prevent your housemate from stealing the wad of cash, you'll probably lose $500 (impact). Well, what could you do? What steps could you take to protect your asset (safeguards)? You could move out of the place, but that's an expensive proposition. Maybe it would cost you $2,000 (moving costs, deposit on a new place, etc.) to protect that $500. That safeguard wouldn't be cost-effective. It would cost more to protect your asset ($2,000) than the value of the asset itself ($500). What other safeguards could you institute? You could install a lock on your bedroom door. It would cost you only $50, but it would probably keep him out.

Of course, in a full-blown risk analysis of the range of threats arrayed against your wad of cash, you would have to factor in the possibility of a professional thief who could pick the lock to steal your $500 while everyone was gone from the house. You would have to decide whether you could do anything to mitigate the risk from natural threats like a fire or a flood.

Maybe you would convince yourself that a fireproof strongbox was cost-effective. Maybe you would bury your money in the backyard. That would be a good safeguard against the fire or the professional thief, but it would probably be ineffectual against the flood.

Maybe you would just throw in the towel and put the money in a bank account.

That's really the essence of risk analysis.

(Well, it's the essence of qualitative risk analysis. Quantitative risk analysis would use numeric estimates for the frequencies of a housemate stealing someone's wad of money from under the mattress as well as for the professional thief picking the lock, as well as for the fire and the flood. You see the problem with quantitative risk analysis, don't you? How meaningful could those numeric estimates be? And how hard would they be to procure?)

Tom Peltier, CISSP, of Netigy Corporation and a CSI faculty member, is a leading proponent of risk analysis. He teaches CSI's course on "Facilitated Risk Analysis Process (FRAP)."

According to Peltier, "Qualitative risk analysis is a technique that can be used to determine the level of protection required for applications, systems, facilities, and other enterprise assets. It is a systematic examination of assets, threats, and vulnerabilities that establishes the probabilities of threats occurring, the cost of losses if they do occur, and the value of the safeguards or countermeasures designed to reduce the threats and vulnerabilities to an acceptable level. The qualitative methodology attempts to prioritize the various risk elements in subjective terms."

There are 12 steps in a qualitative risk analysis:

1. Develop a plan.
2. Develop application priority.
3. Identify and evaluate assets.
4. Identify threats.
5. Evaluate threats.

6. Estimate potential losses.

7. Calculate risk factors.

8. Analyze vulnerabilities.

9. Identify safeguards.

10. Perform cost/benefit analysis of safeguards.

11. Rank safeguards in priority order.

12. Write risk-analysis report.

FRAP is a methodology driven by the owner of the application or system and conducted by a facilitator. It is a subjective process that obtains results by asking questions. The results of the FRAP are a comprehensive document that has identified risks, issues, threats, and controls to mitigate those risks and an action plan created by the owner.

For example, let's say a particular business unit within a large corporation is going to roll out an e-commerce application. During a FRAP session, a facilitator would lead the "owners" of the proposed e-commerce application through a discussion or series of discussions.

First, the "owners" must clearly define the asset and place a dollar value on it (i.e., asset identification). Second, every conceivable, viable threat and vulnerability the asset will be exposed to must be articulated (i.e., threat and vulnerability analysis). The interested parties gathered for the FRAP will brainstorm about everything from DDoS to financial fraud by insiders to theft of the credit card database by intruders to sabotage of the e-commerce servers. They will prioritize the risks in terms of likelihood. Third, they will explore the range of controls to limit the risk from each kind of threat. They will consider the cost of the appropriate controls. They will weigh the likelihood and impact of each threat against the cost of relevant control. They will try to come up with a reasonable, cost-effective approach to reducing the scope of the risks involved (i.e., safeguard selection).

According to Peltier, FRAP has several advantages over other types of risk analysis. Other types of risk analysis are often perceived as major tasks performed by consultants. They are big-budget items drawn out over an extended period of time. The process usually overlooks in-house expertise and results in a series of recommendations that are not acceptable to the client.

FRAP, on the other hand, is driven by the asset's owner and engages the in-house expertise. In this way, the FRAP facilitator wins his or her buy-in, which is essential to the success of the task. Furthermore, a FRAP could end up taking minutes instead of months or years. (Indeed, Dan Erwin of Dow Chemical, one of the fathers of FRAP, used to teach "30 Minute Risk Analysis" at CSI conferences.) FRAP is cost-effective.

The success of a risk analysis strategy, Peltier says, depends on the following ingredients:

- Senior management commitment
- Skills and experience in identification of risks and development of effective risk controls
- Close working relationship between risk management team and business units to identify and manage information asset risks
- Risk analysis as an ongoing process
- Use of a consistent risk analysis process
- Regular reporting of performance to gauge whether safeguards are meeting the needs of the organization

Perhaps FRAP's greatest strength is that it establishes a method to prioritize the identified risks into categories of minor, moderate, or major. No organization has sufficient resources to control every identified risk. According to Peltier, where an effective risk analysis gains support is when it attempts to ensure that limited corporate resources are spent where they will do the most good.

"Risk analysis is a necessary and cost-effective part of an effective information security program," he says. "It will support management in fulfilling its mandate to exercise due diligence in protecting the assets and resources of the enterprise."

Baseline Controls Versus Risk Analysis

The FRAP method is widely used and highly regarded among information protection practitioners in large corporations and government agencies. But not everyone buys into risk analysis (facilitated or not).

For example, Atomic Tangerine's Donn Parker is adamantly opposed to it.

"I have participated in security reviews for more than 250 organizations during the past 30 years," he says, "and I have interviewed more than 200 computer criminals and their victims. I can assure you that risk analysis or assessment does not work, and it is mostly a waste of time. (See my book, *Fighting Computer Crime: A New Framework for Protecting Information* [Wiley, 1998] for a complete debunking of this methodology.) There may be some value in a risk analysis that forces owners and users to examine their vulnerabilities and to be more aware of the need for security, but I can easily show the fallacies of conclusions from any risk analysis that would materially change the results.

"First and foremost," he continues, "you want to be sure that your organization has the prudent, well-known controls that other well-run organizations are using under circumstances similar to yours. Then you can deal one at a time with the new threats and vulnerabilities that are not yet solved by existing accepted controls. Almost all organizations have the same threats against the same kinds of information and similar systems, especially those in the same business." Parker says that you can find most of the controls to meet these threats in the new British Standards Institute BS7799-1:1999 *Information Security Management* and the Information Systems Audit and Control Foundation CobiT Report with over 300 control objectives.

"Go to the CSI conferences and security product shows to find the latest due care controls," he advises. "Do benchmark studies to compare your progress with others. Test for vulnerabilities and the effectiveness of your present controls. You will find the prudent due care controls developed and proven from 30 years of experience that will keep your organization busy implementing for the next five or ten years. And you will be moving toward the safe harbor of due care where you, your job, and your organization's managers will be safe from accusations of negligence when and if an abuse or misuse occurs.

"It is not possible to know whether a risk analysis is effective," Parker continues, "because you don't know the losses that your security kept from happening. However, it is possible and practical to determine the effectiveness of meeting a standard of due care by conducting a benchmark study that compares your progress with other well-run, similar organizations and comparing your implemented security with that found in the extensive literature of our art. Several large international corporations have adopted the baseline due care and best practice method. Shouldn't you give this some consideration before wasting your efforts on risk analysis or risk assessment?"

Sound Practices

Whether you rely on risk analysis or baseline controls or incorporate elements of both, you'll want to get your hands on a body of sound practices (i.e., tried and true controls and countermeasures). Here are some examples.

Sixteen Sound Practices Learned from Leading Organizations

In Chapter 17, I highlighted some of the security assessments performed by the U.S. GAO from 1996 onward. But during that span of time, the GAO wasn't just rattling doorknobs and diagnosing digital disorders. It was also trying to articulate a bold, broad message of how to get healthy and stay healthy in cyberspace.

In May 1998, the GAO released *Information Security Management: Learning from the Leading Organizations* (GAO/AIMD-98-68), the results of a GAO study of private-sector organizations with reputations for having superior security programs undertook to identify practices that could be adopted successfully by federal agencies.

The study involved eight organizations that had developed robust, enterprise-wide information-security programs. (In selecting the organizations, the GAO relied primarily on the Computer Security Institute and one or two of the big public accounting firms.)

All the organizations involved were successful and high-profile. They included a financial services corporation, a regional electric utility, a state university, a retailer, a state agency, a non-bank financial institution, a computer vendor, and an equipment manufacturer.

The user population in these organizations ranged from 3,500 to 100,000. Four of the organizations had far-flung global operations.

Of course, the organizations weren't referred to by name in the study. They could well have become targets simply by being touted as having exemplary information-security programs. Someone out there in the netherworld would have wanted to test his mettle against them.

Although the nature of their businesses varied widely, all eight organizations had chosen to build on the foundation of the following five risk-management principles:

- Assess risk and determine needs.
- Establish a central management focal point.
- Implement appropriate policies and related controls.
- Promote awareness.
- Monitor and evaluate policy and control effectiveness.

The senior security managers that the GAO interviewed saw these five principles not as disconnected abstractions but as ongoing processes in a cycle of activity that guaranteed that information-security policies and controls would stay relevant and sharp-edged by ceaselessly confronting new risks.

The straw that stirred the drink, according to those who had built these worthy programs, was the recognition and commitment of senior management.

> The single most important factor in prompting the establishment of an effective security program was a general recognition and understanding among the organization's most senior executives of the enormous risks to business operations associated with relying on automated and highly interconnected systems. However, risk assessments of individual business applications provided the basis for establishing policies and selecting related controls. Steps were then taken to increase the awareness of users concerning these risks and related policies.

The effectiveness of controls and awareness activities was then monitored through various analyses, evaluations and audits, and the results provided input to subsequent risk assessments, which determined if existing policies and controls needed to be modified. All of these activities were coordinated through a central security management office or group the staff of which served as consultants and facilitators to individual business units and senior management.[1]

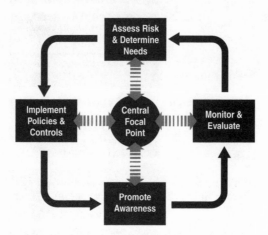

Figure 18.1 Risk management cycle.

Source: GAO/AIMD-98-68 Information Security Management report.

Working with the five risk-management principles, the eight organizations had developed their own bodies of practices over time.

The GAO study articulated sixteen such practices common to the success of all eight organization's information-security programs:

All these practices feed off the five risk-management principles.

Information Protection Assessment Kit (IPAK)

The CSI Hotline gets a lot of calls from people just trying to get their minds around the scope of the information-security problem. "Where do I begin? How do I know where to start?"

---

1. Information Security Management: Learning from the Leading Organizations, GAO report GAO/AIMD-98-68, May 1998.

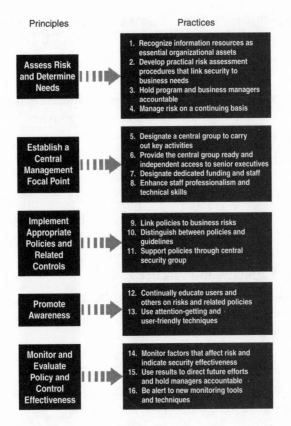

Principles   Practices

Assess Risk and Determine Needs

1. Recognize information resources as essential organizational assets
2. Develop practical risk assessment procedures that link security to business needs
3. Hold program and business managers accountable
4. Manage risk on a continuing basis

Establish a Central Management Focal Point

5. Designate a central group to carry out key activities
6. Provide the central group ready and independent access to senior executives
7. Designate dedicated funding and staff
8. Enhance staff professionalism and technical skills

Implement Appropriate Policies and Related Controls

9. Link policies to business risks
10. Distinguish between policies and guidelines
11. Support policies through central security group

Promote Awareness

12. Continually educate users and others on risks and related policies
13. Use attention-getting and user-friendly techniques

Monitor and Evaluate Policy and Control Effectiveness

14. Monitor factors that affect risk and indicate security effectiveness
15. Use results to direct future efforts and hold managers accountable
16. Be alert to new monitoring tools and techniques

Figure 18.2 Sixteen practices employed by leading organizations to implement the risk cycle.

Source: GAO/AIMD-98-68 Information Security Management report

The Hotline also gets a lot of calls from more experienced practitioners who are simply looking for some credible, independent source to reference in some ongoing internal dispute about whether to install some control. "Okay, you wanted me to prove it to you; here, read this!"

Other callers are just looking for a practical, inexpensive way to communicate to executive management just exactly what the information-security program was doing.

I decided to dust off the old CSI Compliance Test, a relic from the mainframe computing era, to overhaul it, retool it, and put it in the hands of earnest information-security practitioners everywhere.

We threw it to the wolves. We let two successive CSI advisory councils tear away at it. We doled out individual segments to subject matter experts like Rik Farrow, Charles

Cresson Wood of Baseline Software, Tom Peltier, and Dan Erwin of Dow Chemical. We developed a consensus on 20 important, widely acknowledged controls in 11 critical areas of information security, and then we added a scoring system to it so that you could prioritize your needs and plot your progress.

Renamed the Information Protection Assessment Kit (IPAK), this tool has worked well for many information security practitioners as a means with which to get some leverage to lift a heavy load.

Here is one sample control from each of the 11 categories.

A. Information Protection Program and Administration

Each business unit, department, agency, etc. has been designated an individual responsible for implementing the IP program for that organization.

B. Personnel Policies and Practices

Exit interviews are conducted with terminating employees to recover portable computers, telephones, smart cards, company equipment, keys, and identification badges and to identify morale problems if they exist.

C. Physical Security

Documents containing sensitive information are not discarded in whole, readable form; they are shredded, burned, or otherwise mutilated.

D. Business Process Controls

A formal change-control procedure, which includes security testing, is used to manage all software modifications to any software running in production on all platforms.

E. Backup and Recovery Measures

Backups for critical LAN-based systems are produced regularly, stored both on-site (at servers) and off-site, and tested.

F. End-User Controls

Users must sign an Internet usage and responsibility agreement prior to gaining World Wide Web or Internet e-mail access, acknowledging that they understand what they should do (e.g., access the Internet only for legitimate work-related purposes) and should not do (e.g., no downloading of games, no "spamming") with their on-line privileges.

G. Network Security Controls

Transmission of sensitive information between security domains in the network or outside the organization's network is encrypted.

H. Internet Security Controls

Firewalls log all traffic passing through them. Logs identify hosts or users, Web sites visited, optional names of files transferred, and amount of data transferred.

I. Web Security Controls

Web servers with public content are not placed on the internal network but on a separate network protected by a firewall (often dubbed a demilitarized zone, or DMZ); and CGI or ASP scripts are used to make requests from databases or e-commerce systems on the internal network.

J. Telecommunications and Remote Access Security Controls

Sensitive data stored on portable computers (e.g., notebooks) is encrypted via a standardized, simple-to-use product and portable computer users have been trained in its use.

K. Internet Commerce Controls

Staff members with access to the Internet commerce system are given special in-depth background checks.

One of the greatest information protection challenges that your enterprise faces today is how to secure its electronic commerce activities. So take a look at the full list of IPAK Internet commerce controls and use the scoring sheet provided in Figure 18.3 to get a feel for how well your organization fares in addressing the fundamental issues. But remember, IPAK isn't meant to be a sum total of every countermeasure that you should be taking, only a list of controls that you simply shouldn't proceed without.

1. A detailed and up-to-date contingency plan for storefront computer outages has been developed.

2. A contingency plan for storefront computer outages is tested on a regular basis with exercises more detailed than tabletop scenarios.

3. A computer emergency response team (internal CERT) has been designated, trained, and periodically drilled to deal with problems like hacker intrusions.

4. An uninterruptible power system (UPS) is employed to provide necessary power in case of a power outage that lasts several hours or longer.

5. Communications with the telephone company are supported by lines to two or more central offices.

6. A mirror site provides geographical diversity for contingency planning purposes as well as increased performance.

7. Redundant equipment such as RAID (redundant array of inexpensive disks) ensures that a single hardware fault will not bring the commerce system down.

8. Internet commerce systems are physically isolated from other computers in a data center machine room via locked wire cages, separate locked rooms, etc.

9. Internet commerce systems are protected from hackers with respected firewall (and the most recent version of this firewall is installed).

10. Access controls are used to limit what individual internal users can read, write, or execute based on actual business need.

11. Card numbers sent over communications lines are encrypted using SSL or a stronger encryption process.

12. Backup tapes are encrypted and stored off-site in a locked container or room.

13. A fraud detection system is used to catch suspicious credit card orders before the order is filled.

14. A publicly accessible digital certificate is provided for all customers to verify that they have reached a legitimate server.

15. All communications between internal machines that make up the Internet commerce suite are encrypted and supported by digital certificates.

16. An intrusion detection system provides instant notification of hacker attacks and related problems.

17. A network management system provides real-time information about system load, response time, system downtime, and other performance issues.

18. A vulnerability identification system identifies configuration and setup problems before hackers can exploit them.

19. Staff with access to the Internet commerce system are given special in-depth background checks.

20. A specific individual is defined as the manager who "owns" the Internet commerce system (and who by extension is responsible for security thereon).

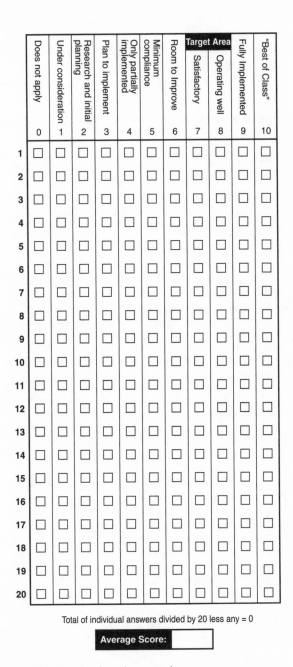

Total of individual answers divided by 20 less any = 0

Average Score:

Figure 18.3 Sample IPAK controls and answer sheet.

Source: Computer Security Institute

Policies and Procedures

A comprehensive body of well-crafted information security policies will spell out what is expected of everyone in the organization. Here are two worthy examples of how good policy can help.

Net Abuse

In September 1999, Patrick Naughton, then a 34-year-old executive vice president of Infoseek Corp. and Disney's GO Network, was arrested after he arranged to meet what he thought was a 13-year-old girl after seven months of sending her lewd e-mail messages through an on-line chat room. The "girl" turned out to be an undercover FBI agent. While on-line with the undercover agent, Naughton acknowledged that he was chatting from his office computer.

My guess is the day of the arrest was a bad one for Disney's PR flacks and for Naughton's colleagues on Disney's version of "Mahogany Row." But it could have been worse. If Naughton had worked at the White House or maybe a major metropolitan Roman Catholic Archdiocese, I doubt the organization he worked for would have gotten off so lightly in terms of bad publicity. "How could this have happened? Who is responsible for monitoring this kind of behavior? How many others are there in your organization?" Disney is a giant of the family entertainment industry. It is a premiere purveyor of content for children. Ah yes, but it is also a media giant. It owns one of the major networks now.

Abuse of Net privileges isn't just the threat of a PR disaster. It is also a big productivity drain.

According to a study from Net Partners Internet Solutions, employees reading the intimate details of the relationship between President Bill Clinton and Monica Lewinsky on the Internet cost American companies almost $500 million in lost productivity. The firm said about 13.5 million workers downloaded independent counsel Kenneth Starr's report or the President's grand jury testimony at work.

The following policy document was authored by Jacqueline Smick, CISSP, of Southwestern Bell (St Louis). Smick is one of CSI's lifetime achievement award winners.

The policy illustrates how an organization could position itself to thwart a potential Naughton early on, long before the PR disaster begins to unfold with the click of the handcuffs.

Internet access for employees[2]

Scope

These policies and guidelines apply to all employees in all business units of the company and any of its affiliated companies. In this document we will refer to each simply as "Internet users" and "the company." The policy covers all usage of the Internet including access to the World Wide Web, e-mail, file transfers (including both uploading to and downloading from the Internet), and postings to USENET news groups. As with all company policies, this Policy also applies to independent contractors who perform work for the company on company premises or using company provided resources.

This policy will be distributed to all contractors and agents of the company and adherence to this policy by such contractors or agents will be incorporated into their written contracts with the respective business unit.

This policy is the responsibility of the Corporate Human Resource organization.

Specification and oversight of security technologies is the responsibility of the Corporate Information Security organization. Investigations and monitoring of Internet access logs for appropriate business usage are the responsibility of the Asset Protection organization.

Employee Use Guidelines

As with other corporate assets, access to the Internet is provided for the pursuit of legitimate company-related business. Users must adhere to the following guidelines:

- Comply with all applicable FCC regulations.
- Abide by copyright laws and licensing agreements.
- Do not access, download, e-mail, store or print material that could be considered inappropriate, offensive or disrespectful to others. Only legitimate business-related material should be accessed.
- Do not disclose any information that could be considered proprietary, restricted proprietary, or company confidential.
- Do not express personal opinions or in any way conduct yourself in a manner that could be embarrassing to the company.
- Protect your workstation and the information on it while accessing the Internet. Use caution when downloading files through the use of a company approved virus detection package.

---

2. Computer Security Alert, #196, July 1999

- Read and comply with all company guidelines and bulletins regarding Internet security.

Management Responsibility

Local management is responsible for ensuring all Internet users are aware of their responsibilities as described in this policy. Managers must review this policy with their subordinates and should make it a part of the annual coverage of corporate policies (for example, the Code of Business Conduct).

Individual Accountability

Each Internet user is responsible for understanding and complying with this policy. As with all company resources, the Company reserves the right to monitor access to and usage of the Internet. This will be accomplished through UserID/Password or other approved authentication technology at the Internet access point (firewall).

Access to the Internet

All Internet access from corporate networks will be through authorized Internet gateways. Authorized Internet gateways must be registered with and approved by Corporate Information Security. (It is anticipated that there will be a minimal number of authorized Internet gateways.) Firewall(s) at these gateways will be managed, either directly or indirectly, by the Corporate Information Security organization. In all cases, Corporate Information Security and Asset Protection must have access to, and authority on, firewall(s), in order to accomplish their mission of security oversight for these gateways. Any access to the Internet from an official Company location using facilities other than the authorized Internet gateways is strictly prohibited. Employees needing Internet access from other than an official Company location may accomplish it using approved company dial-in facilities with token authentication at the dial-in access point and userID/password or other approved authentication technology at the Internet access point (firewall).

E-Mail Abuse

In December 1999, the Associated Press reported that the *New York Times* had fired 23 people for sending offensive e-mail at the Shared Services Center in Norfolk, Virginia, a hub for processing payroll, invoices, and benefits. The fired employees "all transmitted clearly inappropriate and offensive material, which left no doubt as to the discipline required." Other employees received disciplinary warnings.

Meanwhile, another case of abused e-mail privileges at the Naval Inventory Control Point in Mechanicsburg, Pennsylvania, led to the questioning of 1,000 civilian and military personnel, 500 of whom were disciplined. Investigators had found e-mail messages that contained sexually explicit cartoons and photographs, as well as dirty jokes and lewd stories. The official letters of reprimand read, "This poses a threat not only to the overall sexual harassment free climate, but to the public trust reposed in us all to use government resources (including duty time) wisely."

In March 1998, e-mail messages characterized as racist embroiled Morgan, Stanley, Dean Witter and Co. in a $30 million civil suit.

Nor does e-mail have to contain something prurient or hateful to cause an organization trouble. Just ask Oliver North or Bill Gates. Archived e-mail figured prominently as evidence of wrongdoing in both the Iran-Contra investigation and the Microsoft antitrust case.

In June 1996, UOP, a joint venture of Allied Signal and Union Carbide, sued Anderson Consulting, one of the then "Big Six" accounting firms, for $100 million alleging fraud and breach of contract. UOP computer analysts had read the e-mail messages Anderson consultants left behind on UOP hard drives. The messages revealed the misgivings of some Anderson consultants about their own colleagues. "He should be taking classes at a community college," one consultant e-mailed in reference to another working on the UOP account.

The following excerpt from an e-mail security policy developed by Principal Financial Group (another one of CSI's Information Security Program of the Year Award recipients) articulates many of the issues that organizations need to address up-front with their employees in order to avoid such problems.

E-Mail Security[3]

Management Responsibilities

Managers are responsible for the following:

- Ensuring employee e-mail options are appropriately set to cover unexpected absences
- Appropriately securing electronic departmental bulletin boards
- Ensuring their employees comply with e-mail policies

---

3. Computer Security Journal, Vol. XV, No. 1, Winter 1999

Employee Responsibilities

Each employee is responsible for understanding the following corporate policies:

- The e-mail systems of the company are to be used for business purposes. The company reserves the right to monitor all electronic mail messages.

- Any views expressed by individual employees in electronic mail messages are not necessarily those of the company.

- Any e-mail messages sent to non-employee groups, systems, or individuals must include a disclaimer stating the views of the message are the sender's and do not necessarily represent the views of the company.

- Failure to follow the policies of this manual could result in disciplinary action up to and including termination of employment.

Each employee is responsible for complying with the following corporate policies:

- Do not share e-mail passwords.

- Establish appropriate precautions when sending e-mail. Send information with the assumption that other people may read it.

- Establish appropriate precautions when receiving e-mail. If a message is marked confidential, do not send it to other people.

- E-mail messages can be made to appear as though they came from someone other than the actual sender (spoofing). When a message is marked confidential or contains sensitive information, call the apparent sender to confirm its origination.

- Forward requests you receive for proprietary or confidential information to the area responsible for releasing the information.

- Do not send confidential messages to public networks or bulletin boards. Use a secure method, such as the phone, registered mail, or a secure fax to send confidential information.

- Do not send confidential or proprietary information through a public network such as the Internet or AOL.

- Do not send or post messages containing medical information on any e-mail system. This practice is against federal regulations and can result in lawsuits.

- Messages sent to public newsgroups, listservs, or other public discussion forums must have the following disclaimer:

  Any opinions expressed in this message are not necessarily those of the company.

- Do not forward all e-mail to any Internet e-mail addresses (including your Internet e-mail address).

- For your own personal security, we recommend you do not provide information such as your home phone number, address, or cell phone number in the product's personal configuration.

Appropriate E-Mail Use

E-mail is used primarily for business correspondence. Employees should limit their use of e-mail for sending personal messages.

Examples of acceptable uses of e-mail include the following:

- Business messages
- Messages about company-sponsored events
- Short personal messages deemed necessary (for example, meeting someone for lunch or after work) when calling or physically visiting would take more time

Unacceptable Use of E-Mail

Examples of unacceptable use of e-mail include the following:

- Messages interfering with the normal conduct of business
- Messages involving solicitation or for-profit personal business activity
- Sending chain letters or electronic art
- Messages containing lewd, harassing, or offensive information

Abuse of E-Mail

Managers who suspect an employee is using e-mail in an unacceptable manner can monitor the employee's e-mail use. Managers cannot monitor messages for misconduct without Human Resources approval. After the manager contacts the Human Resources Counselor assigned to the area, Human Resources sets up the monitoring through Information Protection.

Legal Implications

Certain words, phrases, and messages, often seemingly harmless on e-mail, could lead to accusations of slander, defamation, or discrimination. E-mail messages have been used as evidence in recent and varied legal cases. When using e-mail, express facts clearly and be careful when expressing opinions. Avoid sending messages laced with anger, humor, or irony, which can easily be misunderstood.

Deleting Messages

Sensitive messages should be deleted from your inbasket and your trash file the day you receive the message. In some e-mail systems, deleting your message from your inbasket only does not mean the message is gone. The message remains in your trash file until you delete it or until nightly system maintenance deletes the trash file. If you do not delete the message from your trash file the day you receive it, the message remains on a backup tape. Although the intent of the company is not to retrieve messages from the backup tapes, there is a potential, in extreme circumstances, to retrieve this information (for example, lawsuits).

Sharing E-Mail Passwords

Employees are responsible for their e-mail account and the messages sent from this account. Therefore, employees must not share e-mail passwords. Once an employee has shared the password with another person, the other can log on to e-mail in the employee's name, send messages from the employee's name, read the employee's incoming messages (including confidential messages), and access the employee's e-mail files.

Security Awareness

Imagine buying an expensive burglar alarm system that your employees simply forget to switch on when they go home at night. Or imagine instead that they do indeed activate the burglar alarm but willingly offer up the four-digit code to disarm it to any stranger who requests it from them. There is an awful lot of damage that clueless, careless users can do to your organization's information security posture.

Clueless, careless users turn off their antivirus software because it slows down their accessing of files.

Clueless, careless users turn over their passwords to unfamiliar voices on the other end of a telephone line.

Clueless, careless users leave their computers logged on and unattended.

Clueless, careless users write their password down on a yellow sticky note and affix to their terminal.

Clueless, careless users download and execute unsolicited attachments.

The litany of woes goes on and on.

Effective information security programs go to great lengths to heighten the security awareness of the organization's user population. Trinkets like key chains, coffee mugs, and mouse pads with information security slogans on them are distributed. Day-long events featuring videos and guest speakers are held.

Contests to find every information security violation in a mock workspace have been developed. Wall posters reminding users to change their passwords and back up their data are hung in the lunchrooms.

World-class information security programs have put together robust intranet sites with plenty of fascinating content for users to draw on as a resource.

	Presentations	Slides, Viewgraphs	Posters	Pamphlets, Brochures	Internal Manager Newsletter	Security Newsletter	Alert Memos	Intranet Web site	Videos
Upper Management									
Financial Managers									
Operation Managers									
Support Group Managers									
Technicians									
Customer Support									
Data Processing									
Application Programmers									
Network Users									
Macintosh Users									
PC Users									
New Hires									

Figure 18.4   Security awareness tools and target audiences.

Source: Computer Security Institute

Frontline

Several years ago, CSI Director Patrice Rapalus had a brilliant idea.

She instructed me to produce a quarterly newsletter on information security targeted at users. Corporations and government agencies could then buy it from CSI, include a bit of content specific to their computing environment, and slap their own logos on the publication.

Dubbed *Frontline*, this quarterly newsletter developed into a powerful security awareness tool. *Frontline*'s approach is to not talk down to the reader, but rather to involve them, to help them understand that they are indeed the first line of cyberdefense in many ways.

Each issue features a cover story on some current high-profile computer crime. Each issue also contains an in-depth checklist of do's and don'ts in different aspects of information security (for example, tips on how to thwart social engineering attacks or tips on how to prevent laptop theft). There is also an update on the latest nasty computer virus as well as collection of real-world horror stories of hack attacks, insider abuses, financial fraud and trade secret theft from around the world.

The following "Seven Steps to Success" is an example of how to enlist your users as an integral part of the solution instead of leaving them to remain a big part of the problem.

Seven Steps to Success[4]

"You've got to be more than street-wise"

Let's take a look at what it means to be "street-wise" in cyberspace. Security is one area of high-tech expertise that information workers struggling to get ahead often overlook. But more and more managers are not only hoping for greater sophistication about information security from their workers, they're expecting it. If you add the following seven steps to success in information security to your portfolio, you will have taken another giant leap into excellence and career advancement.

Step 1: Don't be victimized by social engineering hackers or competitive intelligence operatives.

Hollywood's vision of the stereotypical hacker may be a tattooed youth with purple hair and multiple body piercings, flaying away at his laptop and using some sophisticated software he wrote on his spring break to bring down the Pentagon's computers from a phone booth somewhere. Hollywood's vision of an industrial spy may be a heartthrob leading man in Ninja-black commando fatigues descending from the ceiling via a razor thin wire to escape detection by the infrared sensors and using his pocket camera to photograph the schematics for some far-fetched technological wizardry. But in the real world, both hackers and industrial spies are almost always going to try the weakest link first: that's right, you.

Have you ever answered some unusual question about the configuration of your desktop system from someone on the phone claiming to be from the "Help Desk" or "Tech Support" and felt a wave of paranoia or puzzlement pass over you after you hung up? You might have been scammed by a hacker trying to glean information about your organization's computer systems through social engineering to save himself some time and trouble.

Hackers revel in developing adroit "social engineering" skills. They pose as telephone repair men, they pose as cable installers, they pose as long distance operators, they pose as co-workers you have never met. They will cajole or bully you, depending upon which they sense will get the best results. The questions they ask could be as simple as "What version of the operating system is installed on your system? We're doing an enterprise-wide update." The questions could be as brazen as "Could you tell me your password? We need to reconfigure your user account. There's been some file corruption and we can't retrieve your ID info."

Have you ever found yourself halfway through some telephone "marketing survey" and wondered, "Why did I ever agree to answer these questions?" Someone conducting competitive intelligence operation against your organization has probably scammed you. (*Competitive intelligence* is a pleasant phrase for activities just short of outright industrial espionage: i.e., legal or quasi-legal vs. clearly illegal information gathering.)

To avoid being duped, follow two simple rules:

- Don't provide information about your organization's information systems to strangers over the phone (or even in person). If the request is unusual, be suspicious. Turn their query around, start asking them a lot of questions. "Who are you? What is your title? What is your extension? Who is your supervisor?" Tell them you'll have to call them back, then contact your manager or your organization's information security personnel.

- Never answer "marketing surveys," whether they come at you over the phone, through the mail or via the Internet. If it's a telephone query, string the caller along: Ask for the person's name and phone number, that person's company's name and address, the title and purpose of the survey, etc. But don't answer questions. Tell the caller he or she should call back, then report the incident to your manager or your organization's information security personnel. Perhaps he or she will want you to forward the call to them if the surveyor calls back—but they probably won't call back. If you receive a "marketing survey" through the mail, hand it over to them. If you receive it via the Internet, forward it to them.

Step 2: Don't do or say anything on-line that you wouldn't want to read in the newspapers or hear on the evening news.

Remember that Web-surfing with anonymity is harder than walking on rice paper without a trace. Your employer will know how much time you spend at www.x-rated.com. And so will the local newspaper should you ever decide to run for public office. Remember that sending an e-mail message over the Internet is like sending a paper-based communiqué in an open envelope to be passed from hand-to-hand by one stranger after another until it reaches its destination. It's not a good means for professing illicit love or venting pent-up rage.

People are disarmed by the false intimacy of e-mail and Web-surfing. For example, the publisher of *Wired* magazine abruptly canceled plans to take the company public because of a tepid reception by investors. There was speculation that a leaked e-mail memo from a *Wired* chief executive might have contributed to the collapse of the offering. The memo, which was intended only for employees but found its way on to the Internet, appeared to violate federal regulations prohibiting companies from touting stock offerings from the time an offering is first planned to 25 days after they are completed.

Think twice before you surf somewhere on the Web. Think twice before you fire off an e-mail message. The safest approach is simply to never use either the Web or e-mail for personal purposes from work. You will not only be limiting your organization's exposure to civil liability or even criminal complaints, you'll also be protecting your own job. The consequence of failing to abide by this rule of thumb can range from embarrassing to costly to dire.

Step 3: Don't overlook physical security.

Most people do! But if you take physical security seriously, you will limit your exposure to hackers, industrial spies and other dark-siders. Think about it. You don't take your own personal physical security lightly, do you? You don't leave your keys in your car when it's parked on the street. You don't leave the garage door open when you drive off to work. Well, there are plenty of analogies in the work place. If you don't leave your keys in the ignition when you park the car, why do you leave your password scrawled on a yellow Post-it Note on your computer monitor? If you don't leave the garage door open when you drive off to work, why do you leave your computer on and your e-mail account open when you go home at night?

Hackers, industrial spies, and common thieves will always try the door and locks of your physical locale before they ever try to scale the firewall protecting your organization's patch of cyberspace. Why? It's easier. For example, a personal computer was stolen from a Visa International office that processes charges on a number of different credit card brands. Its memory included information on about 314,000 credit card accounts, including Visa, Master Card, American Express, Discover, and Diner's Club.

Step 4: Backup your files frequently: at the very least, once a day.

If you're dealing with word processing documents, databases, or other files that you update often in the course of the day, it would be much better to back up at sensible intervals during the course of the work day. Simply back up whatever files you've worked on just before your coffee breaks. By setting up this rhythm, you'll ensure that you never lose more than two or three hours of work.

If you've backed up adequately, when the system crashes, you'll be the hero. If you've failed to back up in a timely and thorough manner, you'll be the fall guy. Note that I say *"When* the system crashes..." rather than *"If* the system crashes..." It will crash. And you'll probably get no warning at all.

If you had come into work this morning and your system hadn't started up or if your previous days' work had been destroyed by a virus or even accidentally deleted, would you have had a backup of critical files and ongoing work so that you could pick up where you left off? Or would you have to start all over again from scratch?

Don't skip backup because you're in a hurry. Ever! And leave yourself reminders lest it slip your mind. Tailor your backup scheme to the needs of your specific work. For example, if you're an editor facing a deadline, it is wise to back up the particular files that you need for the deadline frequently throughout the day (even more than once an hour if the time is really tight).

But don't only save it to your system's hard disk, or even to the network. Save it to a diskette as well. If your hard disk crashes, you're out of luck. Or if the network goes down, your system will likely go with it. But with a current version on diskette, you can move to any other workstation or even to the 24-hour business center and finish your work!

Step 5: Don't engage in software piracy, and don't allow others to do it on your watch.

You wouldn't shoplift, would you? Well, software piracy is shoplifting in cyber-space. It is ethically wrong, and getting caught could be terribly embarrassing. If you're caught, your organization could pay steep fines. You will probably pay too...with your job.

Step 6: Always use anti-virus software on your computer (whether desktop or mobile).

Take a personal interest in how your computer systems scans for viruses. Is the anti-virus software set up to scan disks as they're inserted? If not, why not? If it is, never disable it, never allow others to disable it. Look at the version number and corresponding date. Has the anti-virus software been updated recently? Are you using the latest release? If the anti-virus software has not been updated recently, there is an excellent chance that your system could fall victim to a newer virus and spread it throughout the network.

Step 7: Create strong passwords and change your passwords frequently.

Don't think of your password as a way to get into your computer, think of it as a way to keep others out. Don't think of your password as a free ticket, think of it as an expensive, highly prized, easily pocketed item coveted by dishonest insiders, malicious hackers and unethical competitors alike. Your password should be a mix of letters and numbers and you should change it frequently (for example, at least every 30 days). Ask your manager or your organization's information security staff for password guidelines.

Security Technologies: Few Solutions, Lots of Snake Oil, and No Silver Bullets

International Data Corp. (IDC) projects that the security software market will grow from $2 billion to $7.4 billion in 2003 and the security hardware market will grow from $500 million to $1.9 billion in 2003. IDC also reports that the market for Virtual Private Networks (VPNs) will grow from $700 million to $5 billion in 2003 and that the market for Public Key Infrastructure (PKI) will grow from $197 million to over $1.3 billion in 2003.

Yes, indeed, there is a lot of money to be made selling security technologies and services. But will your networks or the data that flows over them be any more secure? It depends. Is this good news for the purveyors of security technologies? Of course, it is. Is it good news for those deploying them with the hope of a more robust information security posture? It depends on how good the products are, how well they are implemented and administered, and whether other vital issues (for example, adequate levels of staffing and training for information security personnel) are addressed seriously.

For example, in 2000, 100% of respondents to the *CSI/FBI Computer Crime and Security Survey* reported the use of anti-virus software, and yet, 85% also report incidents of virus contamination.

The number of CSI/FBI respondents reporting the use of intrusion detection systems (IDS) rose from 35% in 1998 to 50% in 2000. The number of CSI/FBI respondents reporting the use of digital IDs rose from 20% in 1998 to 36% in 2000. The number of CSI/FBI respondents using encrypted logins rose from 36% in 1998 to 50% in 2000. The number of those using encrypted files also rose from 50% in 1998 to 62% in 2000. Indeed, the overwhelming majority of respondents reported use of firewalls, access control, and physical security; and yet, 95% of respondents reported some type of cyberattack within the last twelve months, and 70% reported some kind of financial losses due to those cyberattacks.

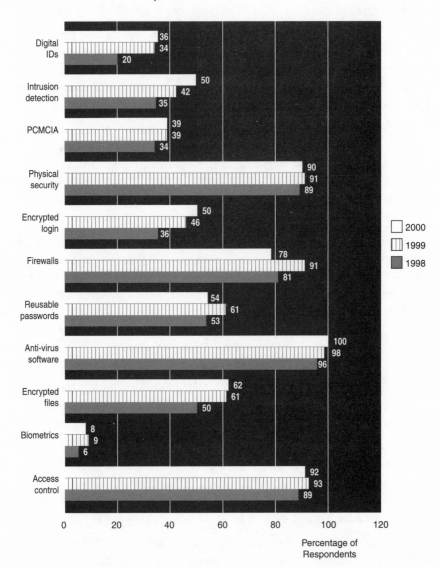

Figure 18.5 Security technologies used.

Source: CSI/FBY 2000 Computer Crime and Security Survey

A lot of hyperbole is swirling around about the various security technologies mentioned here. Whole rainforests have been felled to extol their praises. Many naive IS managers and corporate executives believe that information security equals PKI plus VPN plus firewalls plus IDS, etc.

This kind of thinking is very dangerous.

Wave after wave of enthusiasm for information security technologies have washed over the marketplace in the last five or six years: firewalls, VPNs, IDS, PKI,...

When the business world woke up to the potential of the Internet and the WWW, the demand for firewalls grew dramatically. It was a very hot marketplace. From the beginning, I tried to steer CSI's editorial content toward practical, hard-nosed advice on the relative strengths and weakness of the different types of firewalls as well as how to evaluate and select the best product for a particular environment.

For example, the CSI Firewall Matrix, which I developed with Rik Farrow, is a free, on-line resource available for those who want to compare the features of various firewalls. The site also offers an archive of *Computer Security Journal* articles by Farrow, Marcus Ranum, and Dr. Eugene Schultz. These articles and interviews from the formative period of the firewall marketplace provide an excellent context to come to your own understanding of what firewalls can and can't do for you.

Do you need firewalls for your Internet connections? Yes, of course. But how many and where? You may need more than one firewall that guards your gateway to the Internet. You may decide that you need two or three or even more internal firewalls to strengthen your defenses around vital systems in order to thwart attacks from disgruntled, dishonest insiders or outsiders who have somehow found a way to circumvent your Internet firewall. And which type of firewall? How do you select a firewall? An application gateway or stateful inspection firewall? What should you look for in regard to vendor support? Perhaps you'll decide on one type of firewall for your Internet defenses and another type of firewall for your internal defenses.

"Just having a firewall is not enough to prevent penetration," comments Rik Farrow. "Many firewalls are not configured correctly: for example, permitting direct connections to internal systems without strong authentication and encryption.

"Some firewalls exist only in name," he adds, "their configuration is so weak that all they do is slow down network traffic without providing any security at all. Keep in mind, also, that the best way into an organization's network may not be the 'front door,' but via a modem into some desktop running PC Anywhere."

In October 1998, I attended a panel discussion on IDS, moderated by Dr. Eugene Spafford of CERIAS. (See Appendix C for more information on Spafford and CERIAS and the vital work he is doing there.)

The room was packed, even though it was stiflingly hot. Everyone's attention was riveted on the discussion.

Afterward, I said to Spaf, "Didn't that IDS session remind you of something?"

"Yes," Spaf, smiled and agreed, "some firewall panel circa 1995–1996."

Okay. So it wasn't my imagination.

Everyone had bought and installed firewalls, but they were still in need of more technology to deter, detect, and thwart unauthorized activity on their networks.

The IDS wave was cresting and about to break over the marketplace. What could CSI offer our readers and conference attendees to help them sort out the truth from the hyperbole?

Should you deploy IDS to supplement your firewall? Yes, of course, but how do you evaluate them? Should your IDS be host-based or network-based? And where should you place it?

One of the experts I turned to was Marcus Ranum of Network Flight Record (NFR), who responded by delivering a double session at NetSec 1999 on the strengths and weaknesses of various IDS models.

The host-based IDS paradigm is to collect the data from someplace on the system. Typically, you are going to collect it from audit logs, system logs, application logs, and local watchdogs (i.e., daemon processes that record who's logged in and what they're doing).

The advantage of host-based IDS, according to Ranum, is that the quality of information is extremely high. Once you've pulled that information out, you pretty much have the information that you need. You don't need to do any further post-processing on it.

But there are several disadvantages to host-based IDS.

For example, they are also very system-specific. "The typical host-based IDS will support one or two platforms," Ranum says, "maybe three on the outside. What you'll get is NT and then one or two flavors of UNIX."

Furthermore, you may experience some performance degradation, according to Ranum, because you have to send the logs off the host to do some processing somewhere else.

But the biggest problem Ranum cites in regard is that the hosts are the target of the attack. "You don't attack a network as a whole," he contends. "You wind up attacking a system, even if it is just a router, on the network."

In the network-based approach, Ranum explains, you're pulling the traffic off of something, either from the wire in passive mode or out of a hub or off a switch or some other kind of an infrastructure device.

"You're looking at the contents of the traffic as information," Ranum states. "You're looking at packet headers, you're looking at packet data, you're trying to reassemble it into something that makes sense. You're trying to determine what's happening from the contents of the traffic."

One of the pros of network-based IDS, as Ranum sees it, is zero performance impact. The network-based IDS will not affect your host platforms because they're not on your host platforms.

"That also means that they have a lower management impact," Ranum explains. "If you're trying to monitor six subnets with 5,000 machines—I guess it would be more than six subnets, let's say a couple hundred subnets for a couple thousand machines. You do not need to install software on a couple of thousand desktops."

But one of the disadvantages of network-based IDS, Ranum observes, is that it could lose packets on flooded networks. That's a big one. If you're looking at network-based IDS and evaluating them, be very careful about whether it can handle the traffic load on your network.

Ranum believes that it isn't a simple "either/or" decision. For him, it is a "both/and" decision.

"You need to have them both," he says. "But you have some vendors that are host-based and some that are network-based. In five years, the host-based vendors will also be looking at the network and the network-based vendors will also be looking at the hosts. It's the stupid ones that are going to tell you that one or the other one stinks without thinking that they're going to be doing it in a couple years."

Of course, whether to use host-based or network-based IDS is only one of the issues. You have many other considerations in evaluating various IDS products.

The point is that information security is not (and probably never will be) an area in which you will be able to plug something in and forget about it.

In the *Computer Security Journal* (Vol. XVI, No. 1, Winter 2000), I ran an article by Counterpane's Bruce Schneier and Intel's Carl Ellison that highlighted "Ten Risks of Public Key Infrastructure: What You're Not Being Told About PKI." The piece caused a firestorm of debate on-line. I ran rebuttals and responses in two ensuing issues of the Alert, CSI's monthly publication.

What was all the furor about? Well Schneier and his colleague (I confess that I urged them on) simply brought up some of the vulnerabilities in PKI at a time when everyone was embracing it as the panacea. Of course, the PKI vendors weren't doing too much to disabuse their potential customers of their unrealistic expectations. There are probably still a lot of IS managers out there in cyberspace who think that they can avoid pouring money and human resources into enterprise-wide information security by simply deploying PKI.

Is PKI a part of the puzzle? Certainly, it will, if used properly and maintained adequately, reduce some risks of on-line business to business transactions. But it can't substitute for a comprehensive information security program. No technology can.

Here is a list of questions I suggest you ask:

- Where does information protection (IP) report within your organization?
- Do you have adequate IP staffing levels?
- Is your IP staff adequately trained?
- Do you conduct risk analysis?
- Have you attained a body of sound practices?
- Have you developed a body of IP policies and procedures?
- Do you have a security awareness program for your employees?
- Do you include IP in job performance review?
- Do you conduct security assessments or penetration tests?
- Do you have an emergency response team?
- Do you have a business continuity/disaster recovery plan?
- Do you know your adversaries?
- Have you taken advantage of available security technologies, such as strong authentication (for example, smart cards), encryption, firewalls, intrusion detection, anti-virus scanners, etc.?

If you answer "yes" to that last question on security technologies, but "no" to any of the previous ones, you're wasting your money and are very vulnerable to attack.

The lesson to be learned is simple: Security technology does not equal a security program. While the deployment of security technologies is essential to securing information systems, it is not the only step that is required. Organizations need comprehensive information protection (IP) programs. Such programs include an adequate, well-trained IP staff, an all-encompassing body of IP policies and procedures, a creative and engaging security awareness program, and an overarching information security architecture based in many cases on a body of "sound practices" specific to an industry segment or computing environment.

Security technologies and an overarching security architecture are only one-third of the equation. The other two-thirds relate to organizational issues, human resources, policies, and user education.

For some expert advice on the strengths and weaknesses of IDS, PKI and VPN, you can consult CSI's free, on-line Editorial Archive (www.gocsi.com/excerpt.htm).

Outsourcing? Yes and No

Information protection, as you can see, is not as simple as plugging in an assortment of security technology products. Even if you win the turf war over where your IP unit should report, even if you develop policies and procedures that have some teeth to them, your effort can still be understaffed, inadequately funded, or simply over-whelmed by the scope of the problem. There is another way. Increasingly, corporations are outsourcing certain aspects of their information protection program.

Consider what Bruce Schneier's Counterpane Internet Security (www.counterpane.com) offers its clients: 24-7 "security-event" monitoring and response of their networks.

If you sign up for their service, Counterpane places sentry systems on your network. These sentries take the pulse of your servers, routers, firewalls, etc., and send the relevant data back to Counterpane's Secure Operations Centers (SOCs), where it is monitored by bonded expert analysts who have undergone background checks and psychological testing and sit behind biometrically controlled locks.

A service-level agreement, tailored to your environment, will spell out how to deal with "security events" that fall into the range from "interesting" (for example, "single, isolated port scans") to "relevant" (for example, multiple port scans from the same source IP address) to "suspicious" (for example, "connection attempts to ports or services from suspect sources") to "critical" (for example, "successful connections from suspect sources").

Not only would such a service help you detect unauthorized activity early on, it would also help you determine the best approach to dealing with the problem as it develops.

Of course, when you consider outsourcing anything, particularly information security, you must ask yourself how sure you are that you can trust the outsourcing service.

Bruce Schneier is a force in the industry. For example, his Twofish algorithm is among the five finalists being considered for the Advanced Encryption Standard (AES) by the

National Institute of Standards and Technology (NIST). Schneier's scathing product analysis of Microsoft's PPTP (undertaken in collaboration with Mudge from L0pht Heavy Industries) exposed numerous vulnerabilitites. And Schneier is a frequent and significant contributor to CSI's editorial content and annual conferences as well as those of other reputable organizations. So perhaps there is a comfort level with Schneier and those he would bring with him that would simply not exist if the principles of the potential outsourcing service were unknown to you.

Cost justification is perhaps the biggest problem. Whether you can justify the cost of such a service depends on several factors:

- How much you really have to lose financially and in terms of public relations
- How good you are at quantifying what you have to lose
- How much it would cost your enterprise to build your own in-house 24-7 monitoring operation (assuming you really could do it)
- Whether your management understands that your enterprise is at risk
- Whether you are really serious about avoiding the kind of problems documented in *Tangled Web*

But remember, although outsourcing certainly could supplement and complement some of your in-house strengths as well as mitigate some of your in-house weaknesses, it cannot substitute for building your own in-house cadre of IP professionals.

The Human Factor

People sometimes ask, "How did you get into computer security? How did you get that journalistic beat?" Well, I just wandered into it really, and I was intrigued.

Perhaps I have thrived in the field because the subject matter has to do with the shadow side of the psyche. The themes of espionage and criminality make for fascinating content.

Great novels will come from the world of cybercrime and infowar. Someone must write a *Cybercrime and Punishment*, which probes the tortured mind of some digital Raskolnikov. Someone must write an *Infowar and Peace*, a sweeping epic in which whole political systems and economies hang in the balance on a digital battlefield.

But *Tangled Web* sticks to the "facts on the ground." Each of the case studies I've included could have been a book of its own. *Tangled Web* itself could have been 1,000 pages. I have not answered every question or highlighted every detail. But I hope I've given you a strong sense of some of the dangers and challenges of the Internet revolution.

My editors asked me for an introduction, but I said that an epilogue would serve our purposes better. Why? Well, everything in this field is moving so fast. It is like a train hurtling by. Before the ink dries, there will be another whole manuscript worth of stories that should be added in. So an epilogue is really more appropriate.

Imagine that train roaring on. This epilogue is like the caboose at the rear end of it. It is a platform on which I can stand to holler a few final words of warning to you as the train hurtles forward into the long tunnel.

One Term I Never Heard In Silicon Valley

I only knew one thing about computer security before I started working at CSI in 1994, but that one thing was very telling. I had worked for successful Silicon Valley technology developers for ten years, and I had never heard the term *computer security* once.

Indeed, that little realization was a very significant one.

One of the fundamental problems in regard to securing your organization's computer networks and the information that flows over them is that operating systems and applications that you need to use are inherently flawed in regard to security issues. They are not built with security in mind. The engineers who designed them have not studied information security in any serious, disciplined way. Despite what the marketing hype might promise you, most products (even most security products) are broken from their inception.

When I worked down in Silicon Valley, the buzzwords we used were *speed, interoperability*, and *ease of use*. Today, they've all added another buzzword, *security*. But it is often little more than something that is said because you want to hear it.

Microsoft is a prime example. When Windows NT was introduced in the mid-1990s, it was promoted as "the secure operating system," a viable alternative to Unix, which in all its many flavors had been the repeated victim of hacker exploits for years by that time. Well, it didn't take hackers (both white and black hat) to find and expose NT's numerous and glaring vulnerabilities to the public eye.

Frankly, the technical experts who I respect most almost unanimously recommend Unix over NT for security reasons alone.

Nevertheless, NT has taken the lion's share of the market.

Why? Well, it is easier to use. But perhaps the Justice Department's antitrust division could provide a better answer to that question.

Porous operating systems and applications are a big part of the overall problem. Their deployment means that security is too often an add-on, something that you have to lay on top of something else, rather than an inherent element of the system architecture. Marcus Ranum described the problem to me as "trying to change the hull of a ship at sea."

Hopefully, the next generation of software engineers will understand the problem better. (Indeed, one of the reasons why Gene Spafford's CERIAS program at Purdue University is so important is that its computer science students are being inculcated with the higher principles of information security.)

Meanwhile, buyer beware.

Infosec du Soleil

In the course of covering cybersecurity beat, I have met some extraordinarily talented and insightful individuals: for example, Dr. Fred Cohen of Sandia National Laboratory.

Cohen is sometimes referred to as the "father of the computer virus," a somewhat misleading moniker. Cohen did, indeed, write his first paper on the subject in November 1983. His musings grew into a thesis and led to his Ph.D. from University of Southern California in 1986. The first computer viruses appeared "in the wild" in 1987 and 1988. Of course, Cohen isn't responsible for the scourge of the computer virus, he simply was forward-thinking enough to see them coming and wonder "what if…"

I was flying back to the West Coast from a conference in Chicago a couple of years ago. Cohen plopped down in the seat across the aisle.

Fred is perspicacious, to many maddeningly so. Way back in 1995, with my encouragement, Cohen came up with "50 Ways to Attack Your Web Site," which I published in the *Computer Security Alert*.

Within a year or two, they had almost all been demonstrated.

Thinking of the three-and-a-half-hour flight from Chicago to San Francisco, I challenged him to come with "50 Ways to Attack Your Intrusion Detection System." He said, "No problem."

The subsequent publication of the piece in the *Alert* infuriated some of the IDS vendors and some other self-proclaimed Internet security experts as well. I invited rebuttal, but I didn't receive any. I did, however, begin to see white papers and presentations by others that reflected Cohen's insights (although they would never admit it).

PKI is the current belle of the ball. Everyone wants to dance with PKI. Well, I called Cohen again, at 4:07 one afternoon and laid down the gauntlet once again.

"50 ways," Cohen mused, "53 minutes of free time, no problem." He had fired them off to me by 4:57, just in time to take his kids to a soccer game.

You can review these and other "50 Ways…" lists on Cohen's own Web page (http://www.all.net).

I have also encountered some charlatans and hucksters.

No, I am not going to mention any names.

But consider some of the following comments that I collected from conference sessions and news items along the way.

One "information security consultant" boasts that he can assemble a HERF gun from parts purchased off the shelf at Radio Shack.

Another "information security consultant" boasts that he could "teach a chimpanzee to hack" in two hours.

A third "information security consultant" boasts that he could bring down the Internet in one day.

Well, I would love to call the bluff of these blusterers.

My vision is to hold a special three-ring circus event called "Infosec du Soleil" at a CSI conference. An invitation to perform their feats in public would be extended to these three "information security consultants."

On a big screen in the center ring, a remote video camera would follow the first "information security consultant" on a shopping trip to Radio Shack for HERF gun parts.

Meanwhile, in one of the side rings, in a soundproof room with a one-way mirror, the second "information security consultant" would be teaching a chimpanzee to hack. On the wall behind them, a large clock would be ticking off the two hours he said would be required to teach the ape to hack.

In the other side ring, the third "information security consultant" would sit at a keyboard in an isolation booth. Only his silhouette would be visible to the audience. Above the isolation booth, another clock would be ticking off the 24 hours he said would be required to bring down the Internet.

The ticking of the two clocks would thud ominously throughout the auditorium.

The remote video camera would follow the first "information security consultant" back into the auditorium where he would then assemble the HERF gun for a live demonstration of its awesome "infowar" power.

The chimpanzee would not be able to learn to hack in two hours. The Internet would probably not be brought down in twenty-four hours (although someone could probably significantly limit its availability). The homemade HERF gun would at best disrupt a desktop PC from close range.

Beware of the idle boasts of self-promoters.

Joseph's Robe of Many Colors Was Made of Patches

Most of the big headline-grabbing hacker stories of the last decade (for example, the three major cases detailed in Chapter 6) involved the exploitation of known vulnerabilities for which patches existed.

Are you curious about this pervasive carelessness? Does it seem crazy to you? Do you wonder, "Why don't they just patch the damn holes?" Well, what does it mean to patch the holes? And why doesn't it happen with more alacrity?

"There are a lot of problems," Gene Schultz explains. "It is a major organizational commitment and expense to install these patches. People have real operational cycles. They have to upgrade operating systems, install new applications, tune networks, etc. They don't like it when security people start crying wolf about all these patches. They don't perceive the risk. They often don't have the tools it takes to do massive automatic install of patches.

"Tivoli, for example, would do that quite easily but it is very expensive" he continues. "You can use a lower-grade tool, but God help you. Sometimes the patches are wrong. You install a patch and two weeks later the vendor tells you to install another one. Sometimes patches cause systems to break. 'Who installed this patch? We need this system up and running?' In the real world, there are a lot of reasons that people get conservative about installing patches. Unless you have the money and resources to dedicate to it, it is not an easy road."

Like the issues surrounding how your InfoSec unit is organized, where it reports, and how well it is staffed and budgeted (discussed in Chapters 15 and 18), the failure to install security-related patches is a serious problem, but also a solvable one.

Beware of excuses.

Another Patsy Named Lee?

I tracked the Los Alamos nuclear weapons lab spy story for well over a year from Spring 1999 through Summer 2000. I kept an exhaustive file of news items related to the case, but I refused to write anything about it or even cover it in CSI publications. There was plenty of copy on it elsewhere. I just wanted to hold off for awhile. I just wanted to watch it unfold. It struck me as a weird, disingenuous, and flawed story. I knew it would have some twists and turns before it began to flow straight and true.

Don't misunderstand me. I do not doubt that Chinese intelligence is actively engaged in stealing any nuclear weapons secrets it can't buy outright. (Of course, I also believe that the United States would be doing the same if it felt itself vulnerable to a more powerful potential adversary.) But the way in which the story was handled in the mainstream media and by politicians inside the beltway was very disturbing.

Here are some of the highlights (lowlights?) of this sad affair.

In 1996, the FBI launched an investigation into the theft of W-88 Trident submarine missile warhead designs. It targeted Wen Ho Lee, a Los Alamos scientist who had come to its attention because of his contacts with a Taiwanese nuclear scientist and suspected spy. In 1997, the FBI requested a search warrant from the Department of Justice to search Lee's computers. But Justice, citing a lack of evidence, rejected the FBI's request. Twice.

According to *Time* magazine (June 7, 1999), the FBI finally got to look inside Lee's computer hard disk drive, just before the story broke into the newspaper headlines. And investigators discovered that Lee had downloaded the "legacy codes" containing "all the most important data the U.S. had amassed from years of nuclear testing."

On April 21, 1999, the *New York Times*, in anticipation of an intelligence study expected to be delivered to the White House and Congress, reported that U.S. intelligence officials had concluded that China did indeed steal "design information related to America's most advanced nuclear warhead" from Los Alamos.

On May 17, 1999, the *Washington Post* reported that, according to a select congressional committee chaired by Representative Christopher Cox (R-California), China had gained "design secrets of America's five most modern nuclear warheads through pervasive spying at the nation's nuclear laboratories."

On May 25, 1999, the *Los Angeles Times* reported that, according to the Cox committee, China had "stolen the design secrets of seven U.S. nuclear warheads, including every weapon in the current U.S. nuclear arsenal, through spying" at four U.S. government research labs including Los Alamos and Livermore.

On December 11, 1999, the Associated Press (AP) reported that Wen Ho Lee had finally been arrested and charged with "removing nuclear secrets from highly secure computers" at Los Alamos although "there was still no proof that he passed information to China."

On December 15, 1999, the AP reported that a "team of foreign policy analysts" at Stanford University's Center for International Security and Cooperation had concluded that the Cox committee study was "misleading, inaccurate and damaging to U.S.-China relations." The Stanford analysts cited six significant flaws in the Cox report.

On December 20, 1999, the AP reported that Wen Ho Lee was going to file a lawsuit against the FBI, the Department of Justice, and the Department of Energy for violating his privacy and "wrongly portraying him as a Chinese spy."

However, with Wen Ho Lee accused, incarcerated, but still not on trial, Los Alamos' security problems were again dominating the headlines in the mainstream media.

On June 13, 2000, the *New York Times* reported that investigators had discovered that two computer hard disk drives "containing nuclear weapons data and other highly sensitive material stored in a vault" were missing at Los Alamos.

The hard disk drives, which had disappeared from a locked compartment inside a locked bag that was kept inside a heavily guarded vault, were found three days later tucked behind a photocopy machine.

On June 25, 2000, the *New York Times* reported that an inventory of all classified data at Los Alamos revealed that "two 10-year-old floppy disks containing classified information" were missing. The two misplaced diskettes were found a day later, attached to a paper report in a secured area nearby.

On July 7, 2000, the *Los Angeles Times* ran a story with the following lead:

> Federal prosecutors have concluded that fired Los Alamos engineer Wen Ho
> Lee was trying to boost his job prospects with research institutions in Europe
> and Asia when he allegedly copied virtual archive of nuclear weapons secrets.[1]

Were vital nuclear weapons secrets compromised? Were reports of egregious lapses in information security, personnel security, and physical security ignored? Were the details of an ongoing counterintelligence investigation leaked to the media? Were the findings of a congressional inquiry exaggerated or distorted for partisan political motives?

The Los Alamos affair is worthy of a book of its own.

My point here is that Lee, whether he is guilty or not of espionage, was a patsy.

The security problems at Los Alamos and the other nuclear weapons labs are chronic, systemic, and severe. In an environment in which computer security, personnel security, and physical security are so very broken, it is ludicrous to treat a single suspect as public enemy number one. (Remember Julius and Ethel Rosenberg?)

In April 1999, the General Accounting Office (GAO) issued a report on security at the U.S. Department of Energy (DOE), "Key Factors Underlying Security Problems at DOE Facilities" (GAO/T-RCED-99-159). The study articulated "security-related problems" in several areas.

---

1. "Prosecutors Give Theory in Case of Jailed Scientist," by Bob Drogin and Eric Lichtblau, *Los Angeles Times*, Friday, July 7, 2000

- "Ineffective controls over foreign visitors to DOE's most sensitive facilities." For example, in 1997, at two particular DOE facilities, only five percent of visitors from all sensitive countries, and less than two percent of visitors from China, had undergone background checks.

- "Weaknesses in efforts to control and protect classified and sensitive information." For example, one DOE facility could not account for 10,000 classified documents.

- "Lax physical security controls, such as security personnel and fences...." For example, "at one DOE facility, 78 percent of security personnel failed a test of required skills."

- "Ineffective management of personnel security clearance programs has been a problem since the early 1980s. Backlogs were occurring in conducting security investigations, and later when the backlogs were reduced, the GAO found that some contractors were not verifying information on prospective employees."[2]

Furthermore, funding for counterintelligence activities at Energy facilities during the mid-1990s could only be considered minimal. Prior to fiscal year 1997, Energy provided no direct funding for counterintelligence programs at its facilities. Consequently, at eight high-risk facilities, counterintelligence program funding was obtained from overhead accounts and totaled only $1.4 million and 15 staff.

But perhaps the most damning evidence of lax security at Los Alamos and other Energy sites relates to the state of computer security.

> Security problems identified by DOE's own internal security oversight staff often go unresolved, even today. For example, issues related to the inadequate separation of classified and unclassified computer networks were identified at Los Alamos in 1988, 1992, and 1994. This problem was only partially corrected in 1997, as classified information was discovered on Los Alamos' unclassified computer network in 1998.[3]

In April 1999, with the Lee scandal in full bloom, Energy suspended use of classified computers at Los Alamos, Sandia, and Livermore labs because those labs had received a less than satisfactory security rating for 1998.

On April 7, 1999, the *New York Times* reported that thousands of scientists and other researchers who rely on classified computer networks were forced to attend training sessions on cybersecurity.

---

2. "Key Factors Underlying Security Problems at DOE Facilities" (GAO/T-RCED-99-159). Statement of Victor S. Rezendes, Director, Energy, Resources, and Science Issues, Resources, Community, and Economic Development Division, April 20, 1999

3. Ibid.

The classified computers are connected together but not linked to the outside world. Ever since the U.S. stopped testing nuclear weapons, the work of modeling the reliability of weapons designs has been done with these networks.

One security flaw is that secret information about nuclear weapons can be copied from the sensitive computers and onto a computer disk and then sent as e-mail among thousands of e-mails that leave the lab through separate unclassified computer systems.[4]

The possibility that someone would send classified material in or attached to an e-mail message (even inadvertently) isn't the only problem. There is also the danger that a user's e-mail account could be snooped or that the e-mail traffic itself could be monitored.

Two weeks later, Secretary of Energy Bill Richardson authorized the resumption of work on the classified computer networks.

The real question in the Los Alamos affair is not "How did the Chinese get these secrets?" The real question is "Who else got them?" That's how porous the environment of those labs has become.

In November 1999, *Brill's Content* ran a piece excoriating the *New York Times* for its coverage of the Wen Ho Lee story.

The *Times'* initial story on Lee and Los Alamos ran on March 6, 1999 with the headline: "Breach at Los Alamos: A Special Report; China Stole Nuclear Secrets For Bombs, U.S. Aides Say." And as Robert Schmidt observed, the *Times* story "sparked an immediate firestorm in the media, in Congress and in the White House."

"The *Times* onslaught," Schmidt wrote, "continued for five months."

"In a series of front-page articles written mostly by Jeff Gerth and James Risen, the *Times* pressed the case against Lee, insinuating that he was guilty of various nefarious deeds. Along the way, the Times drew an ever-tightening noose around the Clinton administration, accusing it of minimizing and downplaying the alleged espionage."[5]

Schmidt recounts that the tenor changed, however, in early September, when the *Times* published an article by science reporter William Broad.

Broad's article shed new doubt on both the case against Lee and the whole spy scandal itself as it had been reported in the *Times*. "The lost secrets," Broad had written," were available to hundreds if not thousands of people."

---

4. "Computer Work Is Halted At Nuclear Weapon Labs," by James Risen. *New York Times*, April 7, 1999.

5. "Crash Landing," by Robert Schmidt. *Brill's Content*, November 1999.

"Broad's story," Schmidt remarked, "was meticulously reported. But it left out one salient fact: The *New York Times* itself had been largely responsible for fueling the scandal and portraying Wen Ho Lee as a traitor."

There are two important lessons to be learned from the Los Alamos fiasco. First, never underestimate computer security, personnel security, or physical security. Second, beware of fear-mongers and muckrakers whether in the press and in elected office.

From the Red-Eye to the Russell Office Building

In 1996, as I mentioned in Chapter 3, I testified in the U.S. Senate hearings on "Security in Cyberspace" held by then-Senator Sam Nunn (D-Georgia), chairman of the Permanent Subcommittee on Investigations of the Committee on Governmental Affairs.

I flew the red-eye from the West Coast, didn't pack a bag, wore my suit on the plane, hailed a cab to the Russell Office Building, passed through the metal detectors without incident, and wandered around until I stumbled on Senator Nunn's office.

Two bright, confident, and friendly men, Jim Christy and Keith Rhodes, were waiting for me there with hot black coffee and a laptop to load my presentation into.

Later that morning, the three of us sat together with Rich Pethia of CERT at the witness table—with a bank of cameras and lights off to the side, a roomful of press behind us—answering the questions of Nunn, Senator John Glenn (D-Ohio), and others.

Christy testified on the investigation into the Rome Lab intrusion (see Chapter 6), Rhodes testified on the GAO report on the Defense Department's cybersecurity problems (see Chapter 17), and I testified on the results of the second annual CSI/FBI survey.

Recently, I asked Rhodes to comment on the most important InfoSec-related events or contributions of the last few years.

"I would say that those hearings held by Nunn were the key," Rhodes told me. "It seems to me that the combination of Nunn's influence, Glenn's support, Daniel Gelber's counsel, and Jim Christy's and Mark Webster's legwork was what started the ball rolling.

"The other events were aftereffects," he continued. "They are not minor, but they were aftereffects. The one point that I think galvanized the hearings was the combination of your data on financial losses and our estimate that Defense was being hit (250,000 times per year). You gave them real dollars and we gave them a large and plausible number. That combination together with the succession of people at very high levels of government and industry who all came in to testify, 'Yes, this is real and we should be really worried,' made the hearings important."

At the time of the hearings, Rhodes worked for GAO as a technical assistant director in the chief scientist's office. Then he became the technical director, and then the director of the Office of Computer and Information Assessment. Currently, he is the GAO's chief technologist, or in other words, its chief technology officer (CTO).

At the time of the hearings, Christy, the AFOSI investigator who had worked the Rome Lab case, was assigned to Nunn's committee. Afterward, he was assigned to NIPC during its formative development and then to the Defense Information Assurance Program (DIAP) to organize the Defense Department's effort to solve its own InfoSec problems.

Rhodes and Christy exemplify the intelligence and dedication of those with whom I have been honored to interact over my years in covering the InfoSec beat. Their stories are strong threads throughout *Tangled Web*.

Like Spafford, Ranum, Denning, Farrow, and others cited in this book, Rhodes and Christy are proof that people are the greatest resource in the defense of cyberspace. Not firewalls, not crypto, not IDS, not policies, not background checks, not biometrics. People.

It is people who will build and maintain the defenses of cyberspace to ensure that it is a commons in which the planetary population can communicate with, inform, educate, express, liberate, empower, and enrich itself.

Appendices

alert   A formatted message describing a circumstance relevant to network security.

ankle-biter   A person who aspires to be a hacker/cracker but has very limited knowledge or automated information systems. This term is usually associated with young teens who collect and use simple malicious programs obtained from the Internet.

anomaly detection model   A model where intrusions are detected by looking for activity that is different from the user's or system's normal behavior.

assurance   A measure of confidence that the security features and architecture of a system accurately mediate and enforce the security policy.

attack   The act of trying to bypass security controls on a system. An attack can be active, resulting in the alteration of data, or passive, resulting in the release of data. The fact that an attack is made does not necessarily mean that it will succeed.

audit   The independent examination of records and activities to ensure compliance with established controls, policy, and operational procedures, and to recommend any indicated changes in controls, policy, or procedures.

audit trail   In computer security systems, a chronological record of system resource use. This includes user login, file access, other various activities, and whether any actual or attempted security violations occurred, legitimate and unauthorized.

authenticate   To establish the validity of a claimed user or object.

authentication   To positively verify the identity of a user, device, or other entity in a computer system, often as a prerequisite to allowing access to resources in a system.

availability   Assuring information and communications services is ready for use when expected.

back door   A hole in the security of a computer system deliberately left in place by designers or maintainers. Synonymous with *trap door*; a hidden software or hardware mechanism used to circumvent security.

biometrics   The biological identification of a person, which includes eyes, voice, handprints, fingerprints, retina patterns, and hand-written signatures. Biometrics is a more foolproof form of authentication than passwords or even using smart cards, which can be stolen.

black hat   Term generally used to refer to a hacker with nefarious intent.

bomb   A general synonym for crash, normally of software or operating system failures.

breach   The successful defeat of security controls that could result in a penetration of the system. A violation of controls of a particular information system such that information assets or system components are unduly exposed.

bridge   A device that connects two network segments together, which may be of similar or dissimilar types.

buffer overflow   This happens when more data is put into a buffer or holding area than the buffer can handle. This is due to a mismatch in processing rates between the producing and consuming processes. This can result in system crashes or the creation of a back door leading to system access.

bug   An unwanted and unintended property of a program or piece of hardware, especially one that causes it to malfunction.

C2   Command and control. C2 functions are performed through an arrangement of personnel, equipment, communications, facilities, and procedures employed by a commander in planning, directing, and controlling forces and operations in the accomplishment of a mission.

C2W   Command and control warfare. A U.S. military term to denote warfare related to command and control.

C4   Command, control, communications, and computers. A U.S. military term to denote relevant organizations and activities.

C4I   Command, control, communication, computers, and intelligence. A U.S. military term to denote relevant organizations and activities.

Certified Information Systems Security Professional (CISSP) The professional accreditation designation of the information security industry.

CGI scripts Allow for the creation of dynamic and interactive Web pages. They also tend to be the most vulnerable part of a Web server (besides the underlying host security).

Check Password A hacking program used for cracking VMS operating system passwords.

computer abuse The willful or negligent unauthorized activity that affects the availability, confidentiality, or integrity of computer resources. Computer abuse includes fraud, embezzlement, theft, malicious damage, unauthorized use, denial of service, and misappropriation.

computer fraud Computer-related crimes involving deliberate misrepresentation or alteration of data in order to obtain something of value.

confidentiality Assuring information will be kept secret, with access limited to appropriate persons.

countermeasure Any action, device, procedure, technique, or other measure that reduces the vulnerability of or threat to a system.

Crack A popular hacking tool used to decode encrypted passwords. System administrators also use Crack to assess weak passwords by users in order to enhance the security of the system.

cracker Some call a hacker who breaks into systems to steal or destroy data rather than simply for the adventure and the knowledge gained a *cracker* instead of a *hacker*.

crypto Cryptography. The conversion of data into a secret code for transmission over a public network. The original text is converted into a coded equivalent called *ciphertext* via an encryption algorithm.

crypto keys Algorithms used to encrypt and decrypt text.

daemon Pronounced "demon." A computer (Unix) program that executes in the background ready to perform an operation when required.

DARPA Defense Advanced Research Projects Agency.

data-driven attack A form of attack encoded in innocuous-seeming data that is executed by a user or a process to implement an attack. A data-driven attack is a concern for firewalls, since it may get through the firewall in data form and launch an attack against a system behind the firewall.

DEC   Digital Equipment Corporation.

Demon Dialer   A program that repeatedly calls the same telephone number. This is benign and legitimate for access to a BBS or malicious when used as a denial of service attack.

denial of service (DoS)   Actions that prevent any part of a system from functioning in accordance with its intended purpose. In distributed denial of service (DDoS), the impact of the attack is magnified by hitting the target from multiple directions.

digital certificate   The digital equivalent of an ID card used in conjunction with a public key encryption system. Also called *digital IDs*, digital certificates are issued by trusted third parties known as certification authorities (CAs). Driver's licenses, notarization, and fingerprints are examples of documentation required.

digital signature   An electronic signature that cannot be forged. A digital signature is unique for every transaction.

DNS   Domain Name System. Software that lets users locate computers on the Internet by domain name. The DNS server maintains a database of host names and their corresponding IP addresses.

DOR   Department of revenues.

dumpster diving   Searching for access codes or other sensitive information in the trash.

electronic warfare (EW)   Any military action involving the use of electromagnetic and directed energy to control the electromagnetic spectrum or to attack the enemy. The three major subdivisions within electronic warfare are electronic attack, electronic protection, and electronic warfare support.

EMP   Electromagnetic pulse capable of disrupting computers.

EMP/T Bomb   A device similar to a HERF gun but many times more powerful.

fault tolerance   The capability of a system or component to continue normal operation despite the presence of hardware or software faults.

file transfer protocol (ftp)   A popular way to transfer files over a network (Internet, Unix, etc.). It includes functions to log on to the network, list directories, and copy files.

finger   A computer command widely used on the Internet to find out information about a particular user.

firewall A system or combination of systems that enforces a boundary between two or more networks. A gateway that limits access between networks in accordance with local security policy. The typical firewall is an inexpensive micro-based Unix box kept clean of critical data, with many modems and public network ports on it, but just one carefully watched connection back to the rest of the cluster.

hacker Originally described a person who pursued knowledge of computer systems for its own sake—for example, someone willing to "hack through" the steps of putting together a working software program. However, it has come to mean a person who breaks into other people's computers with malicious intent.

hacking Unauthorized use, or attempts to circumvent or bypass the security mechanisms of an information system or network.

HERF High Energy Radio Frequency.

HERF gun A device that can disrupt the normal operation of digital equipment such as computers by directing HERF emissions at them.

hijacking An action whereby an active, established, session is intercepted and co-opted by the unauthorized user. Hijacking, or IP splicing, attacks may occur after an authentication has been made, permitting the attacker to assume the role of an already authorized user. Primary protections against this type of attack rely on encryption at the session or network layer.

information operations (IO) Actions taken to affect adversary information and information systems while defending one's own information and information systems. Another term for *information warfare.*

information security The result of any system of policies or procedures for identifying, controlling, and protecting from unauthorized disclosure, information whose protection is authorized by executive order or statute.

information warfare Actions an organization takes to achieve information superiority by affecting adversary information, information-based processes, and information systems, while defending its own information, information-based processes, and information systems. Any action an organization takes to deny, exploit, corrupt, or destroy the enemy's information and its functions; protect itself against those actions; and exploit its own information functions.

Internet Relay Chat (IRC) A very large multiple-user live chat facility. A number of major IRC servers around the world are linked to each other. Anyone can create a "channel." Private channels can (and are) created for multiperson "conference calls."

Internet service provider (ISP)   A company that provides access to the Internet for a fee.

Internet worm   A worm program (see *worm*) that was unleashed on the Internet in 1988. It was written by Robert T. Morris as an experiment that got out of hand.

intrusion   Any set of actions that attempt to compromise the integrity, confidentiality, or availability of a resource.

intrusion detection   Pertaining to techniques that attempt to detect intrusion into a computer or network by observation of actions, security logs, or audit data. Detection of break-ins or attempts either manually or via software expert systems that operate on logs or other information available on the network.

intrusion detection systems (IDS)   Tools that monitor and analyze network traffic to let network operators and security specialists protect their networks against unauthorized use and/or abuse and determine how their networks are being utilized.

IP spoofing   An attack whereby a system attempts to illicitly impersonate another system by using an IP network address.

keystroke monitoring   A specialized form of audit trail software, or a specially designed device, that records every key struck by a user and every character of the response that the system returns to the user.

leapfrog attack   Use of user ID and password information obtained illicitly from one host to compromise another host. The act of Telneting through one or more hosts to preclude a trace (a standard cracker procedure).

letterbomb   A piece of e-mail containing live data intended to do malicious things to the recipient's machine or terminal.

local area network (LAN)   A computer communications system limited to no more than a few miles and using high-speed connections (2–100 megabits per second).

logic bomb   A resident computer program that, when executed, checks for a particular condition or particular state of the system that, when satisfied, triggers the perpetration of an unauthorized act.

mailbomb   The mail sent to urge others to send massive amounts of e-mail to a single system or person, with the intent to crash the recipient's system. Mailbombing is widely regarded as a serious offense.

malicious code   Hardware, software, or firmware that is intentionally included in a system for an unauthorized purpose—e.g., a Trojan horse.

National Information Infrastructure (NII) The nationwide interconnection of communications networks, computers, databases, and consumer electronics that make vast amounts of information available to users. The NII encompasses a wide range of equipment, including cameras, scanners, keyboards, facsimile machines, computers, switches, compact discs, video and audio tape, cable, wire, satellites, fiber-optic transmission lines, networks of all types, monitors, printers, and much more. The friendly and adversarial personnel who make decisions and handle the transmitted information constitute a critical component of the NII.

non-repudiation Method by which the sender of data is provided with proof of delivery and the recipient is assured of the sender's identity, so that neither can later deny having processed the data.

Operations Security (OPSEC) A process of identifying critical information and subsequently analyzing friendly actions attendant to military operations and other activities to achieve several purposes:

- Identify those actions that can be observed by adversary intelligence systems.
- Determine indicators that hostile intelligence systems might obtain that could be interpreted or pieced together to derive critical information in time to be useful to adversaries.
- Select and execute measures that eliminate or reduce to an acceptable level the vulnerabilities of friendly actions to adversary exploitation.

packet A block of data sent over the network transmitting the identities of the sending and receiving stations, error-control information, and message.

packet filter Inspects each packet for user-defined content, such as an IP address but does not track the state of sessions. This is one of the least secure types of firewall.

packet sniffer A device or program that monitors the data traveling between computers on a network.

passive attack Attack that does not result in an unauthorized state change, such as an attack that only monitors and/or records data.

password cracker A software program that hackers use to gain unauthorized access to an organization's computer network. Such programs contain whole dictionaries of words that are used in automated logon attempts. They are remarkably proficient at discovering matches for weak passwords.

password grabber   A software program that captures and stores ID and password combinations. Hackers surreptitiously plant password grabbers in an organization's computer network. Later, the collected ID/password combinations are retrieved and used to attack the network.

pen register   A device that records the telephone number of calls received by a particular telephone.

penetration   The successful unauthorized access to an automated system.

penetration testing   The portion of security testing in which the evaluators attempt to circumvent the security features of a system. The evaluators may be assumed to use all system-design and implementation documentation, which may include listings of system source code, manuals, and circuit diagrams. The evaluators work under the same constraints applied to ordinary users.

perpetrator   The entity from the external environment that is taken to be the cause of a risk. An entity in the external environment that performs an attack: e.g., hacker.

phracker   An individual who combines phone phreaking with computer hacking.

phreak(er)   An individual fascinated by the telephone system. Commonly, an individual who uses his knowledge of the telephone system to make calls at the expense of another.

phreaking   The art and science of cracking the phone network.

physical security   The measures used to provide physical protection of resources against deliberate and accidental threats.

piggyback   The gaining of unauthorized access to a system via another user's legitimate connection.

Pretty Good Privacy (PGP)   A freeware program primarily for secure electronic mail.

privacy enhanced mail (PEM)   A standard for secure e-mail on the Internet.

private branch exchange (PBX)   An in-house telephone switching system used in many organizations to connect telephone extensions to each other, as well as to the outside telephone network.

probe   Any effort to gather information about a machine or its users for the apparent purpose of gaining unauthorized access to the system at a later date.

Psychological Operations (PsyOp)   Planned operations to convey selected information and indicators to foreign audiences to influence their emotions, motives, objective reasoning, and ultimately the behavior of foreign governments, organizations, groups, and individuals. Psychological operations induce or reinforce foreign attitudes and behavior favorable to the originator's objectives.

public key infrastructure (PKI)   The policies and procedures for establishing a secure method for exchanging information within an organization, an industry, a nation, or worldwide. It includes the use of certification authorities (CAs) and digital signatures as well as all the hardware and software to manage the process.

replicator   Any program that acts to produce copies of itself. Examples include programs, worms, and viruses. Some even claim that Unix and C are the symbiotic halves of an extremely successful replicator.

risk assessment   A study of vulnerabilities, threats, likelihood, loss, or impact, and theoretical effectiveness of security measures. The process of evaluating threats and vulnerabilities, known and postulated, to determine expected loss and establish the degree of acceptability to system operations.

Rootkit   A hacker security tool that captures passwords and message traffic to and from a computer. A collection of tools that allows a hacker to provide a back door into a system, collect information on other systems on the network, mask the fact that the system is compromised, and much more. Rootkit is a classic example of Trojan horse software and is available for a wide range of operating systems.

router   An interconnection device that is similar to a bridge but serves packets or frames containing certain protocols. Routers link LANs at the network layer.

rules-based detection   The intrusion detection system detects intrusions by looking for activity that corresponds to known intrusion techniques (signatures) or system vulnerabilities. Also known as *misuse detection*.

Security Administrator Tool for Analyzing Networks (SATAN)   A tool for remotely probing and identifying the vulnerabilities of systems on IP networks. A powerful freeware program that helps to identify system security weaknesses.

security audit   A search through a computer system for security problems and vulnerabilities.

security perimeter   The boundary where security controls are in effect to protect assets.

security policies   The set of laws, rules, and practices that regulate how an organization manages, protects, and distributes sensitive information.

smart card   An access card containing encoded information and sometimes a built-in microprocessor. The information on the card, or the information generated by the processor, is used to gain access to a facility or a computer system. It is more secure than a magnetic stripe.

smurfing   A denial of service attack in which an attacker spoofs the source address of an echo-request ICMP (ping) packet to the broadcast address for a network, causing the machines in the network to respond en masse to the victim thereby clogging its network.

sniffer   A program to capture data across a computer network. Used by hackers to capture user ID names and passwords. Software tool that audits and identifies network traffic packets. Also used legitimately by network operations and maintenance personnel to troubleshoot network problems.

social engineering   A term used to denote various hacker scams to elicit information from naive or gullible employees through deception, disguise, and coercion.

spam   To crash a program by overrunning a fixed-site buffer with excessively large input data. Also, to cause a person or newsgroup to be flooded with irrelevant or inappropriate messages.

spoofing   Pretending to be someone else. The deliberate inducement of a user or a resource to take an incorrect action. Attempt to gain access to a system by pretending to be an authorized user. Impersonating, masquerading, and mimicking are forms of spoofing.

STU-III   Secure telephone unit, third generation. A terminal used for the protection of national security classified or sensitive but unclassified telephone communications.

subject matter expert (SME)   A person with extensive knowledge on a specific topic.

subversion   Occurs when an intruder modifies the operation of the intrusion detector to force false negatives to occur.

superuser   A person with unlimited access privileges who can perform any and all operations on the computer.

SYN flood   When the SYN queue is flooded, no new connection can be opened.

sysadmin   Systems administrator. Generally, the person who manages a multiuser computer system.

telnet   (noun and verb) A process commonly used on the Internet that allows a computer user to log onto a remote device and run a program.

TEMPEST   The study and control of spurious electronic signals emitted by electrical equipment. (TEMPEST is not an acronym but a military code name.)

threat agent   Methods, materials, tools, weapons, forces of nature, etc. used to exploit a vulnerability in an information system, operation, or facility: fire, natural disaster, and so forth.

Tiger Team   Government and industry-sponsored teams of computer experts who attempt to break down the defenses of computer systems in an effort to uncover, and eventually patch, security holes.

trace packet   In a packet-switching network, a unique packet that causes a report of each stage of its progress to be sent to the network control center from each visited system element.

tradecraft   The techniques and procedures of espionage.

Transmission Control Protocol/Internet Protocol (TCP/IP)   The suite of protocols the Internet is based on.

trap and trace device   A generic term that may encompass pen registers and dialed-number recorders. Technically a trap is placed on a telephone number in advance, while a trace is conducted while the call is in progress.

trap door   A hidden software or hardware mechanism that can be triggered to allow system protection mechanisms to be circumvented.

tripwire   A software tool for security. Basically, it works with a database that maintains information about the byte count of files. If the byte count has changed, the tripwire will identify it to the system security manager.

Trojan horse   An apparently useful and innocent program containing additional hidden code that allows the unauthorized collection, exploitation, falsification, or destruction of data.

user ID   User identification. The name a person uses to identify himself or herself when logging onto a computer system.

van Eck monitoring   Monitoring the activity of a computer or other electronic equipment by detecting low levels of electromagnetic emissions from the device. Named after Dr. Wim van Eck.

virtual private network (VPN)   A private network that is configured within a public network. VPNs enjoy the security of a private network via access control and encryption, while taking advantage of the economies of scale and built-in management facilities of large public networks.

virus   A program that can "infect" other programs by modifying them to include a possibly evolved copy of itself.

war dialer   Hacking software to detect dial-in access to computer systems. War dialers are usually run from outside an organization's environment and control. From a modem-equipped computer, the hacker enters starting and ending phone numbers and the program sequentially dials each number in the range, seeking a computer and modem with an active phone line.

warez   Pronounced *wares*. Slang for pirated software traded in violation of copyright and license.

white hat   Term used to refer to a hacker whose goals are not criminal in intent.

wiretapping   Interception of communication signals with the intent to gain access to information transmitted over communications circuits.

worm   Independent program that replicates from machine to machine across network connections often clogging networks and information systems as it spreads.

APPENDIX A

U.S. Laws and International Treaties

Computer Fraud and Misuse Act

US Code as of: 01/05/99

Sec. 1030. Fraud and related activity in connection with computers

(a) Whoever -

(1) having knowingly accessed a computer without authorization or exceeding authorized access, and by means of such conduct having obtained information that has been determined by the United States Government pursuant to an Executive order or statute to require protection against unauthorized disclosure for reasons of national defense or foreign relations, or any restricted data, as defined in paragraph y. of section 11 of the Atomic Energy Act of 1954, with reason to believe that such information so obtained could be used to the injury of the United States, or to the advantage of any foreign nation willfully communicates, delivers, transmits, or causes to be communicated, delivered, or transmitted, or attempts to communicate, deliver, transmit or cause to be communicated, delivered, or transmitted the same to any person not entitled to receive it, or willfully retains the same and fails to deliver it to the officer or employee of the United States entitled to receive it;

(2) intentionally accesses a computer without authorization or exceeds authorized access, and thereby obtains -

(A) information contained in a financial record of a financial institution, or of a card issuer as defined in section 1602(n) of title 15, or contained in a file of a consumer reporting agency on a consumer, as such terms are defined in the Fair Credit Reporting Act (15 U.S.C. 1681 et seq.);

(B) information from any department or agency of the United States; or

(C) information from any protected computer if the conduct involved an interstate or foreign communication;

(3) intentionally, without authorization to access any nonpublic computer of a department or agency of the United States, accesses such a computer of that department or agency that is exclusively for the use of the Government of the United States or, in the case of a computer not exclusively for such use, is used by or for the Government of the United States and such conduct affects that use by or for the Government of the United States;

(4) knowingly and with intent to defraud, accesses a protected computer without authorization, or exceeds authorized access, and by means of such conduct furthers the intended fraud and obtains anything of value, unless the object of the fraud and the thing obtained consists only of the use of the computer and the value of such use is not more than $5,000 in any 1-year period;

(5)

(A) knowingly causes the transmission of a program, information, code, or command, and as a result of such conduct, intentionally causes damage without authorization, to a protected computer;

(B) intentionally accesses a protected computer without authorization, and as a result of such conduct, recklessly causes damage; or

(C) intentionally accesses a protected computer without authorization, and as a result of such conduct, causes damage;

(6) knowingly and with intent to defraud traffics (as defined in section 1029) in any password or similar information through which a computer may be accessed without authorization, if -

(A) such trafficking affects interstate or foreign commerce; or

(B) such computer is used by or for the Government of the United States; [1]

(7) with intent to extort from any person, firm, association, educational institution, financial institution, government entity, or other legal entity, any money or other thing of value, transmits in interstate or foreign commerce any communication containing any threat to cause damage to a protected computer; shall be punished as provided in subsection (c) of this section.

(b) Whoever attempts to commit an offense under subsection (a) of this section shall be punished as provided in subsection (c) of this section.

(c) The punishment for an offense under subsection (a) or (b) of this section is -

(1)

(A) a fine under this title or imprisonment for not more than ten years, or both, in the case of an offense under subsection (a)(1) of this section which does not occur after a conviction for another offense under this section, or an attempt to commit an offense punishable under this subparagraph; and

(B) a fine under this title or imprisonment for not more than twenty years, or both, in the case of an offense under subsection (a)(1) of this section which occurs after a conviction for another offense under this section, or an attempt to commit an offense punishable under this subparagraph;

(2)

(A) a fine under this title or imprisonment for not more than one year, or both, in the case of an offense under subsection (a)(2), (a)(3), (a)(5)(C), or (a)(6) of this section which does not occur after a conviction for another offense under this section, or an attempt to commit an offense punishable under this subparagraph; and [2]

(B) a fine under this title or imprisonment for not more than 5 years, or both, in the case of an offense under subsection (a)(2), if -

(i) the offense was committed for purposes of commercial advantage or private financial gain;

(ii) the offense was committed in furtherance of any criminal or tortious act in violation of the Constitution or laws of the United States or of any State; or

(iii) the value of the information obtained exceeds $5,000;

[3]

(C) a fine under this title or imprisonment for not more than ten years, or both, in the case of an offense under subsection (a)(2), (a)(3) or (a)(6) of this section which occurs after a conviction for another offense under this section, or an

attempt to commit an offense punishable under this subparagraph; and
(3)(A) a fine under this title or imprisonment for not more than five years, or
both, in the case of an offense under subsection (a)(4), (a)(5)(A), (a)(5)(B),
or (a)(7) of this section which does not occur after a conviction for another
offense under this section, or an attempt to commit an offense punishable
under this subparagraph; and (B) a fine under this title or imprisonment for
not more than ten years, or both, in the case of an offense under subsection
(a)(4), (a)(5)(A), (a)(5)(B), (a)(5)(C), or (a)(7) of this section which occurs
after a conviction for another offense under this section, or an attempt to
commit an offense punishable under this subparagraph; and [4]

(d) The United States Secret Service shall, in addition to any other agency having
such authority, have the authority to investigate offenses under subsections
(a)(2)(A), (a)(2)(B),

() The United States Secret Service shall, in addition to any of the United States
Secret Service shall be exercised in accordance with an agreement which shall
be entered into by the Secretary of the Treasury and the Attorney General.

(e) As used in this section -

(1) the term "computer" means an electronic, magnetic, optical, electrochemical,
or other high speed data processing device performing logical, arithmetic, or storage functions, and includes any data storage facility or communications facility
directly related to or operating in conjunction with such device, but such term does
not include an automated typewriter or typesetter, a portable hand held calculator,
or other similar device;

(2) the term "protected computer" means a computer -

(A) exclusively for the use of a financial institution or the United States
Government, or, in the case of a computer not exclusively for such use, used
by or for a financial institution or the United States Government and the conduct constituting the offense affects that use by or for the financial institution
or the Government; or

(B) which is used in interstate or foreign commerce or communication;

(3) the term "State" includes the District of Columbia, the Commonwealth of
Puerto Rico, and any other commonwealth, possession or territory of the United
States;

(4) the term "financial institution" means -

(A) an institution, with deposits insured by the Federal Deposit Insurance
Corporation;

(B) the Federal Reserve or a member of the Federal Reserve including any Federal Reserve Bank;

(C) a credit union with accounts insured by the National Credit Union Administration;

(D) a member of the Federal home loan bank system and any home loan bank;

(E) any institution of the Farm Credit System under the Farm Credit Act of 1971;

(F) a broker-dealer registered with the Securities and Exchange Commission pursuant to section 15 of the Securities Exchange Act of 1934;

(G) the Securities Investor Protection Corporation;

(H) a branch or agency of a foreign bank (as such terms are defined in paragraphs (1) and (3) of section 1(b) of the International Banking Act of 1978); and

(I) an organization operating under section 25 or section 25(a) [5] of the Federal Reserve Act. [6]

(5) the term "financial record" means information derived from any record held by a financial institution pertaining to a customer's relationship with the financial institution;

(6) the term "exceeds authorized access" means to access a computer with authorization and to use such access to obtain or alter information in the computer that the accesser is not entitled so to obtain or alter;

(7) the term "department of the United States" means the legislative or judicial branch of the Government or one of the executive departments enumerated in section 101 of title 5; and

[7]

(8) the term "damage" means any impairment to the integrity or availability of data, a program, a system, or information, that -

(A) causes loss aggregating at least $5,000 in value during any 1-year period to one or more individuals;

(B) modifies or impairs, or potentially modifies or impairs, the medical examination, diagnosis, treatment, or care of one or more individuals;

(C) causes physical injury to any person; or

(D) threatens public health or safety; and

(9) the term "government entity" includes the Government of the United States, any State or political subdivision of the United States, any foreign country, and any state, province, municipality, or other political subdivision of a foreign country.

(f) This section does not prohibit any lawfully authorized investigative, protective, or intelligence activity of a law enforcement agency of the United States, a State, or a political subdivision of a State, or of an intelligence agency of the United States.

(g) Any person who suffers damage or loss by reason of a violation of this section may maintain a civil action against the violator to obtain compensatory damages and injunctive relief or other equitable relief. Damages for violations involving damage as defined in subsection (e)(8)(A) are limited to economic damages. No action may be brought under this subsection unless such action is begun within 2 years of the date of the act complained of or the date of the discovery of the damage.

(h) The Attorney General and the Secretary of the Treasury shall report to the Congress annually, during the first 3 years following the date of the enactment of this subsection, concerning investigations and prosecutions under subsection (a)(5).

Footnotes

[1] So in original. Probably should be followed by "or".

[2] So in original. The word "and" probably should not appear.

[3] So in original. Probably should be followed by "and".

[4] So in original. The "; and" probably should be a period.

[5] See References in Text note below.

[6] So in original. The period probably should be a semicolon.

[7] So in original. The word "and" probably should not appear.

Economic Espionage Act of 1996

[As published in the Congressional Record of October 2, 1996]

(Only relevant parts of the Act are included.)

SECTION 1. SHORT TITLE.

This Act may be cited as the "Economic Espionage Act of 1996".

TITLE I — PROTECTION OF TRADE SECRETS

SECTION 101. PROTECTION OF TRADE SECRETS

(a) IN GENERAL. — Title 18, United States Code, is amended by inserting after chapter 89 the following:

"CHAPTER 90 - PROTECTION OF TRADE SECRETS

"§1831. Economic espionage

"(a) IN GENERAL. — Whoever, intending or knowing that the offense will benefit any foreign government, foreign instrumentality, or foreign agent, knowingly -

"(1) steals, or without authorization appropriates, takes, carries away, or conceals, or by fraud, artifice, or deception obtains a trade secret;

"(2) without authorization copies, duplicates, sketches, draws, photographs, downloads, uploads, alters, destroys, photocopies, replicates, transmits, delivers, sends, mails, communicates, or conveys a trade secret;

"(3) receives, buys, or possesses a trade secret, knowing the same to have been stolen or appropriated, obtained, or converted without authorization;

"(4) attempts to commit any offense described in any of paragraphs (1) through (3); or

"(5) conspires with one or more other persons to commit any offense described in any of paragraphs (1) through (4), and one or more of such persons do any act to effect the object of the conspiracy, shall except as provided in subsection (b), be fined not more than $500,000 or imprisoned not more than 15 years, or both.

(b) ORGANIZATIONS. —Any organization that commits any offense described in subsection (a) shall be fined not more than $10,000,000.

§1832. Theft of trade secrets

"(a) Whoever, with intent to convert a trade secret, that is related to or included in a product that is produced for or placed in interstate or foreign commerce, to the economic benefit of anyone other than the owner thereof, and intending or knowing that the offense will, injure any owner of that trade secret, knowingly -

"(1) steals, or without authorization appropriates, takes, carries away, or conceals, or by fraud, artifice, or deception obtains such information;

"(2) without authorization copies, duplicates, sketches, draws, photographs, downloads, uploads, alters, destroys, photocopies, replicates, transmits, delivers, sends, mails, communicates, or conveys such information;

"(3) receives, buys, or possesses such information, knowing the same to have been stolen or appropriated, obtained, or converted without authorization;

"(4) attempts to commit any offense described in paragraphs (1) through (3); or

"(5) conspires with one or more other persons to commit any offense described in paragraphs (1) through (3), and one or more of such persons do any act to effect the object of the conspiracy, shall, except as provided in sub-section (b), be fined under this title or imprisoned not more than 10 years, or both.

"(b) Any organization that commits any offense described in subsection (a) shall be fined not more than $5,000,000.

§1833. Exceptions to prohibitions

"This chapter does not prohibit -

"(1) any otherwise lawful activity conducted by a governmental entity of the United States, a State, or a political subdivision of a State; or

"(2) the reporting of a suspected violation of law to any governmental entity of the United States, a State, or a political subdivision of a State, if such entity has lawful authority with respect to that violation.

§1834. Criminal forfeiture

"(a) The court, in imposing sentence on a person for a violation of this chapter, shall order, in addition to any other sentence imposed, that the person forfeit to the United States —

"(1) any property constituting, or derived from, any proceeds the person obtained, directly or indirectly, as the result of such violation; and

"(2) any of the person's property used, or intended to be used, in any man-ner or part, to commit or facilitate the commission of such violation, if the court in its discretion so determines, taking into consideration the nature. scope, and proportionality of the use of the property in the offense.

"(b) Property subject to forfeiture under this section, any seizure and disposition thereof, and any administrative or judicial proceeding in relation thereto, shall be governed by section 413 of the Comprehensive Drug Abuse Prevention and Control Act of 1970 (21 U.S.C. 853), except for subsections (d) and (j) of such section, which shall not apply to forfeitures under this section.

§1835. Orders to preserve confidentiality

"In any prosecution or other proceeding under this chapter, the court shall enter such orders and take such other action as may be necessary and appropriate to pre-serve the confidentiality of trade secrets, consistent with the requirements of the Federal Rules of Criminal and Civil Procedures, the Federal Rules of Evidence, and all other applicable laws. An interlocutory appeal by the United States shall lie from a decision or order of a district court authorizing or directing the disclosure of any trade secret.

§1836. Civil proceedings to enjoin violations

"(a) The Attorney General may, in a civil action, obtain appropriate injunctive relief against any violation of this section.

"(b) The district courts of the United States- shall have exclusive original jurisdiction of civil actions under this subsection.

§1837. Applicability to conduct outside the United States

"This chapter also applies to conduct occurring outside the United States if -

"(1) the offender is a natural person who is a citizen or permanent resident alien of the United States, or an organization organized under the laws of the United States or a State or political subdivision thereof; or

"(2) an act in furtherance of the offense was committed in the United States.

§1838. Construction with other laws

"This chapter shall not be construed to preempt or displace any other remedies, whether civil or criminal, provided by United States Federal, State, commonwealth, possession, or territory law for the misappropriation of a trade secret, or to affect the otherwise lawful disclosure of information by any Government employee under section 552 of title 5 (commonly known as the Freedom of Information Act).

§1839. Definitions

[(a)] "As used in this chapter -

"(1) the term 'foreign instrumentality' means any agency, bureau, ministry, component, institution, association, or any legal, commercial, or business organization, corporation, firm, or entity that is substantially owned, controlled, sponsored, commanded, managed, or dominated by a foreign government;

"(2) the term 'foreign agent' means any officer, employee, proxy, servant, delegate, or representative of a foreign government;

"(3) the term 'trade secret' means all forms and types of financial, business, scientific, technical, economic, or engineering information, including patterns, plans, compilations, program devices, formulas, designs, prototypes, methods, techniques, processes, procedures, programs, or codes, whether tangible or intangible, and whether or how stored, compiled, or memorialized physically, electronically, graphically, photographically, or in writing if -

"(A) the owner thereof has taken reasonable measures to keep such information secret; and

"(B) the information derives independent economic value, actual or potential, from not being generally known to, and not being readily ascertainable through proper means by, the public; and

"(4) the term 'owner', with respect to a trade secret, means the person or entity in whom or in which rightful legal or equitable title to, or license in, the trade secret is reposed

(b) CLERICAL AMENDMENT. — The table of chapters at the beginning part I of title 18, United States Code, is amended by inserting after the item relating to chapter 89 the following:

(c) REPORTS. — Not later than 2 years and 4 years after the date of the enactment of this Act, the Attorney General shall report to Congress on the amounts received and distributed from fines for offenses under this chapter deposited in the Crime Victims Fund established by section 1402 of the Victims of Crime Act of 1984 (42 U.S.C. 10601).

SECTION. 103 WIRE AND ELECTRONIC COMMUNICATIONS INTERCEPTION AND INTERCEPTION OF ORAL COMMUNICATIONS.

Section 2516(l)(c) of title 18, United States Code, is amended by inserting "chapter 90 (relating to protection of trade secrets)," after "chapter 37 (relating to espionage),".

Council of Europe - Draft Convention on Cybercrime

PC-CY (2000) Draft N° 19

EUROPEAN COMMITTEE ON CRIME PROBLEMS (CDPC)

COMMITTEE OF EXPERTS ON CRIME IN CYBER-SPACE (PC-CY)

Draft Convention on Cyber-crime (Draft N° 19)

Prepared by the Secretariat Directorate General I (Legal Affairs)

DRAFT CONVENTION ON CYBER-CRIME (Draft N° 19)[1]
Preamble

The member States of the Council of Europe and the other States signatory hereto,

---

1. For more information, go to http://conventions.coe.int/treaty/en/projets/cybercrime.htm

Considering that the aim of the Council of Europe is to achieve a greater unity between its members;

Recognising the value of fostering co-operation with the other States signatories to this Convention;

Convinced of the need to pursue, as a matter of priority, a common criminal policy aimed at the protection of society against cyber-crime, inter alia by adopting appropriate legislation and fostering international co-operation;

Conscious of the profound changes brought about by the digitalisation, convergence and continuing globalisation of computer networks;

Concerned at the risk that computer networks and electronic information may also be used for committing criminal offences and that evidence relating to such offences may be stored and transferred by these networks;

Believing that an effective fight against cyber-crime requires increased, rapid and well-functioning international co-operation in criminal matters;

Convinced that the present Convention is necessary to deter actions directed against the confidentiality, integrity and availability of computer systems, networks and computer data, as well as the misuse of such systems, networks and data, by providing for the criminalisation of such conduct, as described in this Convention, and the adoption of powers sufficient for effectively combating such criminal offences, by facilitating the detection, investigation and prosecution of such criminal offences at both the domestic and international level, and by providing arrangements for fast and reliable international co-operation, while ensuring a proper balance between the interests of law enforcement and respect for fundamental human rights.

Welcoming recent developments which further advance international understanding and co-operation in combating cyber-crimes, including actions of the United Nations, the OECD, the European Union and the G8;

Recalling Recommendation N° R (89) 9 on computer-related crime providing guidelines for national legislatures concerning the definition of certain computer crimes and Recommendation N° R (95) 13 concerning problems of criminal procedural law connected with Information Technology, calling for, inter alia, the negotiation of an international agreement to regulate trans-border search and seizure;

Having regard to Resolution No. 1 adopted by the European Ministers of Justice at their 21st Conference (Prague, June 1997), which recommended the Committee of Ministers to support the work carried out by the European Committee on Crime Problems (CDPC) on cyber-crime in order to bring domestic criminal law provisions closer to each other and enable the use of effective means of investigation concerning such offences;

Having also regard to the Action Plan adopted by the Heads of State and Government of the Council of Europe, on the occasion of their Second Summit (Strasbourg, 10 - 11 October 1997), to seek common responses to the development of the new information technologies, based on the standards and values of the Council of Europe;

Have agreed as follows:

Chapter I - Use of terms

Article 1 - Definitions (1)

For the purposes of this Convention:

a. "computer system" means any device or a group of inter-connected devices, which pursuant to a program performs automatic processing of data [or any other function] (2);

b. "computer data" means:

- any representation of facts, information or concepts in a form suitable for processing in a computer system, or

- set of instructions suitable to cause a computer system to perform a function (3);

c. "service provider" means any public or private entity that provides to users of its services the ability to send or receive electronic communications;

d. "traffic data" means:

1. a code indicating a network, equipment or individual number or account, or similar identifying designator, transmitted to or from any designated point in the chain of communication;

2. the time, date, size, and duration of a communication;

3. as to any mode of transmission (including but not limited to mobile transmissions), any information indicating the physical location to or from which a communication is transmitted;

a. "subscriber data"(4) means:

- any information possessed by the service provider necessary to identify and determine the physical address of a subscriber, user, or account-payer of a service provider's communications services, and

- any information associated with such subscriber, user, or account-payer possessed by the service provider relating to a network, equipment or individual number or account or similar identifying designators, services, fees;

the physical location of equipment, (5) if known and if different from the location information provided under the definition of traffic data;

Chapter II - Measures to be taken at the national level

Section 1 - Substantive criminal law

Title 1 - Offences against the confidentiality, integrity and availability of computer data and systems

Article 2 - Illegal Access

Each Party shall adopt such legislative and other measures as may be necessary to establish as criminal offences under its domestic law when committed intentionally (6) the access to the whole or any part of a computer system without right. A Party may require that the offence be committed either by infringing security measures or with the intent of obtaining computer data or other dishonest intent.

Article 3 - Illegal Interception

Each Party shall adopt such legislative and other measures as may be necessary to establish as criminal offences under its domestic law when committed intentionally the interception without right, made by technical means, of non-public (7) transmissions of computer data to, from or within a computer system, as well as electromagnetic emissions from a computer system carrying such computer data.

Article 4 - Data Interference

Each Party shall adopt such legislative and other measures as may be necessary to establish as criminal offences under its domestic law when committed intentionally the damaging, deletion, deterioration, alteration (8)or suppression (9) of computer data without right (10).

Article 5 - System Interference

Each Party shall adopt such legislative and other measures as may be necessary to establish as criminal offences under its domestic law when committed intentionally the serious hindering without right of the functioning of a computer system by inputting, [transmitting,] damaging, deleting, deteriorating, altering or suppressing computer data.

Article 6 - Illegal Devices

Each Party shall adopt such legislative and other measures as may be necessary to establish as criminal offences under its domestic law when committed intentionally and without right:

    a. the production, sale, procurement for use, import, distribution or otherwise making available of:

        1. a device, including a computer program, designed or adapted [specifically] [primarily] [particularly] for the purpose of committing any of the offences established in accordance with Article 2 - 5;

        2. a computer password, access code, or similar data by which the whole or any part of a computer system is capable of being accessed with intent that it be used for the purpose of committing the offences established in Articles 2 - 5;

    a. the possession of an item referred to in paragraphs (a)(1) and (2) above, with intent that it be used for the purpose of committing the offenses established in Articles 2 - 5. A party may require by law that a number of such items be possessed before criminal liability attaches.

Title 2 - Computer-related offences

Article 7 - Computer-related Forgery

Each Party shall adopt such legislative and other measures as may be necessary to establish as criminal offences under its domestic law when committed intentionally and without right the input, alteration, deletion, or suppression of computer data, resulting in inauthentic data with the intent that it be considered or acted upon for legal purposes as if it were authentic (11), regardless whether or not the data is directly readable and intelligible. A Party may require by law an intent to defraud, or similar dishonest intent, before criminal liability attaches.

Article 8 - Computer-related Fraud

Each Party shall adopt such legislative and other measures as may be necessary to establish as criminal offences under its domestic law, when committed intentionally and without right, the causing, without right, of a loss of property to another by:

    a. any input, alteration, deletion or suppression of computer data,

    b. any interference with the functioning of a computer [program] or system, with the intent of procuring, without right, an economic benefit for himself or for another.

Title 3 - Content-related offences
Article 9 - Offences related to child pornography

1. Each Party shall adopt such legislative and other measures as may be necessary to establish as criminal offences under its domestic law when committed without right (12) and intentionally the following conduct:

    a. offering (13), distributing, transmitting or [otherwise] making available child pornography through a computer system;

    b. producing child pornography for the purpose of its distribution through a computer system (14);

    c. possessing child pornography in a computer system or on a data carrier (15);

2. For the purpose of paragraph 1 above "child pornography" shall include pornographic material (16) that visually depicts:

    a. a minor engaged in a sexually explicit conduct (17);

    b. a person appearing to be a minor engaged in a sexually explicit conduct;

    c. realistic images representing a minor engaged in a sexually explicit conduct.

3. For the purpose of paragraph 2 above, the term "minor" is to be defined by each Party, but shall include in any case all persons under [14] (18) years of age.

Title 4 - Copyright and related offences
Article 10 - Copyright and related offences

1. Each Party shall adopt such necessary legislative and other measures as may be necessary to establish as criminal offences under its domestic law the reproduction and distribution, by means of a computer system, of works protected by copyright, as defined under the law of that Party, [in conformity with the Bern Convention for the Protection of Literary and Artistic Works, the TRIPS Agreement and the WIPO Copyright Treaty], where such acts are committed intentionally on a commercial scale, without right.

2. Each Party shall adopt such legislative and other measures as may be necessary to establish as criminal offences under its domestic law the reproduction, distribution or similar acts, by means of a computer system, of works, items or equivalent creations protected by neighbouring rights, as defined under the law of that Party [in conformity with the WIPO Performances and Phonograms Treaty], where such acts are committed intentionally on a commercial scale, without right.

Title 5 - Ancillary liability and sanctions

Article 11 - Attempt and aiding and abetting

Each Party shall adopt such legislative and other measures as may be necessary to establish as criminal offences under its domestic law, when committed intentionally:

a. attempt to commit any of the offences established in accordance with Articles [..];(19)

b. aiding or abetting (20) the commission of any of the offences established in accordance with Articles 2 - 10 above.

Article 12 - Corporate liability

1. Each Party shall adopt such legislative and other measures as may be necessary to ensure that legal persons can be held liable for the criminal offences established in accordance with this Convention, committed for their benefit by any natural person, acting either individually or as part of an organ of the legal person, who has a leading position within the legal person, based on:

- a power of representation of the legal person; or
- an authority to take decisions on behalf of the legal person; or
- an authority to exercise control within the legal person;
- as well as for involvement of such a natural person as aidor or abettor, under Article 11, in the above-mentioned offences.

2. Apart from the cases already provided for in paragraph 1, each Party shall take the necessary measures to ensure that a legal person can be held liable where the lack of supervision or control by a natural person referred to in paragraph 1 has made possible the commission of the criminal offences mentioned in paragraph 1 for the benefit of that legal person by a natural person under its authority.

3. Liability of a legal person under paragraphs 1 and 2 shall not exclude criminal proceedings against natural persons who are perpetrators, aidors or abettors of the criminal offences mentioned in paragraph 1.

Article 13 - Sanctions and measures

1. Each Party shall take the necessary measures to ensure that the criminal offences established in accordance with Articles 2 - 11 are punishable by effective, proportionate and dissuasive sanctions and measures. In particular, each Party shall ensure that the offences established in accordance with Articles [..](21) and those referred to in Article 21, paragraph 1, when committed by natural persons, are punishable by penalties involving deprivation of liberty which can give rise to extradition.

2. Each Party shall ensure that legal persons held liable in accordance with Article 12 shall be subject to effective, proportionate and dissuasive criminal or non-criminal sanctions, including monetary sanctions.

Section 2 - Procedural law

Article 14 - Search and Seizure of Stored Computer Data

1. Each Party shall take such legislative and other measures as may be necessary to empower its competent authorities to search or similarly access:

a. a computer system or part of it and computer data stored therein; or

b. a medium in which computer data may be stored

[in its territory or other place over which it exercises its sovereign powers] (22) for the purposes of criminal investigations or proceedings.

2. Each Party shall take such legislative and other measures as may be necessary to ensure that where its authorities search or similarly access a specific computer system or part of it, using the measures referred to in paragraph 1 (a), and have grounds to believe that the data sought is stored in another computer system or part of it in its territory or other place over which it exercises its sovereign powers, and such data is lawfully accessible from or available to the initial system, such authorities shall be able to expeditiously extend the search or similar accessing to the other system.

3. [If the computer system or a part thereof or computer data accessed according to paragraphs 1 or 2 are found out to be inadvertently accessed in the jurisdiction of another Party, the competent authorities of the Party conducting the investigation shall act as provided for in article [..]] (23)

4. Each Party shall take such legislative and other measures as may be necessary to empower its competent authorities to seize or similarly secure computer data accessed according to paragraphs 1 or 2 in view of their possible use in criminal investigations and proceedings. These measures shall include the power to:

a. seize or similarly secure a computer system or part of it or a medium in which computer data may be stored;

b. make and retain a copy of those computer data;

c. maintain the integrity of the relevant stored computer data;

d. render inaccessible or remove those computer data in the accessed computer system.

5. Each Party shall take such legislative and other measures as may be necessary to empower its competent authorities to order for the purposes of criminal investigations and proceedings any person who has knowledge about the functioning of the computer system or measures applied to secure the computer data therein to provide all necessary information, as is reasonable, to enable the undertaking of the measures referred to in paragraphs 1 and 4.

6. Where measures referred to in paragraphs 1 and 2 have been taken in respect of a computer system or part of it, or computer data stored therein, the person in charge of (24) the computer system shall as soon as reasonably practicable be duly informed about the executed measures.

7. The powers and procedures referred to in the present Article shall be subject to conditions and safeguards as provided for under national law.

Article 15 - Production Order

1. Each Party shall take such legislative and other measures as may be necessary to empower its competent authorities to order a person in its territory or other place over which it exercises its sovereign powers to submit specified computer data under this person's control stored in a computer system or a medium (25) in which data may be stored in the form required by these authorities for the purposes of criminal investigations and proceedings.

2. The power referred to in paragraph 1 of the present Article shall be subject to conditions and safeguards as provided for under national law.

Article 16 - Expedited preservation of data stored in a computer system

1. Each Party shall adopt such legislative and other measures as may be necessary to enable its competent authorities to order or otherwise obtain, for the purpose of criminal investigations or proceedings, the expeditious preservation of data that is stored by means of a computer system, at least where there are grounds to believe that the data is subject to a short period of retention or is otherwise particularly vulnerable to loss or modification.

2. Where a Party gives effect to paragraph 1 above by means of an order to a person to preserve specified stored data in the person's possession or control, the Party shall adopt such legislative and other measures as may be necessary to oblige that person to preserve and maintain the integrity of that data for a period of time as may be ordered pursuant to national law.

3. Each Party shall adopt such legislative or other measures as may be necessary to oblige a person to whom the procedures of preservation referred to in this Article

are directed, to keep confidential the undertaking of such procedures for a period of time as permitted by national law.

4. The powers and procedures referred to in the present article shall be subject to conditions and safeguards as provided for under national law.

Article 17 - Expedited preservation and disclosure of traffic data

1. Each Party shall, with respect to undertaking the procedures referred to under article 16 in respect of the preservation of traffic data concerning a specific communication, adopt such legislative or other measures as may be necessary to:

   a. ensure the expeditious preservation of that traffic data, regardless whether one or more service providers were involved in the transmission of that communication; and

   b. ensure the expeditious disclosure to the Party's competent authority, or a person designated by that authority, of a sufficient amount of traffic data in order to identify the service providers and the path through which the communication was transmitted.

2. The powers and procedures referred to in the present article shall be subject to conditions and safeguards as provided for under national law.

Article 18 - Interception

(under discussion)

Section 3 - Jurisdiction

Article 19 - Jurisdiction

1. Each Party shall take such legislative and other measures as may be necessary to establish jurisdiction over any offence established in accordance with Articles 2 - 11 of this Convention, when the offence is committed

   a. [in whole or in part] in its territory or on a ship, an aircraft, or a satellite(26) flying its flag or registered in that Party;

   b. by one of its nationals, if the offence is punishable under criminal law where it was committed or if the offence is committed outside the territorial jurisdiction of any State.

2. Each State may, at the time of signature or when depositing its instrument of ratification, acceptance, approval or accession, by a declaration addressed to the Secretary General of the Council of Europe, declare that it reserves the right not to apply or to apply only in specific cases or conditions the jurisdiction rules laid down in paragraph 1 b of this article or any part thereof.

3. If a Party has made use of the reservation possibility provided for in paragraph 2 of this article, it shall adopt such measures as may be necessary to establish jurisdiction over a criminal offence referred to in Article 21, paragraph 1 of this Convention, in cases where an alleged offender is present in its territory and it does not extradite him to another Party, solely on the basis of his nationality, after a request for extradition.

4. This Convention does not exclude any criminal jurisdiction exercised in accordance with national law.

5. When more than one Party claims jurisdiction over an alleged offence established in accordance with this Convention, the Parties involved shall, where appropriate, consult with a view to determining the most appropriate jurisdiction for prosecution.

Chapter III - International Co-operation

Article 20 - General principles relating to international co-operation

The Parties shall co-operate with each other, in accordance with the provisions of this chapter, and through application of relevant international instruments on international co-operation in criminal matters, arrangements agreed on the basis of uniform or reciprocal legislation, and national laws, to the widest extent possible for the purposes of investigations and proceedings concerning criminal offences related to computer systems and data, or for the collection of electronic evidence of a criminal offence.

Article 21 - Extradition

1. The criminal offences established in accordance with Articles 3 - 5 and 7 - 11 of this Convention shall be deemed to be included as extraditable offences in any extradition treaty existing between or among the Parties. The Parties undertake to include such offences as extraditable offences in any extradition treaty to be concluded between or among them. With respect to the criminal offence established by Article 2, the following criteria may be required for qualifying that offence as extraditable:

- [the access without right must be made with the intent to breach the confidentiality of data or impair the integrity or availability of data or a computer system, or]

- [the access without right must impair the integrity or availability of data or a computer system.]

2. If a Party that makes extradition conditional on the existence of a treaty receives a request for extradition from another Party with which it does not have an extradition treaty, it may consider this Convention as the legal basis for extradition with respect to any criminal offence referred to in paragraph 1 of this Article.

3. Parties that do not make extradition conditional on the existence of a treaty shall recognise the criminal offences referred to in paragraph 1 of this Article as extraditable offences between themselves.

4. Extradition shall be subject to the conditions provided for by the law of the requested Party or by applicable extradition treaties, including the grounds on which the requested Party may refuse extradition.

5. If extradition for a criminal offence referred to in paragraph 1 of this Article is refused solely on the basis of the nationality of the person sought, or because the requested Party deems that it has jurisdiction over the offence, the requested Party shall submit the case to its competent authorities for the purpose of prosecution unless otherwise agreed with the requesting Party, and shall report the final outcome to the requesting Party in due course. Those authorities shall take their decision in the same manner as in the case of any other offence of a comparable nature under the law of that State.

6. (a) Each Party shall, at the time of signature or when depositing its instrument of ratification, acceptance, approval or accession, communicate to the Secretary General of the Council of Europe the name and addresses of each authority responsible for the making to or receipt of a request for extradition or provisional arrest in the absence of a treaty. [Designation of an authority shall not exclude the possibility of using the diplomatic channel.](27)

(b) The Secretary General of the Council of Europe shall set up and keep updated a register of authorities so designated by the Parties. Each Party shall ensure that the details held on the register are correct at all times.

Article 22 - Mutual Assistance

1. The Parties shall afford one another mutual assistance to the widest extent possible for the purpose of investigations and proceedings concerning criminal offences related to computer systems and data, or for the collection of electronic evidence of a criminal offence.

2. Each Party shall also adopt such legislative or other measures as may be necessary to carry out the obligations set forth in Articles 24 - 29.

3. For the purpose of providing cooperation under articles 24 - 29, each Party shall, in urgent circumstances, accept and respond to mutual assistance requests by expedited means of communications, including [voice], fax or e-mail, to the extent that such means provide appropriate levels of security and authentication, with formal confirmation to follow where required by the requested State.

4. Except as otherwise specifically provided in Articles 24 - 29, mutual assistance shall be subject to the conditions provided for by the law of the requested Party or by applicable mutual assistance treaties, including the grounds on which the requested Party may refuse cooperation.(28)

5. Where, in accordance with the provisions of this chapter, the requested Party is permitted to make mutual assistance conditional upon the existence of dual criminality, that condition shall be deemed fulfilled, irrespective of whether its laws place the offence within the same category of offence or denominates the offense by the same terminology as the requesting Party, if the conduct underlying the offense for which assistance is sought is a criminal offense under its laws.

Article 23 - Procedures pertaining to mutual assistance requests

1. Where there is no mutual assistance treaty or arrangement on the basis of uniform or reciprocal legislation in force between the requesting and requested Parties, or the Parties concerned do not have national laws under which to provide mutual assistance to one another, the provisions of paragraphs 2 through 10 of this article shall apply. The provisions of this article shall not apply where such agreement, arrangement or legislation is available, unless the Parties concerned agree to apply any or all of the remainder of this Article in lieu thereof.

2. (a) Each Party shall designate a central authority or authorities that shall be responsible for sending and answering requests for mutual assistance, the execution of such requests, or the transmission of them to the authorities competent for their execution.

(b) The central authorities shall communicate directly with each other.

(c) Each Party shall, at the time of signature or when depositing its instrument of ratification, acceptance, approval or accession, communicate to the Secretary General of the Council of Europe the names and addresses of the authorities designated in pursuance of this paragraph.

(d) The Secretary General of the Council of Europe shall set up and keep updated a register of central authorities so designated by the Parties. Each Party shall ensure that the details held on the register are correct at all times.

3. Mutual assistance requests under this Article shall be executed in accordance with the procedures specified by the requesting Party except where incompatible with the law of the requested Party.(29)

4. The requested Party may, in addition to conditions or grounds for refusal available under Article 22 (4), refuse assistance if it believes that compliance with the request would prejudice its sovereignty, security, ordre public or other essential interests.

5. The requested Party may postpone action on a request if such action would prejudice investigations, prosecutions or related proceedings by its authorities.

6. Before refusing or postponing assistance, the requested Party shall, where appropriate after having consulted with the requesting Party, consider whether the request may be granted partially or subject to such conditions as it deems necessary.

7. The requested Party shall promptly inform the requesting Party of the outcome of the execution of a request for assistance. If the request is refused or postponed, reasons shall be given for the refusal or postponement. The requested Party shall also inform the requesting Party of any reasons that render impossible the execution of the request or are likely to delay it significantly.

8. (a) Without prejudice to its own investigations or proceedings, a Party may, within the limits of its domestic law, without prior request, forward to another Party information obtained within the framework of its own investigations when it considers that the disclosure of such information might assist the receiving Party in initiating or carrying out investigations or proceedings concerning criminal offences established in accordance with this Convention or might lead to a request for cooperation by that Party under this chapter.

(b) Prior to providing such information, the providing Party may request that it be kept confidential or used subject to conditions. If the receiving Party cannot comply with such request, it shall notify the providing Party, which shall then determine whether the information should nevertheless be provided. If the receiving Party accepts the information subject to the conditions, it shall be bound by them.

9. (a) The requesting Party may request that the requested Party keep confidential the fact and substance of any request made under this Chapter except to the extent necessary to execute the request. If the requested Party cannot comply with the request for confidentiality, it shall promptly inform the requesting Party, which shall then determine whether the request should nevertheless be executed.

(b) The requesting Party may request that the requested Party not, without the prior consent of the requesting Party, make use of the substance of the request, nor of the information obtained pursuant to having executed the request, for purposes other than those for which it was obtained or for criminal investigations and related proceedings. If the requested Party cannot comply with the request, it shall promptly inform the requesting Party, which shall then determine whether the request should nevertheless be executed.

(c) The requested Party may request that the requesting Party not, without the prior consent of the requested Party, transmit or use the materials furnished for investigations or proceedings other than those stated in the request. If the requested Party accepts the materials subject to the conditions, it shall be bound by them. If the requesting Party cannot comply with the conditions, it shall promptly inform the requesting Party, which shall then determine whether the materials should nevertheless be provided.

10. (a) In the event of urgency, requests for mutual assistance or communications related thereto may be sent directly by judicial authorities, including public prosecutors, of the requesting Party to such authorities of the requested Party. In any such cases a copy shall be sent at the same time to the central authority of the requested Party through the central authority of the requesting Party.

(b) Any request or communication under this paragraph may be made through the International Criminal Police Organisation (Interpol).

(c) Where a request is made pursuant to subparagraph (a) and the authority is not competent to deal with the request, it shall refer the request to the competent national authority and inform directly the requesting Party that it has done so.

(d) Requests or communications made under this paragraph that do not involve coercive action may be directly transmitted by the competent authorities of the requesting Party to the competent authorities of the requested Party.

(e) Each Party may, at the time of signature or when depositing its instrument of ratification, acceptance, approval or accession inform the Secretary General of the Council of Europe that, for reasons of efficiency, requests made under this paragraph are to be addressed to its central authority.

Article 24 - Provisional measures: Expedited preservation of stored computer data

1. A Party may request another Party to order or otherwise obtain the expeditious preservation of data stored by means of a computer system, which is located within the territory of that other Party [or other places over which it exercises its sovereign

powers] and in respect of which the requesting Party intends to submit a request for mutual assistance for the search or similar access, seizure or similar securing, or disclosure of the data.

2. A request for preservation made under paragraph 1 shall specify:

a. the authority that is seeking the preservation;

b. the offence under investigation and a brief summary of related facts;

c. the stored data to be preserved and its relationship to the offence;

d. the necessity of the preservation;

e. that the Party intends to submit a request for mutual assistance for the search or similar access, seizure or similar securing, or disclosure of the data.

3. Upon receiving the request from another Party, the requested Party shall take all appropriate measures to preserve expeditiously the specified data in accordance with its domestic law. For the purposes of responding to a request, dual criminality shall not be required (30) as a condition to providing such preservation, but may be required as a condition for the disclosure of the data to the requesting Party.

4. A request for preservation as described in paragraph 2 may only be refused if the requested Party believes that compliance with the request would prejudice its sovereignty, security, ordre public or other essential interests.

5. Where the requested Party believes that preservation will not ensure the future availability of the data or will threaten the confidentiality of, or otherwise prejudice the requesting Party's investigation, it shall promptly so inform the requesting Party, which shall then determine whether the request should nevertheless be executed.

6. Any preservation effected in response to the request referred to in paragraph 1 shall be for a period not less than 40 days in order to enable the requesting Party to submit a request for the search or similar access, seizure or similar securing, or disclosure of the data. Following the receipt of such request, the data shall continue to be preserved pending a decision on that request.

Article 25 - Expedited disclosure of preserved traffic data

1. Where, in the course of the execution of a request made under Article 24 to preserve traffic data concerning a specific communication, the requested Party discovers that a service provider in a third State was involved in the transmission of the communication, the requested Party shall expeditiously disclose to the requesting Party a sufficient amount of traffic data in order to identify that service provider and the path through which the communication was transmitted.

2. Disclosure of traffic data under paragraph 1 may only be withheld if the requested Party believes that compliance with the request would prejudice its sovereignty, security, ordre public or other essential interests.

Article 26 - Mutual Assistance Regarding Accessing of Stored Data

1. A Party may request another Party to search or similarly access, seize or similarly secure, or disclose data, stored by means of a computer system, which is located within the territory of that other Party [or other place over which it exercises its sovereign powers], including data that has been preserved pursuant to article 24.

2. Upon receipt of a request referred to in paragraph 1, the requested Party shall execute the request as expeditiously as possible, by:

a) Where permitted by its domestic law, ratifying or endorsing any judicial or other legal authorisation that was granted in the requesting Party to search or seizure the data, thereupon executing the search or seizure and, pursuant to its mutual assistance treaties or laws, as applicable, disclosing any data seized to the requesting Party; or

b) Responding to the request and disclosing any data seized, pursuant to its mutual assistance treaties or laws, as applicable; or

c) Using any other method of assistance permitted by its domestic law.]

Article 27 - Transborder Access to Stored Data Not Requiring Mutual Legal Assistance

[Notwithstanding anything in this Chapter, a Party may, when acting in accordance with its domestic law [and without obtaining the authorisation of another State or providing notice to another State]:

a) access publicly available [open source] data, regardless of where the data is geographically located;

b) access or receive stored data located in another State, if the Party [has been in contact with a person located within its territory and] acts in accordance with the lawful and voluntary consent of a person who has the lawful authority to permit the Party access to, or to disclose to the Party, that data.] (31)

Article 28 - Interception

[under discussion]

Article 29 - 24/7 Network

1. Each Party shall designate a point of contact available on a 24 hour, 7 day per week basis in order to ensure the provision of immediate assistance for the purpose of the investigation of criminal offenses related to the use of computer systems and

data, or for the collection of electronic evidence of any criminal offense. Such assistance shall include facilitating, or, if permitted by its domestic law and practice, directly carrying out:

1. providing technical advice;
2. preservation of data pursuant to Articles 24 and 25; and
3. the collection of evidence, giving of legal information, and locating of suspects.

2. (a) A Party's point of contact shall have the capacity to carry out communications with the point of contact of another Party on an expedited basis.

(b) If the point of contact designated by a Party is not part of that Party's authority or authorities responsible for international mutual assistance or extradition, the point of contact shall ensure that it is able to coordinate with such authority or authorities on an expedited basis.

3. Each Party shall ensure that trained and equipped personnel are available in order to facilitate the operation of the network.

Chapter IV - Follow-up

Chapter V - Final Provisions

. . .

Footnotes:

(1) The Drafting Group agreed at its 10th meeting (February 2000) that most definitions under Article 1 should be placed either in relevant parts of the Convention or in the Explanatory report and accordingly deleted from this Article definitions 1/e to 1/n. The remaining definitions (1/a - 1/e) need to revised by the DG.

(2) The explanatory report should specify that "computer system" refers to the function of data processing and therefore may include any system that is based on such a function, e.g. telecom systems, and that the "inter-connection" referred to in the definition encompasses radio and logical connections. The Chairman noted that in the jurisdiction provision(s), the PC-CY will have to determine to what extent States will be able to claim jurisdiction over acts occurring in the whole or part of such a "computer system".

(3) The concept of computer data includes computer programs. The Drafting Group agreed that the Explanatory Report should specify, either under Article 1 or another provision, that a "program" is understood as "data suitable for further processing".

(4) The explanatory report should clarify that subscriber data does not include traffic data nor the content of any communication.

(5) The explanatory report should clearly exclude electronic surveillance, this being a separate legal issue.

(6) In the understanding of certain members of the Drafting Group, "intent" may also cover "dolus eventualis". For common law countries, this notion would be similar to "recklessness", i.e. that a person is aware of the high risk that a certain result may occur and knowingly accepts it. The Drafting Group agreed that the interpretation of "intent" should be left to national laws, but it should not, where possible, exclude "dolus eventualis".

(7) The Drafting Group agreed, at its 9th meeting (January 2000) on the principle that the terms "non-public" relate to the transmission (communication) process and not necessarily to the data transmitted. It agreed to keep the term in the text temporarily and to try to find some alternative language.

(8) The Drafting Group agreed at its 8th meeting (November 1999) that the Explanatory Report should specify that "Alteration" also includes tempering with traffic data (spoofing).

(9) "Suppression of data" has two commonly agreed meanings for the Drafting Group: 1) delete data so that it does not physically exist any longer; 2) "render inaccessible", i.e. prevent someone from gaining access to it while maintaining it. As the latter, second meaning covers "rendering inaccessible", which appeared separately in previous versions of this Article, this element was deleted on the understanding that an explanation will be included on this in the Explanatory Report.

(10) One delegation noted that it would need some extra-qualifyer (serious damage or harm) to make this offence extraditable.

(11) The Explanatory Report shall specify that the term "authentic" refers to the issuer of the data, regardless whether the content of the data is true or not.

(12) The Explanatory Report should clarify that the terms "without right" include legal defenses, excuses or similar relevant principles that relieve a person of responsibility under specific circumstances. For example, with respect to paragraph (2)b, a State may provide that a person is relieved of criminal responsibility if the accused proves that the person depicted is not a minor.

(13) The Drafting Group agreed at its 8th meeting (November 1999) that the Explanatory Report should specify that "offering" also includes giving information about hyperlinks to child-pornography sites.

(14) The Explanatory Report should clarify that this provision by no means is intended to restrict the criminalisation of the distribution, etc, of child pornography to cases making use of a computer system, but the Convention establishes this only as a minimum standard and States are free to go beyond it.

(15) Some delegations wished to further consider their position on this paragraph and hold further consultations with domestic authorities. However, a number of delegations viewed it as a provision necessary to prevent the sexual abuse of children when such material is created.

(16) The Explanatory Report should clarify that that the term "pornographic material" is governed by national standards pertaining to the classification of materials as obscene, inconsistent with public morals or similarly corrupt.

(17) The Explanatory Report should specify that a "sexually explicit conduct" covers at least actual or simulated: a) sexual intercourse, including genital-genital, oral-genital, anal-genital or oral-anal, between minors, or between an adult and a minor, of the same or opposite sex; b) bestiality; c) masturbation; d) sadistic or masochistic abuse; or e) lascivious exhibition of the genitals or the pubic area of a minor.

(18) Several alternatives were discussed at the 7th Plenary (March 2000), i.e. 14, 16 or 18 years.

(19) The Plenary agreed that once the list of criminal offences will be finalised in the draft convention, it will return to this provision on "attempt" to determine to which offences it will apply. Delegations have already expressed concern about applying a provision on "attempt" to illegal access under article 2(1) and copyright and related offences under article 4 (since attempt is not covered by the TRIPS agreement).

(20) The Plenary agreed to that Explanatory Report should clarify the double-intent requirement for establishing as criminal offences aiding and abetting, i.e. that the intent has to cover both aiding and abetting and the underlying offence. The Explanatory Report will specify that "aiding and abetting" is to be interpreted in a large sense, also covering, notably, instigators and accessories.

(21) Further consideration will have to given to the offences to be included under this provision once the list of criminal offences is finalised. At present, many States do not consider illegal access to be an extraditable offence, nor will attempt always be an extraditable offence.

(22) At its 7th meeting (March 2000), the Plenary requested the Drafting Group to find some alternative language to describe the concept of "territory".

(23) The Drafting Group did not discuss this provision at its 10th meeting (February 2000) as it is closely related to the provision on trans-border search.

(24) The Drafting Group agreed at its 10th meeting (February 2000) to use this term and clarify in the Explanatory Report that it referred to persons having an actual (physical) control over the computer (system). This would normally include the owner of the premises where the computer is located or the owner/user of the computer itself.

(25) At its 7th meeting (March 2000), the Plenary requested the Drafting Group to find some alternative language that could replace this term.

(26) Further clarification is required with regard to the inclusion of satellites, in particular as to whether this provision would require a State that has responsibility for a satellite (or shares such responsibility with other States) to establish jurisdiction over an offence where the only nexus with that State is that data related to the offence has been transmitted through that satellite. Other international instruments should be examined to determine how they affect the jurisdiction of States with respect to satellites.

(27) This provision has been limited to situations in which there is no extradition treaty in force between the Parties concerned. Where a bilateral or multilateral extradition treaty is in force between the Parties concerned (such as the 1957 European Convention on Extradition), the Parties will know to whom extradition and provisional arrest requests are to be directed without the necessity of a burdensome registration requirement. The language between brackets governing use of diplomatic channels is modeled after article 5 of the second additional protocol to the European Convention on Extradition.

(28) The Drafting Group was, for the moment, unable to reach an agreement on this provision.

(29) The explanatory text should specify that the mere fact that its legal system knows no such procedure is not sufficient grounds to refuse to apply the procedure requested by the requesting State.

(30) The Plenary agreed at its 7th meeting (March 2000) that further consideration was necessary on this matter, given that certain delegations expressed their reservation as to the possibility of giving up the requirement of dual criminality.

(31) This paragraph assumes that the accessing State will limit its own contact to persons within its territory (though such persons may themselves need to contact people in other territories in order to obtain such consent or authority). This could be explicitly added by the insertion of the bracketed text or be explained in the explanatory memorandum.

Excerpt from Criminal Affidavit in the Ardita Case

The following excerpt from the criminal affidavit in the Ardita case (see Chapter 6), submitted and sworn to by Peter Garza, Special Agent, Naval Criminal Investigative Service in March 1996, provides a fascinating glimpse into a real-world cyberinvestigation.

22. On August 25, 1995, an individual using the user identification "chult" accessed the NCCOSC computer host named mindy.nosc.mil. "Chult"[8] accessed mindy.nosc.mil from the FAS Harvard host. "Chult" installed several files onto mindy.nosc.mil.[9] Included in the files installed by "chult" was a program referred to in the industry as a "sniffer" program, a program used frequently by computer intruders to capture packets containing user identification and associated passwords for network access. The sniffer program actually intercepts electronic communications as they are transmitted over the network and then stores a selected portion of each communication. In this case, the sniffer program installed by "chult" was designed to store the first 256 bytes of the communications, which often include the user's account name and password. "Chult" named this program "sni256."

---

8. Most Internet computers use the UNIX operating system, which is case sensitive. The case sensitivity will be respected throughout this affidavit except at the beginning of sentences, where the first letter will be capitalized to conform with normal grammatical form.

9. A directory of network hosts referred to in this Affidavit is appended.

23. The "sni256" program installed by "chult" created a file named "test." This file served as the repository for the illegally intercepted user names and passwords. "Chult" also installed a program named "zap." Most Internet host computers use the UNIX operating system. UNIX, in turn, has a utility program named "who" which is used to identify other users currently logged into the network. Information pertaining to users on a UNIX host, used by the "who" utility, is stored on the UNIX host and a continuously updated log is created. The "zap" program installed by "chult" deleted references to his access in the "who" log. "Chult" also installed a program named "pinga" which, upon review, has been confirmed to obtain "root," or unlimited, access on the compromised network host. With "root" access, the user has the authority to view, alter and install files anywhere on the network host. Such access generally is limited to system administrators.

24. "Chult" was a legitimate user identification which actually belongs to a NCCOSC system administrator. However, this NCCOSC system administrator did not install the programs on August 25 and did not direct or authorize anyone to use his account to do so.

25. The Intruder from FAS Harvard host repeatedly accessed mindy.nosc.mil using the user name "chult" on August 25, 1995. During one session, the Intruder used mindy.nosc.mil to access another network host named dax.nosc.mil which is the network host for another NCCOSC computer system located in Arlington, Virginia. While accessing dax.nosc.mil, the Intruder installed his "sni256," "test" and "zap" programs and files.

26. The placement of unauthorized files and programs on mindy.nosc.mil was discovered by a NCCOSC system administrator on August 28, 1995. On August 29, 1995, a more comprehensive audit program was activated on mindy.nosc.mil.

27. On August 29, 1995, the Intruder logged into mindy.nosc.mil as "chult" from FAS Harvard host. Specifically, Broersma related that computer records for the NCCOSC network indicate a connection was established by an intruder from FAS Harvard host on August 29, 1995. These records show that an intruder from FAS Harvard host logged into a user account called "chult" on the NCCOSC host known as mindy.nosc.mil. Broersma said the Intruder executed commands to determine who was on the network and then executed the "zap" program to remove records concerning his own access. The Intruder then copied the contents of his "test" file, containing illegally obtained user names and passwords, to his terminal. The Intruder then deleted the contents of the "test" file and restarted the illegal wiretap program, "sni256."

28. Broersma also related that he had detected no intrusion into the NCCOSC network from FAS Harvard host before the intrusion into the host known as irc.nosc.mil, which occurred on or about August 24, 1995. This host also contained the signature "sni256, "test" and "zap" programs and files which had been installed on August 24, 1995. According to Broersma's records, the original connection to mindy.nosc.mil at NCCOSC appears to have occurred via the "chult" user account on irc.nosc.mil, on or before August 25, 1995.

29. On September 4, 1995, the Intruder also used his mindy.nosc.mil connection to access another NCCOSC network host, at the Naval Command Control and Ocean Surveillance Center at San Diego, California, named fountainhead.nosc.mil. Because the Intruder accessed a user name other than "chult" after using "chult" to access the results of the sniffer file installed on mindy.nosc.mil, it is my opinion, based upon my training and experience, that the Intruder used a new account name obtained from his sniffer file on mindy.nosc.mil to give him access to fountainhead.nosc.mil.

30. On September 19, 1995, I spoke with Special Agent Deborah Rocco of the Naval Criminal Investigative Service, who informed me of an interview which she had conducted earlier that day with Darryl Cleveland, the System Manager of the Army Research Lab ("ARL") in Edgewood, Maryland. Darryl Cleveland informed Special Agent Rocco that an intruder from FAS Harvard host had attempted to gain unauthorized access to one of the host computers on ARL's computer network on or about August 12, 1995, between 4:16 p.m. and 4:19 p.m. Darryl Cleveland related that the attempt appeared to have been unsuccessful. Darryl Cleveland could not pinpoint the user account on FAS Harvard host from which the intrusions had originated.

31. On September 20, 1995, I spoke with Special Agent Gary Walker of the Navy Criminal Investigative Service, who informed me of an interview which he had conducted on September 19, 1995 with the system manager of the Army Research Lab in Aberdeen, Maryland. The system manager informed Agent Walker that an intruder from FAS Harvard host had made approximately ninety attempts to gain unauthorized access to different branches of the ARL's computer network, at different locations throughout the United States. According to the system manager, these attempts took place from August 12, 1995 until August 16, 1995 and appeared to have been unsuccessful. The system manager could not pinpoint the user account on FAS Harvard host from which the intrusions had originated.

32. On October 11, 1995, I spoke with the systems manager for the Electrical Engineering Department of the California Institute of Technology in Pasadena, California ("Caltech"). He explained that on October 4, 1995, he discovered a

"sniffer" program called "sni256" was running on a Caltech network host computer known as scrooge.systems.caltech.edu. It was located in a hidden subdirectory called "..." which also contained files called "test" and "zap". As described in this affidavit, "sni256," "test" and "zap" are signature files used by the Intruder. The systems manager also stated that on the following day, October 5, 1995, the Caltech network host was probed unsuccessfully twice from FAS Harvard host.

Efforts to Identify and Localize the Intruder Within the FAS Harvard Host

33. During the latter part of August, September and October, extensive efforts were undertaken to localize and identify the Intruder. Those efforts evidenced defining behaviors including:

   (a) The Intruder was accessing and attempting to access without authorization an overlapping set of government and education network hosts from several different accounts at FAS Harvard host; and

   (b) The Intruder, once he had obtained unauthorized access to other network hosts, had created files and implanted programs with unique names in a number of those hosts.

34. As summarized herein, the Intruder repeatedly had used changing accounts of the FAS Harvard host to gain unauthorized access to an overlapping group of victim networks. Once on many of the victim networks, the Intruder had installed similar files with identical names, performing similar functions. These files were peculiar to the performance of unauthorized functions associated with "hackers,"[10] in that they enabled the Intruder to gain unauthorized access to accounts on the victim computers and to conceal the intrusions themselves from system managers who might otherwise detect the intrusions through routine audits of the computer logs. The unique names of the files utilized by the Intruder included "sni256," "test,"[11] "zap," "pinga," "ropt," "roption," "HotterThanMojave InMyHeart," and "InfamousAngel."[12] Searches of the archives on the Internet have not revealed files performing the same unauthorized functions to have been published on the Internet under the names "sni256," "test," "zap," or "pinga." Further, a check with Special Agent Jolene Smith Jameson at the National Computer Crime Squad, FBI Washington Metropolitan Field office, Washington, D.C., has revealed that none of these file names have been associated with other groups or individuals involved with "hacker" activity.[13]

---

10. A "hacker" is a slang term frequently used to refer to a person who breaks into computer systems with wrongful intent.

11. As his unlawful activity continued, "sni256" would be abbreviated as "sni" and "test" would be abbreviated as "tst."

12. The Intruder created for his files and programs a subdirectory with a unique name, as well, "...".

13. The file names "ropt," "roption," "HotterThanMojaveInMyHeart," and "InfamousAngel" have been found to be used by at least one other group, which has made them publicly available over the Internet.

35. On September 8, 1995, I spoke with Ron Holland, Networking and Computer Security Group with NASA's Jet Propulsion Laboratory, Pasadena, California. Holland related that he found files similar to those which had been described as being installed by the Intruder at the NCCOSC network. Holland checked a subdirectory called "/bin" on merlin.jpl.nasa.gov and found the file called "pinga". Mr. Holland said systems administrators examined this file and it was found to be written to exploit system vulnerabilities and obtain "root" privileges on this host computer. Holland also found a hidden subdirectory named "... " (that is, three dots) which contained files named "sni256," "test" and "zap." Holland confirmed that the "sni256" file was a program that first intercepted users' identification and password commands to the host computers and then recorded the intercepted information to another file called "test." Holland said the file called "zap" had been examined and was found to delete records used by the UNIX "who" program on this host computer; the "zap" file on the JPL/NASA hosts was similar to the "zap" program installed on the NCCOSC network host computers, specifically mindy.nosc.mil and dax.nosc.mil.

36. On September 14, 1995, I spoke with Special Agent Thomas Gilchrist, NCIS Los Angeles Field Office, who related that he had re-interviewed Holland, who provided additional information regarding the Intruder's activity. Review of information provided by Mr. Holland confirmed a FAS Harvard host user identified as "margolin" obtained unauthorized access to the "debabani" account on the JPL/NASA network host called merlin.jpl.nasa.gov on or about September 8th. Before or during that session, the file "sni256" had been installed on the system. This unauthorized connection to merlin.jpl.nasa.gov originated from FAS Harvard host.

37. During subsequent discussions and electronic mail communications with Ed Chan, who is the Ames Network Security Manager responsible for ssal.arc.nasa.gov, I learned that on September 8, 1995, a user from FAS Harvard host connected to an account with a user identification of "yuen" on an Ames network host known as ssal.arc.nasa.gov. Mr. Chan told me that he had contacted the authorized user of the account, and the authorized user had reported finding an unfamiliar file named "ropt" in his home directory.[14] Mr. Chan related that examination of the "ropt" file revealed that when executed, it attempted to exploit a known vulnerability in the UNIX operating system to obtain root privileges on the host computer. Root privileges enable a user to control the host computer, allowing the user to run programs such as the sniffer programs found on previous compromised hosts.

---

14. A home directory is a user's assigned work space on the host computer and enables the user to store his own computer files and programs.

38. Mr. Chan's review of the "ropt" file indicated that the file executed commands contained in two files named "HotterThanMojaveInMyHeart" and "InfamousAngel." The script file looked for these files in a subdirectory called "/tmp." The "/tmp" subdirectory is a standard subdirectory in UNIX for temporary files which are deleted if the UNIX computer is restarted. Mr. Chan related the records which were available for the sal.arc.nasa.gov host indicate that the "ropt" script file and the "HotterThanMojaveInMyHeart" and "InfamousAngel" files in the "/tmp" subdirectory were used in the attempt to gain root privileges with a technique that exploits a known vulnerability in UNIX systems.

39. On September 20, 1995, I spoke with Special Agent Gary Walker, NCIS, Dahlgren, Virginia, who related the following information he received from Randy Taylor, Network Engineer, Naval Research Laboratory (NRL), Washington, DC.

40. On August 6, 1995, a user from FAS Harvard host successfully gained access to an account named "guest" on a host called i714Orr.itd.nrl.navy.mil and later logged in again on this host to a user account named "wang." Taylor related the account named "shuang" was being used at FAS Harvard host to access the NRL network. Once the "shuang" user from FAS Harvard host gained access to a valid account on i714Orr.itd.nrl.navy.mil, the 42 other network host computers on this network would allow connections using the "wang" account. A search of the computer hosts on this network revealed the file called "pinga" on the hosts known as i714Orr.itd.nrl.navy.mil and abyss.itd.nrl.navy.mil at NRL. This file was used by the "shuang" intruder to obtain root access to i714Orr.itd.nrl.navy.mil on August 7, 1995 and to obtain root access on abyss.itd.nrl.navy.mil on September 11, 1995. In addition the "shuang" intruder created a subdirectory called "..." in the "/usr/etc/" subdirectory, where he installed a file called issl3.jue. This issl3.jue file is a publicly available computer security scanning program which scans a UNIX computer for security vulnerabilities.

41. During my earlier discussions with Broersma he had related a similar file called "pinga," used to obtain root access, was found on mindy.nosc.mil and dax.nosc.mil. Broersma had also described the use of a subdirectory called "..." on mindy.nosc.mil and dax.nosc.mil, where the Intruder attempted to hide files he had installed on the compromised systems.

42. On September 18, 1995, I contacted a system administrator at the Centro de Computo Academico, Departamento de Fisica, Universidad de Sonora (Academic Computing Center, Physics Department, University of Sonora), Hermosillo, Sonora, Mexico. The system administrator related that on August 25, 1995, computer logs for network host fisica.uson.mx at the University of

Sonora Mexico showed that, earlier that day, an unauthorized user had logged into a user account named "garibay" from FAS Harvard host. The system administrator related that the Intruder from FAS Harvard host installed a script file called ".roption" in the "garibay" user's home directory on fisica.uson.mx. The "roption" file contained instructions to use the files "HotterThanMojaveInMyHeart" and "InfamousAngel," located in a subdirectory called "/tmp," to gain root access on fisica.uson.mx using the above described vulnerability.

43. In my conversations with the administrators for the network hosts which have been compromised, I have been told that there are no legitimate users which are known to use a host at Harvard University. None of the people responsible for compromised hosts at the arc.nasa.gov, jpl.nasa.gov, and the nosc.mil domains have reported that there are users who would have had legitimate connections from FAS Harvard host.

44. On October 16, 1995, I interviewed the systems manager, Mathematics and Statistics Department, University of Massachusetts ("UMASS"), Amherst, Massachusetts ("the UMASS system manager"), regarding computer intrusions into the UMASS network host known as comet.phast.umass.edu. The UMASS systems manager related he had been informed by NASA's Ames Research Center ("ARC") , Moffett Field, California on September 18, 1995 that an account named "yuen," on the ARC host named ssal.arc.nasa.gov, had been accessed by an unknown intruder. The UMASS systems manager was informed that the UMASS network may have been compromised because Yuen also had an account on a UMASS network host computer and the Ames Research Center's network had been probed from UMASS.

45. The UMASS systems manager said that his computer logs reflected that someone had gained unauthorized access to comet.phast.umass.edu. and had installed the files "pinga," "sni256," and "zap" on August 29, 1995 at approximately 23:40. The logs further showed that the "sni256" sniffer file was activated on October 10, 1995, when the unauthorized user gained access to the computer after establishing a telnet connection from an internet network host in Texas. This file again was activated on October 12, 1995, at approximately 00:58, when the intruder used the telnet protocol to connect to comet.phast.umass.edu from the FAS Harvard host, where the intruder was logged in under the user account called "margolin."

46. The UMASS systems manager discovered and terminated the "sni256" file on October 12, 1995. The UMASS systems manager then copied the file called "test" which had been created by the "sni256" program and removed the "test" file from comet.phast.umass.edu. On October 14, 1995, the intruder connected

from the "margolin" account on the FAS Harvard host and ran the "pinga" program and logged out.

47. The UMASS system manager stated that the computer system logs for comet.phast.umass.edu also evidenced that an unauthorized user logged into the "rmillang" account from the "margolin" account on the FAS Harvard host. After discovering this, the UMASS systems manager reviewed the ".history" file information for the user "rmillang". The UNIX operating system creates a file called ".history" (the word history preceded by a dot) in a user's home directory which maintains a running log of a certain number of commands issued by a user. The UMASS systems manager stated that his review of the ".history" file information for the user account called "rmillang" shows the intruder logged in, ran the identifying program "pinga," and then logged out.

48. The UMASS systems manager explained the legitimate user of the "rmillang" account is a first year graduate student in the UMASS Mathematics and Statistics department. He regularly accesses his account during the day, and is not known to access his account during the late night hours. The UMASS systems manager's review of the comet.phast.umass.edu system's logs, which record all logins, did not reveal any record of a login to the "rmillang" account during the times the Intruder connected with comet.phast.umass.edu from the FAS Harvard host, or, in fact, from June 10, 1995 to October 1995. The UMASS systems manager stated that he knows the legitimate "rmillang" user did regularly access his account on comet.phast.umass.edu during that period. The UMASS systems manager opined that the Intruder used the "zap" program which deleted not only the Intruder's sessions, but all sessions when the "rmillang" account was accessed from the computer system's records up through October 1995.

Real-Time Monitoring of the Intruder's Activities in November and December, 1995

49. Based on the probable cause established in the initial phase of the investigation, the United States applied for and obtained court authorization to conduct electronic surveillance of the Intruder's electronic communications to and from the FAS Harvard host. The orders further directed Harvard University to furnish the FBI and NCIS with the information, facilities and technical assistance necessary to accomplish the interceptions unobtrusively and with a minimum of interference to the persons whose communications might be intercepted. As a result of these court authorized interceptions, the government was able to locate the city from which the Intruder appeared to be

accessing the Internet and to partially identify the Intruder through a unique moniker he had given himself. The Intruder - "griton" - was accessing the Internet initially from Buenos Aires, Argentina.

50. A network monitoring program was obtained from the Automated Systems Security Incident Support Team (ASSIST), Defense Information Systems Agency, Washington, DC, and was used to aid in the interceptions and to minimize the interception of electronic communications other than those evidencing the Intruder's criminal activity. The network monitoring program was designed to monitor packets of information transmitted across a network and can be configured to store selected, captured packets for later review. once stored, the captured data can be searched for particular words, phrases or other information (called "text-strings") and the packets containing these strings can be reassembled to reconstruct the network sessions in which they were created. These reconstructed sessions can then be replayed to a computer monitor to depict the timing and combination of "keystrokes" typed during the selected session, or the captured session can be copied to a text file.

51. The network monitoring program was installed on a computer located on the network connection between the FAS Harvard host and the router at the Harvard University Faculty of Arts and Sciences Computer Center ("the FAS Harvard router"). It was configured to monitor all transmissions between the FAS Harvard host and FAS Harvard router, searching for one of a limited set of file and account names and computer addresses typed by the user and associated with the Intruder. The file and account names and computer addresses which the network monitoring program was set up to detect included the names of accounts and addresses of Internet hosts which the Intruder was believed to have compromised, as well as certain commands he was believed to have executed and the names of files he was believed to have installed at sites to which he had gained unauthorized access from FAS Harvard host.

52. Communications across the network link between the FAS Harvard host and FAS Harvard router are transmitted at up to ten megabits per second, that is 10,000,000 ones or zeroes which form pieces of information, per second. While the monitoring program executed its detection function, communications flowed continuously through the computer's RAM, or short-term, memory. The network monitoring program did not capture, display or permanently store the communications which it monitored.

53. Once the network monitoring program detected an occurrence of one of the targeted file names and words, it displayed and recorded a text-string (particular words, phrases or other information) of up to approximately eighty

characters identifying the context in which the target word or command was intercepted. At the same time, it isolated and recorded the computer session of the user who typed in the text-string until the user terminated his connection to the FAS Harvard host.

54. The government initially sought to distinguish, and thus avoid review of, any session by anyone other than the Intruder by examining the logged text-string context of the triggering file name, which was automatically recorded as discussed above. The only sessions examined by law enforcement agents were those sessions where the displayed text-string or a secondary scan by computer utility programs for key words strongly indicated evidence of unlawful activity by the Intruder.

55. On November 20, 1995, the text string "/usr/bin/pinga" was detected by the network monitoring program. This text string indicated that the "pinga" program used by the Intruder was executed via the FAS network. Accordingly, I extracted this and related data streams (electronic communications one direction or the other between the FAS Harvard host and FAS Harvard router) which made up communications believed to be the Intruder's into a readable text form. Review of the transcript of these data streams revealed that the Intruder established a connection to the FAS Harvard host from the Internet host with the Internet protocol address of 200.3.40.17, which belongs to an Internet host known as clirisc.telecom-com.ar registered to Telecom Argentina, Buenos Aires, Argentina, and then established a connection from the FAS Harvard host during this session to the Internet protocol address of 134.75.138.3. This address is registered to the System Engineering Research Institute ("SERI"), Seoul, Republic of Korea. When the Intruder connected to the FAS Harvard host from Telecom Argentina and accessed SERI in Seoul, the Intruder executed programs known to have been used by the Intruder on several computer systems described earlier in the affidavit. While logged into SERI in Seoul the Intruder executed the "pinga" program to obtain control of the computer system, ran "zap" to conceal that he was logged in under the account name of "wgchoe," and copied the "test" file, which contained the results of a previously installed sniffer program, named "sni", which captured, among other information, user identifications and passwords.[15] The sniffer program believed to be used by the Intruder in past intrusions was called "sni256"; it appears that the Intruder chose to shorten the name of the program to "sni."

15. On this occasion, the Intruder copied approximately 31 user identification and password combinations which had been intercepted by the sniffer program.

56. Ten data streams[16] believed to be associated with the Intruder were intercepted on November 22, 1995. The word which triggered interception of each of these ten data streams was again "pinga" embedded in the text string "/usr/bin/pinga." The text string indicated that the "pinga" program, described earlier in my affidavit as a program known to be used by the Intruder, was executed via the FAS Harvard host. Accordingly, I extracted these data streams into readable text form.

57. The transcript of the November 22, 1995 data streams revealed that the Intruder again established a connection to the FAS Harvard host from the Internet protocol address of 200.3.40.17, which belongs to an Internet network host known as clirisc.telecom.com.ar, registered to Telecom Argentina in Buenos Aires, Argentina. During this session into the FAS Harvard host, the Intruder established connections to the Internet network hosts known as venus.fisica.unlp.edu.ar, which is registered to Universidad de La Plata, La Plata, Argentina; splinter.coe.neu.edu, which is registered to Northeastern University, in Boston, Massachusetts; and orac.wes.army.mil, which is registered to the U.S. Army Engineer Waterways Experimentation Stations, in Vicksburg, Mississippi.

58. The transcript of these connections revealed that the Intruder executed the same programs for illegally intercepting computer passwords and for disguising his presence which he had previously used in other computer networks, as detailed earlier in my affidavit. Specifically, the Intruder executed the "pinga" program to obtain control of each of the computer systems which he accessed from the FAS Harvard host. He also executed a command to list the contents of a subdirectory named "... " (three dots), which contained the files "sni," "test," and "zap." While logged into compromised accounts on each of the three target sites, the Intruder searched the "test" file, which contained the passwords and user identifications captured by the previously installed sniffer program named "sni." After searching the contents of the "test" file, the Intruder copied the contents to his terminal. The Intruder then re-started the sniffer program

---

16. The number of data streams intercepted is very likely to overstate the number of computer sessions which were intercepted because of the manner in which the triggering mechanism of the network monitoring software works. For example, when the Intruder, as described below, sent an electronic communication from one Internet host through the FAS Harvard host to a third Internet host, the network monitoring software saw this as up to four electronic data streams or communications one from the Intruder into the FAS Harvard host, one from the FAS Harvard host out to the third Internet host, and two complementary streams if the third host responded through the FAS Harvard host to the Intruder - rather than a single computer session.

to capture further user identifications and passwords. Before logging off, the Intruder ran "zap" to conceal the account names he was using on each of the targeted systems.[17]

59. Review of the data streams for the Intruder's session on November 22, 1995, confirmed the Intruder retrieved user identification and passwords which had been intercepted on venus.fisica.unlp.edu.ar, splinter.coe.neu.edu, and orac.wes.army.mil by the sniffer programs planted in them. On the Internet host known as venus.fisica.unlp.edu.ar the Intruder copied approximately fourteen user account and password combinations which had been intercepted and stored in the "test" file. On the Internet host named splinter.coe.neu.edu the Intruder copied the output of the "test" file which contained approximately fourteen user identification and password combinations, in addition to the user account he used to access splinter.coe.neu.edu. While connected to the Internet host known as orac.wes.army.mil the Intruder copied approximately nine user identification and passwords which had been intercepted by the sniffer program and stored in a file called "test."

60. Computer logs containing connection information for the Intruder on the FAS Harvard host revealed that on November 20 and November 22, 1995, the Intruder accessed an account named "qrr2" on the FAS Harvard host from the Internet host with the Internet protocol address of 200.3.40.17 (clirisc.telecom.com.ar registered to Telecom Argentina). Comparison of the intercepted data streams with this login information indicated that the Intruder used this "qrr2" account during the sessions intercepted by the network monitoring software on those dates.[18]

61. The command "pinga" was executed again via the FAS Harvard host on November 30, 1995. I have extracted two data streams associated with this communication into readable text form. Review of the corresponding text files indicated that on November 30, 1995, the Intruder again accessed the FAS Harvard host from the Internet host bearing the Internet protocol address of 200.3.40.17 (clirisc.telecom.com.ar registered to Telecom Argentina).

---

17. The captured data streams nonetheless enabled us to identify the accounts he was using on each of the targeted systems. On venus.fisica.unlp.edu.ar the Intruder accessed an account named "torres." On splinter.coe.neu.edu the Intruder accessed the account "arambel." On orac.wes.army.mil the Intruder accessed an account named "lichvar."

18. Computer logs containing connection information for the Intruder on the FAS Harvard host revealed the Intruder logged into the FAS Harvard host under the user account "qrr2" on December 19, 1995, as well, during a period when the monitoring system had been shut down temporarily. During this session the Intruder connected to the Fas Harvard host from the Internet network host with the host name of "tsl-e0.starnet.net.ar," which is on the commercial network operated by Startel S.A., an Internet access provider in Buenos Aires, Argentina.

62. The command "pinga" was executed again via the FAS Harvard host on December 5, 1995. The intercepted data streams composing this session revealed the Intruder logged into the FAS Harvard host from an Internet host computer with the Internet protocol address ("IP address") of 200.26.8.22, which is registered under the name of tsl-ppp5.starnet.net.ar. The tsl-ppp5.starnet.net.ar host is one of several network hosts operated by a commercial Internet access provider known as Starnet in Buenos Aires, Argentina. Review of the Intruder's activity documented in these data streams revealed that the Intruder was logged into the FAS Harvard host as "qrr2" and accessed a network host with the IP address of 140.115.45.105. This host is registered to the Ministry of Education Computer Center, Taipei, Taiwan, Republic of China. While logged into the 140.115.45.105 host under the account name of "sm5OO2" the Intruder executed the "pinga" program to obtain root privileges and ran the "zap" program to conceal that he was logged on the "sm5OO2" account. The Intruder then executed the "who" command and changed the directory he was working in to a subdirectory called (three dots). The Intruder then listed the contents of the sub-directory to his terminal. Intruder connected to the FAS Harvard host from the Internet network host with the host name of "tsl-e0.starnet.net.ar", which is on a commercial network operated by Startel S.A., an Internet access provider in Buenos Aires, Argentina.

63. The "..." subdirectory included a further sub-directory dated September 5, 1995, which indicates the Intruder may have been using this account at least since that date. Among the files which were listed in the "... " subdirectory was an executable program file called "iss," which is a program known as Internet Security Scanner and is designed to scan a series of IP addresses and check for known security flaws. Such flaws could enable the Intruder to gain unauthorized access to additional Internet sites.

64. During the Intruder's December 5, 1995 session the Intruder viewed the contents of the file called "test" which contained text which indicated it was the output of the Internet Security Scanner program and listed the results of a security scan of a range of IP addresses from 200.9.104.1 to 200.9.254.254. The file listed three sites in that range that appeared to have vulnerabilities which could be exploited by the Intruder: the Internet network hosts with the IP addresses of 200.9.112.130, 200.9.112.65, and 200.9.115.2. The Internet network hosts with the IP addresses of 200.9.112.130 and 200.9.112.65 are both on a network registered to the Escola Paulista de Medicina, a medical school in Sao Paulo, Brazil. The IP address of 200.9.115.2 is registered under the Internet host name of ns.cast.edu.jm, operated by the University of the West Indies. A fourth IP address, 200.9.112.137, which is registered under the name

tapera.bf.epm.br and is also at the Escola Pualistade Medicina, was listed by the iss program as using an older version of electronic mail software which has known, but correctable, vulnerabilities.

65. December 6, 1995, the Intruder executed the program named "ropt," which exploits a vulnerability in some versions of the UNIX operating system to obtain access to an Internet host as a "root" user. Network monitoring software triggered on the target word "roption" which is embedded in the "ropt" program and captured a series of data streams which indicated that the Intruder logged into the FAS Harvard host from an Internet network host named tsl-e0.starnet.net.ar with the IP address of 200.26.3.18. While logged into the FAS Harvard host from the tsl-e0.starnet.net.ar host, the Intruder had established a connection to an Internet network host with the IP address of 200.9.151.173 under the account name of "operador." This host is registered with the host name of chiloe.chilepac.com which is on a network operated by a company, known as Chilepac S.A. in Santiago, Chile.

66. While the Intruder was logged into the chiloe.chilepac.com host the Intruder viewed the file containing the computer program called "ropt." I saw that the instructions in this program referred to program files called "HotterThanMojaveInMyHeart" and "InfamousAngel" which were to be written to a subdirectory called "/tmp." This "/tmp" sub-directory is a standard area where certain versions of the UNIX operating system store temporary files which are deleted if the system is restarted. Both "HotterThanMojaveInMyHeart" and "Infamous Angel" have been associated with the Intruder in the past, as detailed earlier in my affidavit. The Intruder executed the "ropt" program in an unsuccessful attempt to gain access to a host with the IP address of 151.10.81.10, using the user name "No1InParticular." The Intruder then executed the "ropt" program, unsuccessfully targeting a host named ciro.chilepac.com, again using user name "No1InParticular." The Intruder continued attempts to gain access to the following Internet hosts with the "ropt" program under the user name of "No1InParticular:" palborno.chilepac.com, with the IP address of 200.9.151.131; aklenner.chilepac.com, with the IP address of 200.9.151.171; ealbornoz.chilepac.com, with the IP address of 200.9.151.144 and a host with the IP address of 140.115.45.105 on a network registered to the Ministry of Education Computer Center Taipei, Taiwan, Republic of China. In reviewing the Intruder's activity on chiloe.chilepac.com, I saw that he viewed, installed and edited a program called "mailscript." As he was editing "mailscript," the program displayed an explanation that it exploits a flaw in a particular version of sendmail software on computers using the UNIX operating system in order to obtain root access. The Intruder also appeared to have

installed the files called "sni" and "zap," with which he has been associated repeatedly in the past.

67. While logged into the chiloe.chilepac.com host the Intruder also established a telnet connection to an Internet host with the IP address of 200.9.151.160, with the host name of gte.chilepac.com, and logged in under the user name of "operador". While on gte.chilepac.com, the Intruder viewed the contents of the password file for this host and a file which lists all hosts on its network. The Intruder then disconnected from gte.chilepac.com and listed the contents of a subdirectory called "..." (three dots) on the chiloe.chilepac.com hosts. This "..." subdirectory contained the files called "sni," "tst" and "zap." Just as the Intruder appears to have shortened the name of his sniffer file from "sni256" to "sni," he appears to have shortened the name of his output file from "test" to "tst." The Intruder viewed the contents of the "tst," which contained portions of sessions intercepted by the "sni" program on chiloe.chilepac.com.

68. Later in the same session, the Intruder used the telnet protocol to connect from the FAS Harvard host to the host with the IP address of 140.115.45.105 at the Ministry of Education Computer Center, Taipei, Taiwan, R.O.C., where he logged into the account named "sm5O02." There, the Intruder executed the program called "pinga," to obtain root privileges, and ran the program called "zap," to conceal the account name he was using. The Intruder viewed the contents of the subdirectory called "..." and viewed the path for the current working directory, which was "/homel/5002/ ..."

69. Another set of data streams intercepted on December 6, 1995, documented a session when the Intruder logged into Internet Relay Chat ("IRC") under the nick-name of "griton" and joined a channel called "#hack.br." IRC allows users to engage in communications over the Internet in the interactive nature of a conversation, rather than sending stored communications such as electronic mail to each other. It is the practice on IRC to assign yourself a nick-name when you log onto an IRC server (an Internet host computer which is linked to a worldwide network of IRC servers to facilitate the "chat" sessions). Communications take place over channels which are either public for all to see and join in if they wish - or private - open only to invited participants. Based on my training and experience, I am aware that computer intruders, commonly referred to as "hackers," use public IRC channels to "advertise" that they are active and then invoke the "private" message facility in IRC to exchange interactive messages directly. During those interactive messages, users can communicate and also transfer files.

70. Later in the evening of December 6, 1995, an additional session for the Intruder was intercepted by the monitoring computer. Data streams for this

session indicate the Intruder logged into the FAS Harvard host from the IP address of 200.3.40.17, which is a host on a network operated by Telecom Argentina, Buenos Aires, Argentina. While logged into the FAS Harvard host the Intruder established a connection to a host with the IP address of 200.9.151.173, which is chiloe.chilepac.com. While on chiloe.chilepac.com, the Intruder executed the "pinga" program and then changed to a sub-directory called ".... " where he executed the "zap" program to conceal that he was logged into the account named "operador." The Intruder then accessed IRC and joined a channel called "#argentine" under the nick-name of "griton."

Identification of "Griton," the Intruder, in Buenos Aires, Argentina

71. "Griton" has now been identified as Julio Cesar Ardita through two independent means. First, "griton" made several descriptive postings on a computer bulletin board known as "yabbs," including an open invitation to visit his own computer bulletin board in Buenos Aires. The location of griton's computer bulletin board has been traced by the Argentine Federal Police to Ardita's residence in Buenos Aires. Second, Telecom Argentina has confirmed that the Intruder into the FAS Harvard host from their computer system, in turn, had broken into their system from a telephone number located at Ardita's residence.

72. A search of files accessible to the public through the Internet disclosed that "griton" previously had posted a number of communications on a computer bulletin board known as "yabbs." On a computer bulletin board, a user can post messages accessible to all other users of the bulletin board service, just as an individual might tack a note to a cork bulletin board in a common club room. On August 23, 1993, Griton invited readers of the yabbs bulletin board to contact the "Scream!" bulletin board service of which he was the "sysop" (systems operator) at a telephone number in Buenos Aires, Argentina. In pertinent part, at 00:10:34 on that day he posted:

```
      Call to:
      Scream! BBS
      +54.[0]1.72.6305
      24-8 east time.
   h/p, Pc Music, Cracks, VGA Stuff, friends ...
   To C001 Axes:
      Name: INTER
      pw: NET
      Your sysop ...
   El Griton
```

Based on my training and experience, the first paragraph of this posting lists the time and telephone number at which the Scream! bulletin board service ("BBS") can be reached. The second paragraph gives a brief description of the types of information exchanged on the board. "H/p" is an abbreviation for "hacking" and "phreaking;" "cracks," a reference to "cracking." "Hacking" and "cracking" are slang terms for identifying and using systems' vulnerabilities to crack the security of computer systems and obtain unauthorized access to them. "Phreaking" refers to "phone phreaking," which is the practice of breaking into and misusing telephone systems. Phone phreaking includes obtaining unauthorized access to telephone exchanges which can be used to access computer networks and make long distance telephone calls without charge.[19]

The final paragraph gives an account name ("name") and password ("pw") through which a reader of the bulletin board posting on yabbs can access the Scream! bulletin board service.

73. In subsequent postings on the yabbs bulletin board in November, 1993, griton[20] sought information on how to "hack" into (break into) a particular kind of computer system, and described himself as a computer science student in his first year of study, and, in an aside, stated what a nice city he thought Chicago was.

74. The Federal Police of Argentina have determined that telephone number 72 6305, the number given by "griton" for his Scream! bulletin board, was in service in August, 1993, at the residence of Julio Rafael Ardita, his wife, their 21 year old son, Julio Cesar Ardita, and three minor children.[21] The Federal Police also have confirmed that Julio Cesar Ardita was more recently a student in applied sciences, a discipline which includes the computer sciences.

---

19. On February 22, 1996, FBI Special Agent James Hegarty and I contacted Carlos E. Maldonado, who is the Business Electronic Security Coordinator based in the United States for E.I. DuPont de Nemours and Company, Wilmington, Delaware with responsibility for coordinating electronic information security for DuPont in countries including Argentina. Maldonado confirmed he had contacted Harvard University regarding phone calls made from a DuPont Company telephone PBX (a private telephone switching system) into the FAS Harvard modem pool. DuPont has been conducting an internal investigation of the compromise and misuse of a PBX which services a DuPont Company plant in Mercedes, Argentina. Maldonado related that Jarvas V. Torres, a DuPont Company Manager located in Brazil responsible for Argentina, has reviewed telephone records for their PBX in Argentina and has determined that an unknown intruder obtained access to their PBX from outside the company and had made numerous telephone calls from Argentina to the FAS Harvard modem pool number at (617) 495-0635, to a residence in Chicago, Illinois and to other telephone exchanges in at least April and May, 1995.

20. Ardita referred to himself both as "griton" and "El Griton." The return address line on the bulletin board postings read "griton@yabbs;" when the postings were signed, they were signed "El Griton."

21. The oldest of these minor children, now 16, would have been approximately 14 at the time of the yabbs bulletin board postings.

75. Julio Cesar Ardita and Julio Rafael Ardita both applied for United States visas in January, 1995. On that occasion, Julio Rafael Ardita listed his date of birth as July 9, 1946 and his occupation as retired military, consultant to Argentine Congress. On the same occasion, Julio Cesar Ardita listed his date of birth as March 28, 1974 and his occupation as student. Records of the Immigration and Naturalization Service indicate that only Julio Cesar Ardita travelled to the United States at that time and he listed his U.S. address during his stay as Chicago, Illinois.

76. Telecom Argentina has confirmed that someone broke into their computer network and from there accessed the FAS Harvard host during late 1995. While on the Telecom Argentina network, the Intruder installed files including the identifying "InfamousAngel" and "HotterThanMojaveInMyHeart," among others.

77. Telecom Argentina has determined that the intrusions into their host computer originated in Buenos Aires from a telephone number located in the apartment residence of Julio Cesar Ardita and his family. The telephone line from which the intrusions originated - 832 6305 - is the same as that on which the bulletin board service had been operated earlier - 72 6305. The exchange was changed to 832 from 72 after August, 1993, during a restructuring of telephone service in Argentina.

Peter Garza, Special Agent, Naval Criminal Investigative Service

Subscribed and sworn before me this day of March, 1996.

MARIANNE B. BOWLER, UNITED STATES MAGISTRATE JUDGE

Resources and Publications

The following is a brief list of suggested World Wide Web sites, publications, and other sources of material pertaining to information security and high-technology crime. It is by no means complete but will prove useful to computer security professionals and those wanting to learn more.

General Information

Center for Education and Research in Information Assurance and Security (CERIAS)

http://www.cerias.purdue.edu/

This is the foremost university center for multidisciplinary research education in areas of information security (computer security, network security, and communications security). The site contains many, many useful links.

NIST Computer Security Resource Clearinghouse

http://csrc.ncsl.nist.gov/

The Computer Security Resource Clearinghouse (CSRC), sponsored by the National Institute of Standards and Technology, is designed to collect and disseminate computer security information and resources to help users, systems administrators, managers, and security professionals better protect their data and systems. A primary goal of the CSRC is to raise awareness of all computer system users, from novice to expert, about computer security.

Computer Crime Research Resources

http://mailer.fsu.edu/~btf1553/ccrr/states.htm

Here you will find many state statutes pertaining to crimes involving computers, information, and telecommunications.

The following are some interesting individual sites from some of the information security industry's most notable names.

Rik Farrow

http://www.spirit.com/

Bruce Schneier and Counterpane Systems

http://www.counterpane.com/

Lincoln Stein's WWW Security FAQ

http://www.genome.wi.mit.edu/WWW/faqs/

Bill Cheswick's Home Page

http://cm.bell-labs.com/who/ches/index.html

Alec Muffet's Home Page

http://www.users.dircon.co.uk/~crypto/

Marcus Ranum's Home Page

http://www.nfr.com/

Fred Cohen & Associates

http://all.net/

Dr. Dorothy Denning's Home Page

http://www.cs.georgetown.edu/~denning/

Dan Farmer's Home Page

http://www.fish.com/

Sarah Gordon's Home Page
http://www.badguys.com/

George Smith, *The Crypt Newsletter*
http://sun.soci.niu.edu/~crypt/

U.S. GAO Cybersecurity Assessments

Information Security: Computer Attacks at Department of Defense Pose Increasing Risks
http://www.gao.gov/AIndexFY96/abstracts/ai96084.htm

Information Security: Computer Attacks at Department of Defense Pose Increasing Risks
http://www.gao.gov/AIndexFY96/abstracts/ai96092t.htm

Information Security: Computer Hacker Information Available on the Internet
http://www.gao.gov/AIndexFY96/abstracts/ai96108t.htm

Information Security: Opportunities for Improved OMB Oversight of Agency Practices
http://www.gao.gov/AIndexFY96/abstracts/ai96110.htm

IRS Systems Security and Funding: Employee Browsing Not Being Addressed Effectively and Budget Requests for New Systems Development Not Justified
http://www.gao.gov/AIndexFY97/abstracts/ai97082t.htm

IRS Systems Security: Tax Processing Operations and Data Still at Risk Due to Serious Weaknesses
http://www.gao.gov/AIndexFY97/abstracts/ai97049.htm

IRS Systems Security: Tax Processing Operations and Data Still at Risk Due to Serious Weaknesses

http://www.gao.gov/AIndexFY97/abstracts/ai97076t.htm

Air Traffic Control: Weak Computer Security Practices Jeopardize Flight Safety

http://www.gao.gov/AIndexFY98/abstracts/ai98155.htm

Computer Security: Pervasive, Serious Weaknesses Jeopardize State Department Operations

http://www.gao.gov/AIndexFY98/abstracts/ai98145.htm

Executive Guide: Information Security Management— Learning From Leading Organizations

http://www.gao.gov/AIndexFY98/abstracts/ai98068.htm

FAA Systems: Serious Challenges Remain in Resolving Year 2000 and Computer Security Problems

http://www.gao.gov/AIndexFY98/abstracts/ai98251t.htm

Information Security: Serious Weaknesses Place Critical Federal Operations and Assets at Risk

http://www.gao.gov/AIndexFY98/abstracts/ai98092.htm

Information Security: Serious Weaknesses Put State Department and FAA Operations at Risk

http://www.gao.gov/AIndexFY98/abstracts/ai98170t.htm

Information Security: Strengthened Management Needed to Protect Critical Federal Operations and Assets

http://www.gao.gov/AIndexFY98/abstracts/ai98312t.htm

Department of Energy: Key Factors Underlying Security Problems at DOE Facilities

http://www.gao.gov/AIndexFY99/abstracts/rc99159t.htm

Information Security: The Melissa Computer Virus Demonstrates Urgent Need for Stronger Protection Over Systems and Sensitive Data

http://www.gao.gov/AIndexFY99/abstracts/ai99146t.htm

High-Risk Series: An Update HR-99-1

http://www.gao.gov/pas/hr99001.pdf

Information Security: Many NASA Mission-Critical Systems Face Serious Risks

http://www.access.gpo.gov/cgi-bin/
getdoc.cgi?dbname=gao&docid=f:ai99047.txt.pdf

Anti-Virus Information

Virus Bulletin

http://www.virusbtn.com/

Virus Bulletin: The International Publication on Computer Virus Prevention, Recognition and Removal is the technical journal on developments in the field of computer viruses and anti-virus products.

Rob Rosenberger's Computer Virus Myths

http://www.kumite.com/myths/

European Institute for Computer Antivirus Research (EICAR)

http://www.eicar.org/

EICAR combines universities, industry, and media plus technical, security, and legal experts from civil and military government and law enforcement as well as privacy protection organizations. EICAR's objectives are to unite efforts against writing and proliferating malicious code such as computer viruses or Trojan horses, based on a code of conduct.

Datafellows Virus Information Center

http://www.datafellows.com/virus-info/

Henri Delger's Virus Help

http://pages.prodigy.net/henri_delger/index.htm

Eddy Willems Free Anti-Virus Consultancy

http://www.wavci.com/

Incident Response Information

Computer Emergency Response Team (CERT)

http://www.cert.org/

The CERT Coordination Center is part of the Survivable Systems Initiative at the Software Engineering Institute at Carnegie Mellon University. It was started by DARPA (the Defense Applied Research Projects Agency, part of the U.S. Department of Defense) in December 1988 after the Morris worm incident crippled approximately 10% of all computers connected to the Internet.

Forum of Incident Response and Security Teams (FIRST)

http://www.first.org/

This coalition brings together a variety of computer security incident response teams from government, commercial, and academic organizations. FIRST aims to foster cooperation and coordination in incident prevention, to prompt rapid reaction to incidents, and to promote information sharing among members and the community at large.

Computer Incident Advisory Capability (CIAC)

http://ciac.llnl.gov/

CIAC provides on-call technical assistance and information to Department of Energy (DOE) sites faced with computer security incidents.

This central incident handling capability is one component of the all-encompassing service provided to the DOE community. The other services CIAC provides are awareness, training, and education; trend, threat, vulnerability data collection and analysis; and technology watch. This comprehensive service is made possible by a motivated staff with outstanding technical skills and a customer service orientation. CIAC is an element of the Computer Security Technology Center (CSTC), which supports the Lawrence Livermore National Laboratory (LLNL).

Federal Bureau of Investigation, National Infrastructure Protection Center (NIPC)

http://www.nipc.gov/

Postal Address	935 Pennsylvania Avenue N.W.
	Washington, D.C. 20535-0001
Telephone	(202) 323-3205
Fax	(202) 323-2079
E-mail address	nipc@fbi.gov

The FBI's Washington Field Office Infrastructure Protection and Computer Intrusion Squad (WFOIPCIS) is responsible for investigating unauthorized intrusions into major computer networks belonging to telecommunications providers, private corporations, United States Government agencies, and public and private educational facilities. The squad also investigates the illegal interception of signals (cable and satellite signal theft) and infringement of copyright laws related to software information warfare.

President's Commission on Critical Infrastructure Protection (PCCIP)

http://www.info-sec.com/pccip/pccip2/info.html

PCCIP is the first national effort to address the vulnerabilities created in the new Information Age. The Commission, established in July 1996 by Presidential Executive Order 13010, was tasked to formulate a comprehensive national strategy for protecting the infrastructures we all depend on from physical and cyberthreats. For more information contact P. O. Box 46258 Washington, D.C. 20050-6258.

What Is Information Warfare? by Martin Libicki

http://www.ndu.edu/inss/actpubs/act003/a003.html

Information Warfare Resources

http://sac.saic.com/io/io_l.htm

Institute for the Advanced Study of Information Warfare

http://www.psycom.net/iwar.1.html

Organizations and Associations

Computer Security Institute (CSI)

http://www.gocsi.com/

CSI is the world's leading membership organization specifically dedicated to serving and training the information, computer, and network security professional. Since 1974, CSI has been providing education and aggressively advocating the critical importance of protecting information assets. CSI sponsors two conferences and exhibitions each year, NetSec in June and the CSI Annual in November, and seminars on encryption, intrusion management, Internet, firewalls, awareness, Windows, and more. CSI membership benefits include the ALERT newsletter, quarterly journal, and Buyers Guide. CSI also publishes surveys and reports on topics such as computer crime and information security program assessment.

American Society for Industrial Security (ASIS)

http://www.asisonline.org/

ASIS is an international organization for professionals responsible for security.

Postal Address	1625 Prince Street
	Alexandria, VA 22314-2818
Telephone	(703) 519-6200
Fax	(703) 519-6299

The Information Systems Security Association (ISSA)

http://www.issa-intl.org/

ISSA is a nonprofit international organization of information security professionals and practitioners. It provides education forums, publications, and peer interaction opportunities that enhance the knowledge, skill, and professional growth of its members.

Federal Information Systems Security Educators' Association (FISSEA)

http://csrc.nist.gov/organizations/fissea.html

Founded in 1987, FISSEA is an organization run by and for federal information systems security professionals. FISSEA assists federal agencies in meeting their computer security training responsibilities.

International Information Systems Security Certification Consortium, Inc. (ISC)^2

http://www.isc2.org/

(ISC)^2 is an international organization dedicated to the certification of information systems security professionals.

Electronic Frontier Foundation (EFF)

http://www.eff.org

EFF is a nonprofit, nonpartisan organization working the public interest to protect fundamental civil liberties in the arena of computers and the Internet.

High Technology Crime Investigation Association

http://www.htcia.org

An association for peace officers, investigators, and prosecuting attorneys engaged in the investigation and prosecution of criminal activity associated with computers and advanced technologies.

USENIX

http://www.usenix.org/

USENIX is the Advanced Computing Systems Association. Since 1975, the USENIX Association has brought together the community of engineers, system administrators, scientists, and technicians working the cutting edge of the computing world. The USENIX conferences have become the essential meeting grounds for the presentation and discussion of the most advanced information on the developments of all aspects of computing systems.

The SANS (System Administration, Networking, and Security) Institute

http://www.sans.org/

The SANS Institute is a cooperative research and education organization through which system administrators and network administrators share the lessons they are learning and find solutions for challenges they face. SANS was founded in 1989.

International Computer Security Association (ICSA)

http://www.icsa.net/

ICSA provides security assurance services for Internet-connected companies. It supports both corporate users as well as the vendor community. ICSA publishes *Information Security Magazine* and is a Gartner Group affiliate.

Books and Publications

Arquilla, John and David Ronfeldt. In Athena's Camp: *Preparing for Conflict in the Information Age*, Santa Monica, Calif.; RAND, 1997, ISBN: 0-8330-2514-7.

Denning, Dorothy E. *Information Warfare and Security*. New York: ACM Press; Reading, Mass.: Addison-Wesley, 1999. ISBN 0-201-43303-6.

Garfinkel, Simson. *Database Nation: The Death of Privacy in the 21st Century*, Cambridge, Mass.; O'Reilly and Associates Inc., 1999, ISBN: 1-56592-653-6.

Garfinkel, Simson and Gene Spafford. *Practical UNIX & Internet Security, 2nd Edition*. Cambridge, Mass.: O'Reilly & Associates, Inc., 1996. ISBN 1-56592-148-8.

Hafner, Katie and John Markoff. *Cyberpunk: Outlaws and Hackers on the Computer Frontier.* New York: Touchstone Books, 1995. ISBN 0-6848-1862-0.

Icove, David; Karl Seger; and William VonStorch. *Computer Crime: A Crimefighters Handbook.* Sebastopol, Calif.: O'Reilly & Associates, Inc., 1995. ISBN 1-56592-086-4.

Littman, Jonathan. *The Fugitive Game: Online with Kevin Mitnick*. Boston: Little, Brown and Company, 1996. ISBN 0-316-52858-7.

McCarthy, Linda. *Intranet Security: Stories from the Trenches*, Upper Saddle River, N.J.; Prentice Hall, 1998, ISBN: 0-13-894759-7.

Parker, Donn B. *Fighting Computer Crime: A New Framework for Protecting Information*. New York: John Wiley & Sons, Inc., 1998. ISBN 0-471-16378-3.

Schneier, Bruce. *Secrets and Lies: Digital Security in a Networked World*, New York; John Wiley and Sons, 2000, ISBN: 0-471-25311-1.

Shimomura, Tsutomu with John Markoff. *Takedown: The Pursuit and Capture of Kevin Mitnick, America's Most Wanted Computer Outlaw—By the Man Who Did It*. New York: Hyperion, 1996. ISBN 0-7868-6210-6.

Smith, George. *The Virus Creation Labs: A Journey into the Underground*. Tucson, Ariz.: American Eagle Publications, 1994. ISBN 0-929408-09-8.

Sterling, Bruce. *The Hacker Crackdown: Law and Disorder on the Electronic Frontier*. New York: Bantam Books, 1992. ISBN 0-553-56370-X.

Computer Security Journal, published by the Computer Security Institute, is a quarterly journal offering comprehensive, practical articles; case studies; reviews; and commentaries written by knowledgeable computer security experts.

SC Magazine (www.scmagazine.com) is the largest-circulation information security magazine.

Infosecurity Magazine (www.icsa.net), published monthly, is an industry-leading source for news, analysis, insight, and commentary on today's infosecurity marketplace. It includes features and case studies, news coverage, op-ed commentary, and product reviews.

On-Line News Sources

SecurityFocus and Security Portal

http://www.securityfocus.com/

SecurityFocus is designed to facilitate discussion on security-related topics, create security awareness, and provide news, books, tools, and products.

Security Portal is a Web site and information services provider dedicated to providing corporate security professionals with the information needed to protect their networks.

APBonline

http://www.apbonline.com/

APBonline is a source for news, information, and data on crime, justice, and safety.

Security Mailing Lists

AUSCERT Australian Computer Emergency Response

Contact: auscert@auscert.edu.au

The AUSCERT mailing lists are restricted to registered sites. Registration is free for AARNet members and affiliates. Registration forms are available from ftp://ftp.auscert.org.au/pub/auscert/auscert-registration-p?.ps

CERT Advisory Mailing List Computer Emergency Response Team

For receiving CERT advisories.

Contact: cert-advisory-request@cert.org

CIAC Mailing List

For receiving CIAC security informational documents.

Contact: E-mail ciac-listproc@llnl.gov with `subscribe` `list-name` `LastName`, `FirstName` `PhoneNumber` as the body of the message (`list-name` is either `CIAC-BULLETIN` or `CIAC-NOTES`).

Cypherpunks Mailing List

For discussion of cryptography.

Contact: E-mail majordomo@toad.com with `subscribe` `cypherpunks` as the body of the message.

Firewalls Mailing List

For discussions of Internet firewall security systems and related issues.

Contact: E-mail Majordomo@GreatCircle.com or Firewalls-request@GreatCircle.com with `subscribe` `firewalls` as the body of the message.

Academic-Firewalls Mailing List

For discussion of firewalls in the academic environment.

Contact: E-mail Majordomo@net.tamu.edu with `subscribe` `academic-firewalls` as the body of the message.

FWall-users Mailing List

For TIS's Firewall Toolkit users.

Contact: E-mail fwall-users-request@tis.com

Firewalls Wizards

http://www.nfr.net/firewall-wizards/

BugTraq Mailing List

For full disclosure discussion of UNIX security issues.

Contact: E-mail bugtraq-request@fc.net with subscribe bugtraq as the body of the message.

RISKS-LIST

Forum on risks to the public in computer and related systems (comp.risks). ACM Committee on Computers and Public Policy, Peter G. Neumann, moderator.

E-mail risks-request@csl.sri.com with SUBSCRIBE (or UNSUBSCRIBE) in the body of the message. Include your Net address if it differs from the address in the FROM field.

Newsgroups

comp.unix.programmer - UNIX programming issues

comp.protocols.tcp-ip - TCP/IP issues

comp.protocols.nfs - NFS issues

comp.security.unix - General UNIX security issues

comp.security.misc - Misc security issues

comp.security.firewalls - Internet firewall security issues

comp.security.announce - Security announcements

alt.security - General security

alt.hackers - Hacking discussions

alt.2600 - Hacking around the world

Conferences and Training

Computer Security Institute

http://www.gocsi.com/

CSI hosts conferences and a broad range of training programs. Its annual Fall Conference and Exhibition is the largest commercial computer security conference and trade show and is held each November. Each June, CSI hosts NetSec: The Technical Dimensions of Network Security. In addition, CSI offers public and private training in all areas of information security, both technical and nontechnical in scope.

The Federal Law Enforcement Training Center (FLETC)

http://www.treas.gov/fletc

The Federal Law Enforcement Training Center is a partnership of federal law enforcement organizations. Their mission is to provide quality, cost-effective training for law enforcement professionals. They accomplish their mission by using law enforcement and training experts; providing quality facilities, support services, and technical assistance; conducting law enforcement research and development; and sharing law enforcement technology.

National Cybercrime Training Partnership

http://www.nctp.org/

The NCTP, developed by the U.S. Department of Justice, provides guidance and assistance to local, state, and federal law enforcement agencies in an effort to ensure that the law enforcement community is properly trained to address electronic and high-technology crime.

MIS Training Institute

http://www.misti.com/

MIS Training Institute provides training for audit and information security and has offices in the United States, United Kingdom, and Asia. System Security Ltd., a U.K. division of MIS, provides hands-on audit and security training.

National Information Systems Security Conference

http://www.nist.gov

Cosponsored by the National Computer Security Center and National Institute of Standards and Technology (NIST), this conference is held annually each fall. The National Information Systems Security Conference audience represents a broad range of information security interests spanning government, industry, commercial, and academic communities.

For more information, contact:

> National Information Systems Security Conference
> National Computer Security Center
> FANX III
> STE 6765 9800 Savage Road
> Fort George G. Meade, MD 20755-6765

Computer Underground

2600 Magazine: The Hacker Quarterly

http://www.2600.com/

Postal Address	2600 Magazine
	P.O. Box 752
	Middle Island, NY 11953
Telephone:	631-751-2600
Fax:	631-474-2677

The magazine also sponsors the Hackers on Planet Earth (HOPE) conferences.

Attrition

http://www.attrition.org/

Site that archives defaced Web pages.

DefCon

http://www.defcon.org

The granddaddy of hacker conventions, it meets every summer in Las Vegas, organized by the Dark Tangent.

L0pht Heavy Industries

http://www.l0pht.com

L0pht provides tools, services, and numerous advisories related to computer system vulnerabilities.

Phrack

http://www.phrack.com/

Phrack is an online magazine for and by the hacking/phreaking community.

Cult of the Dead Cow (cDc)

http://www.cultdeadcow.com/

A quasi-underground computer security organization.

AntiOnline

http://www.antionline.com/

AntiOnline has archives, a daily news search engine, and more.

Hacker News Network (HNN)

http://www.hackernews.com/

The Hacker News Network reports the activities of the computer underground, updated every weekday.

Computer Underground Digest

http://www.soci.niu.edu/~cudigest/

This is a more-or-less weekly digest/newsletter/journal of debates, news, research, and discussion of legal, social, and other issues related to computer culture.

INDEX